CONTESTED STATEHOOD

Contested Statehood

Kosovo's Struggle for Independence

MARC WELLER

OXFORD

UNIVERSITY PRESS

OXFORD

UNIVERSITY PRESS

Great Clarendon Street, Oxford, OX2 6DP,
United Kingdom

Oxford University Press is a department of the University of Oxford.
It furthers the University's objective of excellence in research, scholarship,
and education by publishing worldwide. Oxford is a registered trade mark of
Oxford University Press in the UK and in certain other countries

Published in the United States of America by Oxford University Press
198 Madison Avenue, New York, NY 10016, United States of America

British Library Cataloguing in Publication Data

Data available

ISBN 978-0-19-956616-7

This book is dedicated to Nora, who showed her trust in peace
when life had to begin anew, and who chose love
and justice over retribution.

Preface

The Kosovo crisis lasted for twenty years. That period saw the application of the entire arsenal of diplomatic tools available for crisis management, including good offices, negotiation, mediation through proximity talks and shuttle diplomacy, high-level conference diplomacy, action at the United Nations Security Council, and even the use of force. Despite this level of engagement, the provisional end result was the very one the organized international community had most wanted to avoid: independence for Kosovo. This book traces international diplomatic attempts to grapple with the crisis against the backdrop of Kosovo's struggle for statehood. It asks how Kosovo managed to achieve its aims and what this result will mean for the future of international relations. The relevance of this latter aspect—the impact of the Kosovo episode on the international system—was demonstrated most recently by Russia's actions over South Ossetia and Abkhasia. In that episode, Russia quite clearly set out to construct a parallel with the Kosovo case, however forced that parallel might have been.[1]

This book has two primary aims. On the one hand, it seeks to chronicle and analyse the development of the crisis and the international responses it elicited. On the other hand, it also considers more generally the impact of the crisis on developments in international relations and, notably, in international law, including the evolution of our thinking about human rights, self-determination, non-intervention and forcible humanitarian action.

As this is the first expansive work on the Kosovo crisis undertaken to date, its narrative is structured chronologically, so as to assist the reader in navigating the period's historical twists and turns. However, at times, this format might inhibit slightly the wider analytical ambitions of the book—a sacrifice that was felt necessary to secure clarity of presentation. Moreover, while the author is a legal specialist, an overly technical legal analysis was avoided lest it deter the reader with a more general interest in the development of this episode. Nevertheless, both the conclusions drawn, as well as the overall thesis advanced, endeavour to address the wider issues raised by events occurring in and around Kosovo, and to consider the legal dimension at least to some extent. For those with more specialized legal interests, references are made to alternative sources where the author has addressed the international legal issues more comprehensively.

---

[1] See Marc Weller and Jonathan Wheatley, *The War in Georgia: Great Power Politics and Failed Conflict Prevention* (London and New York: Hurst Publishers and Columbia University Press, forthcoming).

The focus of the presentation is very much on international attempts to engage with the crisis, which means that other interesting aspects have not been fully covered. For instance, very little space is devoted to the conduct of hostilities between NATO and Yugoslavia in 1999,[2] and the international administration of Kosovo under UNMIK remains unaddressed—the latter a potentially vast area of interest that will undoubtedly occupy many specialist monographs in years to come.[3] An attempt has been made, however, to offer a fairly comprehensive bibliography, to assist the reader seeking to pursue these and other areas.

This book covers the period of 1988 to 2008, ranging from the initial attempts by the Belgrade government to reduce the autonomy of Kosovo to the latter's eventual independence. As it went to press, somewhat ambiguous arrangements had just been made outside of a formal, new United Nations Security Council mandate for the incoming EULEX presence in the territory. Given the absence of agreement at the level of the Council, the modalities for implementation of 'supervised' independence were not yet fully in place. Still, the basic shape of developments in this respect had become visible and it seemed better to proceed with publication than await further events. This brings the period covered in the book to twenty years, almost exactly to the day.

The author acted as adviser to Kosovo in many, if not most, of the various peace processes and negotiations analysed in the book. An attempt has been made to offer a neutral, scholarly perspective on these events. Most of the historical documents on which this work relies have been assembled and published by the author in the *International Documents and Analysis Series*. Permission was granted by the Royal Institute of International Affairs to draw on an article addressing the Rambouillet Conference published in *International Affairs*, in Chapter 8.

The author gratefully acknowledges the support given to this publishing project by the staff of the European Centre for Minority Issues. Ms Katherine Nobbs offered research assistance, acted as sub-editor for this volume and compiled the chronology and index with her usual amazing efficiency. Adrian Zeqiri, the Director of the ECMI office in Kosovo, and Arben Osmani also rendered invaluable assistance to this project. Mr William McKinney provided materials for the bibliography. Ambassador Tore Bøgh, a key international actor in this episode, kindly read the manuscript and offered valuable suggestions, as did the anonymous readers at Oxford University Press. Ms Gill Colver proofread the initial version of the manuscript. Ms Maj-Britt Risbjerg Hansen and Ms Gisa Marehn at ECMI headquarters offered further support. Important points and suggestions were made by Ms Leonora Weller.

[2] See, for instance, Ivo Daalder and Michael O'Hanlon, *Winning Ugly: NATO's War to Save Kosovo* (Washington: Brookings Institution Press, 2000).
[3] An early, critical monograph on this issue is provided by Ian King and Whit Mason, *Peace at Any Price. How the World Failed Kosovo* (London: Hurst Publishers, 2006).

Once again, the author acknowledges the efficiency, speed and kindness of John Louth, Alex Flach, Christopher Champion, and Lucy Page at Oxford University Press in accepting this book and arranging for its expeditious production.

Marc Weller

Cambridge
August 2008

Contents

Table of Cases

Table of International Instruments and Domestic Legislation

List of Abbreviations

CSCE/OSCE	Conference on Security and Cooperation in Europe/ Organization for Security and Cooperation in Europe
CSO	Committee of Senior Officials
EC/EU	European Community/European Union
EULEX	European Union Rule of Law Mission in Kosovo
FRY	Federal Republic of Yugoslavia
ICRC	International Committee of the Red Cross
JIAS	Joint Interim Administrative Structure
KDOM	Kosovo Diplomatic Observer Mission
KLA	Kosovo Liberation Army
KVM	Kosovo Verification Mission
LBD	United Democratic Movement of Kosovo
LDK	Democratic League of Kosovo
NAC	North Atlantic Council
NATO	North Atlantic Treaty Organization
OSCE	Organization for Security and Cooperation in Europe
PCG	Pre-Constitutional Working Group
PDK	Democratic Party of Kosovo
PISK	Provisional institutions of self-government in Kosovo
SFRY	Socialist Federal Republic of Yugoslavia
UN	United Nations
UNHCR	United Nations High Commissioner for Refugees
UNMIK	United Nations Mission in Kosovo
UNOSEK	UN Office of the Special Envoy for the Future Status Process for Kosovo
UNPREDEP	UN Preventative Deployment Force in Macedonia
UNSG	United Nations Secretary-General
UNSC	United Nations Security Council
(UN)SRSG	Special Representative of the UN Secretary-General
VJ	Yugoslav armed forces
WEU	Western European Union

Chronology

1987

24 April — Future president Slobodan Milosevic rallies a crowd of Kosovo Serbs, who are alleging harassment by the majority Albanian community.

1989

23 February — Serbian Parliament unanimously adopts proposals for amendment of the 1974 Constitution, stripping Kosovo of autonomy rights.

22 March — Constitutional amendments approved by the provincial government of Kosovo, installed through Serb political intervention.

1990

26 June — Law on Special Circumstances permits the direct administration of Kosovo affairs by the Republic of Serbia.

5 July — Serbian Assembly votes to close the Kosovo Assembly permanently and to assume its responsibilities.

28 September — New Serbian constitution enters into force, which states that Kosovo is a province of Serbia.

26 December — Slobodan Milosevic is elected President of Serbia.

1991

25–6 June — Slovenia and Croatia declare independence.

7 July — Signature of the Brioni agreement, which ended the war in Slovenia and froze Croatian and Slovenian independence for three months.

7 September — Initial meeting of key interested governments at The Hague, chaired by Lord Carrington.

22 September — Kosovo formally declares independence.

25 September — UN Security Council (SC) imposes arms embargo against Federal Republic of Yugoslavia (FRY) (although with its consent).

23 December — Deadline for constituent units of the SFRY to submit their applications to the Badinter Commission, for recognition as sovereign states.

1992

15 January — Recognition of Croatia and Slovenia by the EU and other states.

6 April — Bosnia and Herzegovina is accorded recognition.

24 May — Elections take place in Kosovo. The Democratic League of Kosovo (LDK) wins a majority of seats in the assembly and its leader, Ibrahim Rugova, is elected President. Results are not recognized by Serbia.

8 July — Yugoslavia suspended from participation in the CSCE.

14 August — UN Special Rapporteur for Yugoslavia is established (initially Tadeusz Mazowiecki).

	Establishment of the CSCE Missions of Long Duration in Kosovo, Sandjak and Vojvodina.
26–28 August	Conference on Yugoslavia takes place in London.
7 September	Work of the permanent Conference on Yugoslavia begins in Geneva.

1993

25 May	SC Resolution 827 (1993) establishing the International Criminal Tribunal for the former Yugoslavia (ICTY).
July	OSCE Mission of Long Duration is withdrawn after FRY refusal to prolong mission.
9 August	Passage of SC Resolution 855 (1993), the only Council action to be targeted specifically at Kosovo between 1988 and 1998.
20 December	Milosevic is re-elected President of Serbia.

1995

27 July	Mazowiecki resigns as UN Special Rapporteur in protest at inaction by Western powers over Bosnia and Herzegovina. He is replaced by Elisabeth Rehn.
14 December	Dayton Peace Accords are signed in Paris.

1997

15 July	Milosevic is elected President of the FRY.
24 September	Contact Group (CG) expresses concern at situation in Kosovo, and calls for a solution based on 'enhanced autonomy' (but expressly not independence).

1998

25 February	A CG statement again rejects independence as a solution to unrest in Kosovo, but expresses concern at the deteriorating situation.
22 March	Elections take place in Kosovo. LDK win a majority and Rugova is re-elected as President. Results are not recognized by Serbia.
31 March	Adoption of SC Resolution 1160 (1998), calling on states to prevent the sale of arms to the FRY, including Kosovo.
16 June	Boris Yeltsin invites Milosevic to Moscow in an attempt to ward off military intervention in Kosovo.
8 July	Bonn Meeting of the CG.
23 September	SC Resolution 1199 (1998), adopted under Chapter VII UN Charter, affirms that the situation in Kosovo constitutes a threat to peace and security in the region.
1 October	Presentation of first Hill draft.
16 October	Signature of the Kosovo Verification Agreement, which led to the establishment of the Kosovo Verification Mission (KVM).
20 October	US Ambassador Holbrooke concludes agreement with Milosevic. NATO bombing narrowly avoided.
25 October	NATO-Serbia/FRY Meeting in Belgrade. OSCE establishes KVM.
1 November	Presentation of revised Hill proposal. Deadline for political settlement on the basis of the Holbrooke

	Agreement, upon which the Kosovo delegation had not been consulted.
18 November	Parallel conference organized by Serbia and attended, inter alia, by representatives of the 'national communities' in Kosovo. Counter-proposal to the Hill drafts issued.

1999

15 January	Discovery of Racak massacre.
22 January	CG meets in London to lay the groundwork for Rambouillet.
27 January	Final Hill draft put forward.
29 January	NATO issues a summons to the parties to negotiate at Rambouillet.
30 January	NATO issues a statement announcing that it is prepared to launch air strikes against Yugoslav targets 'to compel compliance with the demands of the international community and [to achieve] a political settlement'.
	The CG issues a set of 'Non-Negotiable Principles', effectively calling for the restoration of Kosovo's pre-1990 autonomy within Serbia, plus the introduction of democracy and supervision by international organizations. It also calls for a peace conference to be held in February at Rambouillet in France.
6–23 February	Parties convene at Chateau Rambouillet in France, led by the UK and French foreign ministers.
15–19 March	Follow-on conference in Paris.
18 March	Signature of Rambouillet Accords by Kosovo Albanian delegation. FRY/Serbia refuses to sign.
22 March	Negotiators travel to Belgrade in a last-ditch attempt to persuade the FRY/Serbia to accept the interim agreement.
23 March	Parliament in Belgrade votes to reject interim agreement.
24 March	NATO launches bombing campaign.
12 April	Germany presents the 'Fischer' peace initiative.
6 May	G-8 adopts set of agreed principles at Petersburg.
7 May	NATO bombs hit Chinese embassy in Belgrade.
24 May	ICTY issues indictment against top FRY/Serbian leadership.
29 May	FRY/Serbia accepts G-8 principles.
9 June	Conclusion of the Military Technical Agreement, establishing a detailed plan for FRY/Serbian withdrawal from Kosovo.
10 June	UN adopts Resolution 1244 (1999), placing Kosovo under UN interim administration (UNMIK) and authorizing a NATO-led peace force (KFOR) to enter the territory.
11 June	Termination of NATO bombing campaign.
24 September	Presidential elections take place in the FRY, with Milosevic and Vojislav Kostunica as clear front-runners. Although the regime-sponsored Federal Electoral Committee maintained that no candidate had won over 50 per cent of the vote, its results were subject to charges of irregularity.
5 October	Large-scale protests at perceived election-rigging by the Milosevic regime are dubbed the 'Bulldozer Revolution'.

Yugoslav Constitutional Court annuls the elections results and declares Kostunica the winner.

6 October	Milosevic resigns.
7 October	Kostunica is sworn in as President of FRY.

2001

15 May — Constitutional Framework for Provisional Self-government is issued as UNMIK Regulation 2001/9.

2002

4 March — Ibrahim Rugova is re-elected as President by the Kosovo Assembly, after ethnic Albanian parties reach a power-sharing deal. Bajram Rexhepi becomes Prime Minister.

24 April — Declaration of 'standards before status' policy by Special Representative of the UN Secretary-General (UNSG) Michael Steiner.

2003

14 October — First direct talks between Serbian and Kosovo Albanian leaders since 1999. These end with no agreement.

12 December — UNSC formally endorses status review process, to be effected concurrently with standards implementation.

2004

16–17 March — Violent riots erupt in Serb-majority area of Mitrovica and other parts of Kosovo.

31 March — UNMIK releases 117-page Kosovo Standards Implementation Plan, two years after announcement of 'standards before status' policy.

3 December — Parliament re-elects President Rugova and elects former rebel commander Ramush Haradinaj as Prime Minister. The latter's Alliance for the Future of Kosovo Party (AAK) enters into a coalition with the LDK.

2005

13–14 February — Serbian President Boris Tadic visits Kosovo, promising to defend the rights of Serbs in the region.

8 March — Haradinaj resigns as Prime Minister, and answers war crimes charges made by ICTY.

15 March — An explosion rocks the convoy of vehicles in which President Rugova is travelling through Prishtina. He is unhurt.

23 March — Bajram Kosumi takes over as Prime Minister of Kosovo.

13 June — UN Special Envoy Kai Eide delivers his comprehensive review on the situation in Kosovo to the UNSG.

2 July — Blasts go off near UN, OSCE and Kosovo parliament buildings in Prishtina. No-one is hurt.

2006

12 January — UN Special Envoy Martti Ahtisaari invites the parties to discussions in Vienna.

21 January	President Rugova dies in Pristina of lung cancer. He is succeeded in February by Fatmir Sejdiu.
20 February	UN-sponsored talks begin on the future status of Kosovo, presided over by UN Special Envoy Ahtisaari.
1 March	Prime Minister Kosumi resigns following criticism of his performance from within his own party. He is succeeded by former KLA commander Agim Ceku.
24 July	In Vienna, the CG representatives observe the first high-level meeting between ethnic Serbian and Kosovan leaders since 1999.
3 October	Russia sends demarche to the EU Presidency, demanding that the talks be continued in 2007 if no agreement is achieved by the end of 2006.
28–29 October	Voters in a referendum in Serbia approve a new constitution which declares that Kosovo is an integral part of the country. Kosovo's ethnic Albanian majority does not participate in the ballot and UN sponsored talks on the future of the disputed province continue.

2007

21 January	Serbia holds parliamentary elections. Radicals win most votes, but not enough to form a government.
26 January	Ahtisaari presents his plan to CG.
2 February	Ahtisaari presents his draft proposal in Belgrade and Prishtina. Welcomed by Kosovo Albanians but rejected by Serbians, who refuse to receive Ahtisaari.
26 March	The Comprehensive Proposal and Ahtisaari's Report, in which he recommends 'supervised independence' for Kosovo, are officially delivered to the UN Security Council.
19 April	Russia rejects the Ahtisaari proposal in the UN Security Council.
11 May	European members of the UN Security Council circulate a draft UN Security Council resolution that will replace UN Security Council Resolution 1244, endorse Ahtisaari's proposal, and end the UN administration after a transition period of 120 days. The US Permanent Representative to the UN says that the European/US draft has enough support in the Security Council to be adopted unless Russia chooses to use its Security Council veto, which Russia has threatened to do on numerous occasions unless the resolution is acceptable by both sides.
15 June	US President George W. Bush says Kosovo needs to be independent 'sooner rather than later'.
17 July	US and European Union redraft UN resolution to drop promise of independence at Russian insistence, replacing it with a pledge to review situation if there is no breakthrough after four proposed months of talks with Serbia. President Sejdiu says UN-sponsored process has failed and calls for a declaration of independence by the end of the year.
12 July	Russia rejects the latest draft of a UN Security Council resolution on the status of Kosovo.

9 August	Envoys from US, EU and Russia Troika start 120 days of further negotiations between Kosovo and Serbia in attempt to reach an agreement.
17 November	Hashim Thaci's Albanian Democratic Party (PDK) emerges as the winner in general elections. Thaci promises swift independence.
7 December	Final report of the Troika to the UNSG.
	Wolfgang Ischinger, the EU representative in talks on the future status of Kosovo, states that any unilateral declaration of independence by Kosovo will be 'promptly recognized' by the EU and that the EU will reach an agreement on Kosovo in a few days.

2008

3 February	Serbian President Boris Tadic narrowly wins re-election over nationalist Tomislav Nikolic.
16 February	European Council launches the EULEX Kosovo Mission in the wider area of Rule of Law.
17 February	Kosovo declares independence.
	Kostunica vows that Serbia will never recognize the 'false state', but rules out the use of military force.
18 February	US recognizes Kosovo as a 'sovereign and independent state'.
	EU External Relations Council releases statement that 'Member States will decide, in accordance with national practice and international law, on their relations with Kosovo', indicating a split within the EU.
14 March	Serbian opponents of independence seize a UN courthouse in Mitrovica, and more than 100 people are injured in subsequent clashes with UN and NATO forces. A UN police officer is killed.
9 April	Kosovo Assembly adopts new constitution.
15 June	Kosovo Constitution comes into force.

1

Introduction

I. The Meaning of the Kosovo Episode

The Kosovo crisis has divided the organized international community. Not unlike the war in Iraq, international action in relation to Kosovo has inspired fierce debate among governments and observers of international politics. While one might see in the international response to Kosovo an example of the return to the classical power politics of the 19th century, one could also argue that it is the seedcorn for the emergence of a new-style 21st century international constitutional order informed by universally held values. Or one might detect in the Kosovo episode signs of a breakdown both of the classical system dominated by interest politics of states and of the modern system of collective action organized under the umbrella of the United Nations (UN), heralding a period of post-modern international fragmentation and chaos.

A. A return to the 19th century?

The international handling of the Kosovo crisis might indeed be a turning point, demonstrating that we have returned to the classical system of great power politics. Seen from this perspective, the developments concerning Kosovo appear to confirm the old certainties of the classical, so-called realist or neo-realist paradigm. This is an analysis focusing on the state as the key actor in the international system, pursuing its self-interest through the exploitation of its relative power and influence.

The crisis, it could indeed be argued, unfolded according to the script of 19th-century cabinet diplomacy. Major powers became involved, pursuing their particular interests through traditional politics led by self-interest. The United States (US) was keen to utilize its unipolar dominance at the turn of the millennium and imposed its vision for a solution of the crisis (although one would need to question the element of actual self-interest in this instance). Russia sought to retain or regain influence and prestige on the European continent, struggling to be recognized again as a great power. In the application of classical geopolitics, Moscow also sought to defend Serbia, its only remaining ally in central Europe. At least during the first ten-year period of the crisis, Western European states also seemed to side with some of the Balkan players according to historical alliances, dating back to the Second World War or beyond—a phenomenon particularly visible in relation to the United Kingdom and France. Both states had a historical affinity with Belgrade that was only undermined when the extent of atrocities committed in the wider context of the Yugoslav crisis became apparent. Others were informed in their attitude to the conflict by hard-nosed business interests. Italian companies, for example, obtained lucrative communications licences from Belgrade during the crisis. This had a visible impact on the attitude of the Italian government.

Set against this neo-classical background, the modern institutions for collective action of the post-Second World War international system hardly seemed to matter. According to such a view, they were unmasked as the useless talking shops that political realists had always claimed they were. Instead, we saw the revival of instruments of national or international politics long thought overcome. These included conference crisis diplomacy of leading powers in the mould of Europe's classical balance of power. Peace settlement attempts were conducted in chateaux and castles in a style reminiscent of the 1815 Congress of Vienna or the victors' assembly of Versailles, rather than the sober atmosphere of the cramped UN headquarters building in New York. This classical practice even extended to the issuing of ultimata and the threat and actual use of military force for political ends—terms and concepts thought to have been permanently deleted from the diplomatic dictionary since 1945.

Within this neo-classical environment, according to this view, the US pursued a strategy of seeking to dismantle the Federal Republic of Yugoslavia (FRY) (as it was in 1999). First, the US and its somewhat reluctant allies committed an unwarranted act of aggression. Launching a sustained aerial campaign not only against Kosovo but also extending to much of Yugoslavia, the North Atlantic Treaty Organization (NATO) forced its will on a sovereign state and removed it from control over a significant part of its territory. Then, in a second stage of controversial action, these states conspired with the Kosovo leadership to bring about secession of the territory, in violation of the sovereign rights of Serbia. In both instances, they circumvented international rules and mechanisms designed to address problems of this kind, devaluing the rule of international law and the authority of the United Nations in the process.

B. An emerging international constitutional order

However, this perspective can be countered with reference to a number of innovative developments triggered by the crisis. Seen from a more progressive perspective, Kosovo marks the beginning of a new, more advanced form of international politics—the episode serves as the fountainhead of a new international order, not as a signifier of its demise. Instead of relying on outdated concepts, such as non-intervention and mono-dimensional concepts of sovereignty, Kosovo anticipates a post-modern international constitutional system that is still in the process of establishing itself. In such a world, people matter more than states.

Viewed from this angle, Kosovo made manifest the discovery that states cannot claim rights and privileges that exceed or destroy those of their constituents, the people. After all, the state is nothing more than the aggregation of the powers and competences transferred to it by its constituents. The rights of the people are the true source of state sovereignty. Such sovereignty cannot provide cover, through the doctrine of non-intervention, for the mistreatment, forcible displacement or extermination of the population or a significant segment thereof. Moreover, the argument continues, the state is a voluntary association of its citizens. Nothing can or should prevent citizens from freely disassociating themselves from an existing state with a view to forming a new one. If creating a state is an act of will of its constituents, then leaving the state on the basis of an act of will should also be possible.

In this instance, the organized international community intervened in order to save a population from severe mistreatment by the very authorities purporting to represent it, thereby exercising a responsibility to protect. Seen from this perspective, action by NATO in relation to Kosovo served as a major beacon to guide the nascent international practice of humanitarian action to save threatened populations. Similarly, the eventual secession of Kosovo from Serbia may be taken by some to vindicate the view that a population can exercise its will and leave a state, at least if it is not genuinely represented within it, or after it has suffered sustained and severe repression by the central authorities.

Adherents of this view will point to the fact that the Kosovo crisis demonstrates an international willingness to enforce core values of the international system, even against the 'sovereign will' of governments that disregard these cardinal principles, and even if, as was the case in this instance, no express United Nations mandate was available.

C. Fragmentation and chaos

As always, there is of course a third line of argument. By this reading, we have neither regressed into the brutal but stable classical system of 19th-century power politics, nor have we advanced towards the pursuit of universal values within an emerging international constitutional system of the 21st century. Instead, the example of Kosovo points towards the increasingly complex, difficult, and in some aspects, frightening post-modern world we are now entering. It is a world that has lost the certainties of brutal but stable classical power politics, and of the Westphalian international order, without gaining the benefits of a more advanced international constitutional system of global power regulation.

In such a world, the stabilizing concepts of state sovereignty, territorial unity and non-intervention have been fatally undermined, leaving us in a less predictable position. After all, the very identity of the nation-state—the core unit of the classical, Westphalian system—is being challenged by ethnic populations no longer willing to accept state boundaries which they consider unjust. In addition to challenges to the identity of the state as the key unit of the neo-realist system, its internal powers are also threatened. Populations are resisting the exercise of effective governmental authority. Traditionally, effectiveness was seen as the key legitimizing feature for the authority to govern. In addition, the traditional monopoly of the central state over organized violence has been broken by highly destructive terrorism deployed by movements operating across state boundaries. These transnational movements are motivated by ideological, religious or ethnic considerations that cannot be engaged through reasoned argument or negotiations based on what we perceive to be 'rational' choices.

The Kosovo crisis seems to exhibit all of these features. During the conflict, a population successfully rebelled against the authorities of the central state. While Belgrade continued to rely on the classical doctrine of 'effectiveness' of control over territory and population, its machinery of repression was sidelined for a considerable period. An ethnically-defined group dissociated itself from its territorial sovereign through peaceful resistance. It managed to establish and run a parallel system of governance in response to discrimination and repression, rendering meaningless the claim of supreme authority of the classical sovereign.

Subsequently the Kosovo Liberation Army (KLA) deployed what some considered 'terrorist' tactics. Drawing on financial resources collected through a transnational network ranging all over the Western world, it started a process that propelled international actors into war in Europe in defence of humanitarian interests and in disregard of the classical doctrine of non-intervention. In the wake of this use of force, the ethnic Albanians of Kosovo achieved independence with some international backing, breaking through the hitherto sacred doctrine of territorial unity in relation to the Republic of Serbia. Needless to say, this final status and the settlement that accompanied it in the shape of the Ahtisaari plan were obtained without the consent of the territorial sovereign. After independence, the prospect of secession from secession remains. There is talk about dividing Kosovo, assigning its mainly ethnically Serb-inhabited Northern area to Serbia. Such a step would undermine, again, the hitherto sacred doctrine of territorial unity. According to that doctrine, even a seceding entity is entitled to maintain is pre-existing borders (*uti possidetis*).

Seen from this perspective, Kosovo certainly does appear to break with the certainties of the classical international system, and to prophesy instead its fragmentation. This fragmentation was not balanced in this instance by the conduct of international politics through international institutions. When it came to the crunch, collective security administered through the United Nations was sidelined both in relation to humanitarian intervention and secession. Instead, states answered the challenges of the post-modern world through a reversion to unilateralism and power politics harking back to the classical era.

So where does this leave us in our assessment of the international response to the Kosovo crisis? Is it the worst of all possible worlds—a world where we have to contend with the challenges of the post-modern, fractionated international system, without the benefit of enhanced collective institutions and mechanisms capable of addressing them? Instead of collective action in the face of common challenges, are we seeing a return to classic, unilateral remedies that include the renaissance of the use of force as a means of international politics, as the 2003 action of the United States and her allies in relation to Iraq also seems to suggest? Or is this, after all, an international constitutional order in the making—an order characterized by core values, universally held? While enforcement of such values should occur through collective bodies, such as the UN Security Council, groups of states can act in support of international constitutionally-privileged values if these bodies fail to respond.

Against this background, the twenty-year crisis in Kosovo, starting with Belgrade's unilateral reduction of Kosovo's autonomy in 1988 and concluding, provisionally, with independence in 2008, represents more than a struggle for control over an area of some 10,000 square kilometres. It is also a struggle over the redefinition of the international system as such. This struggle is focused on six principal areas:

- the very concept of the state and state sovereignty in relation to its constituents;
- the question of governance within the state;
- the issue of human rights;
- the debate about the legitimacy and utility of the threat or use of force for humanitarian purposes;
- the problem of opposed unilateral secession;
- the issue of hierarchies and competences among international actors, involving a tension between collective action and unilateralism; and
- the issue of state consent in the settlement of international disputes and in the acceptance of international obligations.

These tensions are by no means mere theoretical constructs established in order to offer a neat frame for the analysis that is to follow. Diplomacy in this instance really was a struggle over whether considerations of human rights or of sovereignty should dominate the debate, whether the will of the people should trump the interests of territorial unity and stability, whether force may or may not be used, whether action can or should only be taken within a multilateral framework of collective security, and whether a settlement can be imposed upon parties to a conflict. In this instance, these tensions did not only underpin the debate, they lay at its heart. This was a debate conducted at the highest level of government, at times involving presidents and prime ministers, along with top national and international diplomats. The key international actors in this episode were keenly aware that they were engaging with the most basic and fundamental structural principles of the international system. They knew that the action they were taking would significantly shape the general international environment of the future, going far beyond this instance.

The principal protagonists, Belgrade and Prishtina, were also fully aware of this struggle over basic principles of the international order. Throughout, they were expressly appealing to the contesting values of the international system in order to strengthen or advance their respective cases. It is therefore worthwhile to explore these competing concepts briefly before turning to an analysis of the flow of events.

II. The Concept of the State

The first area of tension concerns the very definition of the state and its powers. In the early modern age, the state was seen to be the emanation of the sovereign, and sovereignty came in the shape of a person—the king or emperor. Louis XIV really meant it when he proclaimed '*l'état c'est moi*'—he literally was the state. In him, God himself had vested the absolute right to rule over his dominion. Of course, while such rule originated from a sacred grant, with the onset of the modern state system its exercise was no longer bounded by the spiritual authority of Rome. The right to rule really was absolute, restrained only by the personal religious and moral code of the sovereign. Hence, as Jean Bodin put it in his famous definition of 1576, sovereignty denotes supreme power over all subjects and objects in a given territory.[1]

That definition, and the treaties of peace of Augsburg (1555) and of Muenster and Osnabrueck (1648), paved the way for a system of sovereign states that recognized each other's supreme powers in relation to the territory they controlled.[2] This meant that states could profess no interest in the internal affairs of other states. This applied in particular to the religious orientation of the sovereign and the population he controlled. In the wake of the thirty-year religious war that had devastated Europe, such a recognition of the *domaine réservé* of states appeared sensible.

With the enlightenment, the doctrine of popular sovereignty gained currency. According to Jean-Jacques Rousseau, 'each of us puts his person and full power in common under the supreme direction of the general will; and in a body we receive each member as an indivisible part of the whole.'[3] Those who had joined

---

[1] Jean Bodin, *Six livres de la République* (1576).

[2] Leo Gross, 'The Peace of Westphalia, 1648–1948', *American Journal of International Law*, 42(1) (1948), 20–42.

[3] Jean-Jacques Rousseau, 'Of the Social Contract', in Victor Gourevitch (ed.), *Rousseau, The Social Contract and Other Later Political Writings* (Cambridge: Cambridge University Press, 1997), 50.

in such a social contract would be absolutely bound by the general will—the general will that was the expression of sovereignty of the community in question. Hence, sovereignty had been reallocated from the person of the monarch to the polity as a whole. But sovereignty remained absolute. As Rousseau put it:[4]

> Now, the Sovereign, since it is formed entirely of the individuals who make it up, has not and cannot have any interests contrary to theirs; consequently the Sovereign power has no need of a guarantor toward the subjects, because it is impossible for the body to want to harm all its members... The Sovereign, by the mere fact that it is, is always everything it ought to be.

Indeed, with the consecration of the free will as the source of all authority in Enlightenment thinking, sovereignty, being the aggregate of the will of all participants in the social contract, retained its somehow sacred character. The mystification of sovereignty was amplified with the advent of nationalism. The nation state was now seen as the expression of a Hegelian national spirit. The sovereign nation realized its historic destiny through the institution of state. Nothing that would interfere with this mystical process could be permitted. Accordingly, one of the cardinal principles of the classical international system was the principle of non-intervention in the internal affairs of states, however the state organized the internal processes of government.[5] The treatment of the internal affairs of the state as a 'black box' by the international system was only slowly breached. During the League of Nations period, certain restrictions were imposed, and internationally monitored, in relation to the treatment of minorities. However, this only applied to certain states that were subject to special legal regimes. After World War II, human rights gained international currency. However, the process of developing a human rights implementation system that would be truly universal (and therefore also apply to the states most likely to violate human rights) was hesitant.

With the termination of the Cold War, however, the concept of popular sovereignty has been readdressed. In part, the Kosovo episode accelerated this process. In the context of the developments in Kosovo of 1999, the UN Secretary-General pointed to the changing view of the meaning of sovereignty.[6] Sovereignty would henceforth not be identified as an accumulation of the rights of the state as an abstraction. Instead, it would be firmly connected with the entitlements of the state population. Its exercise by the government might be rendered conditional on the performance by the government of its responsibilities towards the governed. This changing outlook was a very important factor underpinning the development of the international response to the Kosovo crisis.

---

[4] *Ibid.*, 52.
[5] As classically analysed and expressed by Ellery C. Stowell, *Intervention in International Law* (Washington, D.C.: John Byrne Co., 1921).
[6] Kofi A. Annan, 'Two Concepts of Sovereignty', *The Economist*, 18 September 1999, 49f.

III. Governance

The principle of popular sovereignty has been formally accepted in international standards since the advent of the modern international system of the United Nations era. As was stated in the Universal Declaration of Human Rights of 1948:[7]

The will of the people shall be the basis of the authority of government; this will shall be expressed in periodic and genuine elections which shall be by universal and equal suffrage and shall be held by secret vote or by equivalent free voting procedures.

Of course, in reality, the majority of governments of the post-World War II world were anything but fully democratic. According to the principle of effectiveness, any government, however constituted, was treated as the authentic representative of a state and its population.[8] In order to maintain the legitimizing myth of popular sovereignty, it was simply presumed that any government was, by definition, representing its constituents.

During the Cold War years, when the question of governance lay at the heart of a life and death struggle among competing ideologies, it made sense to leave the issue of genuine democracy unaddressed. No universal consensus on essential principles of representative governance was possible. Accordingly, the international system strengthened, and further refined the international rule of non-intervention. As was stated in the UN General Assembly Resolution on Non-Intervention:[9]

No State has the right to intervene, directly or indirectly, for any reason whatever, in the internal or external affairs of any other State. Consequently, armed intervention and all other forms of interference or attempted threats against the personality of the State or against its political, economic and cultural elements, are condemned.

The International Court of Justice expanded upon this rule in the Nicaragua case, which involved US armed activities against that state:[10]

... in view of the generally accepted formulations, the principle forbids all States or groups of States to intervene directly or indirectly in internal or external affairs of other States. A prohibited intervention must accordingly be one bearing on matters in which each State is permitted, by the principle of State sovereignty, to decide freely. One of these is the choice of a political, economic, social and cultural system, and the formulation of

---

[7] Universal Declaration of Human Rights 1948, Art. 21(3).

[8] As was stated in the *Tinoco Arbitration (Costa Rica v. Great Britain)* of 13 October 1923: 'The issue is not whether the new government assumes power or conducts its administration under constitutional limitations established by the people during the incumbency of the government it has overthrown. The question is, has it really established itself in such a way that all within its influence recognize its control, and that there is no opposing force assuming to be a government in its place?', 2 ILR 34, 37.

[9] Resolution 2131 (XX), A/RES/20/2131, 21 December 1965, para. 1.

[10] *Nicaragua v. US*, 1986 ICJ 13, 106, 205.

foreign policy. Intervention is wrongful when it uses methods of coercion in regard to such choices, which must remain free ones.

Of course, when the Court addresses the right of 'the State' to decide freely, in reality this is the effective government in power. Accordingly, the principle of non-intervention does not really protect the process of the genuine transmission of the will of the people to its government from external interference. Instead, the principle protects any existing government from external action in relation to its internal activities.

However, in line with the changed appreciation of the doctrine of sovereignty, to which reference was already made above, the doctrine of representative government and of non-intervention was subjected to considerable review during the period of the Kosovo crisis. In particular, the language of the Universal Declaration of Human Rights was rediscovered at the point of the termination of the Cold War. While that point may not have marked the end of history, it did, at least for a certain period, mark the renewed consecration of the doctrine that the authority to govern must be based on the will of the people.[11] While this principle was revived at the universal level, and in other regions, such as the Americas, it was extended with particular vigour to the wider Europe encompassed in the region of application of the Conference on Security and Cooperation in Europe, the CSCE:[12]

The participating States declare that the will of the people, freely and fairly expressed through periodic and genuine elections, is the basis of the authority and legitimacy of all government.

At the universal level, the principle had been acted upon in 1994 when the UN Security Council granted a forcible Chapter VII mandate to remove the undemocratic junta that had seized the government of Haiti.[13] In the Americas, the regional states concluded a formal agreement providing for collective intervention should any one of them suffer a counter-constitutional coup.[14] In Europe,

---

[11] e.g.: General Assembly Resolution 45/150, 18 December 1990, A/RES/45/1501:

... 1. *Underscores* the significance of the Universal Declaration of Human Rights and the International Covenant on Civil and Political Rights, which establish that the authority to govern shall be based on the will of the people, as expressed in periodic and genuine elections;

2. *Stresses* its conviction that periodic and genuine elections are a necessary and indispensable element of sustained efforts to protect the rights and interests of the governed and that, as a matter of practical experience, the right of everyone to take part in the government of his or her country is a crucial factor n the effective enjoyment by all of a wide range of other human rights and fundamental freedoms, embracing political, economic, social and cultural rights;

3. *Declares* that determining the will of the people requires an electoral process that provides an equal opportunity for all citizens to become candidates and put forward their political views, individually and in cooperation with others, as provided in national constitutions and laws; ...

[12] Document of the Copenhagen Meeting of the Conference on the Human Dimension of the Conference on Security and Cooperation in Europe, 29 June 1990.

[13] Security Council Resolution 940 (1994), S/RES/940 (1994).

[14] Organization of American States Declaration on Representative Democracy, 5 June 1991: 'THE GENERAL ASSEMBLY RESOLVES: 1. To instruct the Secretary-General to call for the immediate convocation of a meeting of the Permanent Council in the event of any occurrences

the European Community/European Union (EC/EU), the CSCE and the Council of Europe (CoE) created a mechanism to support and stabilize the transition to democracy of the former communist states of Eastern Europe, known as the Stability Pact for South Eastern Europe.

The question of democratic governance was therefore regarded in a changed light around the time of the actions taken by the Belgrade authority against Kosovo.[15] Those actions appeared to disenfranchise a sizeable proportion of the population of Yugoslavia. While, even now, it is not clear that ethnic population groups that are concentrated in parts of the state territory have a right to territorial autonomy, the situation may be different where autonomy has already been granted,[16] for it is often taken as axiomatic that autonomy cannot be unilaterally revoked by the central government once it has been constitutionally established.[17]

The Kosovo conflict was one of dominance of one segment of the population by another—dominance that became institutionalized in the constitutional system of the state. The rump Yugoslavia (FRY), which emerged after the dissolution of the Socialist Federal Republic of Yugoslavia (SFRY) and consisted of Serbia and Montenegro, boasted a population of approximately 10.3 million. Of these, 62 per cent were ethnic Serbs. Perhaps surprisingly, by far the next largest ethnic group in the FRY was made up of ethnic Albanians. According to a Yugoslav census of 1991, 1.7 million of the overall population (16.6 per cent) were ethnic Albanians—that is over half of the population of Albania itself (3.3 million). In fact, the 1991 census probably underestimated the number of ethnic Albanians, as they had boycotted the census. The number of ethnic Albanians relative to Serbs in the FRY was set to rise further, given the significantly higher birth rate within that community. Most ethnic Albanians are Muslims, while Serbs tend to profess allegiance to their own branch of Christian Orthodoxy.[18]

In Kosovo itself, the number of Serbs had dropped from some 27 per cent in the 1950s to a mere 7 or 8 per cent by the 1990s. Some 90 per cent of the population of just short of 2 million were estimated to be ethnic Albanian. Around

---

giving rise to the sudden or irregular interruption of the democratic political institutional process or of the legitimate exercise of power by the democratically elected government in any of the Organization's member states, in order, within the framework of the Charter, to examine the situation, decide on and convene an ad hoc meeting of the Ministers of Foreign Affairs, or a special session of the General Assembly, all of which must take place within a ten day period.'...Adopted at the fifth plenary session of the General Assembly, 5 June 1991, AG/RES 1080 (XXI-0/91).

[15] e.g., Thomas Franck, 'The Emerging Right to Democratic Governance', *American Journal of International Law*, 86 (1992) 46–91, and Gregory H. Fox and Brad R. Roth (eds), *Democratic Governance and International Law* (Cambridge: Cambridge University Press, 2000).

[16] This question is addressed in Marc Weller, 'Self-determination and Autonomy', Working Paper Commissioned by the Working Group on Minorities of the United Nations Sub-Commission on Human Rights, UN Doc. E/CN.4/Sub.2/AC.5/2005/WP.5.

[17] Otherwise, it would be a matter of decentralization. See Marc Weller and Stefan Wolff, *Autonomy, Self-governance and Conflict Resolution* (London: Routledge, 2005), Chapter 1.

[18] In addition there were 5 per cent Hungarians, 3.3 per cent 'Yugoslavs', and 3.1 per cent Muslims in the FRY.

350,000 ethnic Albanians had left the territory, even before the 1998 hostilities, as a result of economic deprivation and repression exercised by the Serbian government since 1988. In addition, there were small groups of Turks, Bosniaks, Gorani, Roma, Egyptians, Ashkali and others.

Kosovo, along with the autonomous province of Vojvodina, had obtained a strong federal status under the 1974 SFRY Constitution. While it was an autonomous province within Serbia, it was equally represented in the federal organs, including the federal presidency. Governance in Kosovo was also principally independent of Serbia, and the territory enjoyed the right to create its own constitutional structure. The failure of ethnic Serbs to prosper in the territory, and their declining numbers, were taken as a sign of discrimination directed against them by the ethnic Albanian authorities in Kosovo. Slobodan Milosevic rose to power in Serbia on a promise to reverse this situation. Then, towards the end of the 1980s, ethnic politics began to take hold in Serbia. Tito's doctrine of brotherhood and unity among all ethnic groups was progressively replaced by an attempt to recreate a Greater Serbia, initially through Serbian dominance of the entire SFRY. The move to restore direct Serbian control over Kosovo lay at the heart of this policy. While Kosovo had been populated mainly by Albanians for several centuries, official doctrine promoted the view that the territory was in fact the heartland of Serbia, given the presence there of important and ancient religious sites.

Serbia then embarked upon a strategy of reducing Kosovo's independent powers, subordinating them to direct rule by Serbia. At the same time, Belgrade took control of key organs of the overall federation. This move was resisted by other republics in the federation, most strongly by Slovenia, and subsequently also by Croatia. When their attempts to renegotiate federal arrangements failed, they declared independence in June 1991. Armed conflict ensued, leading to the complete dissolution of the SFRY and also bringing independence for Macedonia and for Bosnia and Herzegovina. The hostilities were dominated by the Serbian attempt to ensure that areas inhabited mainly by ethnic Serbs, but lying outside the Serbian Republic, would be detached from the other republics seeking independence.

In the meantime, ethnic politics in Kosovo were initially administered through formal legislation. While Kosovo nominally retained its autonomous status, a new Serbian constitution, adopted in 1990, made permanent the abolition of Kosovo's independent powers which had commenced in 1988. This result was consolidated by a new constitution for the rump Yugoslavia, adopted in 1992. Over those four years, a whole host of openly discriminatory legislative acts had been adopted, directed at the ethnic Albanian population in Kosovo. This new constitutional and legal system was then enforced with some vigour, including by systematic acts of repression. While demographic manipulation was employed to reduce ethnic Albanian population numbers, a formal programme was introduced to encourage Serb settlement in the territory.

Accordingly, since 1988 the Kosovo population was no longer genuinely represented in the overall state. Nor was the Kosovo region governed by individuals who enjoyed local legitimacy. Hence, it was difficult to maintain that governance, at least in that region, was being administered in accordance with the will of the people. The question therefore arose whether the organized international community would seek to overturn this result and act in defence of Kosovo's entitlement to autonomy. In the classical international system, this would have been highly unlikely, as the internal organization of the state was very much treated as part of the *domaine réservé* covered by the doctrine of non-intervention.

IV. Human and Minority Rights

Of course, even in a state that governs itself according to democratic standards, safeguards for the rights of the minority need to be provided. After all, the minority can in principle be consistently outvoted and disenfranchised within the democratic state. Human rights, at the minimum, protect all human beings within the democratic state territory from abuse and discrimination by the state organs.

The theory of natural or inherent restrictions on the rights of the sovereign had been discussed since well before the appearance of Locke's famous *Treatises on Government*.[19] This doctrine was formally acted upon with the adoption of the Bill of Rights by the English Parliament,[20] when the first ten amendments to the US Constitution (also called Bill of Rights)[21] were ratified, and when the Declaration of the Rights of Men and Citizens[22] was consecrated in the course of the French Revolution. But while some of these documents speak of inherent or inalienable rights, in fact these rights were positively granted by the state. Where the state did not voluntarily restrict its sovereignty through a voluntary act, it could still claim perfect and absolute powers of sovereignty.

Over the decades, the doctrine of auto-limitation was established. While it was argued that sovereignty was principally perfect and comprehensive, the fully sovereign state could nevertheless limit some of its powers through an act of sovereign will. Such limitations initially took the form of constitutional compacts, granting fundamental rights to citizens. Later, such entitlements were also enshrined through international treaties as human rights. Of course, such human rights would initially only bind those states that had contracted into human rights treaties. But over time, a corpus of universally recognized human rights developed by virtue of general international customary law. In fact, the most essential rules of human rights, such as the prohibition of genocide, slavery, torture, discrimination and apartheid, crimes against humanity and war crimes, enjoy a special legal status in the international system. These rights apply to all states, whether or not it has been demonstrated that they have positively consented to

---

[19] John Locke, *Two Treatises on Government* (Cambridge: Cambridge University Press, 1988).
[20] 13 February 1689.   [21] 25 September 1789.   [22] 26/27 August 1789.

them through human rights treaties (universality). All states have a legal interest in the performance of these rights by all other states (*erga omnes* effect). States cannot unilaterally remove themselves from the application of these rights, even in times of crisis or emergency (non-derogability). Moreover, they lack the legal power to agree amongst themselves to suspend the application of the rights (*jus cogens* effect). Serious violations of these rules trigger an obligation on the part of other states not to recognize the consequences of the violation, not to assist the offending state in maintaining in place those consequences, and to consult about steps to reverse the situation (serious violations of peremptory norms of international law). Finally, most of the rules in question attract individual criminal responsibility, in addition to state responsibility. That is to say, the overall state that has committed a systematic campaign of crimes against humanity can be held internationally responsible for its conduct. At the same time, the individuals who have engaged in these acts, or commissioned them, can be held criminally liable in the domestic courts of individual states, or before international courts and tribunals.

By the time of the outbreak of the Yugoslav conflict, this set of international legal rules and mechanisms had consolidated into a coherent system for the protection of human rights, at least on paper. However, this design still collided with the traditional conceptions of non-intervention.[23] The Cold War had prevented the development of implementation mechanisms that would apply universally. Now, after the post-communist transition, such universal mechanisms also extended to Eastern Europe. However, the Yugoslav crisis was the first testing ground for the functioning of the interlocking mechanisms of universal, non-derogable *jus cogens* rights having an *erga omnes* effect and attracting individual criminal responsibility as well as an obligation to respond on the part of the wider international community. While it is generally agreed that the test failed in relation to Bosnia and Herzegovina, Kosovo offered a second opportunity for the application of these mechanisms.

In relation to Kosovo, it was clear that persistent and widespread human rights violations were being perpetrated under the auspices of official state policy. In fact, the discriminatory practices of the Belgrade authorities were openly reflected in Serbian legislation. There was also consistent intimidation of the ethnic Albanian majority population, including arbitrary arrests, beatings and other similar acts. The situation deteriorated significantly when armed conflict erupted in the region. In the campaign against the KLA, it seemed that a campaign of ethnic cleansing might be developing against the majority population in certain areas of Kosovo.

---

[23] Danilo Tuerk, 'Reflections on Human Rights: Sovereignty of States and the Principle of Non-intervention', in Morten Bergsmo (ed.), *Human Rights and Criminal Justice for the Downtrodden: Essays on Honour of Asbjørn Eide* (Dordrecht: Martinus Nijhoff, 2003), 753; Karl Zemanek, 'Human Rights Protection vs Non-intervention', in Lal Chand Vorah *et al.* (eds), *Man's Inhumanity to Man, Essays in Honour of Antonio Cassese* (The Hague: Kluwer Law International, 2003), 935.

Belgrade officially suspended some of its human rights obligations in order to provide cover for these actions. It also claimed that it had to engage in limited internal police actions to rout the KLA fighters it considered terrorists. However, it denied that there were significant, widespread human rights violations. Moreover, it strenuously held that the matter was an internal issue, to be addressed only by the Belgrade authorities. External interest represented unlawful interference.

It was at this point that the organized international community came under pressure to prove itself. Could it deploy international mechanisms in such a way that the human rights situation in the territory could be investigated, offering authoritative findings in this instance?

In addition to identifying human rights violations and naming them publicly, there remains of course the question of enforcement. Generally, condemnation of human rights practices is deemed sufficient action at the international level. However, what if the state concerned is impervious to international criticism? The rump Yugoslavia had been deeply involved in campaigns of ethnic cleansing and probable genocide in Croatia and in Bosnia and Herzegovina. This involvement was confirmed in official terms by the highest international human rights bodies and even the UN Security Council. The Council imposed tough and comprehensive economic sanctions against Belgrade. Nevertheless, these practices persisted until 1995, when NATO terminated the Bosnian conflict through a short bombing campaign.

If enforcement in relation to a case as notorious as Bosnia had been wanting, what international action would be taken in defence of human rights in Kosovo? Would Belgrade manage to cover its campaign of ethnic dominance and repression by invoking the doctrine of non-intervention, or would it be possible to pierce the armour of state sovereignty in this instance and to insist on political reconstruction of the state in favour of its disenfranchised population?

V. Forcible Humanitarian Action

Where human rights violations lead to the destruction or forcible displacement of an entire population, the question of an international response becomes even more pronounced. Following the advent of the UN Charter in 1945, the doctrine of humanitarian intervention in cases of extreme emergency was often regarded as a doctrine that would open the door to ceaseless abuse by powerful states against weaker ones.[24] As a result, the atrocities committed by Idi Amin

---

[24] The literature on humanitarian intervention is of course vast. For an overview at the traditional position see, for instance, Ian Brownlie, 'Humanitarian Intervention', in John Norton Moore (ed.), *Law and Civil War in the Modern World* (Baltimore: John Hopkins University Press, 1974), 217; Sean Murphy, *Humanitarian Intervention* (Philadelphia: University of Pennsylvania Press, 1996).

in Uganda and the Khmer Rouge in Cambodia against their own populations were initially left unaddressed during this period. When Tanzania and Vietnam respectively finally intervened, they chose to defend their action as self-defence, rather than invoking the doctrine of humanitarian intervention. It was deemed more important to maintain the international prohibition on the use of force as a means of international policy than to allow a precedent in favour of assisting a persecuted population.

However, with the termination of the Cold War came a re-evaluation of this position. Since 1988, the UN Security Council had become increasingly involved in seeking to oppose attacks by governments or other authorities on populations under their control. Under Chapter VII mandates, international action involving the possibility of the use of force had taken place in over a dozen cases. Determination that action would need to be taken in cases of future threats to populations was redoubled after the disasters of Rwanda and Bosnia and Herzegovina. Close to a million civilians had died in Rwanda while an international peace force mainly withdrew from the territory. In Bosnia and Herzegovina, over 100,000 mainly Muslim individuals had been murdered in a campaign of ethnic cleansing inspired by Belgrade, under the very eyes of a UN protection force.[25] The then incoming UN Secretary-General Kofi Annan had been chief of peacekeeping operations at the time. He, like many leading politicians of Western states, had vowed not to allow similar developments to take place in the future. Instead, a campaign was launched to clarify that state sovereignty could never act as a bar to international action in cases of genuine humanitarian emergency. After all, the population under threat in such circumstances was the actual sovereign, rather than the government seeking to exterminate it.

The Kosovo case fell squarely into this debate. The UN Secretary-General in this context described the:[26]

...dilemma of what has been called 'humanitarian intervention': on the one side, the question of the legitimacy of an action taken by a regional organization without a United Nations mandate; on the other, the universally recognized imperative of effectively halting gross and systematic violations of human rights with grave humanitarian consequences.

The Secretary-General noted that while the world cannot stand aside when gross and systematic violations of human rights are taking place, intervention must be based on legitimate and universal principles. He then admitted that:[27]

This developing norm in favour of intervention to protect civilians from wholesale slaughter will no doubt continue to pose profound challenges to the international community. Any such evolution in our understanding of state sovereignty and individual sovereignty

---

[25] Research and Documentation Centre Sarajevo (RDCS). 'Documenting the victims of conflict' (Sarajevo: RDCS). Available at <http://www.idc.org.ba/aboutus/documenting_the_victims.htm>, accessed 6 October 2008.

[26] Speech to the UN General Assembly, 20 September 1999, SG/SM/7136, GA/9596, at 2.

[27] *Ibid.*, 3.

will, in some quarters, be met with distrust, scepticism and even hostility. But it is an evolution that we should welcome.

While it was increasingly accepted that the UN Security Council might act in relation to humanitarian emergencies, the more controversial question was whether individual states could lawfully mount intervention operations in the absence of a Council mandate. The 1991 armed action by an international coalition to rescue the Kurdish population in Northern Iraq did not trigger significant international condemnation. Similarly, an operation the following year to protect the Shiite population in Southern Iraq, the so-called Marsh Arabs, had not engendered much controversy. Accordingly, it seemed possible to argue that there was now emerging within international practice a new right of humanitarian intervention under certain, strictly limited, circumstances.

When the situation in Kosovo worsened in 1998, there were indications of an impending humanitarian catastrophe. Hundreds of thousands of ethnic Albanians were being displaced from their homes. A large number fled across the border into Albania or Macedonia. There were fears that Belgrade might add extermination of the population to its apparent campaign of forcible displacement, as had occurred in Bosnia. The question arose as to whether the organized international community would now be ready to meet this challenge. If it was, the doctrine of humanitarian action, and of the supremacy of the interests of populations over those of states or governments, would be consolidated. If not, the classical doctrine of sovereignty as a bar to international action might be reinforced, at the cost of significant humanitarian suffering in the territory.

VI. The Issue of Secession

The question of international action in response to the emergency in Kosovo was made more complicated by the self-determination dimension of the case.

If the state is nothing more than the accumulation of public powers assigned to it by its constituents, then why should some of those constituents not be able freely to remove their consent, and to leave the existing state structure to create another? This is a problem with which the international system has grappled for many decades.[28] The answer that was found within the classical system was

---

[28] e.g., Viva Ona Bartkus, *The Dynamic of Secession* (Cambridge: Cambridge University Press, Cambridge, 1999); Harry Beran, 'A Liberal Theory of Secession', *Political Studies* 32 (1984); Nathaniel Berman, 'Sovereignty in Abeyance: Self-Determination and International Law', *Wisconsin International Law Journal*, 7 (1988), 51–105; Sam K.N. Blay, 'Self-Determination: A Reassessment in the Post-Communist Era', *Denver Journal of International Law and Policy*, 22 (1994), 275–315; Lea Brilmayer, 'Secession and Self-Determination: A Territorial Interpretation', *Yale Journal of International Law*, 16 (1991), 177–202; Lee C. Buchheit, *Secession: The Legitimacy of Self-Determination* (Yale University Press, New Haven, CT, 1978); Deborah Z. Cass, 'Rethinking Self-Determination: A Critical Analysis of Current International Law Theories', *Syracuse Journal*

straightforward: unilateral opposed secession is simply not possible, or at least it is not legally privileged. If it occurs, the state under threat can use violent means to defeat secession. However, events in the former Yugoslavia in particular have shown that this simple rule may no longer be adequate to address increasingly complex struggles for identity and control over peoples, for self-determination and statehood. Such conflicts do not disappear by virtue of being ignored.[29]

The classical international system, and the rules which govern it, was created by governments acting on the international plane for their own benefit. It comes as no great surprise, therefore, that all governments in power have a mutual interest in perpetuating the survival of the state they claim to represent, within its existing boundaries. Such an attitude is also seen to bring with it the benefit of international stability. Such stability is achieved through the doctrine of territorial unity which is enshrined in numerous international instruments, including the Helsinki Final Act of the CSCE.

Of course, this doctrine is circumscribed by the right to self-determination. While self-determination has many layers of meaning, its scope of application in the context of unilateral opposed secession has been defined in very narrow terms by governments. Self-determination as a legal entitlement to independent statehood has been made available only to colonial non-self-governing territories and in analogous circumstances (for instance, internal colonialism, alien occupation, racist regimes and secondary colonialism). It is not a right pertaining to a self-constituting people, but applies instead to territorial entities defined through colonial administration to which a population is linked in a more or less incidental way. Furthermore, the right can be exercised only once, at the point of decolonization, within the colonial boundaries.[30]

In this way, the rhetoric of self-determination could be safely embraced by governments, including those of newly independent states (former colonies) from the 1960s onwards, without at the same time endorsing a concept which might be invoked against them at some future stage. However, the attempt by the Baltic republics to re-establish statehood and obtain independence from the Union of Soviet Socialist Republics (USSR) in 1990 foreshadowed the pressure which was exerted on this restrictive view after the unfreezing of international relations upon the conclusion of the Cold War. The unilateral declarations of independence of, initially, Croatia and Slovenia which followed in 1991 were seen to pose a dangerous challenge to the

of International Law and Commerce, 18 (1992), 21–40; James Crawford, 'State Practice and International Law in Relation to Secession', *The British Yearbook of International Law* 69 (1998), 85–117; Marcello G. Kohen (ed.), *Secession*, (Cambridge: Cambridge University Press, 2006); Christian Tomuschat (ed), *Modern Law of Self-determination*, (Dordrecht: Martinus Nijhoff, 1993); Christopher Heath Wellman, *A Theory of Secession* (Cambridge: Cambridge University Press, 2005).

[29] This issue, and novel approaches to it, is addressed at length in Marc Weller, *Escaping the Self-determination Trap* (Dordrecht: Martinus Nijhoff, 2008).

[30] See Marc Weller, 'The Self-determination Trap', *Ethnopolitics*, 4 (2005), 1–42.

doctrine of territorial unity. Hence, when it emerged that these actions could not be undone, governments set about limiting the effect of the precedent they set.[31]

This was achieved by combining two arguments. The SFRY, it was asserted, had not been subjected to secession, but had in fact dissolved entirely. Hence, there was no bar to statehood for the federal republics which emerged free and unencumbered by the doctrine of territorial unity. After all, the beneficiary of that doctrine, the overall federation, had disappeared. In addition, the federal republics were entitled to claim statehood on the basis of a right to self-determination—a right which was located not in general international law but in SFRY constitutional law, for the SFRY Constitution of 1974 had in fact provided for the possibility of secession of its constituent units.

Oddly enough, a wider assertion of the right to self-determination had been made by the rump Yugoslavia. It claimed that the mainly Serb-inhabited areas of Croatia and Bosnia and Herzegovina should be entitled to secede from secession, as it were, and to constitute themselves as independent states. The Yugoslav republics had argued that they, as constitutional self-determination entities had the right to leave. Kosovo argued that it, too, had this entitlement, based on its federal status under the 1974 Constitution. Both of these propositions were consistent with the doctrine of *uti possidetis*, which holds that seceding entities must do so within previously established (in this case, federal) boundaries. Serbia now claimed that any ethnic Serb population should be able to leave, disrupting the territorial unity of the newly independent entities.

This argument was rejected by the Badinter Arbitration Commission, established to advise the International Conference on the Former Yugoslavia on issues of recognition, statehood, and succession. While self-determination also applied to Serbs and others who now found themselves in the minority in these new states, this was a different kind of self-determination. It was not an entitlement to statehood, but instead self-determination in this context was reduced in content to human and minority rights, and to autonomous structures of governance in areas where Serbs constituted a local majority.[32]

It was partially in order to prevent further extension of self-determination claims that the governments involved in the international administration of the collapse of the SRFY, acting through the European Union (or the European Community), the Organization for Security and Cooperation in Europe (OSCE), NATO, and the United Nations Security Council, insisted on the maintenance of Bosnia and Herzegovina as a state within its former SFRY boundaries. Hence, at Dayton it was accepted that the mainly Serb entity of the Republika Srpska would administer itself with a high degree of autonomy, but within the continued territorial unity of Bosnia and Herzegovina. The legal

---

[31] See Marc Weller, 'The International Response to the Dissolution of the Socialist Federal Republic of Yugoslavia', *American Journal of International Law*, 86 (1992), 569–607.
[32] Opinion No. 2 of the Badinter Arbitration Commission (1992) 31 ILM 1497.

management of the creation of new states from the former SFRY thus avoided a precedent in favour of a wider right of secession outside the colonial context.

However, it soon became clear that a concept of self-determination that was based merely on the constitutional status of a republic within a federation was not free of dangers. This became evident with the example of Chechnya.[33] Chechnya had been an autonomous territory within Russia while Russia had been a federal unit of the USSR. With the disappearance of the USSR, Russia achieved statehood. The new Russian Constitution in turn promoted Chechnya to the status of a republic within the Russian Federation. Would Chechnya now be able to claim constitutional self-determination and statehood on the basis of the Yugoslav precedent? The answer provided by other governments was an emphatic no. Chechnya found that it was not accorded the legal protection available under the doctrine of self-determination when it took on the Russian Federation and engaged in an armed struggle for independence.

Instead of insisting on a cessation of repressive measures, the withdrawal of Russian troops, and maintenance of the territorial integrity of Chechnya, the international community merely insisted on compliance by Russia with human rights and humanitarian law while it re-established effective control over the territory. Chechnya's status was only consolidated after Russia effectively lost the armed conflict and had to accept the possibility of Chechen independence in an interim agreement that it concluded voluntarily in 1996. However, when Russia unilaterally abrogated that agreement and forcibly reincorporated the territory after its armed forces had reorganized, international condemnation of the action was muted.

The case of Kosovo was seen to fall squarely on the borderline between the precedent set by the Yugoslav republics and that set by Chechnya. Under the 1974 SFRY Constitution, Kosovo was defined as a part of the Republic of Serbia, but it also had its own separate federal status. It was represented separately on the collective presidency of the SFRY, had its own structures of governance (including a national bank) and its own territorial identity. The international community's hesitation in view of the fact that Kosovo might constitute an unhelpful precedent for other cases made less of an impression on the people of Kosovo, who could not see why a population of 90 per cent Albanians should be left under what they saw as the despotic and arbitrary rule of a small elite of ethnic Serbs in the territory.

Proposals that Kosovo should consider itself a 'colonized' territory entitled to colonial self-determination were however not taken up. While the Kosovars felt as if they were being colonized and subjected to a veritable apartheid regime, governments have developed an understanding which once again limits the application

---

[33] Luke P. Bellocchi, 'Recent Developments: Self-determination in the Case of Chechnya', *Buffalo Journal of International Law*, 2 (1995), 183–91; Tarcisio Gazzini, 'Considerations on the Conflict in Chechnya', *Human Rights Law Journal*, 17 (1996), 93–105.

of this doctrine very significantly. The definition of a 'colonial territory' is very much restricted to classical colonialism, that is, to the occupation of a distant territory by an alien and racially distinct metropolitan state for the purposes of economic exploitation during the time of imperialism.

Kosovo instead based its case on the particularities of the SFRY constitution. In this way, it could avoid invoking a broad reading of the right to self-determination that would necessarily have had to be resisted by other states. Kosovo also pledged to respect the territorial integrity of neighbouring states and to renounce all territorial claims, for example in relation to Macedonia. It ruled out a pan-Albanian agenda, indicating that it was indeed seeking independence, rather than union with Albania. And it indicated a willingness to accept all conceivable human and minority rights standards, and to subject itself to intrusive human rights monitoring, especially in relation to ethnic Serbs and others.

The governments and international organizations involved in responding to this claim opted for the restrictive view of constitutional self-determination and did not accept a right to statehood for Kosovo throughout most of the run of the crisis. In view of Serbia's position, and the fear of confrontation with the Milosevic government, it was held that Kosovo had not had republic status within the Socialist Federal Republic of Yugoslavia, and was thus barred from the entitlement to statehood as claimed by republics. Instead, human rights should be respected in relation to the territory, and there should be meaningful self-administration. The expression of will in favour of independence by the Kosovo population in a referendum of September 1991 and the declaration of independence were ignored in the initial peace settlement conference on Yugoslavia of 1991/2.[34]

However, ignoring a problem will not necessarily make it go away. Whatever the commitment of the organized international community to the principle of territorial integrity and unity in this case, in the end a situation prevailed where independence could no longer be effectively opposed. Indeed, some twenty years after the process of reducing Kosovo's autonomy was initiated by Serbia, independence was declared with some international support. The question remains how this fact can be explained and what impact this action will have on the international system.

VII. Competences and Hierarchies among International Actors

If Kosovo has presented a challenge to the classical restrictions on international action in relation to the domestic sphere of states, then the question arises: who exactly is entitled to address the situation? Clearly, the architecture of the international system establishes a rough hierarchy of actors. At the top of the pyramid

[34] See Marc Weller, *The Crisis in Kosovo 1989–1999* (Cambridge: International Documents and Analysis), 80–89.

sits the UN Security Council. The Council is not restricted in its functions and powers only to ensuring compliance with the prohibition on the use of force enshrined in Article 2(4) of the UN Charter. While states are barred in principle from using force in circumstances other than self-defence against an armed attack, the Council can take effective preventative measures for the maintenance of international peace and security before such a transgression has occurred.

During the 1990s, an expansive view emerged as to which situations could be regarded as threats to international peace and security suitable for Council treatment.[35] In earlier practice, it was thought that the powers of the Council were only applicable to interstate violence. The struggles against colonialism and apartheid expanded this view to cover instances of repression within colonial empires or in South Africa. By the end of the Cold War, it became clear that the external ramifications of internal strife can also constitute threats to international peace. For instance, the outpouring of refugees into neighbouring territories, or the risk of the spreading of internal conflict beyond state borders can trigger Security Council action. Furthermore, since Security Council Resolution 794 (1992) on Somalia, it is also clear that the magnitude of humanitarian suffering of a population under threat of death or displacement can itself be considered a threat to peace.

If the Council can therefore be said to have generated a passport to action through its own practice in relation to internal conflicts, this does not mean of course that it will always act in the same way, even when circumstances would appear to so warrant. Some governments remain hesitant when it comes to the authorizing action that would constitute an intervention in the internal affairs of states. This includes China and Russia—two states equipped with the power to veto Council decisions.

What happens if there is a need for authoritative decisions from the Council, but it is precluded from action due to the veto? In the Kosovo episode, this applied both to the demand for humanitarian intervention that followed Rambouillet, and to the endorsement of the final status for Kosovo proposed by UN Special Envoy Martti Ahtisaari. One view would hold that a failure by the Council to act means that no authority is granted. According to this view, it would be presumptuous to determine that no decision amounts to a failure to decide. Instead, inaction by the Council is in fact a decision of the Council that no action should be taken. Such a decision not to act is just as authoritative as a Chapter VII resolution in favour of action.

An alternative view would hold that it is not realistic to focus on action or inaction in accordance with the day-to-day politics of the major powers with permanent seats on the Security Council. While Council authorization is to be preferred, so as to clarify the legitimacy of an action, the lawfulness of that

---

[35] e.g., Mohammed Bedjaoui, *The New World Order and the Security Council: Testing the Legality of its Acts* (Dordrecht: Martinus Nijhoff, 1994).

action is not dependent on a mandate. A true Chapter VII Security Council mandate would immediately render a humanitarian intervention operation lawful. However, in the absence of a mandate, a legal basis may also be sought in general international law. Hence, for those who believe that Kosovo has strengthened the precedent in favour of a right of humanitarian intervention in general international law, no Council mandate is required.

The same would seem to apply to Kosovo's Declaration of Independence. According to some, unilateral independence against the wishes of a central government is not possible. Only the Council has the power to impose such a result on a government. Others note that statehood is a matter of fact. While the Council can perform an important function in clarifying the situation, the passage of time will have the same effect, as more and more states recognize.

In addition to the powers of the Security Council, another issue concerns the role of defensive alliances and regional organizations.[36] NATO considers itself an alliance which, according to Article 51 of the UN Charter, can use force in self-defence without the need for Council authorization. NATO has sought to preserve its freedom of action even when it is not, strictly speaking, engaging in self-defence. Hence, although NATO's humanitarian intervention in Kosovo was not authorized by the Council, nevertheless, some argue that the collective decision of nineteen NATO states to act under the auspices of the Alliance did accord legitimacy to the operation.

While NATO operations are not subject to a formal veto, the actions of the OSCE are based mainly on consensus decision-making. The OSCE was continually reinventing itself throughout much of the period of the Kosovo crisis. It was created in order to preserve the status quo in Europe throughout the Cold War years. With the sometimes violent dissolution of the former Soviet Union and the former Yugoslavia, it took on a new role of crisis prevention and crisis management. In fact, the OSCE (which is not formally established as a legal organization) was recognized by the UN Security Council as an organization or arrangement of regional security according to Chapter VIII of the UN Charter. This means that it can take on the role of sub-contractor to the Security Council, acting in its stead in the event that a mandate is granted by the Council.

While the OSCE was reinventing itself, the EU was also struggling to develop its identity in the area of foreign and security policy. Its action in relation to the Bosnia crisis was generally considered a failure. The EU was campaigning hard to try again, taking the lead on Kosovo during the second phase of the developing crisis. However, EU policy was prone to internal division among its member states, as was evident throughout. At times, its member states took individual initiatives, stealing the limelight from Brussels. On other occasions, no consensus

---

[36] Tarcisio Gazzini, 'NATO Coercive Military Activities in the Yugoslav Crisis (1992–1999)', *European Journal of International Law*, 12 (2001), 391–436.

could be reached on collective action and the EU had to proceed according to the lowest common denominator.

While action was difficult to coordinate among members of the relevant international agencies, the same was true in relation to coordination of the international organizations. Through the so-called Contact Group—created in 1994 and composed of the US, the UK, France, Germany, Italy and Russia—an attempt was made to combine the differing layers of authority in Europe and beyond. According to the doctrine of 'joined-up international governance', the Group was meant to bring Russia into the picture. Russian support for policy initiatives was deemed essential, as these would ultimately require the approval of either the OSCE or the UN Security Council. Without Russia's approval, there was no chance that these bodies would grant a mandate.

While reliance on this mechanism offered the prospect of coordinated action between the EU, the OSCE, NATO and the UN, it also posed certain risks. Giving Russia a seat at the table would also limit the freedom of action of the EU and NATO on issues where Russia was unwilling to agree. As it turned out, this difficulty would pose significant problems during the second decade of international attempts to come to grips with the Kosovo crisis.

VIII. The Issue of Consent

A final issue to consider relates to the basic operation of the international system. In the classical system, it is unquestioned that a state can only be subjected to legal obligations if it has freely consented to them. Indeed, classically, it would not even be possible to constrain a government to submit a dispute to peaceful settlement processes. As the Permanent Court of International Justice put it:[37]

This rule, moreover, only accepts and applies a principle which is a fundamental principle of international law, namely, the principle of the independence of States. It is well established in international law that no State can, without its consent, be compelled to submit its disputes with other States either to mediation or to arbitration, or to any other kind of pacific settlement.

Throughout the period of the violent dissolution of Yugoslavia, the rule of consent was applied in relation to Belgrade, and it was exploited by the Milosevic government and its successors. As will be noted later in this book, Belgrade refused to renegotiate the SFRY constitution, contrary to the demands of several other republics.[38] Belgrade also refused acceptance of the outcome of the EC Conference on Yugoslavia—an agreement that was meant to provide for the peaceful dissolution of the federation to the extent that this was still

---

[37] PCIJ, Ser B, No. 5, at 27, *Eastern Carelia.*
[38] See Chapter 2, Sections III and IV.

possible at the time. All the other republics accepted. Belgrade also frustrated the mission of the Special Group that followed on from the initial conference process.[39] Moreover, Belgrade withdrew its consent to the presence of the early CSCE missions on the territory of Kosovo, forcing that mission, which was one of the few successful ventures in the administration of this crisis, to close down. Finally, Belgrade opposed the Rambouillet agreement on Kosovo, and it denounced the provisions of the Ahtisaari Comprehensive Proposal. Overall, therefore, Belgrade participated in the various international attempts of generating internationally supported outcomes during the various phases of the crisis, but it never genuinely engaged. Rather, its participation appeared limited to the point of keeping negotiation ventures in place when that appeared useful to deflect international pressure.

After this pattern had run consistently over the two decades of the Kosovo crisis, the question ultimately arose whether the organized international community, which had invested billions in stabilizing the territory through the UN governance mission after the 1999 conflict, would now, finally, be ready to impose a settlement. The outcome of the year-long Vienna negotiations, the Comprehensive Proposal put forward by UN Special Envoy Martti Ahtisaari, had been developed as a balanced solution with the support of the international Contact Group (including Russia) and under the flag of the United Nations. It had been endorsed by the UN Secretary-General. Nevertheless, Belgrade demanded a fresh set of negotiations. This demand, too, was granted through the Ischinger Troika negotiations of 2007, without result. Hence, the question arose whether the organized international community, acting through the UN Security Council, would now have the capacity to impose a settlement without Yugoslav consent.

---

[39] See below Chapter 3, Section II.

2

Background to the Crisis

Kosovo is a territory occupying an area of some 10,887 square kilometres bordering on Serbia, Montenegro, Macedonia and Albania. According to a somewhat contested 1991 census of the Yugoslav authorities, its inhabitants numbered roughly two million, of whom some 89 to 90 per cent were estimated to be ethnic Albanian, 8 to 9 per cent ethnic Serbs, and the remaining number divided among small groups of Bosniaks, Turks, Vlachs, Gorani, Roma, Egyptians, Ashkali and others.

I. Distant History with Modern Consequences

Ethnic Albanians claim that their ancestors, the Illirian tribe of Dardanians, settled in modern-day Kosovo as long as 4,000 years ago. From around 1150 onwards, a Serb kingdom began to establish itself in the central Balkan area. This kingdom encompassed both Serb and Albanian segments of the population. However, as soon as the Serb nation was consolidated into early statehood, it came under severe pressure from the Ottoman Turks. On 15 June 1389, an invading Ottoman army under Sultan Murad I engaged a coalition of forces from the region. While the engagement was in fact militarily inconclusive, historical folklore has turned it into a glorious defeat that inaugurated the centuries of Ottoman rule in parts of the region. Indeed, the military leaders on both sides, Serb Prince Lazar and Murad, fell during the battle at Kosovo Polje (the field of Blackbirds), near Prishtina. Somewhat ironically in view of the subsequent history, ethnic Serbs and a sizeable Albanian element fought side by side against the Turks in this engagement.

Despite increasing Ottoman influence over the region in the wake of the battle, Lazar's son Prince Stephan and his successors retained control over Kosovo for several decades. However, by 1459 Ottoman rule had established itself firmly, leading to the 'final extinction of the medieval Serbian state'.[1]

During Ottoman rule, many ethnic Albanians converted to Islam. Serbs, on the other hand, generally remained committed to their Eastern Orthodox Christian

---

[1] Noel Malcolm, *Kosovo: A Short History* (New York: New York University Press, 1998), 92 (hereinafter Malcolm, *Kosovo*).

religion. Under the Ottoman millet system, religious self-administration was tolerated.

Serbs continued to live in the region under Ottoman rule, although a significant exodus took place in 1690, led by Orthodox Patriach of Pec, Arsenije IV, himself. Some 40,000 Serbs left the area for the Belgrade region in the wake of an ill-fated attempt by Austria to conquer the territory. This attempt had been supported by Serbs. When the Habsburg forces withdrew, they felt exposed to repression and left. Similar events followed the Austro-Turkish war of 1788–91.[2]

From the early 19th century onwards, with the failing attempts of the Ottoman Empire to modernize its structures of governance and to retain control over its territorial possessions, Serb nationalism increasingly manifested itself in sporadic rebellions, often centred in Kosovo. During the period of 1817 to 1840, Serbia regained the status of a semi-autonomous principality. Over subsequent years, an attempt was made to expand the boundaries of this entity, to match those of the former medieval kingdom. Serbian statehood, however, matured within the context of the international administration of the dismantling of the Ottoman Empire, the 'sick man of Europe', through the Concert of Europe system of congress diplomacy. The Congress of Berlin of 1878 set about reordering the Balkans, granting independence for Serbia and Montenegro respectively, after the Ottomans had withdrawn their last garrisons in 1862. Ethnic Albanian inhabited territories were accorded the status of suzereignty as part of the vilayet structure of the Ottoman Empire.[3]

In 1882, a Serbian Kingdom was proclaimed. In the years which followed, Serbia agitated for territorial expansion, demanding the incorporation of Kosovo, still part of the Ottoman Empire, and access to the Adriatic. A movement for the establishment of a Greater Serbia culminated in the establishment of the secret association of the Black Hand or 'Union of Death' under Colonel Dimitrijevic Apis in 1911.

While Serbia had enjoyed a period of medieval statehood principally encompassing all Serbs, the Albanians saw themselves as a people forever denied their national state. The ethnic origin of the Albanians (or Illyrians or Dardanians) is somewhat mysterious.[4] They can be divided into the Ghegs of the northern region, including Kosovo, and the Tosks of southern Albania.

With the crumbling of the Ottoman Empire, hopes for the establishment of an Albanian state were finally raised. However, there also emerged the prospect of the apportionment of mainly Albanian-inhabited territories among the states seeking to profit from dismemberment of the Ottoman Empire. In response

---

[2] Several historians see this exodus as the starting point of the change of the demographic character of the territory in favour of ethnic Albanians, e.g., Barbara Jelavich, *History of the Balkans: Twentieth Century*, II (Cambridge: Cambridge University Press, 1983), 93; Miranda Vickers, *The Albanians: A Modern History* (rev. edn, New York: Tauris, 1997), 13 (hereinafter Vickers, *The Albanians*).

[3] Vickers, *The Albanians*, 70.   [4] Malcolm, *Kosovo*, 22ff.; Vickers, *The Albanians*, 1.

to these pressures, in 1878, the Prizren League was formed, an alliance of ethnic Albanian clans which, in due course, demanded the establishment of a unified Albanian Ottoman province under Albanian administration.[5] During the uprising of 1912, demands for autonomy were transformed into claims for Albanian independence.

The ensuing instability emboldened the regional states of Bulgaria, Serbia, Montenegro, and Greece to launch the first Balkan war later that year. Serbia rapidly expelled the remaining Ottoman forces from Kosovo, advanced on the Adriatic, and wrought significant destruction upon the Albanian population. Montenegro also established control over Albanian-inhabited territories. However, at the London Conference of 1913, the great European powers decreed that some of these successes were to be reversed, leading to the creation of the state of Albania. Kosovo, however, remained under Serbian control. Those who favour its independence point to the fact that it was never formally and constitutionally incorporated into Serbia.[6]

During this period, the excesses of Serbian administration in Kosovo were so shocking to the international community that in 1914 an international commission of enquiry was launched to consider this and other burning issues in the Balkan area. The Commission reported that a veritable policy of ethnic cleansing was in operation:

Houses and whole villages reduced to ashes, unarmed and innocent populations massacred...such were the means which were employed and are still being employed by the Serb-Montenegrin soldiery, with a view to the entire transformation of the ethnic character of regions inhabited exclusively by Albanians.[7]

During the First World War, some of the horrors visited upon the Albanians of Kosovo in the course of the Balkan wars were replayed, although there was also counter-violence. The end of the war left Kosovo within the new Yugoslav Kingdom of the Serbs, Croats, and Slovenes. Serbia once again engaged in repression of the Albanian population, which was also subjected to confiscation of land and other property. An attempt was made to introduce Serb settlers. A resistance movement failed, having been isolated from Albanian support. Instead, Tirana initially developed friendly relations with Belgrade. In 1937, Vaso Cubrilovic, who was to become a leading member of the Serbian Academy, opined: '[a]t a time when Germany can expel tens of thousands of Jews and Russia can shift millions of people from one part of the continent to another, the shifting of a few hundred thousand Albanians will not lead to the outbreak of world war'.[8]

---

[5] Barbara Jelavich, *History of the Balkans: Twentieth Century*, II (Cambridge: Cambridge University Press, 1983), 363.

[6] Malcolm, *Kosovo*, 264ff.

[7] Carnegie Endowment, *Report* (1914), 151, quoted in Malcolm, *Kosovo*, 254.

[8] Quoted in Tim Judah, *The Serbs: History, Myth and Deconstruction of Yugoslavia* (New Haven and London: Yale University Press, 1997), 149f (hereinafter Judah, *The Serbs*).

However, when war did break out, the pendulum of historical injustice swung back the other way. Albania came under Italian tutelage during the first part of the war, which also included Kosovo. Now, the Serbs were persecuted by the Kosovo Albanians.[9] The capitulation of Italy in 1943 brought little relief for the ethnic Serbs in the territory. Germany took over occupation of the area. Many Kosovar Albanians appeared to view the German presence as a kind of liberation from Serb dominance. Throughout the Second World War, acts of revenge drove several tens of thousands of Serbs from the territory. However, not all Kosovo Albanians were collaborators. Some joined in Marshall Tito's partisan movement and a small cadre of communist Albanians was established in Kosovo.

II. Modern Developments

At the end of the Second World War, Kosovo found itself once again under Serbian rule, although within the framework of the new Federal Yugoslavia, consisting of six republics (Bosnia and Herzegovina, Croatia, Macedonia, Montenegro, Serbia, and Slovenia). Given its majority Albanian population and a somewhat ambiguous promise of self-determination made during the war by the national liberation forces, the territory was given autonomous status within Serbia, along with Vojvodina which contains a sizeable minority of Hungarians. Repression by Serbs in Kosovo was severe, with memories of the treatment of Serbs during the war still fresh in the mind of the new regime of the republic.[10] Tens of thousands of ethnic Albanians were persuaded to emigrate, mainly to Turkey.[11]

Yugoslavia underwent several constitutional changes in the years which followed.[12] The position of Kosovo and of its majority population improved in the 1960s, presaging the great constitutional reform of 1974.[13] This development had been induced by increasing restlessness among Kosovo Albanians, culminating in the uprising of 1968—a development which shocked the communist establishment. After all, the official doctrine of brotherhood and unity of peoples, nations and nationalities was supposed to have overcome ethnic differences. By 1969, a new more liberal statute for Kosovo had been issued and other reforms followed. Then, the 1974 Constitution of the Socialist Federal Republic of Yugoslavia brought republic status for the two autonomous provinces of Kosovo and Vojvodina in all but name.

---

[9] S.K. Pavlowitch, *A History of the Balkans, 1804–1945* (London, New York: Longman, 1999), 321.

[10] Judah, *The Serbs*, 131f.

[11] Viktor Meier, *Yugoslavia: A History of its Demise* (London: Routledge, 1999), 27 (hereinafter Meier, *Yugoslavia*).

[12] See Section III below.

[13] John R. Lampe, *Yugoslavia as History: Twice There Was a Country* (Cambridge: Cambridge University Press, 1996), 296.

Ethnic Albanian self-administration was effectively established and guaranteed at the federal level, where the province enjoyed equal representation with the republics in federal organs. Kosovo also established important cultural and educational institutions of its own, leading to a clearer expression of ethnic Albanian identity. This, in turn, fed growing resentment in Serbia. While the leading politicians at the time did not wish openly to attack Tito's policy, Serbia's effective loss of control over Kosovo was increasingly bemoaned.[14] Demographic shifts in the region also took place during this time. According to Yugoslav statistics, in 1953, 27 per cent Serbs and Montenegrins had lived in Kosovo, but by the time of the 1991 census, there were less than 10 per cent. According to the official Serbian view, this development was due to a policy aimed at driving ethnic Serbs out of the province. Others simply observed that some Serbs left due to the economic backwardness imposed upon the region by central economic planning, coupled with the fact that that the birth rate among urban Serb middle classes had fallen below that of the ethnic Albanian majority.

On 11 March 1981, a little less than a year after Tito's death, student unrest broke out in the University of Prishtina, which had been allowed to operate since 1970. While the protest was motivated initially by the bleak prospects of students at the university, the opposition movement was rapidly energized by demands for republic status for Kosovo. Such opposition spread to other cities and towns in Kosovo, triggered by economic and other conditions which the new autonomy had failed to redress.

Over the following year, some 2000 'nationalists' were convicted and official rhetoric about the purported suffering of Serbs in Kosovo increased in vigour. This view was given formal expression in the famous memorandum penned by members of the Serbian Academy of Sciences and Arts in 1985, and published in fragments a year later. By 1987, a move within Serbia to 'unify' the republic through constitutional changes in relation to Kosovo gained momentum. In September of that year, Slobodan Milosevic, at the 8th Plenum of the Serbian Party Central Committee, started the process which led in December to the displacement of his mentor, Serbian Party Chairman Ivan Stambolic. The departure of Stambolic, who stood for the old, integrative ideology of brotherhood and unity, heralded the emergence of a nationalist programme directed primarily against Kosovo.[15]

Serbia then secured an enhanced role for itself in the federal organs by establishing control over Montenegro, Vojvodina and, finally, Kosovo. The leadership of the province was replaced in the autumn of 1988 by what many Kosovo Albanians perceived as 'stooges' of Belgrade, and its federal status was abolished through controversial reforms of the Serbian constitution.[16] When, in 1990,

---

[14] A Serbian *Blue Book* criticizing the reforms was cautiously published in 1977.
[15] Misha Glenny, *The Fall of Yugoslavia* (2nd edn, London: Penguin, 1993), 32.
[16] See Section III below.

Serbia adopted an entirely new constitution which fully subordinated Kosovo to the republic, Kosovo declared sovereignty. There followed a referendum on independence and a declaration of independence in 1991, and the election of a new government led by 'President' Ibrahim Rugova in 1992.[17]

The takeover of Vojvodina and Kosovo, and to some extent of Montenegro, was regarded with great concern, initially by Slovenia, and then also by Croatia. Croatia in particular had special concerns, given the large number of Serbs living in its Krajina region. After all, it appeared that the scheme outlined by the Serbian Academy members was now being implemented. The memorandum had claimed: '[e]xcept for the time under the Independent State of Croatia, the Serbs in Croatia have never before been as jeopardized as they are today. A resolution of their national status is a question of overriding political importance. If solutions are not found, the consequences might well be disastrous, not only for Croatia, but for the whole of Yugoslavia.'[18] Having observed Serbia's actions in relation to Kosovo, Croatia sought to transform the federation, with the support of Slovenia, by preparing a draft for a new federal constitution featuring confederal elements in December of 1990. However, attempts to rescue the federation by restructuring it failed. Serbia was in a dominant position and regarded any changes to the status quo as having only negative implications for itself.

On 25/6 June 1991, Croatia and Slovenia both declared independence, resulting in a short armed confrontation with the latter, and a prolonged armed struggle with the former which left about a third of Croatia, including the Krajina region, under Serbian occupation. Despite attempts by the United Nations to set up so-called UN 'protected areas', a campaign of what was now called 'ethnic cleansing' was pursued, only to be replaced by an exodus of Serbs when Croatia forcibly took the territory again a few years later.

The organized international community, initially acting mainly through the states of the EC, pressed at first for the maintenance of the Yugoslav state. However, after the declarations of independence of Slovenia and Croatia, the EC states rapidly accepted that the SFRY was in the process of dissolution. Recognition of Croatia and Slovenia by EC and other states in January 1992 was followed by the independence of Bosnia and Herzegovina that spring. Once again, the army of the rump Yugoslavia (now composed only of Serbia and Montenegro) occupied a significant part of Bosnia's territory, unleashing a campaign of ethnic cleansing which probably amounted to genocide. It is estimated that over 100,000 mainly Muslim Bosnians were killed, and two million forcibly displaced.[19]

While the international community attempted to address the Yugoslav crisis, Serbia had continued to consolidate its position vis-à-vis Kosovo, adopting a formal legislative programme based on ethnic distinction in Kosovo. At

---

[17] See Section V below.   [18] Quoted in Judah, *The Serbs*, 159.
[19] Research and Documentation Centre Sarajevo (RDCS). 'Documenting the victims of conflict'. Sarajevo: RDCS. At <http://www.idc.org.ba/aboutus/documenting_the_victims.htm>, accessed 6 October 2008.

least 80,000 ethnic Albanians were removed from public office and from leading positions in industry (then still state-run). Legislation was adopted to encourage Serb settlement in the province, and attempts were made to denationalize Kosovo Albanians who had been driven to a life abroad. Repression was fierce in the province, although it did not reach the level of violence exhibited in occupied Croatia and in Bosnia and Herzegovina.

With the outbreak of hostilities in 1998, however, Kosovo itself was subjected to a massive and extraordinarily rapid campaign of ethnic cleansing, which moved over half of its ethnic Albanian population of about 1.7 million out of the territory in a matter of a few weeks, and turned hundreds of thousands more into internally displaced people, seeking to survive in the forests and mountains of Kosovo. The reversal of this action after the conclusion of NATO military operations in June 1999 left Kosovo at least temporarily in the control of the KLA, which had effectively removed the elected leadership of the former province. The massive presence of NATO, and the hesitant arrival of UN civilian administrators and police force, could not prevent revenge attacks against the Serbs of Kosovo, many of whom fled.

III. Constitutional Developments up to 1990

The historical developments chronicled above are naturally reflected in the legislation that was adopted to implement them. By 1943, fascist Italy had withdrawn from the war and capitulated. Albania, then temporarily united with most of Kosovo, gained nominal independence but was placed in effect under German control. While some Kosovo Albanians collaborated with them, so as to avoid a restoration of Slav dominance in the region, others took up the resistance struggle. Some joined the People's Liberation Army, or Partisan Detachments of Yugoslavia, led by Josip Broz Tito and organized according to the model of communist cadres. The Anti-Fascist Council for the People's Liberation of Yugoslavia (AVNOJ) had decided in November 1943 that Kosovo would be accorded autonomous status at the end of the war. However, a few weeks later, the 1st Conference of the National Liberation Council for Kosovo was held in Bujan, attended mainly by ethnic Albanians. A formal resolution was adopted, establishing the modalities of Kosovo Albanian participation in the liberation struggle. For many ethnic Albanians, the Bujan Resolution remains, to this day, a focal point of their national aspirations. The Resolution stated:

Kosova and the Dukajin Plateau is a region in which the majority of the inhabitants are Albanian who today wish to be united with Albania, as they have done. Therefore, we feel it our duty to indicate the right road which [is] the road which the Albanian people must follow to realize their aspirations. The only way for the Albanian people of Kosova and the Dukagjin Plateau to be united with Albania is through joint struggle with the other peoples of Yugoslavia against the blood-thirsty Nazi occupier and its paid lackeys, because this is the only way to win the freedom, in which all peoples, including the Albanian people, will be able to determine their own destiny through the right of self-determination up to secession. The guarantee of this is the National Liberation Army of Albania with which it is closely linked...[20]

This pan-Albanian platform was neither directly endorsed nor disowned by the Tito leadership, which instead cautiously pointed out that developments should not prejudice the close future relations expected with Albania.[21] At the conclusion of the war, the communist cadres in Kosovo, of whom less than a quarter were ethnic Albanian, expressed themselves in favour of 'the annexation of Kosovo-Metohija' to federal Serbia. On 3 September 1945, the Serbian People's Assembly created an autonomous region ('oblast') of Kosovo-Metohija as a constituent part of Serbia. Serbia argues that Kosovo was thus confirmed as an integral part of its territory before the federation was created. Kosovo, on the other hand, asserts that the decision to join was expressly conditional upon a 'federal' Serbia, i.e., Serbia and hence also Kosovo as part of a federal structure. While the legitimacy of the decision to join has been disputed given the limited representativeness of the communist structures at the time,[22] Serbia's view that an annexation was necessary at all is interesting. The timing of this act is irrelevant, at any rate. For even if Serbia, prior to joining the federation, had established itself with Kosovo as a constituent part, this act would not have affected the status which resulted from it joining the post-war Yugoslav federation. In joining the federation, Serbia legally accepted the constitutional status for Kosovo provided in the Federal Constitution of 31 January 1946.

Of course, in the first Yugoslav constitution, there was no evidence of a pledge of self-determination for Kosovo which the Kosovo Albanians had thought they had obtained following the Bujan Declaration. Instead, the People's Republic of Yugoslavia was constructed as a Federation of Serbia, Croatia, Slovenia, Bosnia and Herzegovina, Macedonia, and Montenegro. Each of these republics was seen to be the repository of the sovereign rights of equal 'peoples'. These peoples, organized in the individual republics, retained their right to self-determination and even secession from the federation.[23] That is to say, the source of sovereignty, as it were, resided separately in the individual republics and not in the federation itself. As opposed to a centralist federal constitution, where the federal authorities exercise all authority not expressly granted to the constituent units, in Yugoslavia it is the other way around: 'The sovereignty of the people's republics composing the Federal People's Republic of Yugoslavia (FPRY) is limited only by the

---

[20] Resolution of the 1st Conference of the National Liberation Council for Kosovo and the Dukagjin Plateau, 31 December 1943–2 January 1944.
[21] Meier, *Yugoslavia*, 26.   [22] Malcolm, *Kosovo*, 317.
[23] Constitution of the Federal People's Republic of Yugoslavia, 31 January 1946, in Marc Weller, *The Crisis in Kosovo 1989–1999: From the Dissolution of Yugoslavia to Rambouillet and the Outbreak of Hostilities* (Cambridge: Documents and Analysis, 1999), 51–2 (hereinafter 'Weller, *Crisis in Kosovo*').

rights which by this Constitution are given to the Federal People's Republic of Yugoslavia'.[24]

Not having been promoted to the status of a republic, Kosovo was included instead as an 'autonomous region' within the Republic of Serbia, as had been anticipated in the act of 'annexation' and subsequent Serbian legislation. Under the federal constitution, the rights and scope of the autonomy of autonomous provinces and regions were determined by the constitution of the republic. The people's assembly of an autonomous province or territory could establish its own statute, but required the approval of the republic for such a document, which falls short of a constitution. Despite these limitations, Kosovo nevertheless enjoyed dual status. According to the Federal Constitution, Kosovo's legal personality was not only established within Serbia, but directly in Yugoslavia's founding document—in fact in the same article which consecrates the republics as the sources of sovereignty.[25] That the status of autonomous provinces or regions was not solely a matter for the republics is confirmed in Article 44 of the Constitution. That provision requires federal approval for the establishment of new autonomous provinces or territories.

The ambiguous status of Kosovo, and of Vojvodina for that matter, was rooted in two facts. First, it would not have been realistic to attempt to remove the two territories from the dominance of Serbia. Such *realpolitik* rationale was underpinned by the doctrine of peoples or nations on the one hand, and of nationalities and minorities on the other. The republics are of course not actually the ethnically homogenous home of the one or other ethnic 'people'. In fact, the ethnic identity of all these 'peoples' may not even have been fully established by 1946. However, as the Serbs, Slovenes, Macedonians, Montenegrins, Croats and Bosnians do not have an external kin-state, 'their' republic is considered a sovereign home territory. The Hungarians of Vojvodina and the Kosovo Albanians, on the other hand, share an ethnic appurtenance with the majority population of a neighbouring state and merely constitute a nationality accommodated in an autonomous province or region. Other groups have the even less pronounced status of minority, which is not identified with any particular territory or with any form of self-rule.

The 1953 Constitution also reflected the basic idea of a federation of 'sovereign and equal peoples'.[26] Again, federal powers existed only to the extent granted by the federal constitution. Republic powers, on the other hand, remained self-constituting. Still, the federal constitution imposed an express provision, in

[24] Article 9. Subsequent Yugoslav scholarship has somewhat tortuously argued that this language in fact means the opposite, i.e., that only the Federation is sovereign, as the republics exist within its legal framework; e.g. Reneo Lukic, 'The Sovereignty of the Republics under the Preliminary Draft of the Federal Constitution', *New Yugoslav Law*, 14 (1963), 27.

[25] Vojvodina obtained the original federal status of an autonomous province, possibly a somewhat 'higher' status than that of a region.

[26] Constitution of the Federal People's Republic of Yugoslavia, 1953, Art. 1, in Weller, *Crisis in Kosovo*, 52.

Article 113, which declared that the 'self-governance of the autonomous province of Vojvodina and of the autonomous region of Kosovo-Metohija is guaranteed'.[27] This federal guarantee was, however, balanced by a further sentence in that provision, which derives these powers of self-governance from the Constitution of Serbia.

In 1963, the rather symbolic distinction between autonomous province and region was removed. While some observers see the 1963 Constitution as a significant advance in the status of Kosovo, others have identified it as a regression. The source of this dispute lies in the removal of the specific guarantee of self-governance at the level of the federal constitution. Instead of enjoying such a guarantee, Kosovo was now described as a 'social-political community within the republic'—the significance of which is not clear in itself.[28] However, the federal constitution retained the federal status of autonomous provinces. While these could still be founded by republics, such a decision could, as before, only take effect when constitutionally approved by the federation. And the character of Kosovo as an existing autonomous province remained directly established in the federal constitution. Moreover, the special representation of autonomous provinces along with the republics in the federal Chamber of Nationalities was retained.

The Serbian Constitution of 1963 nevertheless remained quite restrictive in terms of the powers of autonomous provinces. It did refer to the social self-government of the province and assigned to it powers to make regulations concerning matters of general relevance to the province. However, throughout, it is made clear that this authority is based in, and restricted by, the competences of the republic.[29]

The constitutional position of Kosovo was significantly improved towards the end of the 1960s, especially in the wake of riots and demonstrations in the province in 1968. The name was changed from Kosovo and Metohija to Kosovo, to placate the sensitivities of the ethnic Albanians, and significantly more power was devolved to the local level. These developments reached their zenith with the adoption of the SFRY Constitution of 1974. An express right to self-determination, including the right to secession, remained the preserve of the 'nation'. However, both nations and nationalities were now 'free and equal':

The nations of Yugoslavia, proceeding from the right of every nation to self-determination, including the right to secession, on the basis of their will freely expressed in the common struggle of all nations and nationalities in the National Liberation War and Socialist Revolution, and in conformity with their historic aspirations, aware that

---

[27] Also included is a mechanism for separate representation of the autonomous provinces and regions in the Federal Assembly which, along with Assembly members nominated by the republics, form the Chamber of Nationalities.

[28] Constitution of the Socialist Federal Republic of Yugoslavia, 1963, Art. 112, in Weller, *Crisis in Kosovo*, 53.

[29] *Ibid.*, 52–3.

further consolidation of their brotherhood and unity is in the common interest, have, together with the nationalities with which they live, united in a federal republic of free and equal nations and nationalities and founded a socialist federal community of working people—the Socialist Federal Republic of Yugoslavia...

The Constitution actually assigned 'sovereign rights' to nationalities, exercised through the socialist autonomous provinces (SAPs) in conformity with their constitutional rights.[30] Moreover, it expressly provided for the full equality of republics and autonomous provinces in their participation in the federation, determining that federal decisions were to be made 'according to the principles of agreement among the republics and autonomous provinces'.[31]

Although Kosovo was still a constituent part of Serbia, the new status of Kosovo was described by Serb and ethnic Albanian scholars alike as that of a 'quasi republic'.[32] It was fully represented in the federal presidency, had distinct representation in the federal organs and, crucially, it had full freedom to determine its own constitution (no longer merely a statute). Its own organs and powers were state-like, including even a national bank and the power to engage in foreign relations. Like all republics, its assembly had the power to block the coming into force of changes to the federal constitution.

Serbia's Constitution of 1974 also confirmed the equal status of all nations and nationalities in Serbia, determining again that they each enjoyed, individually and collectively, 'sovereignty rights'.[33] Kosovo's own constitution confirmed that its people had freely organized themselves in the form of the SAP on the basis of equality with the nations and nationalities of Yugoslavia.[34] The Kosovo Assembly was given express powers 'directly and exclusively' to decide on amendments to the Kosovo Constitution, and to 'approve' amendments to the Constitution of the Socialist Republic of Serbia.[35]

IV. The Purported Removal of Kosovo's Federal Status

When pressure within Serbia increased to counter what was perceived as the marginalization of Serbs in Kosovo, or even their persecution, many in the still communist leadership sought to argue the case for moderation. In fact, the 1985 Memorandum of Members of the Serbian Academy, which criticized the existing

---

[30] Constitution of the Socialist Federal Republic of Yugoslavia, 1974, 'Basic Principles', in Weller, *Crisis in Kosovo*, 54.

[31] *Ibid.*

[32] Indeed, this argument is frequently used by Serbia to demonstrate that it was necessary to reverse the provisions of the 1974 Constitution.

[33] Constitution of the Socialist Republic of Serbia, 1974, Basic Principles, paras 2, 3, in Weller, *Crisis in Kosovo*, 56.

[34] Constitution of the Socialist Autonomous Province of Kosovo, 1974, Basic Principles, in Weller, *Crisis in Kosovo*, 58.

[35] *Ibid.*, Art. 301, 59.

Yugoslav system and, it can be argued, called implicitly for the re-establishment of Serbian dominance in Kosovo, was initially denounced when its contents were published in 1986/7. 'The physical, political, legal and cultural genocide of the Serbian population in Kosovo and Metohija is a worse historical defeat than any experienced in the liberation wars waged by Serbia from the First Serbian Uprising in 1804 to the uprising of 1941', the Memorandum declared, causing something of a scandal at the time.[36] However, the events which followed saw the gradual isolation and removal of those who still subscribed to Tito's vision of a federation of equal peoples, nations and nationalities. Serb nationalism, as well as the cunning exploitation of party rules, and the reluctance of old-style officials to oppose that which appeared to be emerging as a dominant view, facilitated this process.

Slobodan Milosevic is said to have discovered the Kosovo issue on the occasion of his celebrated visit to the autonomous province, where, on 24 April 1987, he was met by agitated Serbs, demanding action from Belgrade to protect them against ethnic Albanian dominance in Kosovo. His famous declaration that 'no one should dare to beat you' energized both the local crowds and Milosevic himself.[37] He used the purported fate of Kosovo Serbs as the key argument in his purge of Serbia's party chairman Ivan Stambolic and his supporters, which commenced in September 1987 and was concluded in December of that year. From then on, the process of the reintegration of Kosovo was pursued in earnest. In 1988, some 50,000 Serbs in Kosovo signed a petition, demanding closer integration with Serbia and threatening direct action of 'self-defence of our freedom, honour and dignity'.[38] This demand was met when on 11 June 1988 a draft for a new Serbian constitution was put forward. To ensure the eventual adoption of reform proposals, first the leadership of Vojvodina was removed, then measures were taken to ensure that Montenegro would not oppose Serbian action at the federal level either.

While Slovenia remained opposed and was locked in an increasingly bitter struggle with Serbia and the federation increasingly dominated by it, Milosevic initially persuaded leaders in Croatia and Bosnia and Herzegovina to remain silent, on the understanding that Serbia would not seek subsequently to take action in support of the large numbers of Serb inhabitants of those two republics. Macedonia, with its very sizeable ethnic Albanian minority of between 20 and 30 per cent, was also persuaded not to oppose the removal of the Kosovo Albanians from political power. Of course, the position of Croatia would soon change, once it became clear that Serbia was reaching beyond the boundaries of Kosovo, and seeking to dominate the federation as a whole. After all, if Serbia controlled not only its own votes, but also those of Montenegro, Macedonia,

[36] Judah, *The Serbs*, 159.
[37] Laura Silber and Allan Little, *The Death of Yugoslavia* (London: Penguin, 1995), 37ff.
[38] Quoted in Meier, *Yugoslavia*, 73.

Vojvodina, and Kosovo, Milosevic could muster an automatic majority in federal decision-making.

Having ensured that opposition at the federal level would be limited, the next step was to disenfranchise the leadership of Kosovo itself, an act which could be performed from above, given that the communist party structure existed in parallel to the republic/province executive structure. This action took place amid demonstrations of Serbs in Belgrade and Albanians in Prishtina in November 1988, and coincided with completion of the installation of a new, more 'reliable' leadership in Montenegro.[39] On 24 February 1989, the Serbian parliament unanimously adopted proposals for the amendment of Serbia's constitution—no representative from Kosovo in the Belgrade parliament having felt it prudent to vote against. A last-minute change to the amendments which had been put before the plenary of the Assembly two days earlier by its constitutional drafting commission removed from Kosovo the power to oppose any further changes to the constitution.

While Kosovo's assent had previously been necessary for constitutional changes relating to the autonomous province to take effect, it would now only need to be consulted. The relevance of these developments was quickly understood in Kosovo. A hunger strike of miners at Trepca in Kosovo and more widespread demonstrations followed. This was immediately answered by the imposition of a state of emergency by the federal state presidency on 27 February. Federal armed forces and federal police, mostly Serbian, were deployed into Kosovo. The provincial government of Kosovo, which had been installed through Serbian political intervention, approved the constitutional amendments on 22 March. A day later, in an episode which remains controversial, the Kosovo Assembly is also said to have opted for its own disenfranchisement, with only 10 opposing votes out of 187. Kosovo representatives point to the fact that over 15,000 army personnel had been deployed in the province by then, and that the Assembly was surrounded by tanks. Non-members of the Assembly were present, it is alleged, and some of them may have voted. Others are said to have directly intimidated the ethnic Albanian representatives. Kosovo also claimed subsequently that the decision was never effective, having not been published in the official gazette.[40]

The decision of the Assembly provoked widespread rioting, triggering in turn a rough response from the police and army. Serbia then adopted the somewhat Orwellian 'Programme for the Realization of Peace, Freedom, Equality, Democracy and Prosperity of the SAP of Kosovo'. That legislative programme was expressly intended to lay the foundations for the reintroduction of an ethnic Serb majority into the territory. It also sought to ensure that the ethnic Albanian

[39] Meier, *Yugoslavia*, 80–100.
[40] For the Kosovo Albanian view, see Council for the Defence of the Human Rights and Freedoms in Kosovo, *The Ruin of Kosova's Autonomy: Material Proof* (undated), 1ff; Esat Stavileci, Blerim Reka, and Arsim Bajrami, 'Kosova: Political, Constitutional and International Law Arguments', *Kosova Law Review* (1996).

majority in Kosovo would effectively be politically powerless, inasmuch as its representation was to be equalized with that of tiny minorities in the territory, in addition to the Serbs in the province, so as to 'exclude majority votes'.

The restoration of Serbia's constitutional dominance over Kosovo was famously and rather provocatively celebrated in Kosovo itself, when Milosevic addressed the 600-year celebrations of the Serbian defeat at Kosovo Polje, staged on the ancient battlefield on 28 June 1989.[41] Already at that stage, the first examples of direct Serbian legislation for Kosovo had been adopted, revealing openly a public programme of ethnic domination and discrimination directed against the Albanians.

The 1990 Law on Special Circumstances formalized the possible exercise of republic powers in Kosovo. It was activated by a decision of 26 June 1990, which permitted officials of the Serbian Republic to administer the affairs of Kosovo directly and to nullify public decisions that had been taken by Kosovo itself. This included the removal of criminal prosecutions and other judicial functions from Kosovo courts, and the appointment of Serbs to head commercial undertakings in Kosovo, which were still state enterprises at the time. Then, on 5 July 1990, Serbia purported formally to terminate the functioning of the Kosovo Assembly and of its Executive Council.[42]

On 28 September 1990, Serbia gave itself a new constitution.[43] Contrary to the writings of some, the autonomous status of Kosovo was not formally abolished altogether. However, the socialist republic was now no longer a 'state of the Serb nation and parts of other nations and nationalities, which live and exercise their sovereign right in it'.[44] Instead, it became a 'democratic state of the Serbian people'.[45] The same provision recognized the right of other 'nations and national minorities'. That is to say, the status of the Kosovo Albanians as at least a 'nationality' was abolished, and the overwhelming majority of Kosovo Albanians were thus reduced to a 'national minority' in their own territory. The powers of the province were now entirely subordinated to those of Serbia. Its constitution was again reduced to a 'statute' which would be enacted after prior 'approval' of the National Assembly. Again, provisions were made for direct executive action of the republic in Kosovo. The unilateral changes to Kosovo's status would, of course, have required an amendment to the federal constitution of Yugoslavia. Again, such an amendment would have required the consent from Kosovo. However, soon the federation itself was in a process of dissolution. Unsurprisingly, the constitution of the new federal Yugoslavia, adopted after the dissolution of the

[41] Misha Glenny, *The Fall of Yugoslavia* (2nd edn, London: Penguin, 1993), 34.
[42] Law Terminating the Work of the Assembly of the SAP of Kosovo and the Executive Council of the SAP of Kosovo, 5 July 1990.
[43] See Stevan Lilic, 'Die Verfassung der Republic Serbien', in Joseph Marko and Tomislav Boric (eds), *Slowenien–Kroatien–Serbien, Die Neuen Verfassungen* (Vienna: Böhlan, 1991), 286.
[44] Constitution of the SR Serbia, 1974, Art. 1, in Weller, *Crisis in Kosovo*, 57.
[45] Constitution of the SR Serbia, 28 September 1990, Preamble, in Weller, *Crisis in Kosovo*, 62.

SFRY and composed only of Serbia and Montenegro, hardly mentions Kosovo or the collective rights of the Kosovo Albanians. Instead, the status of Kosovo and Vojvodina is downgraded to one of 'territorial autonomy'.[46]

V. The Response in Kosovo

Until the summer of 1990, the elected members of the Kosovo Assembly and Kosovo's representatives in the Serbian and federal assemblies had failed to resist these developments with any vigour. However, in June/July the Serbian Parliament purported to terminate the work of the Kosovo Assembly, and its members were literally locked out of their Assembly building. Gathered on the steps of the Assembly Hall, the elected representatives adopted in response a declaration of sovereignty.[47] That declaration was initially rather modest, anticipating the continued existence of Kosovo within Yugoslavia as an equal constituent unit. It expressly stated that Kosovo would continue to comply with the Yugoslav federal constitution, but not with the changes brought about unilaterally by Serbia. It also annulled the decision of 23 March 1989 which had purportedly legitimized the virtual abolition of Kosovo's autonomous status.

The situation which ensued has been described as one of 'sovereignties in collision'.[48] In the exercise of its (at least former) prerogative of creating its own constitution, the Assembly of Kosovo then drafted and adopted a new constitution for Kosovo. This constitution now in turn defined Kosovo as a democratic, sovereign and independent state of the Albanian people and members of other peoples and national minorities.[49] However, a formal declaration of independence only followed a year later, on 22 September 1991, and was confirmed in a referendum. Some 87 per cent of voters participated (ethnic Serbs were boycotting the poll), with close to 100 per cent opting for independence.[50] This was followed, again a year later, by elections, resulting in the overwhelming victory of the Democratic League of Kosovo (LDK) (76 per cent), led by Ibrahim Rugova. Rugova was then directly elected as President by an even larger margin. A government was formed, under the leadership of Bujan Bukoshi. That government, which also operated in exile, from Germany, could call on very extensive financial support from the ethnic Albanian diaspora, especially in Germany, Switzerland and Sweden. These funds were used to maintain the parallel administrative

[46] Constitution of the Federal Republic of Yugoslavia, April 1992, Art. 6, in Weller, *Crisis in Kosovo*, 64.
[47] Assembly of Kosova, Constitutional Declaration, 2 July 1990, in Weller, *Crisis in Kosovo*, 64–5.
[48] Lenard J. Cohen, *Broken Bonds: Yugoslavia's Disintegration and Balkan Politics in Transition* (Colorado, Oxford: Westview, 1993), 121.
[49] Constitution of the Republic of Kosova, 7 September 1990, Arts 1 and 2, in Weller, *Crisis in Kosovo*, 66.
[50] Central Board of Kosova for the Conduct of the Referendum, 7 October 1991.

structure in Kosovo. Subsequent attempts to build up a military wing under LDK leadership were frustrated by the KLA, which had established itself in the meantime. While 'Prime Minister' Bukoshi was attempting to establish a 'professional' armed formation composed of experienced veterans of the Yugoslav wars, this attempt was opposed by the KLA which would soon come to exercise a decisive influence over events.

VI. Conclusion

The Yugoslav crisis as a whole has given rise to a heated discussion about so-called ancient hatreds that lie in constant and violent competition. This debate has now been largely overcome. It is generally appreciated that ethnic conflict has been engineered within this region, as is the case in other regions. This brief background sketch confirms that the confrontation between Kosovo Albanians and Serbs does indeed reveal a spiral of occasional violence and displacement from which both populations suffered over time. However, the underlying factors and causes of conflict in this instance are not driven by inherent hatreds bred into certain populations. Instead, the struggle over the past hundred years has been underpinned by a contestation over land and control of resources—hard political interests, as opposed to identity issues.

Of course, the nationalism of the 19th and 20th centuries is also relevant. Serbia managed to regain a territorial identity. Kosovo was unable to do so, either through independence or through merger with Albania—a state that came late onto the European scene. After World War II, the communist system addressed the issue in three ways. First, the doctrine of brotherhood and unity sought to lessen nationalist ideology. Second, the 'nations' of the socialist Yugoslav states were nevertheless accommodated through an increasingly decentralized federal system. And third, Vojvodina and Kosovo were accommodated in a compromise that combined quasi-republic status with that of a province within Serbia.

This balancing act was disrupted when nationalist ideology was rediscovered as a tool of politics, initially in Serbia but subsequently also in other parts of the federation. The disaster that would ensue if the federal system were to collapse was widely predicted. Kosovo, the proverbial 'powder keg' of the Balkans, was accorded the key role in these scenarios. However, an internal resolution of the constitutional crisis generated by Serbia's attempt to dominate the federation was frustrated by its increasingly radical leadership. Hence, the question arose whether international action might be taken to contain the crisis before its explosion.

3

Initial Settlement Attempts

The surge of Serb nationalism and Belgrade's efforts at establishing dominance over the SFRY constitutional system resulted in defensive action by some of the other entities within the state. Slovenia and Croatia requested a revision of the 1974 Yugoslav constitution in order to strengthen guarantees of their position. Kosovo, too, demanded restoration of its constitutional position, in view of the unilateral abrogation of its status by Serbia in 1988/9. It later requested promotion to the status of full republic as a means of forestalling similar developments in the future. However, these requests were not accorded much international backing. Initial international action was not focused on persuading the Serbian leadership to restore the previously existing constitutional consensus or to negotiate a new one. Instead, international pressure was brought to bear on Croatia and Slovenia. Both republics, frustrated with abortive attempts of negotiating a new, looser federation, declared 'sovereignty' in 1990. They were clearly moving towards uni-lateral declarations of independence. EC emissaries and US Secretary of State James Baker were dispatched to the region. While supporting requests for greater autonomy, they warned both republics that moves towards independence were not encouraged and would not receive support. Instead, a fruitless confrontation would ensue in which Croatia and Slovenia would lose.

I. The Carrington Plan and the London Conference

On 26 March 1991, the EC adopted a formal declaration supporting territorial unity and warning against the use of force.[1] A so-called 'troika' of EC foreign ministers and other emissaries conducted follow-on missions in April and May, offering significant economic assistance if a constitutional compromise might be achieved.[2] The CSCE was also activated, albeit hesitantly, given the reluctance of the Serbian authorities (and hence the SFRY government) to permit the interna-tionalization of the crisis. Hence, it was principally left to the leaders of the six republics to achieve an agreement and the process turned into something of a

[1] Declaration on the Informal European Political Cooperation Ministerial Meeting on Yugoslavia, Chateau de Senningen, 26 March 1991, 4b/61.
[2] See Geert Ahrens, *Diplomacy on the Edge* (Baltimore, MA: John Hopkins University Press, 2007), 42 (hereinafter Ahrens, *Diplomacy*).

farce.[3] In the meantime, the constitutional crisis deepened, when Serbia refused to facilitate the transfer of the federal presidency to Croatia, which was entitled to assume it according to the system of rotation. Four out of the eight federal entities supported the required change, while Serbia used 'its' four seats (Serbia, Montenegro, Kosovo, and Vojvodina) to oppose it. Final attempts to settle for a revised federal constitution with confederal elements were frustrated in June 1991. Indeed, there were rumours of a deal having been struck between Serbia and Croatia providing for the division of Bosnia and Herzegovina. This deadlock and looming declarations of independence triggered the crisis visit of US Secretary of State Baker to Belgrade on 23 June. However, unimpressed with US intervention in favour of retaining territorial unity, two days later Slovenia and Croatia declared independence.

Belgrade launched a short series of military strikes against Slovenia, targeting border crossings and some other installations.[4] This initial military confrontation triggered a very rapid response from both the CSCE and the European institutions.

At that stage, the CSCE was just about to reconstitute itself as a pan-European crisis management mechanism, having served as a confidence-building mechanism since its founding by the Helsinki Final Act of 1975. The newly established Committee of Senior Officials now became active and, within a few days of the declaration of independence, proposed the launch of a CSCE Good Offices Mission to Yugoslavia—an offer that was however refused by Belgrade. The EC, too, deployed itself in a new posture. It was also seeking to develop its identity as a leading player in the area of foreign and security policy. Both institutions saw the looming crisis in Yugoslavia as a first test of emerging security structures in the New Europe.

By early July, some success seemed to have been achieved. According to the Brioni agreement brokered by the EC Troika, the republics would suspend their independence temporarily, for a period of three months, to permit a peaceful resolution of the crisis.[5] In reality, however, the Brioni accord masked a decision that had been reached in Belgrade. In view of its geographical distance from Serbia, it had been agreed that Slovenian independence would be accepted. However, Croatia would not be able to leave the federation unopposed, at least not within existing boundaries, given the large number of ethnic Serbs, many of whom inhabited the territorially identifiable Krajina region. Serbia, now in control of the federal organs of the rump Yugoslavia, had declared previously that:[6]

The Serbian people...demanded respect and protection of their legitimate national and civil rights. When Croatia decided to secede from Yugoslavia to form its own independent

---

[3] Sabrina P. Ramet, *The Three Yugoslavias* (Washington DC: Woodrow Wilson Centre Press, 2006), 386.

[4] *Ibid.*, chapter 14.   [5] Ahrens, *Diplomacy*, 42.

[6] Address of Dr Borislav Jovic in the SFRY Assembly, 19 March 1991, *Review of International Affairs* (1991), 11f.

state, the Serbs inhabiting their ethnical territories decided to break away from Croatia and remain within Yugoslavia...In such a situation it is essential to protect the Serbian people from extermination.

Essentially, the Yugoslav (Serbian) authorities determined that secession could only occur if the territories inhabited predominantly by ethnic Serbs remained within the rump Yugoslavia, thus constituting, as it were, the Greater Serbia of old. This vision looked as though it might become a reality when the Yugoslav national army, now controlled by Serbia, occupied the Krajina and other, in fact not always Serb-inhabited, territories a short time after signature of the Brioni agreement.

The EC condemned the use of force by Belgrade and confirmed the territorial integrity of Croatia. As early as August 1991, the states of the European Community declared:[7]

The European Community and its member States are dismayed at the increasing violence in Croatia. They remind those responsible for the violence of their determination never to recognize changes of frontiers which have not been brought about by peaceful means and by agreement.... The Community and its member States call on the Federal Presidency to put an immediate end to this illegal use of the forces at its command.

This statement essentially assigned to Croatia and Slovenia state rights, or at least the rights of a self-determination entity entitled to form a state. The central state was no longer to use force by way of an 'internal' police action. Instead, this was considered an 'illegal use' of force at the international level. Moreover, the territorial integrity of the republics was protected from forcible change. While there has been much debate about decisions on recognition of the secessionist states of December and January 1991/2, and Germany's role in particular, in reality this statement of August 1991 had already settled the issue. Both republics were entitled to the protection of the international legal order as states or pre-states long before recognition.

As the nature of Belgrade's armed campaign became clear, the European Community and its members also strongly opposed the brutal policy of ethnic cleansing, which had led to the exodus of thousands of Croats from occupied territories. At the same time, they urged the parties to accept the creation of an EC-sponsored peace conference, supported by an arbitration procedure.[8] This invitation was backed by a threat of the imposition of EC sanctions.

In the meantime, the EC deployed its somewhat infamous European Community Monitoring Mission (ECMM). This consisted of unarmed EC observers conspicuously clad in white, who later became known as 'ice cream suits'. While the monitors were in a position to observe the mounting atrocities

---

[7] EC Declaration on Yugoslavia, 27 August 1991, EPC Press Release, P.82/91.

[8] These developments are detailed in Marc Weller, 'The International Response to the Dissolution of the Socialist Federal Republic of Yugoslavia', *American Journal of International Law*, 86 (1992), 569.

in the escalating conflict, they offered only confidential reports to Brussels and member state capitals. However, in this very early phase of the conflict, the diplomatic leadership of the mission did have a significant, although generally unacknowledged effect in diffusing the situation at least in Slovenia.

The EC Conference on Yugoslavia had its initial meeting at The Hague on 7 September 1991, under the chairmanship of Lord Carrington. The Conference was equipped with a mandate 'to ensure peaceful accommodation of the conflicting aspirations of the Yugoslav peoples, on the basis of the following principles: no unilateral change of borders by force, protection for the rights of all in Yugoslavia and full account to be taken of all legitimate concerns and aspirations'.[9] It was attended by the federal Yugoslav government, the presidents of the six republics and the twelve EC foreign ministers.

While success eluded the Hague conference, it led to the development of an overarching framework for the settlement of the Yugoslav crisis.[10] The plan was premised on the acceptance of the claim of all republics that wished it would obtain independence. However, they would need to accept significant conditions, to be agreed in an overall settlement between the republics. In particular, the perceived concern of Serbia for its ethnic kin within the new states was to be addressed. With this aim in mind, the initial Carrington proposal provided for the creation of autonomous regions or 'special status' areas, applying 'in particular, to the Serbs living in areas in Croatia where they form a majority'.

Without mentioning Kosovo and Vojvodina, the draft added, as something of an afterthought, that the republics would also apply 'fully and in good faith established provisions for the benefit of ethnic and national groups, and for autonomous provinces which were given a special constitutional status'. This formulation was rather ambiguous, inasmuch as Serbia would undoubtedly argue that the 'established provisions' were those contained in its own 1990 Constitution, which had obliterated effective autonomy for those two areas. A second draft added international involvement in monitoring the situation in the special status or autonomy areas. In addition, republics would need to apply fully and in good faith the 'provisions existing prior to 1990 for autonomous provinces'.[11]

Kosovo politicians had noted this rather incidental treatment of their cause with some concern. Even within the Socialist Federal Republic, Kosovo's status had been unilaterally abrogated and very severe discrimination and mistreatment had been applied by Serbian authorities without any significant international opposition. For Kosovo to remain within a rump Yugoslavia, dominated entirely by Serbia and where it relied entirely on the latter's 'good faith' in the application of autonomy provisions, was deemed unacceptable. Moreover, the crucial

[9] EC Declaration on Yugoslavia, 3 September 1991, EPC Press Release.

[10] Carrington Draft Convention for a General Settlement, 18 October 1991, in Weller, *Crisis in Kosovo*, 80.

[11] Second Carrington Draft Provisions for a Convention, 1 November 1991, in Weller, *Crisis in Kosovo*, 80.

changes to its status had taken place prior to 1990, when it lost the right to determine its own constitution and to influence changes in the Constitution of the Serbian Republic. A restoration of the pre-1990 situation would therefore not even re-establish the conditions that had been unilaterally terminated by Serbia.

It seemed that the case of Kosovo was getting lost. The international community was focusing principally on reassuring Serbia in relation to Serbs in Croatia and elsewhere. Clearly, the conference hoped that guarantees of a minority and autonomy regime for these Serbs would render Belgrade's opposition to independence of the republics insubstantial. While this appeared to be a reasonable compromise, it was of course not one which could satisfy the agenda of a Greater Serbia—the unification of the Serb people in one state, while at the same time retaining its strong direct rule over 'minorities' within its own borders. The proposal was rejected by Serbia as unsuitable for discussion,[12] even after the EC threatened the adoption of sanctions in order to achieve Belgrade's acceptance. In a tense showdown provoked by Lord Carrington, all other republics had formally declared their willingness to adopt the draft, with only Serbia refusing to endorse it.

To escape a Serbian veto of the peace plan for all of Yugoslavia, the EC then changed tack. It offered recognition to republics wishing independence, provided they committed themselves unilaterally to certain conditions, including in particular the provisions on human and minority rights proposed in the Carrington draft:[13]

The Community and its member states agree to recognise the independence of all the Yugoslav Republics fulfilling all the conditions set out below. The implementation of this decision will take place on January 15, 1992. They are therefore inviting all Yugoslav Republics to state by 23 December whether:

• they wish to be recognised as independent States;
• they accept the commitments contained in the above-mentioned guidelines;
• they accept the provisions laid down in the [Carrington] draft Convention—especially those in Chapter II on human rights and national or ethnic groups—under consideration by the Conference on Yugoslavia;
• they continue to support the continuation of the Conference on Yugoslavia.[14]

While this paved the way for recognition of the statehood of Croatia and Slovenia, and also of Bosnia and Herzegovina and Macedonia, the decision was disastrous for Kosovo. For effectively, the attempt to achieve a settlement of all questions arising from the dissolution of the Socialist Federal Republic had now been abandoned. Instead, each of the republics seeking recognition would simply commit

---

[12] Report of the United Nations Secretary-General, S/23169, 25 October 1991, para. 23.

[13] EPC Guidelines on Recognition of New States, and EPC Declaration on Yugoslavia, 16 December 1991, in Weller, *Crisis in Kosovo*, 80–1.

[14] See also Christopher Hill and Karen Elizabeth Smith, *European Foreign Policy* (Routledge, 2000), at 282.

itself to the EC conditions and settlement proposals. Since Serbia did not seek recognition, it would not be subject to any settlement and would simply keep control over Kosovo, unchecked by further international action.

After having received applications for recognition by 23 December 1991, these would be subjected to an evaluation by the EC Arbitration Commission attached to the Peace Conference and headed by the distinguished French constitutional jurist Robert Badinter.[15] Kosovo formally applied for recognition in a letter to Lord Carrington, the Chair of the Peace Conference on Yugoslavia, a day before the deadline expired.[16] However, as opposed to the requests of the four republics seeking statehood, the letter from Prishtina was not considered by the Badinter Commission.

Before addressing the four cases accepted for consideration, the Badinter Commission also answered a number of general questions. It confirmed that the Socialist Federal Republic was in a process of total dissolution. Hence, there would not be one state continuing the legal personality of the SFRY, as Serbia had argued. Instead, the SFRY would cease to exist completely, and all the entities emerging from it would be treated as new states. The Commission followed the traditional international legal test of statehood, evaluating as objectively as possible whether or not an entity possessed the traditional attributes of statehood (territory, population and government). In a passage which sounded encouraging for Kosovo, the Commission ruled:

That in the case of a federal-type state, which embraces communities that possess a degree of autonomy and, moreover, participate in the exercise of political power within the framework of institutions common to the Federation, the existence of the state implies that the federal organs represent the components of the Federation and wield effective power.[17]

Under the 1974 Constitution, Kosovo had been a federal entity, represented directly in the federal institutions and possessing more than merely a degree of autonomy. Hence it argued that with the disappearance of the federation, it, too, should emerge as an entity entitled to constitute itself as a state. On no account could it be left within Serbia, without the protection of its status by a strong federation. After all, even under the provisions of the SFRY constitution, Serbia had managed unilaterally to attempt to alter its status considerably. Moreover, under the previous constitutional order, it had been denied representation of its people in the federation.

---

[15] Controversially, Germany announced before that date, on 23 December, that it would recognize Croatia and Slovenia, although it suspended implementation of that decision in compliance with the EC decision.

[16] Letter from Dr Rugova to Lord Carrington, 22 December 1991, in Weller, *Crisis in Kosovo*, 81.

[17] Badinter Opinion No. 1, 31 ILM 1488 (1992).

The pleadings of Kosovo were ignored and remained unanswered.[18] The Badinter Commission applied a restrictive attitude.[19] Despite the thrust of its earlier ruling, it now considered that only republics were entitled to emerge as states from the dissolution of Yugoslavia. Kosovo had enjoyed a federal status, and substantive rights, on a par with the republics. But as it had not been designated a republic, and as it was also subject to the authority of one of the republics, namely Serbia, it fell through the cracks of the system. Of course, this result was convenient and, in the eyes of the decision-makers at the time, realistic. It was clear that Belgrade might ultimately accept independence for the republics, but it was unwilling even to address the Kosovo issue internationally.

A similar attitude was exhibited on the occasion of the second major international attempt to address the Yugoslav crisis. By the summer of 1992, the situation in Bosnia and Herzegovina was dominating the agenda. Shortly before recognition was extended to Bosnia and Herzegovina on 6 April, the Yugoslav People's Army, now entirely under Serbian control, commenced hostilities in the republic and launched a strategy of ethnic cleansing, destruction, and extermination of the mainly Muslim population that surpassed even the brutality of the operation in Croatia, and amounting in all probability to genocide. The situation had been clearly identified by objective international agencies, from the UN Security Council to the General Assembly and special human rights bodies, as one characterized by abhorrent human rights abuses that would have to cease immediately, and have their consequences reversed.[20] However, it had not been possible to take action beyond the adoption of sanctions and the half-hearted deployment of UN peacekeepers, who failed to pursue their mandate aggressively.[21]

In the absence of decisive action, a new diplomatic attempt at resolving the crisis was made in the form of the London Conference on Yugoslavia of August 1992. The conference featured a wider spectrum of participants. The permanent members of the Security Council, representatives from the Organization of the Islamic Conference, the CSCE and six neighbouring states participated

---

[18] Macedonia and Slovenia were found to have fulfilled the conditions for recognition, whereas Croatia and Bosnia and Herzegovina would have to take certain additional steps. However, in the first round of recognitions, Croatia and Slovenia were recognized, followed after some delay by the other two.

[19] On the rulings of the Badinter Comisssion, see Matthew Craven, 'The European Community Arbitration Commision on Yugoslavia', *British Yearbook of International Law*, 66 (1995), 333–411; Alain Pellet, 'L'activité de la commission d'arbitrage de la Conférence européenne pour la paix en Yougoslavie', *Annuaire français de droit international*, 39 (1993), 286–303; and Steve Terrett, *The Dissolution of Yugoslavia and the Badinter Arbritration Commission* (Aldershot: Ashgate, 2000), chapter 6.

[20] e.g., Daniel Bethlehem, and Marc Weller (eds), *The 'Yugoslav' Crisis in International Law: General Issues* (Cambridge: Grotius, CUP, 1997), *passim.*

[21] Marc Weller, 'Peace-keeping and Peace-enforcement in the Republic of Bosnia and Herzegovina', *Heidelberg Journal of International Law [Zeitschrift fuer auslaendisches oeffentliches Recht und Voelkerrecht]*, 56 (1996), 70–177.

along with the parties and the EC member states, plus Japan and Canada. The time was deemed auspicious, as the rump Yugoslavia was being led—for a brief period, and ineffectively as it turned out—by the moderate FRY Prime Minister Milan Panic.

Before the Conference, and in preparation for it, Panic had officially declared to the UN Security Council, after consultations with Lord Carrington, that his government was 'conducting its own investigation into human rights violations of its citizens, particularly in Kosovo'. In relation to Kosovo, he promised careful examination with particular urgency of all laws, regulations and administrative practices to ensure that human rights abuses would cease.[22] There was no mention of the issue of the status of Kosovo, and the promise of an 'investigation' into Serbian practices in relation to that territory certainly struck the Kosovars as a rather cynical exercise.

Still, this statement appeared to indicate that, finally, the Kosovo issue might be addressed at the London Conference. However, despite the comments by Panic, Belgrade remained strongly opposed to such a prospect. Hence, Ibrahim Rugova, who had been elected President of Kosovo after an overwhelming victory in unofficial, parallel elections, received a letter that must surely be somewhat unique in diplomatic history. He was informed that it had been agreed that representatives of 'communities not formally represented at the London conference' would nevertheless be welcome to express their views within the overall framework of the Conference:

If you are planning to be in London at the time of the Conference (from 26–28 August) then I am pleased to inform you that it will be possible for you and your delegation to have access to the Queen Elisabeth II Conference Centre for meetings...As it will not, for practical and other reasons, be possible to grant your delegation access to the Conference chamber itself, the organizers will set up a 'Salle d'écoute' to which the formal Conference proceedings will be relayed live.[23]

This letter avoided issuing an invitation, while claiming to reflect 'strenuous efforts to ensure that the views of the Kosovar Albanians are heard'.[24] This slightly schizophrenic approach reflected a sense on the part of the negotiators that, somehow, the Kosovo issue would need to be addressed. On the other hand, in view of Belgrade's position on the issue, they did not really wish to insist on it.

Kosovo did attend the meeting from what became known as its 'echo chamber', where live television pictures of the proceedings were shown. Occasionally Lord Carrington and other dignitaries would visit the room and listen rather haughtily to the pleas of Rugova and his delegation. However, there was no substantive engagement with the Kosovo issue.

In the end, the entire London Conference proved a failure. Once again, the rump Yugoslavia, and the Serbian Republic individually, committed themselves

---

[22] Letter dated 17 August 1992, S/24452, Annex, in Weller, *Crisis in Kosovo*, 85.

[23] Letter from Lord Carrington to Dr I. Rugova, 17 August 1992, in Weller, *Crisis in Kosovo*, 86.

[24] *Ibid.*

to pledges in relation to Bosnia and Herzegovina which were never fulfilled. The Kosovo issue itself was not really addressed in a substantive manner, although Albania attempted to act as a spokesman for the territory. However, Lord Carrington indicated in a unilateral statement named 'Paper by the Chairman' that Serbia and Montenegro had committed themselves to the restoration of 'the full civil and constitutional rights of the inhabitants of Kosovo'.[25]

The formal statement by the conference Chair avoided a direct commitment by Belgrade. This would have been unacceptable, given Serbia's insistence that Kosovo was an entirely internal affair. Hence, it refused to acknowledge its commitment on the record by issuing its own statement, and it was left to the Chair to reflect this undertaking in his statement. Furthermore, the statement related to the civil and constitutional rights of the inhabitants of Kosovo. This turned the issue into more of a human rights question than a status issue. And finally there was, in any event, little prospect of delivery on the part of the FRY. Instead, the modalities for the restoration of civil and constitutional rights were to be discussed at a follow-on meeting to the London Conference.

II. The Special Group

The Conference was thus to remain in place through a process of follow-on meetings, which would also address the issue of Kosovo. However, Serbia insisted that Kosovo could only be considered under the heading of 'minority issues'. This was strongly rejected by the Kosovo Albanians, who considered themselves to be a majority suffering repression at the hands of a minority in their own homeland. In the end a 'Special Group' was set up to work on the Kosovo issue, which permitted both sides to retain their respective views on status.

The follow-on meetings of the Conference convened that autumn in Geneva, and subsequent meetings were also held in Belgrade and Prishtina. The Kosovo Special Group, chaired by Ambassador Gert Ahrens of Germany, quickly opted to circumvent the difficult issue of status, and attempted to focus instead on practical improvements to life in the territory. This decision was accelerated by the leadership, initially, of Milan Panic, who declared himself ready to address immediately the matters determined to be most pressing by the Kosovo leadership. The issue of education was selected as an area in which progress might be possible, and where there was an urgency of action.[26] In Kosovo, a Serbian curriculum had been introduced, and large numbers of ethnic Albanian teachers and professors had been dismissed. The Rugova government had managed to establish the famous parallel school system. Teachers would continue to exercise their profession, often in private houses, and funded by voluntary contributions,

[25] Co-Chairman's Paper on Serbia and Montenegro, 27 August 1992, in Weller, *Crisis in Kosovo*, 89.
[26] Report of the Secretary-General, 11 November 1992, S/24795, paras 90ff, in Weller, *Crisis in Kosovo*, 89.

or taxes, paid by the majority population. However, given the urgent need to avoid a situation in which an entire generation of young people grew up without more regular schooling, it was felt that progress would be in the interests of both parties. After all, the parallel school system also caused considerable embarrassment to Serbia: on the one hand, it demonstrated the effectiveness of the Rugova administration, while simultaneously highlighting the effects of Serbian repression at the international level.

Initial negotiations in September and October 1992, held amidst rising protests by students and others in Prishtina, seemed promising, with both parties agreeing to 'adopt a pragmatic approach to questions requiring urgent resolution, without prejudice to the positions of the parties on broader political issues.'[27] While the sides appeared ready to provide for the re-opening of schools, the sticking point was the control over the re-admission of the ethnic Albanian teachers who had been dismissed from their positions by the Serbian authorities. Moreover, control over the curriculum was at issue, as well as the recognition of qualifications earned in the parallel school system. In essence, this dispute replayed the larger debate about autonomous powers of Kosovo in relation to a specific issue area.

With the disappearance of Milan Panic from the political scene, the talks quickly became bogged down.[28] Worse than the lack of progress on the education issue may have been that the mere existence of the Special Group gave the impression that the Kosovo problem was now being addressed in an international forum. In fact, due to internal re-organizations of the international conference process, it was not clear for some time if the Special Group had been abolished.[29] In the meantime, at the Edinburgh Council meeting of 12 December 1992, the EC declared that 'the autonomy of Kosovo within Serbia must be restored', confirming to the Kosovo Albanian leadership that their wider interests were not going to be fully represented in an EC-led context, while on the other hand repression under an increasingly radicalized government in Belgrade was set to increase. In fact, the Group soon fell into a two-year period of 'inertia'.[30]

In the end, an education accord was reached some four years after the first meeting of the Special Group, although through the mediation of an NGO, rather than the working group.[31] However, that very brief agreement was never implemented. A final attempt to achieve progress in this limited sector was undertaken when fighting and displacement had already taken hold in Kosovo in the spring of 1998. Serbia, it seemed, wanted to demonstrate that it was, after all, willing to negotiate in good faith.[32] However, the process was halted as a result of the parallel military action, notably when reports of massacres and mass displacement began to emerge.

---

[27] Declaration of 14 October 1942, reproduced in Ahrens, *Diplomacy*, 341.
[28] Report of the Secretary-General, 30 March 1993, S/25490, Weller, *Crisis in Kosovo*, 91–2.
[29] Ahrens, *Diplomacy*, 78.   [30] *Ibid.*, 357.
[31] St Egidio Education Agreement, 1 September 1996.
[32] Agreed Measures of the Implementation of the Agreement on Education, 23 March 1998.

While the Special Group achieved little in the settlement of the Kosovo crisis, its demise contributed to its escalation. Kosovo had attempted to seize the Special Group at the time of the finalization of the arrangements for the implementation of the Dayton agreements at the end of 1995. The Kosovo side (rightly) feared that Dayton would be generally seen as the final point in the settlement of the Yugoslav crisis, with Kosovo being left out of the settlement and subject to unfettered repression by Serbia. While the follow-on process for Dayton initially foresaw the continuation of the work of the Group, this attempt was abandoned by the new head of the Peace Implementation Council, Carl Bild, within a few weeks of signing the agreement.

III. CSCE Monitoring

While negotiations proved fruitless even on practical issues, another international attempt was made to stabilize the situation on the ground. This effort was spearheaded by the Conference on Security and Cooperation in Europe. The CSCE, which transformed itself into the OSCE during the period under review, displayed important activism in relation to the Yugoslav crisis. It deployed many, if not most, elements of the plethora of new CSCE mechanisms adopted at the point of Cold War transition, more or less from the moment of their inception. This included the Vienna and Moscow Human Dimension Mechanisms, the Berlin Emergency Mechanism for Consultation and Cooperation, and the Mechanism for Consultation and Cooperation as Regards Unusual Military Activities. However, action by the high profile High Commissioner on National Minorities, established in 1992 to respond at the earliest possible stage to ethnic tensions with the potential to develop into a conflict, was very limited in view of the advanced stage of the crisis.

CSCE interest in the situation was legitimized by three factors. First, there was the danger of instability spreading from Kosovo into Macedonia, which could possibly lead to a wider confrontation involving Greece and perhaps Turkey. This contingency was addressed with the deployment of a CSCE 'spill-over' mission to Macedonia, in addition to the application of preventative diplomacy. Second, there was a risk that the overall conflict in Yugoslavia would involve some of the other neighbouring states. Hence the application of the emergency Mechanism on Unusual Military Activities. Finally, developments in Croatia and Bosnia, as well as those in Kosovo, posed an obvious challenge to the 'human dimension', which had long been one of the principal pillars of the CSCE.

In fact, among the various actors involved in the Yugoslav crisis, the CSCE was the only one which focused directly, expressly, and at an early stage on the crisis of Kosovo itself, rather than regarding it as a matter incidental to the rest of the turmoil in the former Yugoslavia.

The most significant early CSCE actions were the human dimension exploratory missions and the deployment of the Mission of Long Duration in Kosovo,

Sandjak, and Vojvodina in the exercise of the early warning and preventative action functions. The latter mission started operations on 8 September 1992 and remained in place until June 1993, when Belgrade withdrew its consent in response to the decision to suspend the rump Yugoslavia's from participation in the work of the CSCE.

This action was taken in light of the FRY's grave and severe violations of CSCE principles, especially in Bosnia and Herzegovina, and was in fact already in force by the time the Mission was established.[33] The FRY may have hoped that cooperation with the Mission would assist it in its campaign for restoration of membership privileges. When the Mission failed to fulfil this function, and instead brought unwelcome transparency to Kosovo, it was terminated—thereby highlighting the weakness in the constitutional structure of the CSCE, which continued to require the consent of its participating states for most types of operations.

The initial Human Rights Rapporteur Mission pointed out that while world attention was focused on Croatia, human rights were frequently and systematically being violated in other areas, notably in Kosovo and Sandjak. It rejected the Serbian argument of ethnic differentiation, on the basis of according 'nationality' status to Serbs and treating the Kosovo Albanians according to a different legal regime.[34]

The fact-finding mission undertaken by the Conflict Prevention Centre found that military activities in the territory were not unusual. However, in terms of the allegations of repression, the mission found that there was often no clear distinction between the army and the militia, which was employed primarily for that purpose. The mission was also made aware of ethnic Albanian fears that the situation would eventually give rise to armed conflict, under the guise of which Serbian forces would expel the Albanians from Kosovo altogether: '[i]f it started, it would produce a massacre and vast numbers of refugees'.[35]

The Mission of Long Duration in Kosovo, Sandjak, and Vojvodina was established according to a decision of the CSCE of 14 August 1992, in parallel with the London Conference. The mandate of the mission was:

- to promote dialogue between authorities and representatives of the populations and communities in Kosovo;
- to collect information on all aspects relevant to violations of human rights and fundamental freedoms and promote solutions to such problems;
- to establish contact points for solving problems that might be identified; and

---

[33] Decision by the Committee of Senior Officials (CSO), 7 July 1992, in Weller, *Crisis in Kosovo*, 95.

[34] Report of the Human Rights Rapporteur Mission to Yugoslavia, 24 January 1992, in Weller, *Crisis in Kosovo*, 97–100.

[35] Report of the Conflict Prevention Centre Fact-finding Mission to Kosovo, 5 June 1992, in Weller, *Crisis in Kosovo*, 102–4.

- to assist in providing information on relevant legislation on human rights, protection of minorities, free media and democratic elections.

The Mission of Long Duration gradually established a significant presence in the rump Yugoslavia, including in the field offices of Pec and Prizren. In addition to general reports on the situation, it investigated the removal of most ethnic Albanians from all public functions in the province including the judiciary, the takeover of the infrastructure of organs of the media in the territory (by creating a new state concern regulating access to publishing technology and paper), the running down of ethnic Albanian health care and the exclusion of Albanians from the social security system, the establishment by the ethnic Albanians of parallel administrative structures and of a parallel economy, instances of intimidation and police brutality, and so on.

The Mission also attempted, repeatedly, to persuade the majority population to try and exhaust the legal procedures available under the Serbian administration of the territory. This was supposed to provide a better opportunity for the CSCE and human rights bodies to take up particular cases with the FRY/Serbian government. However, the local ethnic Albanian population lacked enthusiasm for this somewhat unrealistic approach. Seeing this, the Mission then consistently attempted to engage Serbian and Albanian leaders in dialogue, and to arrange for small and practical improvements in the situation. Through its presence, it did manage to alleviate the suffering of elements of the local population and, on occasion, to intercede on behalf of individuals who had been detained and were being mistreated.

Hence, these missions served a broader purpose than merely furnishing CSCE decision-makers—or rather, member governments taking decisions within the framework of the CSCE—with internal reports on the situation. The CSCE presence in Kosovo, while it lasted, went beyond reporting, straying into mediation and the active protection of threatened individuals. Through direct contact with the Yugoslav/Serbian governments, a modicum of accountability was also introduced. However, as with the very detailed reports of the EC/EU monitors who silently witnessed the probable genocide in Croatia and in Bosnia and Herzegovina, an even greater sense of accountability could have been introduced had the findings of the field missions been published by the CSCE.

The value of the mission was recognized in the international protest that marked the termination of its operations by Yugoslavia, which included a call from the United Nations Security Council to readmit the CSCE operation.[36] This resolution was to remain the only Council action targeted specifically at the situation in Kosovo, from the outbreak of the crisis in 1988 to 1998, when open hostilities erupted.

---

[36] Resolution 855 (1993), 9 August 1993, S/RES/655 (1993).

IV. Conclusion

The initial phase of the crisis saw the deployment of the principal European mechanisms for conflict prevention and conflict management, in particular the EC and the CSCE. However, neither of these two had at the time fully developed the institutional equipment to fully play this role. Instead, some of the relevant institutions and mechanisms evolved in parallel with the evolution of the crisis. Moreover, there was no single voice represented through these institutions. Instead, they operated more in the nature of collective cabinet diplomacy, than by way of international or supranational organizations. It took time, and dramatic events, before a collective, aggregated 'will' could emerge that might be represented and implemented through such mechanisms. And where such will existed, it could easily be frustrated by the one or other state, in particular in the consensus-prone CSCE environment. This factor reflected deference to two constraints drawn from the classical international order. The first is the principle of state consent. As Serbia, the principal offending power in relation to the traumatic developments in Yugoslavia (Croatia, and Bosnia and Herzegovina) and in relation to the Kosovo issue, was allowed to claim international representation on behalf of Yugoslavia until its dissolution was confirmed in January 1992, it could frustrate international action simply by refusing to consent to it. Even later, when the rump Yugoslavia (Serbia and Montenegro) was denied the claim to automatic succession to the SFRY, it nevertheless retained the power to cause deadlock in international settlement attempts. In particular, the forced withdrawal of the CSCE mission evidences this fact, which is reinforced by a second classical feature of the international system—the principle of non-intervention. While the United Nations Security Council became increasingly active in view of the threat to peace and security that was evident in Bosnia and Herzegovina and Croatia, it remained very hesitant to involve itself in the Kosovo issue. This was due to the position of states that are, traditionally, particularly sovereignty-conscious, including China. Instead, international diplomacy on Kosovo was focused almost exclusively on the Special Group as part of the International Conference process on Yugoslavia. However, that process never managed to engage the underlying status issue in a significant way. Instead, it focused on one practical issue area, and even in that area there was no real progress over the three years of its existence.

4

Dealing with Human Rights Violations

The increasingly desperate human rights situation in a state which had considered itself part of Western Europe for over a decade could be regarded as an indictment of the European and universal international human rights institutions. However, as was the case with the early involvement of the CSCE in the Yugoslav crisis, the universal international constitutional system for the monitoring and implementation of human rights actually functioned with surprising vigour, both in relation to the Yugoslav crisis in general, and in relation to Kosovo. However, there were important structural limitations to the impact of this activity.

I. Standards and International Interest

Human rights are based in general international law, in universal conventions, and in regional and multilateral/bilateral treaties.[1] The most basic and fundamental human rights obligations, such as the prohibition of genocide, apartheid and torture, are part and parcel of the substantive law of the international constitution (*jus cogens*).[2] That is to say, these obligations of general international law apply to all states, whether or not they have specifically consented to them. States can never derogate from these rights or suspend their operation, even in times of armed conflict or other emergencies.[3] Most of these fundamental obligations are also reflected in international conventions which aspire to universal membership. These human rights conventions, most notably the United Nations Covenants on Human Rights of 1966 and the specialized Convention against Torture 1984,

---

[1] Henry J. Steiner, *International Human Rights Law in Context: Law, Politics, Moral. Text and Materials* (Oxford: Oxford University Press, 2000); Malcolm N. Shaw, *International Law* (5th edn, Cambridge: Cambridge University Press, 2003); Rene Provost, *International Human Rights and Humanitarian Law* (Cambridge: Cambridge University Press, 2002).

[2] Michael Akehurst, 'The Hierarchy of the Sources in International Law', *British Yearbook of International Law*, 47 (1974–5), 273–85; Karol Wolfke, 'Jus Cogens in International Law', 6 *Polish Yearbook of International Law* (1974), 145–63; Nicholas G. Onuf and Richard K. Birney, 'Peremptory Norms of International Law: Their Source, Function and Future', *Journal of International Law and Policy*, 4 (1974), 187–98.

[3] Teraya Koji, 'Emerging Hierarchy in International Human Rights and Beyond: From the Perspective of Non-derogable Rights', *European Journal of International Law*, 12(5) (2001), 917–41; Thedor Meron, 'On a Hierarchy of International Human Rights', *American Journal of International Law*, 80 (1986), 1–23.

also include more specific obligations which operate only in relation to states that have contracted into the relevant treaties. Regional treaties will generally add even greater specificity. After all, it is assumed that states in a given region will share a certain human rights culture, and will be able to advance the level of protection offered in relation to certain rights at the universal level. Finally, a number of individual states may wish to create a legal regime among themselves, in order to address particular human rights concerns of relevance to them. For that purpose, they can establish multilateral or bilateral treaties. It is usually the latter that are concluded in relation to the protection of national minorities.

The human rights obligations binding upon the former Yugoslavia by virtue of general international law and its own specific consent were substantive, wide-ranging and clearly expressed. In addition to having to comply with human rights obligations in general international law, the former Yugoslavia was party to several universal human rights conventions (e.g., the 1966 Covenant on Civil and Political Rights and the Conventions on Genocide, Torture, the Rights of the Child, and the Elimination of Racial Discrimination, of 1948, 1985, 1989 and 1965 respectively). However, Yugoslavia made use of the option of derogating from some of its human rights obligations, declaring to the United Nations that, in view of a public emergency, it would provisionally cease applying provisions on the freedom of movement and of assembly. Moreover, Yugoslavia was not a member of the very sophisticated European regional system of human rights operated under the aegis of the Council of Europe.[4] That system not only contains a very detailed catalogue of rights, but also a highly intrusive and effective machinery of human rights enforcement, at the centre of which is the European Court of Human Rights.

The issue of implementation is the principal weak spot of the universal human rights system. According to classical conceptions of international law, states must consent to specific obligations before they can be legally bound by them (of course, as was noted in the introduction to this volume, this excludes the fundamental human rights contained in general international law, or *jus cogens*). Furthermore, state consent can be conditioned by reservations or national interpretation. States have traditionally demanded the right to determine for themselves whether an international mechanism can consider the extent to which they are actually implementing the obligations they have accepted. For example, many universal conventions contain optional clauses or annexes, through which a state can agree that a special committee shall be entitled to receive petitions from individuals who claim to have been the victim of human rights violations. In the absence of such additional consent, the relevant committee lacks competence even to receive such communications.

---

[4] The former Yugoslav republics signed up to the ECHR only in the aftermath of the dissolution of the federation (Bosnia and Herzegovina in 2002; Croatia in 1996; Slovenia in 1993; the former Union of Serbia and Montenegro in 2003; Macedonia in 1995).

However, the international constitutional system has developed quite significantly over the past decade. A state may no longer consider it an unlawful 'intervention' if another government, or an international organization, criticizes its human rights performance. Hence, the United Nations General Assembly, or specialized United Nations bodies such as the former Commission on Human Rights and its Sub-Commission, would now routinely adopt resolutions condemning the human rights practices of certain states, and demand improvements. Moreover, most of the committees attached to international human rights conventions are entitled to receive and even demand reports on compliance from state parties, and to evaluate these reports critically, without the need of a further act of consent from the state in question. In addition, the United Nations has now established a rather sophisticated system of human rights monitoring, through the United Nations High Commissioner for Human Rights, the Human Rights Council and the innovation of special rapporteurs.

There are two types of special rapporteur. Thematic rapporteurs consider certain types of issues or infractions, wherever they are committed. For example, there are very active rapporteurs who consider allegations of torture, involuntary disappearances or religious intolerance around the world. There are also country rapporteurs, appointed by the United Nations Human Rights Council to consider the situation in specific states in crisis. While the states in question can refuse cooperation with such rapporteurs, they rarely do so. Even states which systematically violate human rights are quite sensitive to international criticism and to the condemnation by the UN's political bodies, including the General Assembly, which a failure to cooperate might occasion.

The staggering situation in the former Yugoslavia, especially in relation to Bosnia and Herzegovina, triggered significant international human rights action. In an unprecedented step, the United Nations Commission on Human Rights met in special session in August 1992. It established a Special Rapporteur for Yugoslavia, initially the high profile Tadeusz Mazowiecki, who was replaced by Elizabeth Rehn upon his resignation in protest at international inaction concerning his findings. Existing thematic rapporteurs, including those on torture and arbitrary executions, were also requested to focus their attention urgently on the situation in the former Yugoslavia.

Subsequently, the Commission, backed by the General Assembly, requested that the Secretary-General make available resources to facilitate continuous monitoring, and in the end, after some Yugoslav resistance, efforts to establish a field office presence were successful. The resulting reports were fed into the Sub-Commission, the Commission itself, the Third (Humanitarian) Committee of the United Nations General Assembly, and the plenary of the Assembly. All of these bodies adopted uncharacteristically strong resolutions, condemning FRY/Serbian practices and demanding cessation of this conduct, with none of the usual diplomatic ambiguities.

In addition to these bodies, established directly under the United Nations Charter, the committees attached to specialized human rights conventions also became active. Yugoslavia was made to report on its conduct and its diplomats were cross-examined by the relevant committees, which then adopted quite strongly worded findings. At first, Yugoslavia cooperated with this procedure. However, by September 1992 the United Nations organs had determined that Yugoslavia could not lay claim to automatic succession of the rights of the Socialist Federal Republic of Yugoslavia. Instead, all the states which had emerged from the dissolution of Yugoslavia would be treated equally and considered to be new states. Hence, the rump Yugoslavia would also have to apply anew for membership in the United Nations, although, in the meantime and in something of a diplomatic fudge, Belgrade was permitted to continue its participation in the work of certain UN bodies.[5]

Some time after this decision, Belgrade refused to engage with the human rights treaty bodies, arguing that it had been wrongfully denied its claimed rights as the universal successor state to the SFRY and had, in consequence, been placed in a position of inequality.[6] This view was rejected by the relevant committees. It was noted that, given their special humanitarian objective, human rights obligations continued to be in force for successor states to a state party. This would include the obligation to continue cooperating with the implementation mechanisms attached to a convention to which the state in question was a party.[7] Hence, the treaty committees continued to question and condemn Yugoslav practices where appropriate, drawing largely on information gathered from outside the state reports.[8]

Given the proliferation of UN bodies involved in the human rights crisis in the former Yugoslavia, the General Assembly asked the Secretary-General to facilitate coordination of these various efforts, through an annual report which summarized the findings across different agencies and described their interlocking efforts. The Secretary-General was also required to monitor the extent to which Yugoslavia complied with the Assembly's demand for cooperation with the relevant United Nations bodies, generating a more visible level of accountability for Belgrade in this respect. Overall, therefore, an integrated and in many ways unprecedented response was developed to address the Yugoslav crisis.

The increasing emphasis on Kosovo is also interesting to note. It is true that the international diplomatic effort remained focused very much on the atrocities in Bosnia and Herzegovina. However, the human rights bodies and the General

---

[5] e.g., Security Council Resolution 777 (1992), 19 September 1992, S/RES/777 (1992).

[6] e.g., Letter from the chargé d'affaires a.i. of the Permanent Mission of the FRY to the UN Office at Geneva to the Chairman of the CERD Committee, 15 February 1995, in Concluding Observation of CERD: Yugoslavia, 15/6 March 1995, in Weller, *Crisis in Kosovo*, 148.

[7] Letter from the Chairman of the CERD Committee, 6 March 1995, in Concluding Observations of CERD: Yugoslavia, 15/6 March 1995, in Weller, *Crisis in Kosovo*, 148.

[8] See Weller, *Crisis in Kosovo*, chapter 6.

Assembly also paid attention to developments in Kosovo, both when addressing the situation in the former Yugoslavia as a whole, and when adopting specific resolutions or decisions in relation to it. Moreover, the language used by these bodies in its determinations was unusually lacking in diplomatic ambiguity, clearly identifying the individual elements of the human rights crisis and demanding similarly clear remedial action.

II. Access

The question of access for international observers dominated international concern for Kosovo, especially after the expulsion of the CSCE long-term monitoring mission in the summer of 1993. This concern was only heightened when the full horror of Serbian practices in Croatia and Bosnia and Herzegovina became apparent. Access is an issue that is generally handled with some care and sophistication by governments under investigation. As long as contact is maintained with human rights investigators, a state can claim to be fulfilling its human rights obligations, evidenced in its decision to permit transparency through the presence of monitors.[9] Often it is also possible to restrict and circumscribe the activities of monitors, to equip them with official guides and make them dependent on governmental transport and security arrangements. Rapporteurs can be fed favourable information which, in the interests of balanced reporting, will feature in their reports, regardless of its credibility. More importantly, the reporting agency will generally be minded to phrase its findings cautiously, for fear of losing the access it has been granted.

In this case, the UN General Assembly itself threw its weight behind the demands for access of the Special Rapporteur and others, and as indicated above, the UN Secretariat was required to report on access at the highest level, directly through the Secretary-General. The Special Rapporteur was sometimes granted access—more frequently after the resignation of Mazowiecki, who had reported in a rather outspoken way on the atrocities in Bosnia and Herzegovina. Often, difficult discussions about the modalities of a visit would precede a particular mission. It was also possible to conduct special investigations, for example of trials of ethnic Albanians, using observers in the field.[10] In February 1996, the FRY government agreed to the establishment of a field office in Belgrade—an action it had resisted since it was first proposed in 1992 by Mazowiecki.

Visits to Kosovo were undertaken by the initially two and later four members of the field office, and further representations were made with a view to establishing a field office directly in that territory. That proposal was overtaken by the events

---

[9] e.g., Letter from the FRY to the Chairman of the Commission on Human Rights, 15 February 1995, Weller, *Crisis in Kosovo*, 134–6.
[10] Special Report: Two Trials of Kosovo, 10 September 1997, in Weller, *Crisis in Kosovo*, 170–7.

of 1998. Nevertheless, during that period, the office of the High Commissioner for Human Rights did manage to maintain a continuous presence in Kosovo, although mobility of the observers was restricted.[11]

III. Substantive Findings

The direct and unsubtle nature of Yugoslav/Serbian action in Kosovo remains startling. When committing grave crimes against humanity in Croatia and Bosnia and Herzegovina, the leadership in Belgrade had attempted to cloak its actions in rather implausible denials. But in relation to Kosovo, repression was conducted very much officially, and under a veritable legislative programme.

Serbia had formally established the purported new and subordinated status of Kosovo in its constitutional law. It had also downgraded the ethnic Albanian majority in Kosovo from a 'nationality' to a 'minority'. More than that, many of the openly discriminatory practices applied within the territory were formally condoned in acts of legislation, duly published in the Republic's official gazette. These even included specific decisions whereby individuals were removed from public office or from positions of responsibility in commercial enterprises. Whether this reflected the strength of conviction in the Serbian cause, was a conscious display of proclaimed ethnic superiority or was merely the result of continuing legislative and administrative practices from the communist era, with its slightly odd insistence on Orwellian pseudo-legality, can probably not be answered by the outsider. But this practice certainly made it easier for international human rights bodies to form their views. It is not possible to summarize the findings of individual bodies. However, the general picture painted below identifies some of the principal areas of concern that were identified.

General discrimination. The existence of large amounts of openly discriminatory legislation was confirmed throughout the crisis in the Special Rapporteur reports and condemned by the General Assembly, the Commission on Human Rights and its Sub-Commission, as well as by the Committee attached to the Convention on the Elimination of Racial Discrimination (CERD/C). That Committee engaged in detailed dialogue with the FRY authorities in relation to these actions. In response, the FRY provided lengthy justifications of its policies. Nevertheless, the Committee concluded that ethnic Albanians were being discriminated against in a way that 'deprived [them] of effective enjoyment of the most basic human rights provided in the Convention'.[12] The General Assembly identified as early as 1993 'discriminatory policies, measures and violent actions committed

---

[11] See Report by the Human Rights Field Operation in the Former Yugoslavia, 29 May 1998. In Weller, *Crisis in Kosovo*, 262–3.

[12] CERD Concluding Observations, 15/6 March 1996, also Concluding Observations, 19 March 1998, in Weller, *Crisis in Kosovo*, 155–6.

against ethnic Albanians in Kosovo', demanding a cessation of 'police brutality, arbitrary searches, seizures and arrests, torture and ill treatment during detention and discrimination in the administration of justice'.[13] The Sub-Commission determined that such actions were 'aim[ed] at forcing ethnic Albanians to leave their land'.[14]

Discriminatory legislation in relation to property. The Law on the Restriction of Real Property Transfers required official authorization for changes of title to real property, initially through a special commission and subsequently though the Serbian Secretary of Finance. These provisions were applied 'unevenly and [were] arbitrarily implemented, depending on the applicant's ethnicity and place of residence'.[15] Violations by ethnic Albanians of the relevant provisions were punished by prison sentences.[16]

Resettlement and demographic manipulation. The 1989 Programme for the Realisation of Peace, Freedom, Equality, Democracy and Prosperity of the Socialist Autonomous Province of Kosovo had decreed that obstacles to the 'return of Serbs and Montenegrins, displaced under pressure, and all the others who wish to come and live in Kosovo' would need to be removed through direct rule. In addition to limiting the transfer of property titles to Albanians, legislation had been adopted encouraging Serbs to acquire property, in particular real estate. Special provisions were put into place to facilitate the acquisition of agricultural land by ethnic Serbs. There were financial assistance schemes in place to attract settlement, and an infrastructure programme to support this venture. On occasion, ethnic Albanians were forcibly removed from houses and apartments to make room for Serbs.[17] Finally, Serb refugees from other areas of the former Yugoslavia were settled directly in Kosovo. On the other hand, ethnic Albanians who had left the territory were to be denationalized in an effort to change the ethnic balance, and some of those who remained were declared illegal immigrants from Albania.

The resettlement programme was not successful. With the exception of Serb refugees from other areas of the former Yugoslavia who had no other option, Kosovo did not prove an attractive place of 'immigration'. Ethnic Serbs remained isolated and despite Serbian control over the 'official' economy, few recent arrivals prospered. While the Serbian media and politicians claimed that Serbs were being subjected to significant repression at the hands of the Albanians, the

[13] General Assembly Resolution 48/153, 20 December 1993, A/RES/48/153.
[14] Sub-Commission Resolution 1995/10, 18 August 1995, in Weller, *Crisis in Kosovo*, 136–7.
[15] CERD Concluding Observations, 19 March 1998, in Weller, *Crisis in Kosovo*, 155–6.
[16] Special Rapporteur Report on the Situation of Human Rights in the FRY, 31 October 1997, in Weller, *Crisis in Kosovo* 177–9.
[17] e.g., Special Rapporteur Report on the Situation of Human Rights in the former Yugsolavia, 1 November 1993, in Weller, *Crisis in Kosovo*, 160–1; Report on the Situation of Human Rights in the former Yugoslavia, 21 February 1994, in Weller, *Crisis in Kosovo*, 161.

human rights bodies found little evidence of a concerted campaign to that end, although there were isolated incidents. The attempt to 'change the ethnic balance'[18] of the territory by removing citizenship from those who had fled or moved for economic reasons was also internationally rejected. Similarly, Serbian population figures based on the assertion that many ethnic Albanians were illegal immigrants from Albania were widely ignored. Hence, by 1990, there were about 90 per cent ethnic Albanians in the territory and perhaps 8 per cent Serbs, and it was generally accepted that this figure remained relatively constant throughout the period of tension of the 1990s.

Removal of ethnic Albanians from public office and from commercial enterprises. Ethnic Albanians had been dismissed wholesale from the Kosovo police force. A new police force was then created, drawing upon non-Albanians from Serbia and Montenegro and from Kosovo itself. Albanian judges and prosecutors were removed from office. Teachers were also dismissed, in many cases after they refused to swear allegiance to the Serbian constitution or to teach a Serbian syllabus decreed by Belgrade. Several Albanian-staffed hospitals were 'consolidated' and effectively closed. Because much of the economic system was still dominated by state enterprises, Serbian control of what would elsewhere be considered the private sector could be established easily under Serbian legislation. In fact, senior and middle-level managers were often removed by formal legislative decree. Some enterprises in Kosovo were merged with undertakings in Serbia. The supply of goods and services was restricted, and registration of new enterprises by ethnic Albanians was also constrained.

Interference with the judiciary. The emergency legislation, later regularized under the umbrella of the new 1990 Constitution of Serbia, permitted direct intervention by Serbian courts in proceedings in the province. The judicial system within Kosovo was ethnically cleansed, through the removal of ethnic Albanian judges and other judicial officers. The conduct of trials by these organs was frequently criticized by human rights bodies as unbalanced and in violation of fair trial safeguards. Equally as important, although perhaps less visible, was Serbian control over special economic courts and administrative review bodies. Again, these were placed at the disposal of Republic of Serbia policies in the region. There were consistent allegations of torture as a means of extracting confessions, resulting occasionally in permanent injury. As the Special Rapporteur noted, by the beginning of 1993, 'all remaining Albanian judges or magistrates have been dismissed. Under such conditions the right to a fair trial and the impartiality of the judiciary can hardly be guaranteed with regard to the Albanian population of Kosovo.'[19]

[18] e.g., General Assembly Resolution 50/190, 22 December 1995, A/RES/50/190.
[19] Report on the Situation of Human Rights in the former Yugoslavia, 26 February 1993, in Weller, *Crisis in Kosovo*, 158–60; also Special Report: Two Trials of Kosovo, 10 September 1997, in *ibid.*, 170–7.

Education. Education establishments were required to teach a Serbian curriculum. A widespread refusal to follow this curriculum led to the wholesale closing down of the education system. Teachers and university professors continued to give instruction, unpaid by the state and often in private houses or other unorthodox venues, although Serbian police raids and other measures were used to inhibit this activity.[20] Some 300,000 children were educated in this way, by many of the 18,000 teachers or more who had been dismissed.[21] The Serbian Academy of Sciences took over the Kosovo Academy, or at least its property, and other ethnic Albanian cultural institutions were closed down.

Freedom of the press. The Albanian broadcast media were cleansed as early as 1990, with 1,300 journalists and technical staff being dismissed.[22] Newspaper offices were frequently raided and many closed. Ethnic Albanian journalists were intimidated or arrested. More profoundly, Serbia took over all the sources of supplies for printing and publishing houses by consolidating the relevant undertakings into one, which was fully controlled by the Republic. Nevertheless, a few publications survived.

Arbitrary arrests. Ethnic Albanians were frequently arrested without charge, often taken from their homes at gunpoint and at night, to participate in so-called 'informative talks'. In one six-month period alone, 1,700 persons were 'subjected to police abuse in connection with the raids'.[23] The Serbian authorities 'have on occasion sealed off entire areas, interrogated and sometimes physically assaulted ethnic Albanians at random' and there were instances of disappearances, i.e., individuals who never returned from police custody.[24] There were also 'hostage arrests', where police detained relatives or family members of persons sought by the police.

Torture and mistreatment. The systematic use of torture and other forms of mistreatment by the militia and police was frequently condemned. Such treatment was applied against the elected ethnic Albanian political leaders,[25] against students, more or less at random, and others crossing the paths of Serbian police patrols, all of which created a general climate of intimidation.[26]

Impunity for perpetrators. Serbian officials accused of torture, harassment or killing were not held accountable in any significant way. Similarly, weapons

---

[20] Special Rapporteur Report, 1 November 1993, in Weller, *Crisis in Kosovo*, 160–1.
[21] Special Rapporteur Report, 25 October 1996, in Weller, *Crisis in Kosovo*, 164–9.
[22] Special Rapporteur Report, 13 December 1994, in Weller, *Crisis in Kosovo*, 162.
[23] Special Rapporteur Report, 4 November 1994, in Weller, *Crisis in Kosovo*, 161–2.
[24] Special Rapporteur Report, 25 October 1996, in Weller, *Crisis in Kosovo*, 164–9.
[25] Special Rapporteur Report, 4 November 1994, in Weller, *Crisis in Kosovo*, 161–2.
[26] Special Rapporteur Report, 31 October 1997, in Weller, *Crisis in Kosovo*, 177–80.

were made available to local groups of ethnic Serbs, who terrorized the ethnic Albanian population. Again, there was no attempt to establish responsibility for these actions, or to suppress this practice, leading to a state of insecurity and terror amongst the population at large.

Disproportionate use of force. Even before the outbreak of hostilities in 1998, CERD/C condemned the disproportionate use of force against the Albanian population, which had resulted in numerous violations of the right to life, destruction of property and in the displacement of a large number of people, many of whom were women and children.[27] Of course, this latter practice increased significantly in late 1997 and early 1998.

IV. Conclusion

The crisis in the former Yugoslavia marked a new challenge for United Nations human rights bodies in the post-Cold War world. Perhaps surprisingly, a coordinated effort was made across the relevant UN organs to address this emergency. Unlike the reporting of the UN Secretary-General in the context of UN peacekeeping concerning Croatia and Bosnia (and later in relation to Rwanda), the human rights bodies were proactive and forthright in their activities. Particular respect is due to the human rights field workers and to the special rapporteurs who had to brave quite uncomfortable circumstances in order to undertake fact-finding missions.

Contrary to previous practice, determinations by human rights bodies were no longer constrained by the submissions of the target government. While information was solicited from Yugoslavia, tough and independent conclusions were reached in relation to the claims put forward by its government, including by the United Nations General Assembly. In fact, all human rights bodies, as well as the General Assembly, consistently tracked the situation in Kosovo, even while Bosnia and Herzegovina dominated the international agenda, and issued strong and appropriate demands to the FRY government.

Of course, in the end, these activities did not result in a marked improvement in the situation in the former Yugoslavia, including Kosovo. However, this is not due to a failing in the existing human rights machinery itself. Instead, the absence of a link between, on the one hand, findings of fact, international condemnation and demands for action and, on the other, an enforcement mechanism to address a situation in which these calls remained unheeded, is to blame for this state of affairs. The failure to feed information on the human rights situation in Kosovo and other parts of the former Yugoslavia into the decision-making process, for example as it concerned the lifting of sanctions vis-à-vis the FRY

---

[27] CERD Decision 3 (53), 17 August 1998, in Weller, *Crisis in Kosovo*, 156.

before and after Dayton, might be noted in this context. The lack of enforcement action in the Security Council, at a time when the human rights situation turned from deplorable into a humanitarian disaster throughout 1998, is also striking. No enforcement action was taken, other than the adoption of an arms embargo that did not much affect Yugoslavia, given that a bilateral arrangement with Russia had enabled it to replenish the supplies it had expended in Croatia and in Bosnia and Herzegovina.

5

The Developing Humanitarian Emergency

In 1997/8, the crisis in Kosovo evolved from a human rights problem into a humanitarian crisis. In response to the dramatic turn of events in Kosovo, the United Nations Secretary-General was requested to submit regular reports on the developing situation to the Council. Drawing on the OSCE, NATO and other bodies, these reports chronicled the events of April to October 1998 and the deployment of the OSCE Verification Mission in Kosovo (KVM).[1] Although he did not have his own sources of information on the ground, Kofi Annan (or rather the UN Secretariat) added his own evaluation of the situation. However, there was no evidence of a great deal of diplomatic activity by the Secretary-General himself in the reports. According to Article 99 of the UN Charter, the Secretary-General enjoys a limited freedom of diplomatic initiative and the scope and scale of the evolving drama might have merited an early response from him. The fact that the Kosovo crisis was still a purportedly 'internal affair' of Yugoslavia may explain this apparent passivity. Other factors might include the dispute in the Security Council itself as to the necessary response to the crisis, and the feeling that the Contact Group was exercising a dominant role in crisis diplomacy. However, towards the end of the summer, the findings of the Secretary-General in his reports became more specific, in line with the ever-increasing drama of the displacement that was occurring.

While the OSCE reported very consistently to the United Nations on developments in the province, the silence of the EU is startling in this respect. Although the EU responded to a request by the Secretary-General and the UN Yugoslav Sanctions Committee for assistance in sanctions monitoring, it did not use its EU monitoring mission to add transparency to FRY/Serbian action at the UN level. This mission had already been severely criticized for failing to issue public reports on the genocide it observed in Bosnia and Herzegovina, and it continued to retain something of a phantom presence during the Kosovo crisis.

[1] See Chapter 4.

I. The Spread of Armed Conflict and the Humanitarian Consequences

The change from repression to military assault which brought about the massive displacement of Kosovo Albanians in 1998 followed the increased activity of the Kosovo Liberation Army (KLA) in the autumn of 1997. That organization had previously consisted of tens or perhaps a few hundred individuals, mounting what were described as 'terrorist' attacks.[2] These attacks were generally targeted against police or other security installations, although the FRY/Serbian authorities indicated, with some justification, that these operations were part of a strategy of intimidation directed against Serb civilians. Attacks against Serb civilians did indeed occur, although they remained relatively isolated incidents from which the KLA dissociated itself.

While the increase in KLA operations was relatively marginal, it resulted in a change of tactic by the FRY/Serbian forces in the territory. Previously, a campaign of intimidation, arbitrary arrests and forced confessions had been employed. By the spring of 1998, however, FRY/Serbian police and military units had established more checkpoints on roads, including in rural areas, to limit the freedom of movement of underground fighters.[3] A sequence of events, familiar from the ethnic cleansing in Croatia and Bosnia and Herzegovina, then followed. Ethnic Albanian villages suspected of collaborating with the KLA were surrounded by regular armed forces, including artillery and tank units, and shelled. Civilians would flee or become casualties. Small units were then sent into the villages, often killing entire ethnic Albanian families, or clans, who had failed to seek shelter in the surrounding countryside. This practice was first exposed in the Drenica region, where several groups of individuals, ranging in numbers from twelve to fifty-three, had been 'liquidated', several shot at close range.[4] The largest group among them included fifteen women, six children and four individuals over the age of sixty-five.

Diplomatic observers from the EU and the Kosovo Diplomative Observer Mission (KDOM), composed of representatives of diplomatic missions accredited to Belgrade, were denied access to areas within which it was believed that FRY/Serbian forces were engaging in operations against villages.[5] Humanitarian supplies were also prohibited on occasion, although initially the humanitarian organizations were permitted to retain some access to provide relief.[6] The conflict then spread further, involving large swathes of territory from which the KLA

---

[2] Tim Judah, 'Kosovo's Road to War', *Survival*, 41(2) (Summer 1999), 5–18, 13.

[3] On the 1998 conflict, see the excellent analysis by Stefan Troebst in *SIPRI Yearbook 1999*, Appendix 1C.

[4] High Commissioner for Human Rights, Human Rights Field Operation in the Former Yugoslavia, April 1998, in Weller, *Crisis in Kosovo*, 259.

[5] On the establishment of KDOM, see Chapter 6, Section III.   [6] *Ibid.*

was progressively displaced, along with much of the ethnic Albanian population. Once more, 'wholesale destruction visited upon the Albanian villages' was reported.[7]

In addition to the increasingly intolerable suffering of the civilian population, reports of the influx of small arms and ammunition from Albania surfaced, raising the prospect of internationalization of the conflict.[8] Moreover, corresponding to the ever larger number of displaced Albanians, and the atrocities which had led to their displacement, the KLA steadily grew in numbers. Rather than deserting the KLA on account of its lack of military success, a sense of national crisis among the Kosovo Albanians generated a feeling of solidarity, which was often transposed to the KLA, an organization that appeared to offer the only recourse in an increasingly desperate situation.

By September of 1988, when NATO was moving towards a threat of force to terminate hostilities, Belgrade asserted that it had defeated secessionist terrorism and would soon cease operations. However, the UN Secretary-General reported on a sharp escalation of military operations as a result of an offensive launched by Serbian forces in central, southern and western Kosovo.[9] In his final report before the issuing of the threat of force by NATO, he indicated that 'the level of destruction points clearly to an indiscriminate and disproportionate use of force against civilian populations', with the civilian population increasingly having 'become the main target of the conflict'.[10] As of mid-September, an estimated 6,000 to 7,000 buildings in 269 villages, if not more, had been destroyed. That estimate was later raised to 20,000 when the OSCE gained access to the territory pursuant to the Holbrooke agreement (of which more presently). There were further reports of mass killings of civilians in several locations, including the mutilation of ethnic Albanian bodies according to the pattern witnessed during the ethnic cleansing in Bosnia and Herzegovina. By mid-October, there were some 280,000 to 300,000 displaced ethnic Albanians whose fate was uncertain, given the imminent onset of winter.

II. The Humanitarian Response

The humanitarian emergency which resulted from the events of 1998 was, in many ways, overwhelming. It was addressed by a whole host of international organizations and agencies. These activities extended to monitoring of the situation, the provision of protection through visits to detainees and the presence of international personnel in particular areas of crisis, intervention on behalf of individuals and groups, the distribution of relief and, ultimately, caring for the

---

[7] OSCE Report, Annex V, in UNSG Report, 2 July 1998, S/1998/608.
[8] *Ibid.*, OSCE Report, Annex 1.
[9] UNSG Report, Annex, 4 September 1998, S/1998/834.
[10] UNSG Report, 3 October 1998, S/1998/912.

refugees who were flooding into neighbouring territories. In contrast to the situation which resulted from the mass deportations undertaken by the FRY/Serbia from March 1999 onwards, many of these agencies were initially allowed to be present in Kosovo.

In relation to humanitarian efforts, the International Committee of the Red Cross (ICRC) exercised a particularly important function, given its special international status. Although the ICRC is a private international organization, it enjoys significant right of access to victims of armed conflict. In addition to its international staff, the organization can also act in cooperation with national Red Cross societies, organized in the International Federation of Red Cross and Red Crescent Societies. In this instance, the Yugoslav national society and those of neighbouring states, including Albania and Macedonia, played a particularly important role in bringing relief to those in need.

While the FRY/Serbia considered the hostilities in Kosovo an internal matter, to be dealt with by way of police action, the ICRC nevertheless managed to expand its presence in the FRY and Kosovo very rapidly, to seventeen expatriates and over fifty locally recruited staff (of both Serb and Albanian ethnicity). The ICRC pressed for access to areas of confrontation and to detained persons, in accordance with its mandate. It was, however, denied access to some regions while they were subject to offensive military operations,[11] and was also not permitted to visit hundreds of detained individuals other than those who had been tried and convicted by the Belgrade authorities.[12] When it was admitted to areas of confrontation, it found many deserted and destroyed villages.[13] Often, groups of internally displaced people were found and food parcels were distributed. In addition, the ICRC sought to establish communication between members of separated families.

The ICRC also engaged in active negotiations to achieve the release of Serbs who had been 'abducted', and to provide assistance to Serb communities isolated as a result of the fighting.[14] The problem of so-called abductions was a peculiar one in Kosovo. On occasion, the KLA or other groups would take Serb civilians hostage and there were significant instances of mistreatment and even death. However, in general the KLA captured members of the FRY/Serbian security forces, at times in combat, and at times under other circumstances. In some instance, Serbian policemen were abducted from their homes at night. The KLA considered itself to be in a state of armed conflict and felt entitled to detain those who were engaged in hostilities against it. In other circumstances of internal armed conflict, combatants would be detained by the 'rebel' force. As an underground force is not always in a position to house and care for those

[11] e.g., ICRC Statements, 11 March 1998, 3 June 1998, in Weller, *Crisis in Kosovo*, 252, 253 respectively.
[12] ICRC Update, 10 March 1998, in Weller, *Crisis in Kosovo*, 252.
[13] e.g., Update, 15 June 1998, in Weller, *Crisis in Kosovo*, 254.
[14] Statement, 29 July 1998, in Weller, *Crisis in Kosovo*, 256.

which it considers 'prisoners of war', they may sometimes be placed in the hands of a neutral power for the duration of the conflict. However, the law of internal armed conflict provides little incentive for irregular forces to care for such prisoners, inasmuch as its own members, when apprehended, will generally be tried and convicted on criminal charges by the government against which they have struggled. Thus, the reciprocity of treatment which underpins the laws of war is absent. As such, the ICRC played a crucial role in protecting Serbs who had fallen into this legal limbo and were in significant danger.

Given the scale of the atrocities, mainly and systematically committed by the FRY/Serbia, the ICRC departed from its earlier practice of not publicly commenting on developments, and issued regular reports on its findings. By September 1998, the situation had reached such proportions that the ICRC issued a formal statement on its position on the crisis in Kosovo. It confirmed that from a humanitarian perspective, 'it has become apparent that civilian casualties are not simply what has become known as "collateral damage". In Kosovo, civilians have become the main victims—if not the actual targets—of the fighting.'[15]

The ICRC reports on events are supplemented by the detailed, sometimes daily reports of the United Nations High Commissioner for Human Rights and the High Commissioner for Refugees (UNHCR). The High Commissioner for Human Rights was then an innovation of the United Nations, coordinating the human rights efforts of the organization at UN headquarters and the UN human rights bodies based in Geneva. Given the host of relevant thematic rapporteurs, the Special Rapporteur for Yugoslavia and various other agencies, and the establishment of a human rights field mission, the need for such coordination soon became evident in the Kosovo crisis, especially with the increase in hostilities in 1998.

Humanitarian efforts were coordinated by the UNHCR, which had already exercised the function of 'lead agency' in relation to previous episodes in the Yugoslav crisis. Coordination among humanitarian agencies has traditionally been a weak point in complex humanitarian emergencies. Even within the United Nations system, various agencies (the World Food Programme, UNESCO, UNICEF, the World Health Organization, the Food and Agricultural Organization, and so on) have fought for autonomy and the right of independent action, to the detriment of effectiveness in specific crises. Despite frequent attempts to reorganize the UN humanitarian structures, this problem has not yet been overcome. Hence the need to designate a lead agency for specific conflicts.

Matters were made more complicated by the increasing number of non-governmental organizations (NGOs). While some of these have a large body of professional staff and possess considerable operational experience, others are still only in the process of developing an adequate infrastructure. NGOs also tend to defend their independence with some vigour in relation to intergovernmental agencies. After all, this independence essentially justifies their very existence

---

[15] ICRC Position, 15 September 1998, in Weller, *Crisis in Kosovo*, 258–9.

and makes operations possible which can, for bureaucratic or other reasons, not be undertaken at an 'official' level. In addition, NGOs have in the past not been given to easy cooperation with one another. Competition for donor money, the religious affiliation of some NGOs and other factors have at times led to wasteful competition.

In view of such a complex environment, the role of the UNHCR in helping to organize the overall humanitarian effort was essential. The High Commissioner's staff could also draw upon established contacts with the Belgrade and regional authorities. In addition, the large-scale outpouring of refugees required its particular expertise, honed during the preceding years of conflict in the Balkans. Moreover, over the past decade, the UNHCR has formally embraced a mandate going beyond the provision of assistance to those driven from their country of origin. As such, in-country protection has become an increasingly important focus of its activities. This area of activity was initially controversial, inasmuch as it was seen to endanger the willingness of third states to accept refugees from an area of crisis. If there existed structures for in-country protection, it could be argued that there was no longer a 'well-founded fear of persecution' on the part of the individuals benefiting from these operations. International refugee status, and the corresponding entitlements vis-à-vis third states that are forthcoming from the designation of such status, depends on the demonstration that there exists such a well-founded fear.

However, the situation in the former Yugoslavia and other recent displacement crises demonstrated that this conceptual dichotomy had to be overcome. While in-country operations can contribute to the improvement of an otherwise desperate situation, they do not necessarily remove the threats and dangers entitling an individual to refugee status. The two concepts have to be applied in a complementary way. It was this more advanced approach that characterized the humanitarian operation during the Kosovo crisis.

In exercising its lead function, detailed and coordinated planning could be undertaken based on a consolidated assessment of humanitarian needs, assembled by a variety of organizations. In this way, the mobilization of quite significant quantities of relief supplies was made possible, as it was acquired and distributed by 'best-placed' agencies, according to expertise and capacity. It was also possible to mount consolidated interagency appeals for emergency funds to cover the operations.

The UNHCR also provided consolidated situation reports, obtained from a range of agencies active in the area. In this way, it was able to chronicle the steady rise in the number of refugees and displaced persons. By the end of September 1998, when serious consideration about the NATO threat of the use of force began, there were close to 200,000 internally displaced people, along with 91,000 refugees in neighbouring countries.[16]

---

[16] UNHCR Update, 30 September 1998, in Weller, *Crisis in Kosovo*, 270–1.

International humanitarian agencies were subject to very harsh criticism when they appeared unprepared for the massive influx of refugees from Kosovo into neighbouring territories from March 1999 onwards. However, at this earlier stage, the organizations performed quite well, indeed heroically at times, in circumstances of considerable danger. Moreover, the coordination arrangements pioneered during 1998 greatly assisted the humanitarian aid community when it tried to address the even greater crisis that was to follow. However, the need in 1999 to rely on the military resources of some states, including NATO, led to considerable soul-searching by a number of humanitarian organizations.

III. UN and EC Sanctions

Given the legal, moral and political uncertainties of military action, sanctions remain the international tool of choice when seeking to compel a government to adhere to key principles of the international constitution. In the absence of realistic alternatives, the fact that it is usually the population of an offending state and not the government itself that suffers the consequences of sanctions is still accepted as a necessary evil, although a few sanctions mechanisms, such as travel restrictions, have recently been directed specifically at public officials. While provision was made for the use of sanctions from the inception of the UN Charter, they have rarely been employed at the universal level since 1945. In view of the automatic deadlock in the Security Council, states—or rather blocks of states or alliances—used sanctions and trade restrictions outside of the UN framework quite extensively during the Cold War years. Obviously, it was principally the powerful industrialized states that employed this technique of economic confrontation, although Western enthusiasm for this weapon waned temporarily when the Arab nations adopted an oil embargo in the 1970s against states cooperating with Israel. In principle, of course, a state is free to determine its own economic and trading relations with other states. However, the universal framework of international economic law, now principally focused on the World Trade Organization (WTO)/General Agreement on Tariffs and Trade (GATT), restricts this freedom. In addition, most states will have in place bilateral and other international arrangements with specific states, committing them to certain modes of conduct in their mutual economic relations. The adoption of sanctions obviously interferes with these legal obligations. However, if covered by a Chapter VII Security Council decision, the states concerned are absolved from responsibility for what would otherwise be an unlawful breach of existing economic relations.

Up to 1990, United Nations sanctions adopted under Chapter VII remained few and far between. Only with respect to the outcasts, Southern Rhodesia and South Africa, could the Cold War veto be overcome and limited but binding sanctions imposed. However, since 1990, United Nations sanctions have pro-liferated, beginning with Resolution 661 (1990), which imposed very com-prehensive sanctions against Iraq and occupied Kuwait. In relation to the former Yugoslavia, the Council initially adopted only an arms embargo in Resolution 713 (1991), somewhat oddly, with the express consent of the target state. However, when conflict broke out in Bosnia and Herzegovina, the rump Yugoslavia and its client in Bosnia and Herzegovina were subjected to a Security Council sanctions regime which was, in some ways, even more comprehensive than the Iraq/Kuwait sanctions. Given the initial reluctance to intervene mili-tarily in the Bosnian crisis, the prospect of lifting sanctions remained one of the few tools at the disposal of the international community for influencing decision-makers in Belgrade. A somewhat symbolic suspension of sanctions occurred in October 1994, when Belgrade ceased its armed support for the Bosnian Serbs.[17] The remaining sanctions were suspended[18] and finally terminated[19] when the rump Yugoslavia signed and implemented the Dayton accords on Bosnia. This action was controversial, inasmuch as the suspension and termination included the arms embargo, despite the fact that Yugoslavia/Serbia remained engaged in an increasingly violent campaign of repression in Kosovo. By March 1998 this position was no longer tenable. In response to the outbreak of widespread fighting, the Security Council prohibited in Resolution 1160 (1998) the sale or supply of arms and related equipment to the Federal Republic of Yugoslavia, including Kosovo.

In accordance with standard practice, a 'sanctions committee' composed of members of the Council and chaired by Celso L.N. Amorim of Brazil was set up to monitor compliance. That committee received reports from governments indi-cating the measures they had taken to implement the sanctions in their domes-tic law. In addition, the UN Secretary-General and the committee drew upon the European institutions to help report on the importation of arms and other proscribed items into the FRY, including Kosovo. The EC, through its monitor-ing mission in the former Yugoslavia (ECMM), the Western European Union (WEU), which had a small presence in Albania, NATO, which was also present in Albania and in Bosnia and Herzegovina, the UN Preventative Deployment Force in Macedonia (UNPREDEP), and the Danube Commission all pledged to offer assistance, although none was in a position to offer a comprehensive mon-itoring mission.[20] Nonetheless, steps were taken to coordinate the monitoring efforts of these various agencies.

---

[17] Resolution 943 (1994), adopted 23 September 1994, effective 5 October 1994, S/RES/943 (1994).

[18] Resolution 1021 (1995), 22 November 1995, S/RES/1021 (1995).

[19] Resolution 1074 (1996), 1 October 1996, S/RES 1074 (1996).

[20] See the documents annexed to the UNSG Reports of 4 June 1998, 2 July 1998, in Weller, *Crisis in Kosovo*, 198–202, 202–5. It should be noted here that UNPREDEP was discontinued in 1999, right before the Kosovo war, following Chinese veto.

Despite media reports indicating otherwise, the international monitoring presence was unable to detect violations of the embargo by Yugoslavia. It did, however, receive consistent allegations of a flow of arms and other items across the Albanian border into Kosovo. It was informed by the governments of Germany, Switzerland and Sweden that attempts were being made to investigate ethnic Albanian fundraising activities in these states, although there was no conclusive evidence to suggest that such activities related to the acquisition of arms for the KLA.[21] As indicated in the previous chapter, it was precisely the fact that the Rugova government refused to fund the KLA which led to considerable tension between the two bodies. However, as the conflict progressed, the KLA reportedly established its own fundraising structure in Europe and the United States.

Faced with the threat of a Russian veto, the Security Council failed to respond to Yugoslavia's non-compliance with Resolution 1160 (1998) and its increase in military operations with a tightening of sanctions. Some further action was taken at the European level, although in a strangely haphazard and half-hearted way, given the emerging dimensions of the humanitarian crisis. The EC had in fact kept in place its own arms embargo, even after Dayton, to ensure the safety of the international peacekeeping mission in Bosnia and parts of Croatia.[22] Of course, this did not prevent the FRY from replenishing its stocks, especially from Eastern Europe and from Russia in particular. When the Security Council re-imposed the arms embargo at the universal level, the EC/EU expanded the scope of the sanctions. In addition to arms, non-lethal police equipment was included. There was a moratorium on government-financed export credit support for trade and investment, including financing for privatization in Serbia, and a list of senior Serbian officials who would be prevented from entering the territories of member states.[23] A freezing of Yugoslav/Serbian state funds and of investment in Serbia was added, when there was no compliance with the demands of the UN Security Council and the Union,[24] and there was a ban on flights by Yugoslav carriers to and from territories of members of the EC.[25] That ban was not implemented by all EU member states with similar enthusiasm. The United Kingdom, controversially, found reason not to comply immediately.

IV. Conclusion

The UN system and other international actors had no difficulty in chronicling the developing humanitarian crisis triggered by the increasingly assertive Serbian

---

[21] Report of the Chairman of the Committee established pursuant to Resolution 1160 (1998), 26 February 199, in Weller, *Crisis in Kosovo*, 227–8.

[22] Common Position, 26 February 1996 [the relevant regulations are also reproduced in this chapter], in Weller, *Crisis in Kosovo*, 222.

[23] Common Position, 19 March 1998, in Weller, *Crisis in Kosovo*, 222–3.

[24] Common Positions, 7 May 1998, 8 June 1998, in Weller, *Crisis in Kosovo*, 225.

[25] Common Position, 29 June 1998, in Weller, *Crisis in Kosovo*, 226.

military campaign in Kosovo. The consequences of this campaign were being made altogether too obvious, given the outflow of very significant numbers of refugees into neighbouring states. Despite problems created, at times, by a host country (in particular Macedonia), monitoring of refugee movements and provisioning for basic needs could be accommodated, although the great numbers significantly strained resources and led to severe living conditions for many. Addressing the plight of the internally displaced became more difficult as time progressed, if not impossible. While the movements of the displaced could be remotely monitored, access to them was increasingly limited. KDOM and the few other institutions with a physical presence in the areas of conflict lacked a mandate and facilities to conduct humanitarian tasks. The inability to provide for the displaced, especially during the circumstances of the harsh Balkan winter, contributed to pressure for action, initially through sanctions and subsequently through military means. However, it proved difficult to establish an effective sanctions regime going beyond an arms embargo. At the UN level, decisive measures were foreclosed by the positions of Russia, a supporter of the Belgrade government, and China, a traditional opponent to 'intervention' in the domestic affairs of states. However, even the EU was unable to muster the political coherence of will to implement an effective sanctions regime outside of the universal context of the UN Security Council. This failing may have contributed to the need, rather sooner than later, to move to military measures in order to address the increasingly desperate humanitarian situation.

6

The Outbreak of Violence and the Hill Negotiations

Despite the identification of grave, widespread and persistent abuses of the fundamental human rights of the Kosovo population by international agencies, international action in relation to the crisis had diminished during the 1990s. The Rugova government had judged it appropriate to restrain its actions to mainly passive resistance. During the period of 1991 to 1995 it was feared that Belgrade might use any provocation as an excuse to launch a massive military campaign in the territory, resulting in slaughter and displacement of the kind exhibited in Bosnia and Herzegovina. The Kosovo leadership hoped that this moderation would also be rewarded by the organized international community. In fact, it believed it had received assurances that the 'Yugoslav crisis' would not be considered settled until the Kosovo issue had also been addressed.

This government was therefore disappointed when the Dayton agreement on Bosnia and Herzegovina was concluded. During the settlement process, Slobodan Milosevic had been allowed to represent the Bosnian Serbs. His signature on the agreement rendered him guarantor of an arrangement that would, finally, bring to a close the carnage in Bosnia. Indeed, he would need to use his authority to ensure that the Bosnian Serbs accepted the agreement and complied with it. His status was thus transformed from that of principal author of war and violence to that of peacemaker.

Milosevic had made it clear that any mention of Kosovo at Dayton would destroy any chance of a settlement. Hence, the eventual agreement addressed only Bosnia, which was regarded internationally as the key element in the conclusion of the entire Yugoslav episode. Sanctions against Belgrade were rapidly lifted. In order to console Prishtina, a so-called 'outer wall of sanctions' was left in place, which related to access to certain international economic institutions. However, this action had little effect on Belgrade and in no way constrained its actions in Kosovo. On the other hand, the conclusion of the Dayton agreement had dramatic effects in the territory.

I. The Move Towards Military Confrontation

The conclusion of the Dayton agreement without reference to Kosovo fundamentally undermined the credibility of the Rugova government. Manifestly, peaceful resistance had failed. Instead of being rewarded for having acted 'responsibly', the Kosovars had been ignored. In this climate of dismay, those who had been arguing for a military solution became increasingly influential. For some time, exiled Kosovars in Switzerland and the US, Albanian elements in Macedonia, parts of the Albanian secret service and opponents in Kosovo of Rugova's LDK party had prepared for the possibility of an armed struggle. Initial armed operations commenced in 1996. Some of these extended to attacks against Serbian police and paramilitary installations. Others would target ethnic Albanian 'collaborators' who were in contact with the Serbian administration. In other instances still, Serb civilian targets such as bars or cafes frequented by ethnic Serbs were bombed. This profile of operations led to condemnation of the KLA, which claimed responsibility for the action, as a terrorist organization by the US and other governments. The UN Security Council also condemned terrorist tactics.

Changes were also afoot within the KLA. It had initially been dominated by a narrow cadre, reputed to maintain links with a Stalinist wing of security service officials who had survived the political changes in Albania. As the KLA grew, however, more leaders rose to prominence in their own native regions. Like most of their troops, they had resorted to arms by force of circumstance, motivated by the desire to defend their homes. Their attitude was less ideological and more pragmatic. In view of the military reverses suffered in the field, they were not always persuaded of the effectiveness of the top military and political leadership of the organization. To complicate matters further still, and contrary to media reports at the time, not all of the funds collected from the ethnic Albanian diaspora abroad were being made available to finance the armed campaign of the KLA. The elected government, in particular, had access to considerable sums and was unwilling to transfer them to the control of an organization which it regarded with some circumspection, for the national emergency in Kosovo had led the KLA to claim not only military but also political leadership in Kosovo.

As a result of the increase in repression that followed, the ranks of the KLA swelled rapidly in number. At night, the KLA managed to establish checkpoints on public roads. It could even declare that it was holding territory to the exclusion of Serbian forces—the so-called 'liberated' areas. Serbia responded to their provocations by increasing its troop presence. It pursued a strategy of attempting to isolate the KLA from its rearward bases on the other side of the Albanian border. As was noted in the previous chapter, it also launched attacks against ethnic Albanian villages thought to be associated with, or under the control of, the KLA. These attacks seemed to resemble ethnic cleansing tactics that had been used by Serbian militias in Bosnia. Villages would be surrounded and shelled, then men of military age would be captured, publicly beaten and removed. Others would be made to leave, as houses were torched.

This pattern of practice was intended to remove any support infrastructure for the KLA from the Kosovo countryside. However, it caused disproportionate suffering and displacement of the civilian population. In addition to internal displacement, significant numbers of refugees began spilling over into neighbouring Albania and Macedonia.

II. Attempts to Isolate the Conflict

Persistent demands for the reintroduction of the CSCE Mission of Long Duration had been ignored since 1993. Instead, an international presence had been building up in Macedonia and Albania. Both countries required international assistance in order to retain or restore domestic stability.

In Macedonia, interethnic relations were often described, along with Kosovo, as a 'powder keg'. If conflict were to erupt in that former Yugoslav state, boasting an ethnic Albanian minority of between 20 and 30 per cent, the entire region would be affected; some analysts were even predicting that the conflict could spread as far as Greece and Turkey. It was feared that continued strife in Kosovo, which shares a border with Macedonia, might spark such an explosion. Although ethnic Albanian leaders in Macedonia were then still pursuing a cautious and moderate policy, there had been some indication that the KLA was obtaining support from ethnic Albanians in that state, most of whom lived in territories contiguous with the Kosovo border. Police raids had uncovered a number of arms dumps and other facilities.

To address concerns about the instability of Macedonia, a small but quietly effective UN peacekeeping force had been deployed to the territory early on in the conflict (UNPROFOR, later UNPREDEP), sparked by the dissolution of Yugoslavia. The OSCE had also established a 'spillover mission', hoping to reduce the risk of the conflict spreading. Relations with those missions were somewhat delicate. On the one hand, their presence was vital to prevent the outbreak of civil strife. However, the missions also added an international dimension to what the Macedonian majority regarded as an internal minority problem, and were seen to embolden demands by ethnic Albanian citizens for equal participation in the political system.[1]

In Albania, the post-communist transition led to the eruption of violence in 1997—which was countered by the deployment of an Italian-led peacekeeping mission (with some enforcement powers) to help restore civil society and governance. That mission was accompanied by OSCE, WEU and even NATO activities

[1] Macedonia officially disputed that there were up to 30 per cent ethnic Albanians on its territory.

designed to rebuild Albania's civil and military institutions. However, just at the point when the mission was about to declare itself a success and start winding down, renewed unrest in the autumn of 1998 seemed to spread across the country and the possibility of further civil strife could not be excluded.

At the same time, Albania came under considerable pressure to curb arms smuggling to Kosovo and to close KLA training and supply bases on its territory. While Albania was in no position to give significant military or financial assistance to the KLA, rumours persisted that it was engaged, somewhat unintentionally, in a two-track approach to the mounting violence in Kosovo. At the official government level, it stoutly defended the rights of the Kosovo Albanians. Indeed, Albania had taken the step of recognizing Kosovo as an independent state upon its declaration of independence. While no other state had followed this example, Albania acted as a conduit for Kosovo into the international diplomatic arena.

However, it was also rumoured that, in addition to the government's position, there existed another tier of cooperation not necessarily controlled by it. The structures of the Albanian intelligence service had been left largely in place after the transition from the previous Stalinist regime in Albania. Some of these elements, it was alleged, were encouraging and supporting a hard-line attitude within a small number of KLA cells that had risen to prominence and positions of control within that organization, and which saw no room for compromise and a peaceful resolution of the Kosovo issue. Instead, a pan-Albanian agenda was pursued by some members of these movements within a rigid ideological framework.

The chaos that followed the collapse of the pyramid investment scheme of 1997 made such activities easier. In particular, the vast arsenals of small arms left over from the Hoxa regime were plundered by angry mobs. Albania was awash with some 700,000 unregistered Kalashnikov rifles, rocket-propelled grenades, mortars and other gear. In this kind of environment, it was not difficult to equip the KLA.

Given the somewhat ambivalent nature of its position, the Albanian government permitted international action designed to restore its own domestic stability. Moreover, it was interested in enough of an international presence to deter Yugoslav raids against KLA facilities on its territory. Hence the number of OSCE personnel and the degree of cooperation with NATO were strengthened significantly, culminating in joint military exercises in August 1998.

Albania, however, remained hostile to the idea of introducing an international force to monitor its border region with Kosovo. This might have disrupted the proclaimed 'unity of fate' between Albania and Kosovo. This strategy was designed to forestall application of the policy of containment, which had previously been applied to the Bosnian conflict by the outside world. That strategy held that strife and ethnic cleansing in Bosnia and Herzegovina could not be influenced from the outside, at least not without significant human cost. Instead, an ineffective UN presence was maintained which relied on the cooperation of the parties. Effective international measures concentrated on isolating the rest of the region from the events in Bosnia, however shocking they may have been. It was only when this strategy of containment finally collapsed, in the wake of the Srebrenica massacre of 1995, and with the determination by Islamic states that they would no longer comply with the arms embargo against Bosnia, that decisive international intervention was mounted which terminated the fighting immediately.

This experience taught the Albanian government (and others) that human suffering alone was not sufficient to generate the international involvement necessary to advance the cause of the Kosovo Albanians, or even to save them from a Bosnia-style campaign of ethnic cleansing and possible genocide. Instead, the prospect of a widening of the conflict had to be maintained—a difficult balancing act, given Albania's own political instability and military and economic impotence. An altogether too intrusive international presence along the border with Kosovo would have limited the necessary freedom of action in this respect and would have fostered the international view that it might be possible, after all, to manage the developing Kosovo crisis through containment alone.

In addition to strengthening its limited monitoring presence in Albania and Macedonia, the OSCE revived its calls for permission to deploy in Kosovo when hostilities erupted in earnest in February and March 1998.[2] Through its Troika of Foreign Ministers (previous, present, and upcoming Chairman-in-Office), it requested cooperation with its own organs and with the EU/OSCE Special Representative Filipe Gonzalez. The FRY reiterated its position that the Mission of Long Duration could not return until the modalities for the resumption of full participation in the OSCE organs had been agreed.[3] Instead, the United Nations Security Council, following upon a suggestion from the UN Secretary-General[4] and an invitation from Skopje, increased the strength of UNPREDEP in Macedonia to 1,050 and extended its mandate to 28 February 1999, 'to continue by its presence to deter threats and prevent clashes, to monitor the border area'.[5]

III. Demands for Negotiation and the Kosovo Diplomatic Observer Mission

Even after Dayton, the European Union kept in place its small civilian observer mission in the former Yugoslavia. This group had become the symbol of European inaction or ineffectiveness, its members clad in pure white attire, passively (and, to the outside world, silently) observing the ethnic cleansing and probable genocide in Croatia and in Bosnia and Herzegovina. The EC/EU also appointed Filipe

---

[2] OSCE Permanent Council Decision No. 218, 11 March 1998, in Weller, *Crisis in Kosovo*, 292.
[3] UN Secretary-General's Report, 4 June 1998, in Weller, *Crisis in Kosovo*, 198–202.
[4] UN Secretary-General's Report, 14 July 1998, in Weller, *Crisis in Kosovo*, 205–6.
[5] UNSC Resolution 1186 (1998), 21 July 1998, S/RES/1186 (1998).

Gonzalez as its Special Representative in this matter.[6] It repeatedly called upon both parties to the conflict to exercise restraint, and to engage in meaningful dialogue about a political settlement. In that context, it continued to emphasize the need to retain the territorial integrity of the FRY.

Key states of the EU were also represented in the Contact Group. That Group, composed of the US, the UK, France, Italy, Germany and Russia, had initially been established in Spring 1994 to help address the Bosnian issue.[7] It began to take a more pronounced interest in Kosovo in September 1997, when the first portents of wider hostilities began to emerge. The Contact Group combined three elements of persuasion: Russia was perceived as a state which could 'deliver Milosevic', due to its general support for the position of the FRY/Serbia; the EU members would be able to dangle in front of Belgrade the carrot of closer economic integration with Europe, and financial incentives; and the US would come to represent the driving force behind tougher action, including the possibility of military force. All three combined could virtually guarantee that the Security Council would back their joint demands, inasmuch as four out of the five permanent members were represented in the Contact Group.

In its statement of 24 September 1997, the Group declared:

Regarding the dispute over Kosovo's status, the position of the Contact Group countries is clear: We do not support independence and we do not support maintenance of the status quo. We support an enhanced status for Kosovo within the FRY. Such a status should fully protect the rights of the Albanian population in accordance with OSCE standards and the UN Charter. As a first step to reduce tension, it is essential that dialogue begins.[8]

In January 1998, before the news of massacres of ethnic Albanian villagers at the hands of Serbian paramilitary forces first seeped out, the Group condemned both violent repression and terrorist action and urged dialogue once again. By March, it also condemned the excessive use of force by Serbian police against civilians. Oddly, and in deference to Russia, it termed the military attacks on ethnic Albanian villages and their destruction 'large scale police actions'.[9] On the other hand, the Contact Group had little difficulty in identifying the armed opposition in Kosovo as terrorists.

The statement was also significant, as it formally recorded a split in the group between Russia and its other members. Russia was unwilling to endorse a call for the denial of visas for senior FRY and Serbian representatives responsible for repressive action by FRY security forces in Kosovo. It also broke the consensus

---

[6] Council Conclusion on Kosovo, 31 March 1998, in Weller, *Crisis in Kosovo*, 229; Joint Action, 8 June 1998, in Weller, *Crisis in Kosovo*, 229–30.

[7] See, e.g., Christoph Schwegman, *The Contact Group and its Impact on the European Institutional Structure.* EU-ISS Occasional Paper 16, June 2000.

[8] Statement, 24 September 1997, in Weller, *Crisis in Kosovo*, 234.

[9] Statement, 9 March 1999, in Weller, *Crisis in Kosovo*, 235–6.

on a moratorium for government finance export credit support for Yugoslavia. However, Russia indicated that it might review its position if Belgrade failed to comply with the demands of the Group. These included cessation of action by its special police units, their withdrawal, the granting of humanitarian access and the beginning of dialogue with the ethnic Albanians.

It was at this time that the UN Security Council also became active. In principle, the United Nations is not authorized by its Charter to 'intervene in matters which are essentially within the domestic jurisdiction of any State or shall require the Members to submit such matters to settlement under the present Charter'.[10] Of course, over time the organization has come to involve itself deeply in 'internal' matters, such as colonialist administration, apartheid, or more generally and more recently, in situations of humanitarian emergency and in the systematic violation of human rights. However, as discussed in Chapter 1, states have been reluctant to involve the organization in self-determination disputes outside of the colonial context.[11] India, for example, has struggled desperately to ensure that the Kashmir problem is not addressed directly by the Security Council.[12] Other states have similar interests.[13] Until the unmistakeable dissolution of the Socialist Federal Republic of Yugoslavia, there were objections to Council involvement in what some states still considered an 'internal matter' for Belgrade. This is precisely why the initial arms embargo against Yugoslavia of September 1991 required the positive consent of the SFRY government—without it, China might have vetoed the resolution.[14]

The exclusion of UN Security Council action in relation to matters falling within the domestic jurisdiction of states is, however, subject to one exception: it does not apply where a situation constitutes a 'threat to the peace, breach of the peace, or act of aggression'. Since 1990, the concept of 'threat to the peace' has undergone significant change. Initially, the Council had to resort to cunning tricks to enable itself to take action in relation to essentially internal matters. It had to claim that internal situations, such as grave humanitarian emergencies, had external ramifications amounting to an international threat to the peace—say, by virtue of refugees destabilizing the region of crisis, or in view of the danger of the spreading of a conflict beyond national borders—in order to be able to act under Chapter VII.[15] This charade, performed mainly for the benefit of China, was at

---

[10] UN Charter, Art. 2(7).

[11] Palestine, Katanga, Eastern Timor, Western Sahara, etc., can be classed in this category.

[12] Oddly, India actually brought the Kashmir issue before the Council when it first arose, in a decision subsequently regretted.

[13] One might think of Sri Lanka, China, states with areas predominantly inhabited by ethnic Kurds, etc.

[14] See the very express reference in the preambular paragraph of Security Council Resolution 713 (1991) of 25 September 1991, to this request.

[15] Early examples include resolutions on the crisis in Liberia and Resolution 688 (1991) on Iraq, although the latter resolution could in the end not be adopted under Chapter VII, because of China's attitude. UNSC Resolution 688 (1991), 5 April 1991, S/RES/688 (1991).

least provisionally abandoned in December 1992, when the Council identified the 'magnitude of the humanitarian tragedy caused by the conflict in Somalia' as a 'threat to international peace and security'.[16] That is to say, humanitarian suffering within a state could, itself, amount to a threat to the peace, permitting the application of the collective security provisions contained in Chapter VII of the Charter.[17]

Despite the humanitarian dimension of the Kosovo conflict, documented by objective international agencies since its very beginning, it was nevertheless perceived by some members of the Council as a self-determination dispute—an 'internal' matter best left to cautious diplomacy and the activities of humanitarian and human rights bodies. Significant action was delayed until humanitarian suffering became altogether too evident to ignore and until the problem had actually gained an international dimension by posing a very active threat to the stability of the region. The opportunity of adopting decisive measures which could have arrested the conflict at a far earlier stage had therefore been lost. That said, when the Council finally did act, after the outbreak of hostilities in the territory and the beginning of the first displacement crisis in March 1998, it did so quite decisively.

Resolution 1160 (1998) of 31 March 1998 was expressly adopted under Chapter VII, although it did not identify the source of a threat to the peace which necessitated such action. In its preamble, the resolution expressly affirmed the commitment of all member states of the UN to the 'sovereignty and territorial integrity of the Federal Republic of Yugoslavia'.

Endorsing the previous initiatives of the Contact Group, the UN Security Council called upon 'the Federal Republic of Yugoslavia immediately to take the necessary steps to achieve a political solution to the issue of Kosovo through dialogue and to implement the actions indicated in the Contact Group statements of 9 and 25 March 1998'.[18] In this context, it expressed support for an 'enhanced status for Kosovo which would include a substantially greater degree of autonomy and meaningful self-administration'. While the language ('calls upon') may not have been directly mandatory, the binding nature of this requirement was clarified in subsequent provisions. In operative paragraph 8, the resolution imposed an arms embargo upon the FRY, including Kosovo. The decision as to whether or not the embargo would be lifted would depend on the following substantive requirements:

• Substantive dialogue with a view to a settlement by the parties, with international involvement;

---

[16] Security Council Resolution 794 (1992), 3 December 1992, S/RES/794 (1992).

[17] Similarly, the gradual promotion of 'humanitarian need' in Bosnia and Herzegovina as an issue which, in itself, permitted Chapter VII action, and Article 39 finding in relation to authorization of the French-led operation in Rwanda.

[18] Resolution 1160 (1998), 31 March 1998, S/RES/1160 (1998), para. 1.

- Withdrawal of special police units and cessation of their actions affecting civilians;
- Humanitarian and human rights monitoring access and the introduction of a new OSCE presence.

With this encouragement on the part of the Council, the attempt to launch an internationally sponsored negotiating process was given a significant boost. Belgrade, however, was prepared for the adoption of the Council resolution. It adopted a two-track strategy. Immediately after the adoption of the resolution, Belgrade answered the request by holding a referendum of its population. On 23 April over 90 per cent of the participating Serbian population proclaimed through the poll that the Kosovo issue was an internal matter that could not be subjected to international action.

This blocking of international initiatives was complemented by an attempt to demonstrate that negotiations could be conducted without international involvement. Previously, as a result of the work of the Geneva Special Group and the efforts of the St Egidio community, a fragmentary agreement had been reached between Kosovo and Belgrade. The 1996 Agreement envisaged the resumption of work by educational institutions in Kosovo.[19] However, this very short text was left unimplemented. In 1997/8, students had started to protest in Prishtina, demanding the reopening of the university by the Serbian authorities as much as by the Rugova government. Belgrade used the fact that Rugova was under pressure on this issue to invite the Kosovo authorities to Belgrade for talks on education issues. This move was represented as the opening of the very negotiations that had been demanded by the Contact Group and the Security Council.

Initially, the Kosovars were reluctant to participate. Rugova, who had just been re-elected President, noted that there was little room to discuss education when the entire territory was being subjected to military operations, in addition to repression. However, he was under heavy pressure from the US and others to attend the talks. His presence in Belgrade and his handshake with Milosevic were much exploited by the Serbian media.[20] Expecting an ongoing dialogue, Kosovo established a team of fifteen advisers and a smaller group of negotiators. However, the talks came to nothing, and the Kosovo leadership withdrew when it became clear that FRY/Serbian offensive military operations would not be discontinued.

In June 1998, the EU condemned the 'wide-spread house-burning and indiscriminate artillery attacks of whole villages [indicating] a new level of aggression on the part of the Serbian security forces'. It expressly identified these practices as the beginning of a new phase of ethnic cleansing.[21] The EU also threatened the imposition of tough measures against the FRY/Serbia but, as noted above, its sanctions were actually quite limited. There was, however, the veiled threat of

---

[19] See above, p. 50.
[20] FRY Statement on Talks, 15 April 1998, in Weller, *Crisis in Kosovo*, 353.
[21] Declaration on Kosovo, 11 June 1998, Weller, *Crisis in Kosovo*, 230.

the use of force, although at that stage it seemed to the Union that such measures would require a Chapter VII mandate.[22] The demands of the Cardiff European Council, which included cessation of operations by security forces affecting civilian populations, as well as the withdrawal of such forces, were later reproduced almost verbatim in Security Council Resolution 1199 (1998). This was balanced by a condemnation of 'violent attacks and acts of terrorism' and a declaration that 'the European Union remains firmly opposed to independence'.

Through the operation of the Contact Group, Russia was aware that the US and the EU states were moving towards more decisive sanctions and, possibly, to action by NATO. To forestall such action, on 16 June 1998 Russia arranged a top-level meeting between President Boris Yeltsin and Slobodan Milosevic. At the meeting, Yugoslavia solemnly committed itself to the implementation of demands made by the Security Council in Resolution 1160 (1998). However, since 1991 the Milosevic government had consistently given assurances in relation to its armed activities which were, in general, not kept. Hence, particular attention was paid to the issue of monitoring implementation of the Yugoslav undertakings.

The Security Council had also demanded the reinstatement of the OSCE Mission of Long Duration to monitor compliance. On that crucial point, the statement merely reiterated the well-known FRY position, which effectively precluded a permanent OSCE presence by linking even the 'beginning' of talks on this issue to the reinstatement of the FRY to full OSCE membership privileges:

To announce the willingness of the Federal Republic of Yugoslavia to begin negotiations with the Organization for Security and Cooperation in Europe (OSCE) on receiving the mission sent by that organization to Kosovo and on the reinstatement of the Federal Republic of Yugoslavia as a member of OSCE.[23]

Given this dilemma, a number of states seized upon a further paragraph in the joint statement. That paragraph referred to the presence of foreign diplomatic representatives in Yugoslavia:

Full freedom of movement on the whole territory of Kosovo will be assured so as to reinforce confidence building measures. There will be no restriction on diplomatic representatives of foreign governments and international organizations accredited in the FRY in order to allow them to acquaint themselves with the situation.[24]

While their number was limited to those 'accredited' to Yugoslavia, this nevertheless gave impetus to the use of resident diplomatic staff in lieu of the OSCE. In contrast to EU monitors whose findings have always been confidential, and

---

[22] '…to consider all options, including those which would require an authorization by the UNSC under Chapter VII'. *Ibid.*

[23] Joint Statement by Boris Yeltsin and Slobodan Milosevic, Moscow, 16 June 1998, in Weller, *Crisis in Kosovo*, 292.

[24] Reproduced in Wolfgang Petritsch, Karl Kaser, and Robert Pichler, *Kosovo, Kosova* (Klagenfurt: Wieser Velag, 1999), 223.

whose public role has been seen as marginal, some of these observers issued regular and public reports on events in Kosovo—especially in the case of the US, which made its reports available on the Internet. In fact, the US element was very substantial in what was to become the Kosovo Diplomatic Observer Mission. At a later stage, the US KDOM was also accorded a special, and less public, role in verifying the Holbrooke agreement.

The KDOM mission developed into something of a cat-and-mouse game. Through intelligence and other sources, KDOM staff would be made aware of ongoing or imminent areas of fighting, including significant atrocities against civilians. KDOM did not operate at night. Hence, it would race towards the nominated areas, attempting to arrive there before damaging evidence could be removed. In some instances, KDOM vehicles were subject to mine or shooting attacks.[25] Such attacks revealed that Serbian intelligence was generally well aware of the probable location of KDOM.

KDOM managed to slightly increase transparency in relation to events within Kosovo. However, by early summer of 1998, the situation had deteriorated to such an extent that its consequences were readily visible to the outside world.

The rise of the KLA during this period was somewhat ironic. Since the spring, Serbian forces had launched a significant offensive, displacing the KLA from several of the areas it had previously claimed to control. It was rumoured that this action had not been internationally opposed, so as to remove the KLA from a dominant role in the upcoming negotiations. However, as a result of this campaign, by early summer Serbian/FRY operations were concentrated in the south-western part of Kosovo, adjacent to the Albanian border, causing the first significant exodus of ethnic Albanians across that border. There were also the first reports of border incidents involving Albania directly.

Although the UN Secretary-General could not find evidence of arms trafficking across the border, the FRY government justified this policy with the need to interdict support to the KLA.[26] The KLA, which had managed to establish control over certain rural regions, was increasingly pushed back in the weeks that followed. It was also internationally isolated, labelled by some governments as a terrorist organization. Its position was not strengthened by reports of KLA elements involved in terrorizing isolated Serb communities in the areas still under KLA control.

These apparent reverses led to a sense on the part of the KLA and Kosovo Albanians that the international community was content to have Belgrade 'teach the KLA a lesson' as it were. Such a strategy, it was thought, would ensure that the KLA was not in a position to obstruct the autonomy deal envisaged by the

---

[25] One such attack occurred on 15 September 1998, against a Canadian KDOM vehicle and its passengers, who were pinned down for several hours by sniper attack after having struck an anti-tank mine until relief arrived.

[26] UNSG Report, 4 June 1998, S/1998/470.

international community.[27] However, this plan, if it existed, failed to consider the nature of the Yugoslav/Serbian military campaign and its consequences. In accordance with the tactics of an underground army which has neither the manpower nor the equipment to meet opposing forces directly, the KLA tended to melt away from villages that came under attack. The principal victims of FRY/Serbian operations remained behind and had to flee, often under very dramatic circumstances, or risk death. With the advance of Serbian/Yugoslav forces, the number of displaced persons increased dramatically, reaching 100,000 by the end of July, and rapidly rising thereafter.[28]

However, while the KLA was suffering these reverses, its public standing had increased rather than decreased. Moreover, the KLA, now organized according to a regionally based system of command that had deep roots among the affected populations, was able to rapidly reoccupy its former positions once the Serbian forces left. Hence, its overall position was not weakened as much as Western intelligence organizations had claimed. Instead, the KLA and the parties supporting it now openly challenged the legitimacy of the Rugova government, arguing that it had never really existed.

IV. The Hill Negotiations

By early summer, the Contact Group called for an enhanced effort to begin negotiations between the parties. The attempt was to be spearheaded by US Ambassador to Macedonia Christopher Hill, who had played a role in the Dayton accords.[29] At its Bonn meeting of 8 July 1998, the Contact Group agreed to recommend to its negotiating team basic elements for a resolution of the question of Kosovo's status, emphasizing again that it supported neither the maintenance of the status quo nor independence for Kosovo. The Group indicated that it had 'set in hand work to define possible further elements for the future status of Kosovo, which would be made available to the authorities in Belgrade and the leadership of the Kosovo Albanian community for a dialogue with international involvement'.[30]

The Contact Group required both sides to cease violence and to commit themselves instead to dialogue and a peaceful settlement. In this context, it also put pressure on the armed opposition in Kosovo, insisting that external support for the KLA had to be terminated.

The Contact Group statement had already indicated that action in the Security Council might follow, if its demands were not met by one or the other party. Moreover, NATO now formally entered the picture. The US government, in

[27] Richard Caplan, 'International Diplomacy and the Crisis in Kosovo', *International Affairs*, 74 (1998), 745–61, 753.
[28] UNSG Report, 5 August 1998, S/1998/712.
[29] See EU Council General Affairs Meeting, 13 July 1998, in Weller, *Crisis in Kosovo*, 231.
[30] Statement issued by the Contact Group, 8 July 1998, in Weller, *Crisis in Kosovo*, 238, para 9.

particular, had started to press for possible military action to end repression in Kosovo. On 12 August, NATO Secretary-General Javier Solana had indicated that the Alliance, in its efforts to support the international community in encouraging a negotiated settlement had:

…today reviewed military planning for a full range of options to bring an end to violence and to create the conditions for negotiations. These include the use of ground and air power and in particular a full range of options for the use of air power alone. They ensure that NATO can act swiftly and effectively should the need arise.[31]

Under pressure from the KLA, the Kosovo government had found it difficult to commit itself to negotiations. However, given the possibility of NATO involvement, it was clear that Kosovo could not be the side that frustrated negotiations. After all, Kosovo had hoped for a long time for international involvement in the crisis. The US intimated to the Kosovo leadership that, if it frustrated this settlement attempt, it might find itself the target, rather than the beneficiary, of such action. Accordingly, the very next day, the NATO Secretary-General could 'welcome the news that the Kosovo Albanians have now formed a new negotiating team. This is a tribute to the skilful leadership of Ibrahim Rugova.'[32]

In fact, Kosovo had merely appointed an informal delegation, led by the soft-spoken and gentlemanly Fehmi Agani who had already participated in the work of the Special Group on Kosovo,[33] and composed of a further six delegates representing mainly the LDK and associated parties. KLA representation was opposed by Belgrade, which declared itself unwilling to negotiate with 'terrorists'. The KLA appointed Adem Demaci as its speaker. He was a figure of considerable authority, having already suffered imprisonment for his stance on Kosovo under the Tito government.

The UN Security Council also issued a Presidential Statement endorsing the action of the Contact Group, and indirectly of NATO. It also praised the fact that Kosovo had appointed a negotiating team and called for meaningful dialogue on the future status of Kosovo.

On 2 September, international negotiations with Milosevic resulted in a declaration which endorsed the aim of reaching:

…an agreement on the basis of which it would be possible to establish [an] adequate level of self-governance, which presumes equality of all citizens and national communities living in Kosovo and Metohija. Being committed to mutual understanding and tolerance, the participants of the dialogue, i.e., the state delegation as well as representatives of all national communities living in Kosovo and Metohija, should express their readiness to

---

[31] Statement by NATO Secretary-General Javier Solana, 12 August 1998, NATO Press Release (98)93. Available at <http://www.nato.int/docu/pr/1998/p98-094e.htm>, accessed 6 October 2008.

[32] Statement by NATO Secretary-General Solana, 13 August 1998, NATO Press Release (98)95. Available at <http://www.nato.int/docu/pr/1998/p98-095e.htm>, accessed 6 October 2008.

[33] See above, Chapter 3, Section II.

make [an] assessment after a certain period, e.g., three to five years, of the implementation of the achieved agreement and to achieve improvement, about which mutual agreement would be reached.[34]

This statement was noteworthy, as it gave the initial indication that Belgrade might accept an interim agreement. However, the fact that such an accord would be assessed after three to five years was not a great step from the perspective of Kosovo, as any change to its structure or substance could only come about after this period with the agreement of Belgrade. Hence, it could exercise a veto over a final settlement. Moreover, in the text of the declaration the Kosovo Albanians were mentioned along with all the other national communities in Kosovo. This seemed to hark back to the Serbian view that the ethnic Albanians were just one of many minorities that needed accommodating.

Accordingly, by early September, the UN Secretary-General had to report to the Council that he was 'alarmed' by the lack of progress in arranging negotiations.[35] When no further advance seemed to be forthcoming, the Council adopted a fresh Chapter VII resolution. The text, adopted on 23 September, now identified the deteriorating situation in Kosovo as a threat to peace and security in the region and, acting under Chapter VII, unequivocally demanded that immediate steps be taken to improve the humanitarian situation and to avert 'the impending humanitarian catastrophe'.[36] It expressed grave concern at the increased fighting, including the:

...excessive and indiscriminate use of force by Serbian security forces and the Yugoslav Army which have resulted in numerous civilian casualties and...the displacement of over 230,000 persons from their homes.

The Council also condemned 'terrorism in pursuit of political goals', referring to the activities of the KLA. Specifically, the Council demanded 'immediate' implementation of:

• Cessation of action by security forces affecting the civilian population, and now also the 'withdrawal of security units used for civilian repression';
• Safe return of refugees;
• Effective and continuous monitoring and humanitarian access;
• 'Rapid progress to a clear timetable' in the 'dialogue with the Kosovo Albanian community with the aim of agreeing confidence building measures and finding a political solution to the problems of Kosovo'.

The Council also threatened further enforcement action, including 'action and additional measures to maintain or restore peace and stability in the region'. This, in UN parlance, was code for the possible authorization of forcible measures.

[34] Petritsch, Kaser, and Pichler, *Kosovo, Kosova*, 229.
[35] Report by the UN Secretary-General, 4 September 1998, S/1998/834, para. 28.
[36] Resolution 1199 (1998), 23 September 1998, S/RES/1199 (1998).

Throughout, the demands for negotiations by the EU and its members, the Contact Group and the Security Council had focused on the 'future status' of Kosovo. However, as it transpired, the actual agenda advanced by Ambassador Hill through a shuttle mission between Belgrade and Prishtina took a different turn. After the Contact Group had presented various options for a settlement to the parties, it was clear that agreement on Kosovo's actual status would be impossible. The FRY/Serbia was unwilling to move, and the Kosovo leadership would not be able to abandon its position on independence, in view of the dramatic developments of the summer. Instead, Ambassador Hill reported to the OSCE that an informal understanding had been reached about a three-year stabilization and normalization period to allow for the re-establishment of democratic institutions, after which a new approach could be envisaged. He stressed the crucial importance of an international presence in Kosovo during the implementation period and the important role that the OSCE would have to play in that area.[37]

Although it appeared that the succession of drafts for a settlement emanated from Ambassador Hill and another veteran of Dayton, the quite brilliant legal adviser Jim O'Brien, the Contact Group as a whole retained considerable influence over the content of those documents. In addition, a draft produced by the Council of Europe Venice Commission for Democracy through Law also proved influential—so influential in fact that the equally gifted and resourceful Director of the Secretariat of the Venice Commission was later seconded to support the EU envoy Wolfgang Petrisch at the Rambouillet talks.

After some further explorations during late summer, the first formal and complete Hill draft was presented to the parties on 1 October 1998. It represented a genuine attempt at balancing the divergent interests of the parties. In particular, it avoided altogether the issue of the status of Kosovo and focused instead on a pragmatic assignment of powers to different levels of administration. For the FRY/Serbia, this approach was painful, inasmuch as it avoided explicit confirmation of the continued territorial integrity and sovereignty of the FRY or even of Serbia. Kosovo was also hesitant. While the draft did not directly prejudice its status, being silent on the issue, it nevertheless had one very significant shortcoming. The source of public power, it seemed, would be located, not in the Kosovo institutions, but in the individual communes or local districts. This meant that Kosovo as an entity would not enjoy any significant element of legal personality—a fact which might seriously damage its quest for enhanced legal status at some future date. In deference to Serbia, the draft also contained very detailed provisions which, it was feared, would subject Kosovo to divisive ethnic politics.

The actual assignment of public authority provided for in the draft was quite complex. Residual authority over all matters not regulated elsewhere would lie with the communes, which were also granted significant powers of direct self-administration. This included the power to arrange for local police that were representative of the ethnic composition of the commune. Moreover, communes could unite to form 'self-administering regions comprising multiple communes'. While most communes in Kosovo had an ethnic Albanian majority, a few had a Serb majority. Hence, this provision appeared to be one which would permit the formation of an ethnic Serb entity within Kosovo based on a collection of communes. Such division had not proved fruitful in the past, bearing in mind the establishment of the Republika Srpska in Bosnia and Herzegovina.

In addition, a further layer of authority was introduced on behalf of 'national communities', that is, all ethnic groups regardless of whether they constituted a majority in a particular commune. These communities would enjoy 'additional rights' going some way beyond traditional minority rights, and would have organs of self-administration, including even courts. Kosovo was much opposed to this concept, which once again appeared to be based on ethnic division rather than a multicultural society with equal rights for all. However, the determination of the FRY/Serbia to ensure a separate status for Serbs—and others also, incidentally— was very strong throughout the negotiations, including the Rambouillet process, and the concept of national communities would be strengthened over time.

Kosovo itself was equipped with a number of organs (assembly, chairman, government, administrative organs, ombudsman) which would exercise the powers established in the draft. The assembly would enjoy quite wide legislative competences in relation to political, economic, social and cultural areas, including the power to adopt 'organic documents' of Kosovo, in other words, its own constitution and associated texts. Voting in the assembly, however, could be obstructed by any national community, again introducing the prospect of ethnic politics into Kosovo.

The chairman would be directly elected and head a government. There was no president—a proposition not engendering immediate support from Rugova. The government would include at least one member from each national community and supervise the functioning of the administrative agencies. A separate annex dealt with law enforcement. It provided for an ethnic Albanian Minister of the Interior and a Serb Deputy, and a similar arrangement for the Chief of Staff for Communal Police Issues. The Kosovo police, confusingly named Kosovo Communal Police, would be limited to a ceiling of 2,500 active duty personnel. The extent of municipal (commune) police would depend on the size of the local population.

The federation would exercise powers in relation to territorial integrity, a common market, monetary policy, defence, and foreign policy. There would also be a federal police presence with jurisdiction over crimes with implications for the federation. Crucially, there was no mention of Serbia in the draft.

A very significant element of the draft related to its concluding provisions. It provided for 'a comprehensive assessment of the agreement, with the aim of improving its implementation and considering proposals by either side for additional steps, which will require mutual agreement for adoption'. This provision meant that the agreement was not, in fact, a genuine interim agreement. It could not be terminated or changed, unless both sides so agreed.

While Kosovo was formulating its response to the initial draft, the Holbrooke agreement, which will be considered in detail in the next chapter, was concluded. That agreement had been obtained early in October by US Special Envoy Richard Holbrooke under the threat of an imminent airstrike against Serbia. In exchange for a suspension of the attack, the agreement provided for a ceasefire between the parties on the ground, the deployment of an OSCE monitoring mission and the rapid establishment of a political settlement. In addition to the undertaking to reach such a settlement by 2 November, a unilateral statement by Serbia outlined the basic points for a political framework which it claimed had been agreed with Ambassador Holbrooke.[38] This eleven-point framework would furnish the basis of a political settlement on the basis of the initial Hill draft, it was claimed. Of course, the Kosovo side had not been a party to the Holbrooke discussions with Milosevic. In contrast to the Hill document, the Serbian text included an express provision respecting the territorial integrity and sovereignty of the FRY. It also provided for harmonization of legal arrangements establishing Kosovo's self-governance within the legal systems of both the FRY and Serbia, implying continued subordination of Kosovo to the latter entity.

While President Rugova ultimately supported the Holbrooke deal, Kosovo issued its own statement on fundamental principles for a settlement on 3 November.[39] Furthermore, on 2 November, the date stipulated in the Holbrooke agreement for completion of an interim settlement, a new, far more detailed Hill draft emerged. That draft had to some extent enhanced the status of Kosovo as a legal entity in its own right: Kosovo would also have a president and the role of the Kosovo courts was developed in greater detail. However, on the other hand, the provisions on communes and national communities, of essential concern to the FRY/Serbia, had also been further entrenched.

Despite the pledge made in the Holbrooke agreement, Serbia did not commit itself by 2 November to the Hill document that was presented.[40] This failure to insist on Serbia's compliance with its undertaking may have squandered a crucial opportunity to achieve a settlement, as this draft might also have been acceptable to Kosovo. Instead, on 18 November, Serbia unilaterally organized its own Kosovo settlement conference, attended, inter alia, by representatives, or purported representatives, of the 'national communities' in Kosovo. Of course, there did not include the genuine representatives of the Kosovo Albanian communities.

This meeting resulted in a counter-proposal, supported by the FRY, Serbia and Kosovo Serb, Gorani, Egyptian, Romani, Turk, and Muslim 'national

---

[38] Serbian Government Endorses Accord Reached by President Milosevic, 13 October 1999, Weller, *Crisis in Kosovo*, 279.

[39] Kosovo Statement, 3 November 1998, in Weller, *Crisis in Kosovo*, 369–70.

[40] FRY Press Release, 10 November 1998, in Weller, *Crisis in Kosovo*, 370.

communities'.[41] While this proposal mirrored some of the language of the Hill texts, it was seen by Kosovo as a cynical attempt to undermine the internationalized Hill process. In addition to substantive changes, in particular in relation to national communities and the position of Serbia, the draft did not provide for signature by Kosovo, but by all individual national communities. To the Kosovo Albanians, this was indicative, once again, of Serbian attempts to turn them into a political minority in a land where they constituted the overwhelming demographic majority. Moreover, Kosovo noted that representatives of the national communities supporting the Serbian text were either members of Milosevic's party, or they had been hand-picked by Belgrade and had, in fact, been partly disowned by the groups they purported to represent in Kosovo.

While rejecting the Serbian draft, Kosovo's chief 'informal' negotiator, Fehmi Agani, went further than before in embracing the Hill process and the progress made thus far.[42] This optimism was to prove premature, in that the following day a new Hill draft was submitted, which provided for express powers for Serbia in relation to Kosovo and appeared to have been shaped to be in harmony with the eleven points Serbia had claimed had been agreed with Holbrooke. In fact, the draft was immediately rejected by both sides and, despite new attempts at shuttle diplomacy by the Hill team to keep the dialogue open, the peace process seemed to have reached a dead end. Belgrade started to mount a personal attack against the mediator—a sign that it had determined that the Hill process did not serve its interests.

A feeling of gloom amongst the representatives of the organized international community was strengthened by the FRY/Serbian Christmas offensive and ensuing hostilities in January.

Despite this setback, the Hill team continued its work and produced one more draft, two days before the Contact Group decision to summon the parties to talks at Rambouillet.[43] This draft was very detailed. Several alternative proposals for provisions previously placed in brackets had been removed. Of particular interest were new provisions relating to the withdrawal of the Yugoslav Army and Serbian special police forces, and to international implementation.

V. Conclusion

The rising temperature of hostilities in Kosovo, and the resulting humanitarian emergency, triggered for the first time significant international engagement with the Kosovo crisis. Western governments established the Kosovo

---

[41] Proposal, 20 November, and Declaration in Support of Joint Proposal, 25 November 1998, in Weller, *Crisis in Kosovo*, 372–5, 375 respectively.

[42] Kosovo Press Release, 1 December 1998, in Weller, *Crisis in Kosovo*, 375–6.

[43] Final Hill Proposal, 27 January 1999 in Weller, *Crisis in Kosovo*, 383–91.

Diplomatic Observer Mission which, in lieu of the OSCE, added a measure of increased transparency to the situation. More decisively, though, the UN Security Council finally was able to adopt Chapter VII measures, adopted in close coordination with the states of the Contact Group. However, the ability of the Council to act was limited by the unwillingness of Russia to threaten strong sanctions against Belgrade. This led to the threat or use of force by NATO and the ill-fated Holbrooke deal. That deal, as it turned out, carried with it the seeds of disagreement regarding the interim settlement that the negotiations led by US Ambassador Hill had attempted to achieve.

7

The Holbrooke Agreement and the OSCE Verification Mission

The United States had threatened the use of force in relation to Kosovo since 1992. 'In the event of conflict in Kosovo caused by Serbian action, the United States will be prepared to employ military force against the Serbs in Kosovo and Serbia proper', then President George Bush wrote to Slobodan Milosevic in December of that year—a threat echoed the following February by the Clinton administration.[1] However, neglect of the Kosovo issue permitted that threat to recede into the background for several years. It was only when hostilities commenced early in 1998 that NATO professed a 'legitimate interest in developments in Kosovo, inter alia because of their impact on the stability of the whole region which is of concern to the Alliance'.[2]

I. Preparatory Moves for the Use of Force

In April, the alliance confirmed its willingness to support UN or OSCE monitoring activities and indicated that it was considering NATO preventative deployments in Albania and in Macedonia, and further 'deterrent measures'.[3] To this end, Partnership for Peace collaborations with Albania and Macedonia were increased. NATO also activated Permanent Joint Council consultations with Russia. In June, there followed joint air exercises in Albania and Macedonia, with the agreement of those two states, involving no fewer than sixty-eight fighter aircraft and seventeen support aircraft from thirteen NATO states. The mission flew up to 15 kilometres from the borders with Yugoslavia/Kosovo.[4] In August and September, joint exercises of land forces were held in Albania and Macedonia,

---

[1] Quoted from a news report in R. Caplan, 'International Diplomacy and the Crisis in Kosovo', *International Affairs*, 74 (1998), 753.

[2] NAC Statement, 5 March 1998, in Weller, *Crisis in Kosovo*, 275.

[3] NAC Statement, 30 April 1998 in Weller, *Crisis in Kosovo*, 275.

[4] Statement on Exercise 'Determined Falcon', 13 June 1998, in Weller, *Crisis in Kosovo*, 277; and Press Release, 15 June 1998, in Weller, *Crisis in Kosovo*, 277.

involving NATO troops, but including contingents from a number of other Partnership for Peace states.[5]

By the end of September, the humanitarian situation was dramatic. Despite the involvement of the Kosovo Diplomatic Observer Mission, the conflict escalated and the number of the displaced and refugees exceeded 300,000. Attention of the international agencies remained focused on containing the conflict, increasing the monitoring and, with ever greater urgency, increasing the provision of humanitarian relief. This prompted the UN Secretary-General, who had held a key position in the UN Secretariat managing peacekeeping operations during the Bosnia debacle, to observe in July that 'the international community risks once again being placed in a position where it is only dealing with the symptoms of a conflict through its humanitarian agencies'.[6] But by September, increased monitoring and diplomatic initiatives had not achieved much. The number of displaced persons and refugees was still climbing, and the onset of winter was increasingly imminent. Kofi Annan noted:

In the last few weeks, the international community has witnessed appalling atrocities in Kosovo, reminiscent of the recent past elsewhere in the Balkans. These have been borne out by reporting by the Kosovo Diplomatic Observer Mission and other reliable sources. I reiterate my utter condemnation of such wanton killing and destruction. It is clear beyond any reasonable doubt that the great majority of such acts have been committed by security forces in Kosovo acting under the authority of the Federal Republic of Yugoslavia. But Kosovar Albanian paramilitary units have engaged in armed action also, and there is good reason to believe that they too have committed atrocities.[7]

Only one-third of the 300,000 displaced persons had made it into neighbouring territories, where adequate relief and shelter could be provided. The others were dispersed in the rugged countryside of Kosovo. With the onset of winter a humanitarian catastrophe was feared.

The day after the Security Council adopted Resolution 1199 (1998), on 24 September, the North Atlantic Council approved the issuing of an 'ACTWARN' decision for both a limited air operation and a phased air campaign in Kosovo, taking NATO to an increased level of military preparedness.[8]

II. The Holbrooke Mission

Against this background, in early October, the United States dispatched its Special Envoy Richard Holbrooke to Belgrade, to obtain, finally, compliance with the mandatory demands made by the Security Council in Resolutions 1160

---

[5] These were exercises 'Cooperative Assembly', 17–22 August 1998, and 'Cooperative Best Effort', 10–18 September 1998.

[6] UN Secretary-General's Report, 5 August 1998, in Weller, _Crisis in Kosovo_, 206–11.

[7] UN Secretary-General's Report, 3 October 1998, in Weller, _Crisis in Kosovo_, 214–8.

[8] Statement by NATO Secretary-General, 24 September 1998, in Weller, _Crisis in Kosovo_, 277.

(1998) and 1199 (1998). He had a reputation for being able to persuade Milosevic, having been the key negotiator at the Dayton conference. On this occasion, however, he failed.

In the meantime, the UK government had prepared a legal case in favour of the use of force. In early October, it circulated a one-page memorandum among NATO allies. While the document noted that the Security Council was of course authorized to mandate the use of force, forcible action 'can also be justified on the grounds of overwhelming humanitarian necessity without a UNSCR'. In that case, it proposed the following criteria:

(a) That there is convincing evidence, generally accepted by the international community as a whole, of extreme humanitarian distress on a large scale, requiring immediate and urgent relief;
(b) That it is objectively clear that there is no practicable alternative to the use of force if lives are to be saved;
(c) That the proposed use of force is necessary and proportionate to the aim (the relief of humanitarian need) and is strictly limited in time and scope to this aim—i.e., it is the minimum necessary to achieve that end. It would also be necessary at the appropriate stage to assess the targets against this criterion.[9]

The note continued:

There is convincing evidence of an impending humanitarian catastrophe (SCR 1199 and the UNSG's and UNHCR's reports). We judge on the evidence of FRY handling of Kosovo throughout this year that a humanitarian catastrophe cannot be averted unless Milosevic is dissuaded from further repressive acts, and that only the proposed threat of force will achieve this objective. The UK's view is therefore that, as matters now stand and if action through the Security Council is not possible, military intervention by NATO is lawful on grounds of overwhelming humanitarian necessity.

US President Bill Clinton then announced that he had instructed his delegation to NATO to vote for authorization 'for military strikes against Serbia if President Milosevic continues to defy the international community'.[10] Secretary of State Madeleine Albright echoed that the Alliance 'has the legitimacy to act to stop a catastrophe', adding:

Milosevic knows what he needs to do to avoid NATO action. He must immediately end all military and police operations in Kosovo; withdraw all units to their bases and cantonments in a way that can be verified; provide international organizations and diplomatic observers unfettered access to Kosovo; agree to a timetable for a political settlement based on the draft that the Contact Group has endorsed; and co-operate with the War Crimes Tribunal.[11]

[9] FCO note of 7 October 1998, 'FRY/Kosovo: The Way Ahead; UK View on Legal Base for Use of Force'. Reproduced in Adam Roberts, 'NATO's "Humanitarian War" Over Kosovo', *Survival*, 41(3) (1999), 102–23.
[10] Remarks by US President, 8 October 1998, in Weller, *Crisis in Kosovo*, 278.
[11] Statement, 8 October 1998, in Weller, *Crisis in Kosovo*, 278.

In the meantime, Richard Holbrooke had journeyed to Belgrade. He spent over a week discussing the details of the Hill plan with Milosevic. Serbia required significant amendments, but eventually news of a breakthrough in his talks emerged. However, rather than terminating its threat of the use of force, at Holbrooke's request NATO increased the pressure.

Whilst Holbrooke thought he had the settled basis of an agreement, he recalled Milosevic's tendency to walk away from his undertakings after a period of reflection. On 8 October, Holbrooke briefed the foreign ministers of the Contact Group, assembled in the tiny VIP lounge at Heathrow airport. Based on the understanding that he was close to an agreement, he obtained a commitment to an enhanced threat of the use of force, in order to ensure that a definite deal would be reached. The consensus was not disrupted by Russia on this occasion.

On 13 October, NATO issued an activation order (ACTORD) for both limited air strikes and a phased air campaign, to commence after the expiry of a period of approximately ninety-six hours. That breathing space was intended to permit the Holbrooke deal to be consolidated.[12]

The issuing of this ultimatum was unprecedented in recent history, not only in the annals of NATO.[13] While the demands of the Security Council had been made in two mandatory Chapter VII resolutions, there was no mandate for the military enforcement of its decisions. Instead, this action could only be justified with reference to the humanitarian emergency in the region. The United Kingdom argued that such authority existed in international law in view of the 'exceptional circumstances of Kosovo'. It added that in such circumstances, 'a limited use of force was justifiable in support of purposes laid down by the Security Council but without the Council's express authorization when that was the only means to avert an immediate and overwhelming catastrophe'.[14] The conditions for humanitarian 'intervention' in general international law expressed here could be married to the facts of this case in the following ways:

Overwhelming humanitarian necessity. In this instance, it was claimed that the lives of tens of thousands of internally displaced people were at stake. The existence of life-threatening distress of a significant magnitude could not really be denied. In addition, the ongoing military operations were likely to increase the number of displaced persons. The Security Council itself had determined that there was a risk of an overwhelming humanitarian catastrophe.

---

[12] Statement of NATO Secretary-General, 13 October 1998, in Weller, *Crisis in Kosovo*, 278.

[13] A number of ultimata had been issued by NATO in relation to Bosnia and Herzegovina. However, in that case there had existed an enforcement mandate from the Council.

[14] See the testimony of Baroness Symons, Hansard HL Dbs, WA 139f, 16 November 1998, *British Yearbook of International Law*, 69 (1998), 593, and the discussion in Michael Wood, 'The Law on the Use of Force: Current Challenges', *Singapore Yearbook of International Law*, 11 (2007), 1, 10.

Imminence. Many of the displaced were already living in very unstable conditions, without food and shelter. The onset of a Balkan winter made a large-scale humanitarian emergency inevitable should the situation not be remedied within a short space of time. Indeed, rapid action was required to ensure that large numbers of people could be moved to areas in Kosovo where their needs would be provided for, especially in light of the extensive destruction of houses and civilian infrastructure.

Objective determination of facts. The existence of an imminent humanitarian catastrophe had been confirmed by disinterested objective agencies, best placed to assess the situation, including the Security Council and UNHCR.

Exhaustion of other options. Throughout the year, attempts had been made to persuade Yugoslavia to accept the demands of the Security Council, by Russia, the Contact Group, the EU Special Representative and finally the US Special Envoy. Given the immediacy of the situation, it could be argued that there was no time for other options, such as the adoption of more comprehensive economic sanctions, to achieve compliance.

Objective determination of legitimate aims. The demands made by NATO were precisely those which had been enunciated repeatedly by the Security Council (cessation of hostilities, withdrawal of forces, humanitarian and monitoring access, substantive dialogue leading to a settlement within a short time frame). Hence, it could not really be argued that NATO was pursuing aims of its own, rather than acting on the basis of genuine humanitarian concern.

Minimum force. Military force would be kept to the minimum necessary to achieve the stated aims. To that end, a strategy using either symbolic or phased strikes was put in place.[15]

In contrast to the actual application of military force some months later, the NATO ultimatum and threat of force did not trigger widespread objection among other governments. This was seen at the time as further confirmation that forcible humanitarian action without a Security Council mandate was politically and legally acceptable. Wider discussion was perhaps precluded by the

---

[15] e.g., the UK view on humanitarian intervention in Iraq: 'the practice of states does show over a long period that it is generally accepted that in extreme circumstances a state can intervene in another state for humanitarian reasons. I think before doing so though a state would have to ask itself several questions. First of all, whether there was a compelling and urgent situation of extreme humanitarian distress which demanded immediate relief. It would have to ask itself whether the other state was itself able or willing to meet that distress and deal with it. Also whether there was any other practical alternative to intervening in order to relieve the stress, and also whether the action could be limited in scope'. Testimony by FCO Legal Counsellor Tony Aust, Parl. Papers 1992–3, HC, Paper 235-iii, 85ff; also reproduced in David J. Harris, *Cases and Materials on International Law* (6th edn, London: Sweet and Maxwell, 2004), 951.

apparent rapid success of the threat, and by the fact that its result was formally endorsed by the Security Council, in Resolution 1203 (1998). However, the issue of a threat or use of force for humanitarian circumstances will be explored in greater detail later.[16]

The actual Holbrooke agreement is rather a complex arrangement, much of which was cast in more formal terms a few days after the Holbrooke mission. The package was negotiated with President Milosevic, who announced on 13 October that a settlement had been achieved that would eliminate the danger of military intervention and was fully in keeping with Yugoslav national interests.[17] It was left to the Serbian government alone to announce its acceptance of an eleven-point political framework for the settlement of the Kosovo issue.[18] This permitted Serbia to continue to argue that the fate of Kosovo lay exclusively within its own hands, and was not a matter for the FRY or indeed for international mediation, although the federation subsequently endorsed this plan. As was noted in the previous chapter, the Serbian statement also contained an undertaking to complete an agreement containing core elements for a political settlement in Kosovo by 2 November, using as its basis the paper proposed by the Contact Group (the first Hill proposal).

With respect to military matters, it was agreed that the FRY/Serbia would withdraw security forces introduced into Kosovo after February 1998. These comprised 10,021 special police (MUP). In addition, heavy weapons brought into the territory or transferred from the Yugoslav Army to the MUP after that date were to be withdrawn. Other heavy weapons would be returned to cantonment areas or police stations. Similarly, Yugoslav armed forces (VJ) and their additional equipment brought into the territory after February would be removed. VJ force levels would thus be limited to approximately 11,300. The remaining VJ units would return to their regular garrisons and remain there, with the exception of three company-sized teams to protect lines of communication. Police forces would also be withdrawn from certain areas and their movements and the use of armoured patrols would be significantly restricted. The Kosovo Diplomatic Observer Mission would receive continuous reports on the activities of VJ and MUP units. These military undertakings were formalized in the 'record of a meeting' in Belgrade between the FRY Prime Minister, a senior official from the Serbian Interior Ministry and NATO Generals Klaus Nauman and Wesley Clark. Strictly speaking, this document, previously excluded from the public domain, was not a formal agreement. Instead, the NATO representatives 'took note' of certain undertakings given by the Yugoslav/Serbian representatives.[19] Hence, Belgrade could argue that it had not consented to a definite

---

[16]   See below Chapter 8, Section I.

[17]   Statement by President Milosevic, 13 October 1998, in Weller, *Crisis in Kosovo*, 279.

[18]   Serbian Government statement, 13 October 1998, in Weller, *Crisis in Kosovo*, 279.

[19]   Record of NATO-Serbia/FRY Meeting in Belgrade, 25 October 1998, in Weller, *Crisis in Kosovo*, 283–4.

international obligation with respect to its troop deployments in Kosovo, but merely informed NATO of its intentions concerning such deployments. Further modalities were agreed in an 'understanding' between the KDOM (in fact the US KDOM Chief) and the Ministry of the Interior of Serbia, concluded on the same day.[20] That understanding provided for the dismantling of specific check-points by security forces, with the exception of twenty-seven 'observation points' which would be created along important lines of communication. In addition, police forces would be withdrawn from certain locations, along certain roads.

While the commitments relating to force deployments were concluded in this circuitous way and remained confidential, two formal agreements had already been concluded, on 15 and 16 October respectively. In the Kosovo Verification Mission agreement, the Federal Republic of Yugoslavia agreed to an 'air surveillance system for Kosovo'. The aim was ostensibly to verify compliance of all parties with the provisions of Security Council Resolution 1199 (1998), although in fact it would enable NATO to monitor compliance with the military arrangements subsequently formalized. The agreement provided for the right of overflight, according to certain modalities, of unarmed NATO reconnaissance platforms (unmanned vehicles, low- and medium-level reconnaissance aircraft and U-2 missions). In contrast to the no-fly zones which had been imposed upon northern and southern Iraq for humanitarian purposes, FRY fighter aircraft continued to be entitled to fly within Kosovo at all times, except when NATO-manned low and medium altitude flights were being undertaken. However, air defence weapons or critical components of such systems would be removed from Kosovo and from a 25 kilometre safety zone along its border.

Finally, an agreement was concluded with the OSCE for the deployment of 2,000 unarmed 'verifiers' plus expert personnel on the ground, again to monitor compliance with the terms of Security Council Resolution 1199 (1998). After completion of these two agreements, NATO issued a statement indicating that it would maintain its readiness to launch air operations.[21]

On 27 October, the NATO Secretary-General could report that substantial force withdrawals were taking place and that the situation was stabilizing. However, 'if we see evidence of substantial non-compliance in the future with UNSC Resolution 1199 we will be ready to use force', he indicated, confirming that the ACTORD remained in place, both for limited air strikes and a phased air campaign.[22] In addition, an 'extraction force' of 1,500 NATO troops would be sent to Macedonia, to ensure the protection and eventual evacuation of the OSCE verifiers, should that become necessary.[23] NATO also emphasized that the

---

[20] Understanding, 25 October 1998, in Weller, *Crisis in Kosovo*, 284.

[21] NAC/NATO Secretary-General's Statement, 16 October 1998, in Weller, *Crisis in Kosovo*, 282.

[22] NATO Secretary-General's Statement, 27 October 1998, in Weller, *Crisis in Kosovo*, 284.

[23] The activation order for that force was adopted on 4 December, see NATO Press Statement on the Extraction Force, in Weller, *Crisis in Kosovo*, 286.

Kosovar Albanian side would need to comply with the terms of Resolution 1199 (1998) and cooperate with the verification mission. The Kosovo Albanians had not been party to any of the agreements that had been reached and were, in fact, not informed of the contents of the military undertakings and the precise nature of the overall package. Nevertheless, there was a commitment to a cease-fire and the KLA participated in arrangements for a cooperative disengagement of forces.

Just as with the eventual use of force by NATO in relation to Bosnia and Herzegovina at the end of the summer of 1995, it appeared to some that decisive action by NATO in threatening force had delivered peace to Kosovo, after ten years of crisis. However, the more astute observers noted that the agreement could also be interpreted by Belgrade as a sign that the threat of force was not, in fact, a real one. The US negotiator, it seemed, had seized upon quite informal commitments by the Yugoslav government, which had not been noted for compliance with its undertakings over the preceding ten years. They also questioned whether the OSCE mission could make a significant impact on the territory, being unarmed and effectively having to rely on FRY/Serbian support. Exclusion of the Kosovo Albanians from the arrangements was also a source of concern, especially as the attitude of the KLA was not unambiguously clear. Given these doubts, the widely shared assessment was that the Holbrooke deal might provide a useful pause which could be used for proper negotiations. It would not in itself resolve the crisis and, unless supplemented by further steps, would merely permit the parties to sit out the winter before resuming armed action.

III. The OSCE Verification Mission

The OSCE had been excluded from Yugoslavia since 1993. Persistent demands for reintroduction of its Mission of Long Duration, made not only by the OSCE organs but also by the United Nations General Assembly and the Security Council, had been ignored. According to the OSCE agreement on implementation of the Holbrooke arrangement, the mission would be established under an OSCE Permanent Council decision, but pursuant to a Security Council resolution. In this way, Yugoslavia could assure itself of a modicum of indirect control over the operation, through Russia's presence on the Security Council. In addition, through these means, the FRY could avoid an all-too-obvious U-turn in relation to its refusal to accept an OSCE mission until its participation in that organization had been fully restored.[24]

The agreement was concluded for one year, with the unusual possibility of unilateral extension at the request of either the FRY or the OSCE. It provided for

---

[24] Of course, FRY participation in the UN itself remained somewhat in limbo, but in a less visible way, as FRY delegates continued to represent the FRY in relation to the Security Council.

the presence of 2,000 unarmed OSCE 'verifiers', based principally in Prishtina (headquarters) and in every municipal district in Kosovo, plus a liaison office in Belgrade. The additional use of experts for election monitoring or other tasks was also permitted, providing the option of deploying significantly more than 2,000 personnel. The functions of the mission were broad, being directed towards verification by all parties of compliance with their commitments under Security Council Resolution 1199 (1998). In addition, the OSCE would 'supervise' rather than monitor elections in Kosovo. As the mission would verify compliance by all parties and would effectively run elections in Kosovo, it is interesting to note that the elected representatives of Kosovo, or indeed any representative of Kosovo, were not consulted about its terms, nor were they invited to accede to it.[25] This fact is all the more surprising, inasmuch as the mission was also supposed to support the establishment of a political settlement, and would assist in the building of political institutions in Kosovo, including a new police force.

The military aspect of the mission's mandate was also somewhat confusing. It was charged expressly with reporting on the maintenance of a ceasefire by all parties and also with verifying the numbers and locations of FRY/Serbian military forces and police forces. However, a significant number of senior members of the mission were not given access to the actual undertakings that had been made by Belgrade in relation to these issues. Instead, it appeared that KDOM, which should in principle have become superfluous with the establishment of the OSCE mission, and its US element would also exercise a verification role in this respect. In fact, rather than winding down its presence, towards the end of the mission the US contributed no fewer than 143 members to KDOM, compared to 33 furnished by all EU states combined.

The OSCE appointed US Ambassador William Walker to head KVM, and formally established the mission on 25 October.[26] By that time, the other elements of the Holbrooke deal had been translated into a series of military undertakings, and the Security Council had endorsed the mission the previous day. UNHCR reported that winter was setting in, the first snowfalls having been observed, and that rapid arrangements needed to be made to provide for the return of the displaced and refugees and to assure that they were supplied with foodstuffs, medicine, stoves and building materials.[27] A detailed survey of the state of villages and buildings was undertaken, to ensure that returnees would receive the support they required. Once again, the coordination of the efforts of the UN agencies, KVM,

---

[25] Hence, there ensued intense US efforts to persuade KLA leaders to abide by the agreement. However, a month after the conclusion of the Holbrooke agreement, the UN Secretary-General reported that the position of Kosovo Albanian paramilitaries remained unclear, although respect for a ceasefire was, by and large, expected. There was evidence that paramilitaries were exploiting the FRY/Serbian withdrawals to enhance their positions and to replenish their supplies. Report, 12 November 1998 in Weller, *Crisis in Kosovo*, 302–8.

[26] OSCE Permanent Council Decision 263, 25 October 1998, in Weller, *Crisis in Kosovo*, 295.

[27] UN Inter-Agency Update, 21 October 1998, in Weller, *Crisis in Kosovo*, 300.

KDOM and non-governmental agencies was impressive, in contrast to much previous experience of humanitarian organizations in complex emergencies.

Almost in parallel with the partial pullout of FRY/Serbian forces from Kosovo or to barracks in Kosovo, the first returns were noted. While the humanitarian situation improved somewhat as a result, it was reported that FRY/Serbian repression continued. The increased international presence resulted in the discovery of corpses, apparently victims of summary execution. Some 1,500 ethnic Albanians remained in detention by FRY/Serbian authorities, their future uncertain. There was also retaliatory action by Kosovo forces, who now enjoyed greater freedom of movement, and by returning villagers, against Serbs.[28] Serbian security measures were increased in November and early December, including the re-establishment of security checkpoints and a heavy security presence, especially in villages along the Albanian border. Arbitrary arrests and the practice of 'informative talks' at Serbian detention centres continued 'on a massive scale', along with 'abductions' of Serb individuals (four reported from mid-October, although the actual figure is likely to be higher).[29] A Serb policeman was shot after having been kidnapped, and on 14 December six Serb teenagers were killed while playing pool when two masked gunmen sprayed a cafe in Pec with bullets.[30]

Early December also saw occasional violations of the ceasefire and localized fighting. The tense situation was not improved by the fact that, by that time, the OSCE had only managed to establish an advance headquarters in Kosovo and to introduce fifty staff. As the OSCE does not have significant staff of its own, and as prospective KVM members had to be seconded from or nominated by participating states, and then trained and familiarized with local circumstances, this is, of course, not altogether surprising.

On Christmas Eve, the UN Secretary-General reported that 100,000 Kosovo Albanians had returned to their homes, while 200,000 remained displaced.[31] While no new 'abductions' had been reported to the Secretary-General, no progress had been made in establishing the fate of 282 Serb civilians and police who had disappeared during the conflict. In turn, the amnesty of detained ethnic Albanians, envisaged by the Serbian government statement issued upon conclusion of the Holbrooke agreement, was not progressing. On the positive side, the presence of the OSCE mission had increased very significantly, with personnel totalling 908, including 392 local staff. Regional OSCE centres had also started to become operational. However, rather than stabilizing, the situation deteriorated dramatically. Over the Christmas period, the FRY/Serbian forces commenced a major offensive, leading to a renewed exodus of refugees, now in the harsh conditions of mid-winter. This operation was perceived by international observers as a test of the determination of the international community, and of

---

[28] UN Secretary-General's Report, 12 November 1998, in Weller, *Crisis in Kosovo*, 302–8.
[29] Secretary-General's Report, 4 December 1998, in Weller, *Crisis in Kosovo*, 309–13.
[30] UN Inter-Agency Update, 24 December 1998.
[31] Report of the Secretary-General, 24 December 1998, in Weller, *Crisis in Kosovo*, 313–4.

NATO in particular, and its timing was viewed as significant in that context. It was also a sign that the FRY/Serbia would not be willing to permit the emergence of a situation in which it would lose effective control over Kosovo to the benefit of the Kosovo military and political leadership.

The OSCE managed to negotiate a truce after four days of renewed hostilities, which were again marked by direct attacks against civilian concentrations, rather than limited counter-insurgency operations. However, in early January further attacks were mounted, culminating in the Racak massacre of 15 January 1999. The massacre of forty-five ethnic Albanians, twenty-two of whom were found together in a gully, apparently killed execution style, and including several elderly men and a child, was immediately condemned by the UN Secretary-General, the OSCE, including its Head of Mission, and other international bodies. The Security Council adopted a Presidential Statement reflecting the view that the FRY was responsible for the atrocity. The Council also noted with concern that 5,500 civilians had fled Racak and deplored the decision of Belgrade to declare the OSCE Head of Mission persona non grata for his clear condemnation of the act. A report of a Finnish/EC forensic team later confirmed that none of the victims appeared to have been 'anything other than unarmed civilians'.[32]

Throughout January further fighting was reported, triggering another Presidential Statement from the Security Council.[33] NATO military commanders journeyed to Belgrade, to impress upon Milosevic NATO's continued determination to use force, if necessary. Nevertheless, NATO reported that armed formations had been re-introduced into Kosovo, in violation of the Holbrooke agreement.

IV. Conclusion

The events related in this chapter must be counted amongst the more unusual in recent diplomatic history. NATO formally threatened the use of force for political ends and came close to launching air strikes against Yugoslavia. This action, prima facie inconsistent with the international prohibition of the use of force, can only be justified with reference to a revival of the doctrine of humanitarian intervention. Indeed, the UK government went to great length to make this case to its NATO allies and others. However, as opposed to the very significant debate on the eventual use of force that was to follow in 1999, there was no international debate or condemnation. Instead, the episode was coordinated with the Contact Group that included Russia and had informal backing, but no mandate, from the UN Security Council. At this stage, the threat of force for humanitarian

---

[32] Report of the EU Forensic Team, 17 March 1999, in Weller, *Crisis in Kosovo*, 333–5.

[33] Statement by the President of the Security Council, 29 January 1999, in Weller, *Crisis in Kosovo*, 323.

purposes appeared to work. The Milosevic government agreed to a cessation of hostilities, and withdrawal or cantonment of forces, a significant international verification presence, and rapid conclusion of a political settlement.

In actual fact, however, the Holbrooke deal was a haphazard collection of ill-thought out and unclear commitments generated in late night negotiating sessions with Milosevic and his advisers. There also appear to have been certain aspects of the military agreements that were not shared among all those involved in the supervision of their implementation. Moreover, and perhaps crucially, the deal had not included the Kosovo side, which did not feel constrained in exploiting the withdrawal of Serbian forces. Finally, the agreement had an important knock-on effect on the Hill negotiations on a political interim settlement. It granted to Serbia a listing of eleven points as a basic framework for the settlement—points that had not been agreed, or even seen, by the Kosovo side. This led to the change in the structure of the Hill draft document that made it unacceptable to the Kosovo side, which had been moving towards an acceptance of the earlier draft version. The eleven points and the Hill document of December reflecting them also flowed into some of the points stipulated by the Contact Group as the basis of discussion at Rambouillet. This, in turn, spelt trouble for that upcoming final opportunity for negotiation.

8

The Rambouillet Conference

The Rambouillet conference represents a unique attempt at enforced negotiation. The venture was supported by the demands of the United Nations Security Council and the actions of the Contact Group, which included Russia, an ally of Yugoslavia. However, the unity of the Contact Group and other actors involved proved fragile. The attempt by leading powers to assume the task of 'reordering the Balkans' and impose a settlement in the face of a significant threat to the survival of a civilian population and to regional stability was thus undermined from the beginning. In some respects, the conference was more of a shambles than a grand design aimed at imposing reason upon the parties. But it was a heroic failure nevertheless, which at one stage even appeared close to success.

I. The Summons to the Conference and the Renewed Threat of Force

By early December 1998, the efforts of US Ambassador Hill and his team to mediate a settlement for Kosovo had reached a dead end. Both parties had rejected the latest incarnation of the Hill draft. Yugoslavia had instead put forward its own draft agreement. While that document was designed to mirror some of the language and content of the mediator's proposals, it preserved Serbia's dominant position in relation to Kosovo and was immediately rejected by the elected leadership of the latter. Kosovo, in turn, had observed that the original Hill project was gradually being modified in accordance with key Yugoslav demands, reflected in the original eleven-point outline presented by Belgrade in the context of the Holbrooke agreement of late October. This development jeopardized the fragile consensus among the parties in Kosovo to participate at least indirectly in the Hill initiative, by way of the informal group lead by Fehmi Agani and loosely connected with the Rugova government. Through that means, the Rugova government had been able to declare that it did not regard the Hill plan as a basis for a settlement, while at the same time seeking to improve it through comments provided by Agani's team. Moreover, it had miraculously been possible to persuade the leadership of the KLA that an interim agreement might, in principle, be acceptable and preferable to outright confrontation. However, increased emphasis on the formal determination of the legal status of Kosovo as part of Yugoslavia and the Serbian Republic in both the Yugoslav and the Hill proposals was seen as evidence of the fact that the Hill process was designed to lure Kosovo into a negotiating process which would ultimately be incompatible with its basic requirements. Those requirements were that any agreement would leave open the question of status and that it would be of a genuinely transitory nature.

A. The impetus for the Rambouillet process

The Contact Group negotiators had been aware that an agreement would need to be reached before spring 1999 when a renewed outbreak of hostilities would be made possible by favourable weather. Now, however, it seemed that their worst fears were being realized ahead of schedule. The Yugoslav military offensive, launched on Christmas Eve, threatened a further outpouring of refugees. Not only did it directly affect the civilian populations of the villages that came under attack but, more profoundly, it appeared to indicate that the Verification Mission was not an effective means of constraining Yugoslav military operations which went significantly beyond the limited measures claimed by Belgrade to be necessary to hunt down 'terrorists' in the territory. In that sense, the Christmas offensive seemed to have been designed to test the resolve and capacity of the OSCE verifiers and, more importantly, of NATO. The Alliance, after all, still maintained the threat of the use of force in order to obtain Yugoslav compliance with the terms of the Holbrooke agreement. Again, the NATO governments did not appear to have an appetite for making good their threats, which in consequence were rapidly losing credibility.

While it is generally assumed that it was the discovery of the Racak massacre which prompted the Contact Group to adopt a more vigorous attempt to achieve a settlement, this is only partially true. In reality, it had already become clear in late December that the Holbrooke agreement would not even succeed in guaranteeing space for further mediation until the beginning of spring. Hence, in early January, before the Racak massacre took place, the members of the Contact Group started a process of informal soundings about the prospects of success for an accelerated move towards a negotiated interim settlement. The idea of a concerted push for such a settlement within a short period of time along the lines of the Dayton conference on Bosnia and Herzegovina was mooted within the Contact Group and, cautiously, in relation to representatives of both sides or other persons in contact with either party. As one diplomat put it at the time, 'We cannot afford failure—that would be too embarrassing; we need a guarantee of success'.

Kosovo indicated that it would be prepared to participate in such a conference, provided that the question of status was not addressed and that the result would be a genuine interim agreement. Yugoslavia, while reiterating its willingness to engage in direct talks with a Kosovo delegation on the basis of the eleven-point plan, expressed reservations about a conference at which the KLA 'terrorists' would be represented. There were also doubts about the obvious international-ization which an international conference would bring to what Yugoslavia con-sidered an internal matter of the Serbian Republic. Hence, there was no advance guarantee of success. In fact, when Contact Group political directors met in London on 22 January to lay the groundwork for the conference, there was not even an assurance that both parties would definitely turn up to such an event.

To increase pressure upon the parties to attend and come to an agreement, it would have been preferable to obtain a Chapter VII resolution, requiring con-structive participation of both delegations in conjunction with a further threat of force from NATO. However, even after the Racak massacre, it was judged unlikely that such direct and significant involvement of the Council would be acceptable to some of its members. Nevertheless, it did prove possible to involve the United Nations, and to some extent Russia, in the unorthodox project of the Rambouillet conference.

On 26 January, Secretary of State Albright met Russian Foreign Minister Igor Ivanov. They issued a Joint Statement, declaring that 'the sides in Kosovo must work harder to achieve an interim political settlement providing substantial autonomy for Kosovo and should engage in meaningful intensive negotiations for that purpose'.[1] The wording was carefully chosen. The term 'meaningful' reflected a demand for talks bringing about real results. 'Intensive' referred to the idea of obtaining such a result within a short and defined space of time. Finally, the use of the word 'negotiations' indicated that the time for shuttle diplomacy had now passed and that a more direct format of discussions was required. In terms of substance, Russia was reassured by a further reiteration of the determin-ation that 'a settlement should respect the territorial integrity and sovereignty of the FRY', which was once again added to the formula of 'substantial autonomy for Kosovo'. There was no indication of any NATO threat of force, however.

Further consultations were then held within NATO, which, two days later, expressed its support for an 'early conclusion of a political settlement under the mediation of the Contact Group, which will provide an enhanced status for Kosovo, preserve the territorial integrity of the Federal Republic of Yugoslavia and protect the rights of all ethnic groups'.[2] That day, the United Nations Secretary-General took the unusual step of giving a statement to the North Atlantic Council at NATO Headquarters, linking together the efforts of the Alliance, the Contact Group, and the UN. That statement was quite strongly worded, drawing upon 'our experience in the Bosnian war' and indicating that the situation in Kosovo was now no longer one where 'horror threatens', but instead where 'it is present, in the lives of hundreds of thousands of the people of

---

[1] Joint Statement by Secretary of State Albright and Russian Foreign Minister Ivanov, 26 January 1999, in Weller, *Crisis in Kosovo*, 414.
[2] Statement to the Press by Dr Javier Solana, 28 January 1999, in Weller, *Crisis in Kosovo*, 414.

Kosovo whose lives have been disrupted violently'.[3] The Secretary-General even appeared to endorse a threat of force by NATO, when targeting his words at 'particularly those with the capacity to act' (in other words, NATO) and referring to the 'need to use force, when all other means have failed'.

B. The Contact Group and NATO decisions

On 29 January, the Contact Group issued its summons to the parties to negotiate.[4] This statement was remarkable in several respects. In terms of substance, it 'insists' that a settlement must be based on principles established by the Contact Group. Those principles were contained in the Hill drafts which, according to the Contact Group, merely required refining on a limited number of points. Of course, at that stage both sides had rejected the Hill draft and elements of the basic approach which underpinned it. In terms of process, the six governments summoned the parties to Rambouillet within a week, to negotiate a settlement with direct involvement of the Contact Group, in principle within a further week. If progress was insufficient, the talks could be extended for a further period of less than a week. The Contact Group concluded by reiterating that negotiations would have to be completed within a total of twenty-one days from the date of its summons: '[t]he Contact Group will hold both sides accountable if they fail to take the opportunity now offered to them.' The Security Council immediately declared in a presidential statement that it 'welcomes and supports' the decisions of the Contact Group.[5] In language reminiscent of a Chapter VII resolution (but not contained in one), it 'demands that all parties should accept their responsibilities and comply fully with these decisions and requirements'.

The somewhat ambiguous determination of the Contact Group to hold both sides accountable was rephrased more aggressively by the North Atlantic Council (NAC) the following day. On the one hand, the NAC reiterated that force might be used in order to obtain compliance with the Holbrooke agreement, in particular, the cessation of hostilities, the reduction and redeployment of Yugoslav military and paramilitary forces and the termination of the excessive and disproportionate use of force by them. On the other hand, NATO added a further requirement, namely a positive response to the demand that a political settlement be achieved within the framework established by the Contact Group. In support of these aims, the 'Council has therefore agreed today that the NATO Secretary-General may authorize air strikes against targets on FRY territory'.[6]

---

[3] Statement by Kofi Annan, 28 January 1999, in Weller, *Crisis in Kosovo*, 414–5.
[4] Contact Group Statement, 29 January 1999, in Weller, *Crisis in Kosovo*, 415–6.
[5] Security Council Presidential statement, 29 January 1999, in Weller, *Crisis in Kosovo*, 416.
[6] Statement by the North Atlantic Council on Kosovo, 30 January 1999, in Weller, *Crisis in Kosovo*, 416.

C. Justification for the threat of the use of force

As was the case when NATO issued its original threat of the use of force which resulted in the Holbrooke agreement of October 1998, the threat raised diffi-cult questions in international law.[7] On the face of it, the action appeared incon-sistent with a key pillar of the international constitutional order contained in Article 2(4) of the United Nations Charter. That provision, which enjoys the highest legal authority and applies to all states under all circumstances, prohibits not only the use, but also the threat of the use, of force. In its Advisory Opinion on the Legality of the Threat or Use of Nuclear Weapons, the International Court of Justice had held only a few years earlier:

> Whether a signalled intention to use force if certain events occur is or is not a 'threat' within Article 2, paragraph 4, of the Charter depends upon various factors. If the envis-aged use of force is itself unlawful, the stated readiness to use it would be a threat prohib-ited under Article 2, paragraph 4. Thus, it would be illegal for a State to threaten force to secure territory from another State, or to cause it to follow or not follow certain political or economic paths. The notions of 'threat' and 'use' of force under Article 2, paragraph 4, of the Charter stand together in the sense that if the use of force itself in a given case is illegal—for whatever reason—the threat to use such force will likewise be illegal.[8]

While NATO was not aiming to secure territory, it was clearly determined to cause Yugoslavia to follow a certain political path. Of course, NATO had been careful to tailor its threat to match demands which had been established by the United Nations Security Council. Initially, in October, NATO's aims reflected the Chapter VII demands contained in Resolutions 1160 (1998) and 1199 (1998). These resolutions had been adopted pursuant to a formal finding that the situation in Kosovo constituted a threat to international peace and security and required, inter alia, the cessation of armed action and repression by Yugoslav military and paramilitary forces, their withdrawal and the commencement of substantive dia-logue on a political settlement. With the conclusion of the Holbrooke agreement, the Alliance could also rely upon Chapter VII Resolution 1203 (1998), which endorsed the deal brokered by the US emissary. That deal itself had included a Serbian undertaking to accept a settlement by November 1998.

D. Absence of an express Security Council mandate to threaten or use force

A finding by the Security Council that a situation constitutes a threat to inter-national peace and security confirms that the matter can no longer be considered an internal one. Demands issued by the Council under Chapter VII are legally binding and require immediate and unconditional compliance. But neither of

---

[7] See Chapter 7, Section 2.   [8] 1996 (I) ICJ 246.

these two elements taken individually, nor both of them taken together, amount to a legal authorization for third states to intervene forcibly, or to implement the demands of the Council through the threat or use of force. In fact, when adopting Resolution 1203 (1998), the Council cautiously emphasized this fact by including an unusual preambular paragraph which stated that, under the Charter of the United Nations, 'primary responsibility for the maintenance of international peace and security is conferred on the Security Council'.

One might perhaps argue that the Council had already exercised its prerogative when it welcomed the decision of the Contact Group to summon the parties to the conference at Rambouillet in its Presidential Statement. The statement clearly endorsed the project as one that was fully in accordance with its previous, repeated calls for negotiations on a political settlement within a short time frame. In fact, the statement may have elevated this request and turned it into a requirement; previous resolutions had used a slightly less mandatory form of words. It 'calls upon' the parties to enter into meaningful dialogue, possibly indicating that this step was merely recommended. In past practice, the Council has been very reluctant to involve itself through the application of Chapter VII powers in the actual settlement of disputes, especially self-determination disputes.

However, Resolution 1160 (1998) had already listed the commencement of substantive dialogue as one of the conditions (in fact the first) which would have to be fulfilled before a lifting of the newly imposed United Nations sanctions could be considered. Hence, it appears that the Council did indeed intend to impose upon the parties a binding obligation to negotiate from the beginning. To that was added, in Resolution 1199 (1998), the requirement of a 'clear timetable, leading to an end of the crisis and to a negotiated political solution to the issue of Kosovo'. In Resolution 1203 (1998), finally, the Council called for implementation of Yugoslavia's commitment, given in the context of the Holbrooke agreement, to complete negotiations by 2 November 1998. This deadline not having been met, the Presidential Statement of 29 January 1999 not only welcomed and supported the decision of the Contact Group of the same day, but also 'demands that the parties should accept their responsibilities and comply fully with these decisions and requirements'.

As this 'demand' was not enshrined in a Chapter VII resolution, it is not possible to argue that it constituted, in itself, an enforcement decision through which the Council directly adopted the Contact Group decision as its own and turned it into a legal obligation, binding upon the parties according to Articles 24, 25 and 103 of the Charter, requiring the parties to attend the talks and reach a settlement. Still, the same result was achieved in a slightly less direct way. Through its Presidential Statement, the Council confirmed its understanding that compliance with the decision of the Contact Group would be required in fulfilment of its previous resolutions. In other words, having been unable to engage in meaningful and successful dialogue over the past year, and given the progressively deteriorating situation, the Council now recognized that constructive participation in the Rambouillet talks would be the only means of fulfilling its previous, more general requirements in this respect. In this circuitous way therefore, the Council endorsed the Contact Group's decision to the full. This is not altogether surprising, inasmuch as Russia was part of the Contact Group which had taken the initial decision now supported by the Council.

E. No express retroactive approval from the Security Council for regional action

NATO's claim to act in support of the aims, not only of the Contact Group, but also of the 'international community' as a whole, in backing the summons to negotiate is therefore not entirely unfounded. Nevertheless, it is one thing to offer political support to a decision which has the backing of the Security Council and another to threaten or use force in order to obtain compliance with that decision. Of course, it might be argued that the Presidential Statement also implied retroactive authorization granted to a regional agency, in place of a formal Chapter VII or Chapter VIII mandate granted in advance.[9] While such informal action has no formal basis in the United Nations Charter, it is in fact established in practice, as recent episodes of regional action in relation to Liberia and Sierra Leone have demonstrated. However, in view of the rather ambiguous formulation adopted by the Contact Group ('will hold both sides accountable') and given the known reluctance to intervene in the domestic affairs of states and the potential use of force of individual members of the Council, legislative intent directed towards the granting of such an informal mandate appears unlikely. The response of some members of the Council after the outbreak of hostilities in March 1999 bears this out. Moreover, the Council Statement followed upon the Contact Group decision, but preceded the NATO decision. It is not clear how the Council could retroactively approve that which had not yet happened.

F. No implied enforcement authority for NATO

Still, NATO's decision was targeted towards the implementation of aims established by the Security Council, and the Alliance claimed it was not threatening the use of force for its own purposes but on behalf of the international community as a whole. It was acting, as it were, as the enforcement agent of the Security Council, albeit a self-appointed one. However, this argument, too, is unpersuasive. After all, only a few months earlier, the members of the Security Council had strongly opposed United States and United Kingdom armed action against Iraq. That action had purportedly been undertaken to enforce demands made

---

[9] In fact, NATO does not formally consider itself a regional organization, although it has exercised mandates typically bestowed upon regional organizations when acting under Council authority in relation to Bosnia and Herzegovina.

by the Security Council relating to Baghdad's obligation to cooperate with UN arms inspectors. Indeed, in that instance, the binding Chapter VII character of the requirements of the Council which were to be enforced was even more clearly established. Nevertheless, the thesis that states or groups of states can bestow upon themselves the authority to use force in pursuit of aims enunciated by the United Nations was rightly rejected.[10]

G. Forcible humanitarian action

While the decisions taken by the Security Council were not in this instance sufficient to justify the threat of force issued by NATO, they were still useful in this context for they added credibility to the final line of argument which could be deployed, again in accordance with the practice evident in the October episode: forcible humanitarian action. As will be considered at greater length in the next chapter, humanitarian 'intervention' is seen by some as a further exception to the prohibition of the use of force in international law. It permits the application of force in response to significant and widespread violations of human rights in a foreign territory, at least when such violations have generated an overwhelming humanitarian emergency. A more advanced view argues that forcible humanitarian action can only occur in very limited circumstances, where a government or effective authority can no longer conceivably claim the exclusive power to represent a population or a constitutionally significant segment thereof. For example, where a government exterminates a large segment of its own population, denies a population that which is necessary for its survival or forcibly displaces it, that government is no longer legally entitled to oppose international action on behalf of that population. Instead, in such circumstances of fundamental dissociation between government and population, the United Nations Security Council, regional organizations or states and alliances can act directly on behalf of the threatened population.[11]

The North Atlantic Council decision of 30 January was at great pains to link the purported aims of the international community, as they had been specifically formulated, to humanitarian need:

The crisis in Kosovo remains a threat to peace and security in the region. NATO's strategy is to halt the violence and support the completion of negotiations on an interim political settlement for Kosovo, *thus averting a humanitarian catastrophe* [emphasis added].

---

[10] In fact, the United Kingdom at least appeared somewhat uncomfortable with this argument, preferring to rely instead on the equally unpersuasive assertion that violation of ceasefire Resolution 687 (1991) had revived the forcible mandate granted to states cooperating with the government of Kuwait in the liberation of that state in 1990.

[11] It is, of course, not possible to reproduce here in full the debate about the legality of humanitarian 'intervention'. However, this question will be addressed in greater detail in Chapter 8. On the theory of fundamental dissociation see Marc Weller, 'Access to Victims: Reconceiving the Right to Intervene', in Wybo P. Heere (ed.), *International Law and The Hague's 750th Anniversary* (The Hague: Kluwer, 1999), 353.

Even for those who support the doctrine of humanitarian 'intervention' in international law, this assertion does not in itself provide full justification for the threat of force in this instance. The doctrine of forcible humanitarian action establishes strong criteria which must be fulfilled before force can be applied. While these criteria—and indeed the existence of a doctrine of humanitarian 'intervention' in international law—are still disputed, one might argue that the threat or use of force for humanitarian purposes must meet the following requirements:[12]

- there must have arisen a fundamental dissociation between population and purported government, manifested by an actual or imminent humanitarian catastrophe of significant proportions;
- this fact must have been identified by a best-placed, competent and objective international agency;
- the action taken must be appropriate, necessary and proportionate; and
- the action must be carried out subject to the requirements of transparency, Security Council review and accountability.

In October, the forced displacement of 300,000 civilians from Kosovo as a result of the military and paramilitary operations of Belgrade was evidence of fundamental dissociation.[13] In other words, the Belgrade government could, at that moment, no longer claim to be fully and exclusively competent to represent internationally the very people it was disenfranchising and persecuting on such a massive scale in Kosovo. Instead, international action could be taken directly on behalf of that population to the extent necessary to preserve it from destruction.

The United Nations Security Council itself had authoritatively identified the situation as a threat to international peace and security, and had established the minimum requirements necessary in order to remedy that threat (cessation of repression, withdrawal of Yugoslav/Serbian military and paramilitary forces, and an expeditious settlement). NATO's threat of force was tailored precisely with the goal of achieving these minimum aims. By January, however, it was argued by some that the emergency had subsided, that most of the displaced had returned to their villages and those unable to return had managed to find shelter over the winter elsewhere. In actual fact, there remained no fewer than 200,000 displaced people in Kosovo and abroad, and the latest round of fighting had already led to renewed displacement of approximately 30,000 people.

H. Preventative humanitarian action

It could therefore be argued that NATO action was in fact a response to a veritable humanitarian emergency. Alternatively, it could be argued that the action anticipated one. The violations by Belgrade of the Holbrooke Agreement, consisting of a renewed use of disproportionate and excessive force against civilians and

[12] See above, pp. 98–100 [13] See above, p. 68.

interference with the Verification Mission, were seen to presage developments which would inevitably lead to a renewed exodus of refugees. In this light, NATO action is accorded a preventative, rather than a palliative, character.

Preventative humanitarian operations can be lawful, provided it is clear that an overwhelming emergency will necessarily arise unless international action is taken. For example, in 1992 an international coalition of states imposed, through the threat of use of force, an aerial exclusion zone over southern Iraq. This action was taken after reliable information had been obtained from an objective and best-placed international agency, which confirmed that the Shiite population of southern Iraq was under imminent threat of a military assault from the Baghdad regime. This limited, preventative action did not trigger significant international criticism.[14]

In the case of Kosovo, the international community appeared to be witnessing a repetition of the practice which had brought about the initial emergency in 1998. Given that experience, it was clear that another displacement crisis of similar proportions—this time under the harsh conditions of mid-winter—would have catastrophic humanitarian consequences. The first requirement for preventative humanitarian action was therefore met, and a good case can be made that a humanitarian crisis of some proportion was in fact already underway.

I. Authoritative determination of an actual or imminent humanitarian emergency

The second requirement for lawful humanitarian action was also met. In order to minimize the risk of abuse of the doctrine of humanitarian action by states for their own purposes, the existence of an actual or imminent emergency of sufficient intensity to generate dissociation between population and government must be confirmed by competent, best-placed and objective international agencies. 'Competent' means that the agencies in question must have a constitutional mandate and recognized expertise in evaluating situations of this kind. 'Best-placed' requires that the agency be in a position to judge the concrete circumstances of the particular emergency. Furthermore, to avoid the allegation of bias, the agency must not represent a particular state, group of states or interest group. Instead, it must have a track record of reliably assessing similar cases on their merits.

Here, the OSCE verifiers, a host of humanitarian organizations and the Security Council itself, through its Presidential Statement of 29 January, confirmed the existence of an imminent humanitarian disaster evidencing a fundamental dissociation between population and government.[15]

---

[14] This development is chronicled in Marc Weller, *Iraq and Kuwait: The Hostilities and Their Aftermath* (Cambridge: Grotius, 1993), 723ff.

[15] Security Council Presidential Statement, 29 January 1999, in Weller, *Crisis in Kosovo*, 416.

J. Appropriate, necessary, and proportionate action

Humanitarian action must be appropriate, in that the action taken must be capable of achieving the desired humanitarian objective. It must be necessary inasmuch as no means other than the threat of use of force must be available to this end, all other options having been exhausted. And it must meet the criterion of proportionality, that is to say, the injury done to the target state must not outweigh the humanitarian good that is being pursued.

The assertion that the achievement of a political settlement was appropriate, necessary and proportionate in order to avert a humanitarian disaster may have been somewhat daring—it was certainly an innovative extension of the doctrine of humanitarian 'intervention'. There had been previous instances when the Security Council had mandated complex United Nations peace support operations, which would include an attempt to bring the parties to a settlement and to reconstruct the constitutional structure of civil society in a state which had suffered from prolonged internal strife. However, in this instance, there was no direct Council mandate; the settlement was to be obtained by a self-selected group of states (the Contact Group, backed by the Alliance) and the terms of the settlement, it appeared, were to be imposed upon the parties, at least in a broad sense. The direct and unambiguous threat of the use of force to obtain acceptance of such a settlement was entirely unprecedented in post-UN Charter history and in some ways reminiscent of the exercise of great power diplomacy in the classical balance of power system of the post-Napoleonic Concert of Europe.

Of course, in this instance, the states involved did not really pursue classical hegemonic policies. Instead, they acted—quite reluctantly—to counter the threat of a humanitarian catastrophe. They may also have been propelled into action by the hope of saving that area of Europe from a military confrontation which might spread beyond Kosovo to Albania and Macedonia and, ultimately, perhaps others. However, this additional motivation does not undermine or necessarily taint the declared humanitarian objective.[16] Still, the question remains as to whether a right of humanitarian action can extend beyond military measures which are directly related to the protection of a civilian population from significant and widespread actual or imminent harm and which were strictly necessary, all peaceful alternatives having been exhausted.

The initial threat of force in October was aimed at terminating the excessive use of force by Yugoslav military and paramilitary forces, by imposing a cessation of hostilities. It is difficult to dispute that cessation of the very acts which were directly causing the refugee flow was strictly necessary in order to terminate the humanitarian emergency and that the threat of the use of force was an appropriate

---

[16] In fact, the threat to peace and stability in the wider region might be considered an independent source of authority to act. However, only the Security Council, acting directly or through a regional organization or arrangement, can authorize forcible responses to such abstract threats.

means of seeking to achieve this aim. Hence, given the failure of other options, and in view of the urgency of the situation, it was legally defensible as a forcible humanitarian action. The ceasefire was to be stabilized by a withdrawal of forces to the level held before the Yugoslav spring offensive of 1998 and by essentially cantoning some of the remaining troops. Again, in view of the treatment which the civilian Albanian population of Kosovo had received, and also in view of the record of Yugoslav actions in Bosnia and Herzegovina, this demand also appears to have been necessary in order to reverse the humanitarian consequences of Belgrade's actions. But was it also reasonable to claim, as NATO did in January, that the acceptance of the Contact Group plan for Kosovo, then encapsulated in the Hill proposals, was strictly necessary to avert a humanitarian catastrophe? And did such a demand not impose upon Belgrade requirements which may have been disproportionate to the purported aim of a strictly humanitarian act?

K. A political settlement as a humanitarian necessity?

Justification for such an expansive approach can only be found in the overall context of this episode. NATO would draw attention to the prolonged and repeated history of ethnic cleansing and perhaps even genocide perpetrated by the government in Belgrade, first in Croatia, then in Bosnia and Herzegovina, and finally in Kosovo. A peaceful attempt to rein in Yugoslav practices had been made in relation to Kosovo since 1992, when it was hoped that the situation could be stabilized through the presence of the OSCE long-term monitoring mission and the parallel negotiations track flowing from the London conference of the summer of 1992. However, Yugoslavia had unilaterally terminated the OSCE presence in Kosovo and the Geneva negotiating track had never been pursued in earnest by Belgrade. Other attempts to arrest the situation of perennial crisis and replace it with political accommodation had also failed, whether driven by non-governmental intercession, such as the St Eugidio initiative,[17] or the formal process of Ambassador Hill's shuttle diplomacy.[18]

The more intrusive and coercive attempt to avert a humanitarian emergency through the initial NATO threat followed by the Holbrooke agreement, with its restrictions on permitted numbers, locations and activities of Yugoslav military and paramilitary forces, also appeared to have failed. And Yugoslavia's pledge in October to facilitate a political settlement within weeks had not been fulfilled, notwithstanding the demands of the Security Council. In fact, the Council had found a settlement to be a necessary condition for the restoration of peace and stability in the region. Hence, NATO could argue that the only remaining avenue for addressing this persistent crisis and its likely humanitarian implications was finally to insist on the achievement of a settlement under international auspices within a very short period of time, before more widespread fighting erupted anew.

---

[17] See above, p. 50.   [18] See above, Chapter 6.

Such a settlement would need to be guaranteed through an effective international implementation presence. Whether the requirement to reach such a settlement was reasonable, or necessary and proportionate, must depend on the actual content of the proposals put forward at Rambouillet, and the process through which agreement in relation to them was achieved.

II. The Conference Process

A. Enforced negotiations

The Rambouillet conference is an odd example of enforced negotiations. As already noted, the presence of Yugoslavia at the talks was to be ensured through the threat of the use of force. Yugoslavia responded to this threat with a formal protest, seeking the protection of the United Nations Security Council.[19] It subsequently compared the Rambouillet process to the Munich conference on Czechoslovakia.[20] Nevertheless, Yugoslavia received United Kingdom Secretary of State for Foreign Affairs Robin Cook and the 'Contact Group Non-Negotiable Principles/Basic Elements' for the talks that he brought with him. In spite of hesitations relating to the presence of KLA representatives at Rambouillet, Yugoslavia decided to participate in the conference and, indeed, attempted vigorously to engage the Kosovo delegation, including the KLA, in direct negotiations. Moreover, Yugoslavia formally accepted the 'Non-Negotiable Principles' during the conference process.

In fact, in many respects, the Non-Negotiable Principles bear a striking similarity to the eleven-point declaration on a settlement made unilaterally by Belgrade on 13 October in the context of the Holbrooke agreement. That declaration was, of course, itself formulated within the context of the initial threat of force by NATO. However, it effectively summarized the points of agreement between the Hill proposals, which had been formulated on behalf of the Contact Group, and Belgrade's position. Hence, the threat of force may have been effective in requiring Yugoslavia to attend a conference with a view to achieving a settlement quickly. However, the terms that were to be 'imposed' upon the parties were largely concomitant with Belgrade's own proposals and with the minimum demands of the Security Council, at least at a level of general principle contained in the Non-Negotiable Basic Elements.

The extent of the efficacy of the threat of force in relation to Yugoslavia can perhaps also be judged in light of the final outcome of the conference. After all, Belgrade ultimately refused to sign the overall agreement which emerged from the talks, in full knowledge of the possible consequences. Thus, decisions made

[19] Letter of 1 February 1999, in Weller, *Crisis in Kosovo*, 418.
[20] Speech by Professor Suy, Counsel and Advocate for Yugoslavia, in the International Court of Justice, CR99/14, 10 May 1999.

by the Yugoslav leadership did not seem to be dependent on the threat. Perhaps in the knowledge of this fact, the negotiations were actually conducted in a way which made very significant concessions to Yugoslavia, in order to obtain its relatively freely given consent.

Yugoslavia was aware of the doubtful credibility of the threat of force. NATO had worked very hard not to have to implement it in October. After the Racak massacre and other significant violations of the terms of the Holbrooke agreement, NATO dispatched its military leaders to Belgrade to demonstrate decisiveness, but no action was forthcoming and the mission may well have proved counter-productive. Whether the political resolve and unity of the NATO states would be sufficient even to launch air strikes in response to Belgrade's failure to sign an agreement was by no means clear. Even if strikes were to be launched, they were likely to be limited and symbolic, targeting relatively isolated military infrastructure assets—more appeared unlikely at that stage, given the hesitations of Italy, Germany, Greece, and others. After all, NATO had committed itself to a graduated plan of military action, which required the consensus of the North Atlantic Council at each stage of escalation. Thus, it appeared that Yugoslavia would be able to absorb whatever strikes might be launched without great sacrifice. Once air strikes had occurred without great impact on the Belgrade leadership, NATO would have played and lost its trump card. Yugoslavia could then have mounted a gradual campaign against the KLA, while offering a settlement on its own terms. Given NATO's offensive military action, its role, or rather the role of NATO members in the Contact Group, could have been minimized in the context of such a settlement. After all, it would have appeared unreasonable to accept as neutral mediators, or as participants in a weakened verification mission, the very forces which only a short time before had been involved in an armed attack against Yugoslavia.

The situation of Kosovo was somewhat different. In principle, the threat of the use of force also applied to it, or perhaps more specifically, to the KLA. In reality, however, it was clear that NATO would not really be able to use military force against a grassroots armed movement such as the KLA, which possessed little in the way of heavy armament or installations that could be easily subjected to air strikes. The military threat against the KLA was therefore an indirect one. NATO states would take effective steps to inhibit further funding of its operations from the ethnic Albanian diaspora around the world, especially from the US and Germany (and, if possible, neutral Switzerland). In a bid to shut down its support network abroad, the KLA would be declared a 'terrorist' organization and legally pursued accordingly. Secondly, pressure would be applied to Albania to close the logistical and training facilities that it was allegedly granting to the KLA. NATO might even patrol the Albania–Kosovo and Macedonia–Kosovo borders, in an attempt to inhibit the continued supply of men and equipment to the organization. It is not clear that such action would have been fully effective, given the nature of the terrain, even if it had been possible to force Tirana to accept such a step. However, if implemented, this would have significantly reduced the KLA's effectiveness as a fighting force. In fact, the organization would probably have had to abandon its ambition of functioning as an organized underground army capable of engaging Yugoslav military and paramilitary forces, and instead would have had to resort to 'terrorist' tactics against the Serbian infrastructure in the territory—a fact which had not escaped its leadership, which was keenly interested in developing the profile of a legitimate political movement.

More damaging still was NATO's political threat. If Kosovo refused to go along with the Rambouillet project, NATO states, including the US, would simply declare the situation hopeless and withdraw their involvement in the crisis. Given the reality of the military situation vis-à-vis Yugoslavia, Kosovo's only hope was to even the odds on the political field through strong international involvement. To lose the element of 'internationalization' of the crisis would have meant a far greater disaster for its leadership than any military reversals. In that sense, the NATO threat and the Contact Group summons represented a grave risk for Kosovo. There really was no option but to participate in the conference. However, being by far the weaker party in the negotiations, participation might well have resulted in an agreement fundamentally inconsistent with the requirements of Kosovo—an agreement Kosovo would not be in a position to reject, but which it would also probably not be able to deliver on, given the position of the KLA.

B. Structural inequality

Kosovo's concerns were reinforced by the structural inequality of the parties. Yugoslavia's insistence on the maintenance of its continued sovereignty and territorial integrity had, from the beginning, been shared by the Security Council, the Contact Group and practically all other agencies involved in the crisis. After all, these two principles were cornerstones of the international order in which all governments had a stake and which none wished to see undermined. The language emphasizing a level of self-governance for Kosovo and the restoration of human rights as the principal aim of a negotiating effort appeared to Kosovo to betray a lack of appreciation of the situation. Yugoslavia had demonstrated over a decade that its human rights practices were unlikely to be constrained by still further international obligations. Promises of self-governance also seemed to ring hollow. Even when Serbia was one of eight republics and autonomous provinces in the Socialist Federal Republic, it had been able unilaterally to modify and then abolish Kosovo's autonomy. Now, with Yugoslavia consisting merely of two republics and that rump Federation being dominated by Serbia, it was feared that a regime for self-governance would be easily undermined by Belgrade.

It was also noted that the international community consistently referred to a restoration of self-governance, or 'meaningful self-administration'. This wording appeared to be chosen to fall below the level of authority which Kosovo had enjoyed as an autonomous province. Hence, it appeared that Serbia's usurpation of authority and the removal of Kosovo's direct federal status would now be legit-imized internationally and a lesser status of self-administration within Serbia would be imposed. To Kosovo's leadership, even full restoration of autonomy was insufficient, in view of the sacrifices its population had made over the past decade and given the absence of a strong federal system which might have pro-tected Kosovo's exercise of autonomous powers from Serbia's desire to restore its supremacy. The attachment of the international community to the principles of territorial integrity and sovereignty therefore made it unlikely that the conference would produce anything which might be acceptable to Kosovo's increasingly radicalized constituents at home.

C. Procedure

Belgrade's eleven-point plan of 13 October had been adopted by the Contact Group, through Ambassador Holbrooke, and turned in large measure into its non-negotiable points. Kosovo had no involvement in its formulation. In fact, Kosovo never actually received a full text of the Holbrooke agreement from the Contact Group. To see the unilateral Serbian points on a political settlement reflected directly in the Non-Negotiable Principles, which had been presented to the parties after the Contact Group decision, seemed designed to reassure Yugoslavia whilst paying little regard to Kosovo's position.

The rules of the conference provided for the tabling of detailed elements of a settlement based on the Non-Negotiable Principles. The Contact Group drafts would stand, unless either party could persuade its mediators that a change was required in order to better implement a specific provision, or if both sides agreed on a change. The inequality in formulating the Non-Negotiable Principles would therefore be directly transposed into the conference proceedings through drafts based upon them, from which there was little room for deviation.

Of course, the devil is in the detail, and much would depend on the precise wording of the Contact Group drafts. The actual drafting was entrusted to a small group of highly skilled legal advisers to the three Contact Group negotia-tors, Ambassadors Hill (US), Petritsch (European Union) and Mayorski (Russia). The drafts were provided on the basis of instructions from the Contact Group and were reviewed by it.

Negotiating theory has identified a number of different models of international mediation. There can be entirely neutral mediators, or there may be one or more 'committed' mediators who have a special and long-standing relationship with one of the parties. The strong links between the United States and Israel serve as an example of the latter in the context of Middle Eastern peace negotiations. In this instance, Russia clearly acted as a 'committed' mediator on the side of Yugoslavia, threatening to disrupt the Contact Group consensus should pro-posals be adopted which appeared inconsistent with Belgrade's basic position. Russia's assumed role as the advocate of Yugoslavia also extended beyond internal

Contact Group discussions and was felt very strongly in the actual negotiations. The nuanced differences between the negotiators' statements at the joint press conferences given during the Rambouillet talks provided faint but visible evidence of this fact.[21]

While Russia acted as Yugoslavia's advocate, its attitude was nevertheless consistently praised by the other members of the Contact Group. The expectation was that Russia would fight Belgrade's corner, and would thus be in a position to persuade the Milosevic government to sign. As will be evident from what follows, in accordance with this plan, the original Contact Group draft was changed significantly so as to persuade Yugoslavia to accept the Rambouillet package. However, in the end, neither these concessions nor Russia's attitude were able to deliver acceptance.

On the other hand, no state within the Contact Group could be considered a 'committed' mediator on behalf of Kosovo, at least at the outset. Instead of seeking to advance Kosovo's position, the other members of the Contact Group acted according to what they regarded as a reasonable compromise when approving or modifying drafts for discussions among the parties. Only towards the conclusion of the Rambouillet conference, when Kosovo appeared unwilling to accept the package on offer, did the United States change tack and start to defend the position of Kosovo to some extent.

D. The initial phase of negotiations

The conference opened at the ancient Chateau Rambouillet on 6 February 1999. The inequality of the parties found symbolic expression in the fact that for a long and anxious period the Belgrade government refused to allow the Kosovo delegation to leave for Paris. However, rather than intimidating the Kosovars, these fretful hours spent awaiting transport actually forced the disparate Kosovo delegation closer together and gave its members a first opportunity to attempt to find some cohesion. This tentative unity was evident when the entire delegation refused to leave without the KLA delegates, as demanded by Yugoslavia.

Once both delegations had arrived safely at the chateau, they were issued with special conference badges. While security badges ordinarily provide access to a conference site, in this instance they indicated to the French security forces guarding the chateau that those unfortunate enough to wear them would not be permitted to leave the grounds, which were surrounded by heavy iron fences. Apparently the plan had been to isolate both delegations from the oxygen of publicity. At the Dayton conference, where a similar policy was attempted with greater success, it had been possible to isolate the delegations to some extent from their constituencies and political headquarters at home.

---

[21] See the materials reproduced in '*The Proceedings of the Rambouillet Conference*', Weller, *Crisis in Kosovo*, section 15.B.

Rambouillet, of course, was different in several respects. It was not located in the isolated vastness of Ohio. Instead, the centre of Paris was just a thirty-minute ride away on the local transport system. The mobile telephone infrastructure of Western Europe provided for direct communication links to the Balkans and to the editorial offices of the *New York Times* and other media present in Paris. However, the crucial difference lay elsewhere. In the case of Dayton, the international community had managed to persuade Slobodan Milosevic, after sustained use of force in Bosnia and Herzegovina, that his position in that territory was crumbling. By August/September 1995, the military forces of the Bosnian Serbs were demoralized by NATO attacks against their infrastructure. Precisely at that moment, an alliance of Bosnian government and Croatian forces was starting to roll back Serbian troops on the ground, taking territory which they had held since the outbreak of hostilities in the spring of 1992. To freeze this situation and prevent further losses, President Milosevic simply abandoned the fiction of a separate Serb 'state' in Bosnia and Herzegovina, headed by Radovan Karadzic and General Ratko Mladic. He simply arrogated for himself the power to represent the 'Republika Srpska' at Dayton and personally determined its future destiny at that conference.

By contrast, at Rambouillet the situation was quite different. Yugoslavia had not been beaten on the ground and the issue of Kosovo was seen to be of far more essential interest to Belgrade than the fate of the Bosnian Serbs might have been. Belgrade had little interest in achieving a settlement which, because of international involvement, would inevitably lead to a result less favourable than the status quo. Hence, in the best possible scenario, the conference would fail, and this failure would be attributed to the Kosovo delegation. In that case, the threat of the use of force would collapse, and Yugoslavia would be left to consolidate its control over the territory.

Given this background, Milosevic did not appear in person at Rambouillet. In fact, the Yugoslav delegation styled itself as the delegation of the Republic of Serbia, led by Professor Ratko Markovic. Although the delegation had the full support of the Yugoslav Federal Foreign Ministry and was run by it, this was meant to indicate that the entire matter was really an internal affair of the Serbian Republic. Hence, the delegation at Rambouillet could negotiate for the best possible deal. The Yugoslav government could then hope to extract further concessions back in Belgrade, when it came to persuading Milosevic to sign a deal. Alternatively, Belgrade could disown any accord at which its negotiators might arrive, hoping that NATO would be lacking in its resolve to use force, or to sustain the use of force.

The Yugoslav/Serbian delegation itself was oddly composed. A significant number of representatives were in fact supposed to be delegates from Kosovo, or rather from the non-Albanian minorities in Kosovo. Picked by Belgrade, several of these delegates were, however, disowned by the ethnic groups back in Kosovo whom they purported to represent.

Nor was the composition of the Kosovo delegation without controversy. The LDK party and Ibrahim Rugova had been elected twice by an overwhelming majority. However, during 1997/8, several former supporters of Rugova had left the party, disillusioned by the lack of success of his non-violent campaign. The United Democratic Movement (LBD) in particular had attracted some important supporters. That party, led by the noted academic Rexhep Qosja, was reputed to be ideologically closer to the KLA. Like the KLA, many of its members attempted to undermine the claims to democratic legitimacy of the elected 'government' and president. In fact, bitter attacks had been mounted against the LDK leadership and its claim to have formed a government which had been active over some seven years was discounted by these groups. By the second half of 1998, when the informal group, led by the LDK under Fehmi Agani, put together a response to the successive Hill drafts, a great deal of pressure was exerted to establish a broader-based negotiating team.

At the same time, the United States was pressing for the establishment of a delegation which would include the KLA directly. It was considered too dangerous to arrive at an agreement, either through the Hill shuttle or later through the Rambouillet conference, which might be opposed by the KLA. This might put any implementation force in the position of being targeted by more radical elements of the KLA—a potential nightmare for the United States, in view of their peacekeeping experiences in Lebanon and Somalia. The 'delivery' of the KLA therefore became a key priority, whatever its credentials at the time in terms of democratic representation of the population of Kosovo. This proposed feat was not made easier by the divergence of views within the KLA on key issues. The views of its political leadership cadre may not have been at all times fully reflective of the commanders in the field, who had risen to arms at a time of national emergency and were less ideologically minded.

The Kosovo delegation consisted in the end of roughly one-third LDK representatives (including elected President Rugova and Prime Minister Bukoshi), one-third LBD and one-third KLA. In addition, there were two independents, Veton Surroi and Blerim Shala, both distinguished journalists and intellectuals. Overall, this meant that the more radical LBD and the KLA representatives dominated the delegation by two to one. Thus, instead of the elected President Ibrahim Rugova, the delegation was led by Hashim Thaci, a then 29-year-old, highly intelligent and determined KLA leader whose *nom de guerre*, 'the snake', had been earned during the previous months of confrontation. He had a reputation for great effectiveness in consolidating previously divergent views within the KLA and was viewed by the Belgrade government with particular hatred.[22]

The conference was opened on 6 February with some ceremony by the President of France, Jacques Chirac, and the two conference co-chairmen, the

---

[22] Belgrade issued wanted posters for Hashim Thaci during the Rambouillet conference and sought his arrest by Interpol.

UK and French foreign ministers Robin Cook and Hubert Vedrine. Both parties were then handed an initial draft, consisting of a framework agreement, a constitutional annex, and annexes on elections and the proposed ombudsman.[23] In fact, the completed political part of the agreement was in the hands of the mediators, but an attempt was made to keep the parties working by releasing them in a piecemeal fashion. The FRY/Serbian delegation used this ploy as an excuse to delay engagement, claiming that it would not offer comments until it had seen the entire political section of the agreement. It was made clear by the mediators that no discussions on implementation would take place, as this was reserved for a second round of discussions that had yet to be scheduled.

On the day the conference opened, a bomb exploded in Prishtina, triggering joint condemnation by both parties.[24] The negotiators considered this a promising sign of a spirit of cooperation and compromise. Both parties also issued general statements of their positions in the first days of the conference. The negotiators then reported to the outside world that the delegations had requested computers and had set to work in a business-like fashion. While computers and other conference equipment had certainly been requested, in fact it was only the Kosovo delegation which demonstrated constructive activity by devising detailed and substantive comments on the drafts which had been put forward by the Contact Group.

The members of the Yugoslav/Serbian delegation became known as the 'Tea Club', as they were seen lounging about the public areas of the castle, enjoying refreshments throughout the day. At one stage, an informal protest was made against the singing of Serbian patriotic songs deep into the night in the Yugoslav/Serbian delegation room, which disrupted the sleep of the sizeable delegations from the Contact Group, the OSCE, the EU, and others who were accommodated in the chateau and needed their sleep. However, the Serbian/FRY delegation did not relent. Instead, it requested and received a piano (this request was heartily supported by the Russian mediator), to help it while away the days and evenings. Bands of purported translators or secretaries were also brought in, to add to the jolly mood of the occasion.

While this conduct undoubtedly diminished the excellent reserves of wine and spirits that were made available to the delegations, it would be unfair to blame the Serbian/FRY delegation alone for the small scandal that would rock the French Republic as talks progressed. Newspapers soon claimed that the consumption of food and wine in the castle would very nearly bankrupt the state. In reality, the fact that the chateau also accommodated the thirsty delegations of the Contact Group states at least doubled the damage done to the wine cellar by the FRY/Serbian team. Towards the end of the second week of negotiations, the organizers

---

[23] Interim Agreement for Peace and Self-government in Kosovo, 18 February 1999, in Weller, *Crisis in Kosovo*, 421–8.

[24] Statement of Both Delegations on a Bomb Explosion in Pristina, 7 February 1999, in Weller, *Crisis in Kosovo*, 428.

cut back on the availability of refreshments. Lunches and dinners also became more modest. The splendid cheese course at the end fell prey to these measures almost entirely. However, the French sense of civilization ensured that it was not abandoned completely. The formerly impressive selection of over twenty different cheeses was now replaced by a single giant Brie. This cheese diplomacy was taken by delegates as a sign that the conference organizers now wished them to come to a more expeditious negotiating result.

In fact, the Kosovo delegation had worked quite intensively throughout. It had formed a small drafting committee, chaired by Agani and consisting of at least one representative of the LDK, the LBD and the KLA and one of the two independent members, plus one of the two external legal advisers who had placed themselves at the disposal of the delegation.[25] That committee went through the drafts which had been submitted and formulated detailed comments in a very draining process, the difficulty of which may not have been fully appreciated by the conference chairs and the negotiators. The draft comments were then subjected to very serious debate in the plenary of the entire delegation and frequently modified. The working language of the delegation was Albanian. However, it was deemed preferable to present the negotiators with an English version, rather than having to rely on the work of translators who might well have misunderstood the very nuanced formulations which had been hammered out. The process of translation was itself not without complexity.[26]

Despite these difficulties, Kosovo managed to submit substantive comments on all documents it received in the first week (an Annex on Economic issues was added on 12 February). It took great care to declare that all these documents were in principle 'acceptable', subject to a limited number of technical amendments which could be negotiated. However, throughout, Kosovo reserved its position, emphasizing that consent could only be achieved in relation to the overall package, which in its view would have had to include robust NATO-led enforcement.

On 14 March, the Contact Group foreign ministers assembled again in Paris, articulating their disappointment with the slow progress, but agreeing to extend the conference for a second week, to terminate on Saturday, 20 February at noon. The ministers also gave the negotiators 'discretion to table the remaining

---

[25] Both delegations had been issued with five revolving badges, which could be used to bring different experts into the chateau every day. This posed considerable problems for Kosovo, as the three parties were keen to introduce as frequently as possible those whom they considered to be 'their' advisers. However, after some initial dispute it was agreed that at least the two external lawyers would need to be present throughout the conference and they were exempted from the daily struggle for badges.

[26] Unfortunately, the comments on the framework agreement had been put forward orally and in Albanian at a time when the legal advisers had not yet been let into the chateau by the vigorous French security forces. As the framework agreement covered crucial issues, including the interim nature of the agreement and provisions for a final settlement, this may have meant that a few, but important, points of divergence were not noted sufficiently early by the negotiators and no discussion took place in relation to them until the very end of the conference.

annexes on the implementation of a settlement'.[27] This was somewhat odd, as it was rumoured at the time that the details of the military implementation annex had still not been fully agreed among the Contact Group and remained instead a source of some controversy. In fact, the implementation annexes were tabled just two days before the supposed final deadline of the conference, amid reports that Russia would not support their content.

The Yugoslav/Serbian delegation maintained its silence until Ambassador Hill travelled to Belgrade, together with one senior member of that delegation, for direct discussions with Milosevic.[28] This unilateral move had not been cleared with the Contact Group. EU Envoy Petritsch roused the German EU Presidency while the pair were en route to the airport, but despite a telephone protest from Foreign Minister Joshka Fischer, the mission departed without additional fellow travellers.

It appears that during those talks Yugoslavia identified the key requirements that would have to be met if its delegation was to engage in serious negotiations at Rambouillet. At that time there emerged, ten days after the conference opened and three days before its scheduled conclusion, a very lengthy FRY/Serbian document which fundamentally challenged the drafts that had been submitted thus far. While the negotiators had not responded in any way to the comments that Kosovo had furnished continually over that period, they now engaged in a feverish effort to refine the detailed Yugoslav/Serbian comments into a list of some eight crucial points which would require discussion.

E. The second phase of negotiations: the draft of 18 February and proximity talks

While the negotiators, or rather their legal experts, had spent difficult hours with the Yugoslav/Serbian delegation, attempting to hone down their voluminous comments to points that might actually be discussed, the Kosovo delegation was still not receiving any feedback whatsoever in response to its comments. An initial meeting between the Kosovo drafting committee and the Contact Group committee of legal experts on 17 February proved rather disappointing for the Kosovo delegation. According to the Contact Group legal experts, very few of the proposals put forward by the delegation seemed to offer realistic possibilities for modifying the initial draft. According to the procedures of the conference, no changes to the original Contact Group draft would be admissible unless they were accepted by the other side, or unless the negotiators were persuaded that they would better serve to implement the provisions of the original draft. There

---

[27] Chairman's Conclusion, Contact Group Meeting, Paris, 14 February 1999, in Weller, *Crisis in Kosovo*, 430–1.

[28] Kosovo protested against this violation of the isolation purportedly imposed upon the delegations. By way of compensation, Mr Thaci was also subsequently permitted to travel to Slovenia for a meeting with KLA spokesman Demaci.

had at that stage been no 'trading' of concessions by either side through the negotiators, as is customary in genuine proximity talks. Yugoslavia/Serbia appeared to
have made proposals which fell significantly outside the parameters of the initial
draft and which could not be considered proposals for its more efficient implementation. Hence it appeared that the original Contact Group proposals would
remain principally unaltered.

The following day, however, the negotiators submitted a revised draft for a political settlement. From the perspective of the Kosovo delegation, the new draft
had been fundamentally changed in accordance with demands which had apparently been put forward by President Milosevic during the Hill excursion as a
precondition for substantive participation in the talks. In essence, the new draft
reintroduced the issue of the legal status of Kosovo into the constitutional settlement, and sought to resolve it firmly in favour of Belgrade. The actual exercise of
authority by the Kosovo organs was also severely limited. A veto mechanism for
members of all national communities was also re-introduced, which would have
effectively paralysed legislative action in Kosovo. By contrast, very few of the suggestions proposed by the Kosovo delegation had been adopted.[29]

The new draft was presented by the negotiators, along with an invitation to the
parties to consider it the final version of a political settlement. This invitation was
declined by both sides. In fact, the Kosovo delegation issued a strongly-worded
protest, indicating that it considered the submission of a substantially new document two days before the scheduled conclusion of the conference—apparently as
the result of talks conducted directly with Belgrade outside of the chateau—to be
a breach of faith, and that it refused even to receive this document.[30] This gesture
was meant to communicate to the negotiators a serious warning that fundamentally changing the draft in favour of the side which had obstructed progress in the
talks until the last minute jeopardized further constructive participation from
the Kosovo delegation, which would not be in a position to accept any settlement
irrespective of its contents, and could not continue to be taken for granted. In
fact, the introduction of the new draft had infused the delegation with a feeling
of betrayal which would be very difficult to overcome in the days that followed.
Once again, it seemed to the Kosovars as if the outside world was conspiring to
deprive the ethnic Albanians of their entitlements.

However, this protest was not understood by the Contact Group as a constructive warning, and was instead severely criticized as impetuous and
ill-founded. As there appeared to be no prospect of reverting to the original
draft, the Kosovo delegation reluctantly prepared a very short non-paper of less
than a page, indicating crucial changes which would have to be made if discussions were to continue with any prospect of success. For its part, the FRY

---

[29] One exception to which the negotiators pointed frequently was the introduction of a technical commission to deal with economic claims.

[30] Statement by Kosovo, 18 February 1999, in Weller, *Crisis in Kosovo*, 444–5.

continued to demand changes on a number of key points. Hence, the day before the deadline for acceptance of the agreement, a significant number of substantive issues had not even been negotiated. Moreover, the crucial annexes on civilian and military implementation had only just been presented by the parties (or at least to the Kosovo delegation).

The reasons for the delay in presenting the military annex appear to have been two-fold. It seems that the Contact Group itself remained divided in relation to the functions, modalities and powers of NATO implementation of the agreement. In fact, Russia remained opposed to military implementation in principle, although certain understandings were reached in the end as to the presentation to the parties of the military annex. It was agreed that the draft might be put forward, but in the absence of the Russian mediator. Russia would not commit itself to its presentation on the part of the Contact Group. In addition, as it had been announced that no proposals for changes to the implementation annexes would be entertained, it may have been considered unnecessary to acquaint the parties with the contents of a document which they were expected to accept without changes, at least at this stage in the discussions.

Whatever the merits of this strategy, it had the disadvantage that the Kosovo delegation, and especially its military elements, had not had the opportunity of discussing in depth, with NATO representatives and others, the way in which the NATO annex would be interpreted in practice.[31] As the annex provided for the demilitarization of the KLA, it could not have come as a surprise to the negotiators that some reassurances as to the implications of this concept would have to be given to a delegation which was effectively dominated by the KLA and a political party close to it. Similarly, the negotiators lost the opportunity of explaining certain provisions to the FRY/Serbian side, which were later presented as evidence of entirely unacceptable demands on the part of the Contact Group, or rather NATO. This was especially true of the famous Annex B concerning military enforcement, of which more will be said later.

Despite these uncertainties, on 20 February, shortly before the expiry of the noon deadline, the parties were presented with a short document of less than a page, in which they were to indicate acceptance of the agreement, subject only to technical changes which would be made later by experts. Unfortunately, at that time the negotiators had not been able to provide the delegations with the actual text of the agreement as it stood at that time. In fact, it was known that negotiations continued with the FRY/Serbian delegation in relation to the further substantive concessions it had demanded, which were manifestly not mere technical changes.

---

[31] There had been one briefing on military implementation before the text of the security annex was made available. That briefing left the KLA and its supporters in a state of shock and was evidently not designed to reassure the military elements of the Kosovo delegation on whose consent the entire process would, ultimately, depend.

When it became obvious a few hours after the expiry of the deadline that neither the FRY delegation nor the Kosovo delegation was in a position to sign the text, the Contact Group decided to prolong negotiations until 3pm on 23 February. It was at this stage that a sense of panic set in amongst some members of the Contact Group (other than Russia). Hitherto, some of its members had watched in awe from the Contact Group office as CNN reports of the deployment of US heavy bombers to pre-strike positions began to emerge. Now, suddenly, it appeared as if the strategy of obtaining a settlement, through the threat of force if necessary, was failing spectacularly. The Western members of the Contact Group had assumed that the Kosovo delegation was fully 'on board'. The fact that they had not really been party to the negotiations was deemed irrelevant. If the Kosovars were smart, the reasoning went, they would accept any political settlement, whatever its content, provided it brought with it a withdrawal of FRY/Serbian forces and the deployment of a NATO implementation force. Under this umbrella, democratic Kosovo institutions could be established which would necessarily be dominated by ethnic Albanians, given the demographics of the region.

To the individual members of the Kosovo delegation, this logic was less persuasive. They would, after all, have to live under the terms of whatever settlement might emerge. They would be held responsible by their constituents for the result of the conference. What appeared to the Contact Group negotiators to be matters of detail, for example, provisions on economic management or voting in the Kosovo Assembly, would actually be of tremendous importance in practice. At a broader level, the Contact Group had failed to engage the Kosovo delegation in dialogue on the two issues which were known from the beginning to constitute the principal points of difficulty, namely: the demilitarization of the KLA and provisions for the period after the expiry of the interim period, in particular the uniform demand of all Kosovo parties for a referendum.

When it became known that Kosovo might not sign the draft agreement, the attention of the Contact Group, and of the US in particular, switched. Over the next few days, Secretary of State Albright spent a significant amount of time in the chateau, summoning key members of the Kosovo delegation to meetings. Encounters with Hashim Thaci, the KLA chairman of the delegation, appeared to be particularly draining. In the end, out of the sixteen-member team of the delegation, only he resisted signing the agreement. He lived through several long hours of being worked over by Albright and other senior representatives, to no avail. In the end, it became clear that the KLA had not given him the mandate to sign, and if he had done so regardless, that might well have been the end of his political life, or even of his life proper.

In this final phase, negotiations on finalizing the political settlement were now suddenly being conducted in the manner of genuine proximity talks. Substantive proposals by one side were transmitted through the group of legal experts. A number of these proposals were accepted by the other side. Where no agreement was forthcoming, the Contact Group representatives would seek to reduce the difference in the respective proposals through very tough and skilful negotiation until compromise provisions became acceptable. In this way, it was hoped that it would be possible to produce a consolidated text of the entire agreement in advance of the expected signature on 23 February.

At the insistence of the FRY/Serbian delegation, that text now no longer consisted of a brief framework agreement, tying together a number of substantive annexes. Instead, all the annexes had been incorporated into an overall document, entitled Interim Agreement for Peace and Self-Government in Kosovo. Some of the provisions from the Kosovo constitutional annex had been moved into the general introductory part of the agreement. This was meant to preclude demands from Montenegro to be accorded similar constitutional safeguards.

A belated but intensive effort was finally begun to persuade the KLA and its supporters of the merits of signing the agreement. This included briefings by military experts, including, at the very final stage of the negotiations, by NATO itself. In fact, in opposition to Russia, high-ranking NATO officials were smuggled into the chateau to offer briefings. Through these contacts, the KLA was to be assured of the actual meaning of demilitarization in practice. One government also offered to record its willingness to contribute to the transformation of the KLA in full compliance with the terms of the accords. Nevertheless, two days before the deadline, a straw poll in the Kosovo delegation resulted in a vote of seven to nine against the agreement, with only the LDK and independent members supporting signature.

An intensive diplomatic effort was then made to persuade the KLA and its supporters to change their position. Albania sent its Foreign Minister Paskal Milo to Paris. Ismail Kadare, a particularly respected Albanian novelist then residing in Paris, sent an important and emotional letter to the leader of the KLA-friendly LBD delegates, urging them to accept the draft.

On the other hand, Albanian exile groups were bombarding the delegation with demands that they refuse a settlement. The FRY/Serbia also increased pressure on the Kosovo delegation. On the ground, it launched further offensive operations leading to significant KLA losses. A request for an arrest warrant against Hashim Thaci was forwarded to Interpol and there were death threats. The FRY/Serbian delegation also reiterated its willingness to formally sign the Non-Negotiable Principles, hoping that the Kosovo delegation would find this inconvenient. An attempt would then have been made to claim that Kosovo was in fact obstructing progress. Demands for direct negotiations were also reiterated, with strong support from the Russian mediator. Such talks, it was hoped, might provoke a Kosovo walkout, shifting the blame for a failure in the negotiations. Kosovo, however, refused to depart from the format of proximity talks.

In terms of substance, a determined effort was made to address the issue of the final settlement, which would take place after an interim period of three years. This attempt was spearheaded by the United States and led to some tension in the

Contact Group. Apparently it had been agreed in the Group that on no account would there be a provision on a referendum after the expiry of the interim period. To the Kosovo delegation, however, this issue was non-negotiable. There was no point in having an interim agreement if there was no prospect of significant change after the interim. To satisfy the requirements of the Kosovo delegation, an important addition was made to the final section of the agreement, referring to 'the will of the people', rather than a referendum.

In addition, as a result of quite dramatic all-night negotiations, the US delegation offered to give bilateral assurances to the effect that this formulation did indeed refer to a right of the people of Kosovo to make manifest their will in relation to the future status of the territory through a referendum.[32] The KLA was also promised assistance in the process of 'transformation' from a military to a civil force, in the hope of inducing it to change its stance.

In the meantime, tense but quite productive proximity negotiations had continued with the FRY/Serbian side. Kosovo, now fully focused on the issue of the referendum, agreed to a number of substantive changes required by that delegation. These related to the political decision-making structure within Kosovo and the special rights of national communities. Despite grave reservations on the part of the Kosovo delegation, the reference to the 'sovereignty and territorial integrity' of the FRY had been retained, although in a slightly modified form. This, probably, was the key non-negotiable demand for the FRY/Serbian delegation. Hence, it appeared that an agreement might, after all, be possible. On the other hand, the possibility of agreement appeared to extend only to the political settlement. The FRY/Serbia still objected to any military presence in Kosovo, not to mention a NATO presence. It argued that the NATO annex had not even been approved by the Contact Group and could therefore not be discussed. It did indicate, however, that it might contemplate an 'international presence' of a civilian character. To the Kosovars, NATO implementation was of course a key element in the overall agreement. Having observed the perpetration of ethnic cleansing and genocide under the very eyes of the UN Protection Force peacekeepers in Bosnia and Herzegovina, only NATO would do.

Despite further direct intervention by US Secretary of State Albright, neither Kosovo nor the FRY/Serbian side was in a position to formally sign the agreement by the deadline of 23 February. In fact, her personal intervention had helped to sway the majority of the Kosovo delegation. This result coincided with a change in the leadership of the KLA in Kosovo itself. But Hashim Thaci was still unable to support signature.[33] As the delegation had agreed at the outset of the talks to act according to the principle of consensus, his vote made formal signature impossible at that stage.

---

[32] Draft provision for Chapter 8, 22 February 1999, in Weller, *Crisis in Kosovo*, 452.

[33] J. Smith, 'Kosovar Rebel Upset Western Strategy', *International Herald Tribune*, 25 February 1999, 6.

On the other hand, Rugova, until then not overly active in the negotiating process, quite courageously offered to sign the agreement himself, not as a member of the delegation's presidency, but in his function as the elected President of Kosovo. All this left the international mediators in a state of considerable bewilderment. They had heard of a vote of sixteen to one in favour of signature, and were sitting in the delegation room expecting a decision according to this clear vote. However, Kosovo could not sign without unanimous agreement. In the confusion which followed, a carefully drafted legal statement announcing the intention of Kosovo to sign was written on the spot in Albanian by Veton Surroi, one of the two independent members of the delegation, and under the eagle eyes of the delegation's chairman. That text was then, perhaps not entirely reliably, translated by US staff into English. A somewhat oddly formulated document emerged, in which Kosovo 'understands that it can sign the agreement in two weeks after consultations with the people of Kosova, political and military institutions'.[34] The declaration also noted that, in order to facilitate such consultations, the delegation had voted in favour of the agreement as presented in the negotiations on 23 February.

The position of the FRY/Serbian delegation was also not free of ambiguity. It was clear that there would be no signature by Belgrade, but the means and modalities of presenting this result depended very much on Kosovo's attitude. If Kosovo failed to sign and its delegation fell apart, as then seemed possible, the threat of the use of force would have been dissipated. In that case, the FRY/Serbia could give some evidence of its own constructive attitude and add further significant demands before signature could be contemplated. If, on the other hand, Kosovo signed there and then, the FRY/Serbia would need to indicate that it, too, had in principle accepted a political settlement, although the modalities of implementation would need to be discussed. This division between the political and military aspects of the agreement would undermine the resolve of the less hawkish NATO states to permit the use of force. Finally, if Kosovo requested further negotiations, then the FRY/Serbia could also display a reasonably constructive attitude, while demanding renegotiation of key aspects of the political settlement. Again, the threat of the use of force would have been dissipated.

In some ways, the evolving actions of the FRY/Serbian delegation were slightly comical. Through a Russian member of the Contact Group, the delegation was periodically updated on the latest twists and turns in the Kosovo delegation chamber, where the mood shifted minute by minute from a break-up of the delegation to the possibility of formal signature. In accordance with this conflicting information, the FRY/Serbia issued no fewer than three versions of its final statement to the Contact Group. The first version appeared when the Kosovo delegation appeared to be nearing collapse. It noted that substantial progress had been made, but also that 'we did not reach an agreement on important elements',

---

[34] Kosovo Statement, 23 February 1999, in Weller, *Crisis in Kosovo*, 471.

adding a lengthy list of points that would need be satisfied.[35] A second state-ment omitted the detailed listing of essential issues of disagreement. Instead, it merely 'pointed to eight vital issues' for the FRY/Serbia and again emphasized the need to 'extend the positive spirit of the meeting' through further talks. The FRY/Serbia also expressly agreed to a discussion of the scope and character of an 'international presence' in Kosovo to implement an agreement. The final state-ment no longer mentioned the eight essential points, but referred instead to the need to clarify the definitions contained in the agreement, so as to facilitate its actual implementation. Again, there was also an offer to discuss an international implementation presence.

Hence, in its final statement, delivered the moment US Ambassador Hill entered the Kosovo delegation room to obtain an undertaking to sign the agreement, the FRY/Serbia appeared to indicate that there had been agreement in principle on the political settlement, although some refining work had yet to be done. The issue of implementation could also be addressed, although there was reference only to an 'international presence' as opposed to an international military presence. However, this formulation was not necessarily inconsistent with the Non-Negotiable Principles of the Contact Group, which had provided for an implementation pres-ence by the OSCE 'and other international bodies as necessary'.

The acceptance, in principle, of the political aspects of Rambouillet con-trasts with the subsequent attitude of the FRY government, which claimed that Rambouillet was an entirely unacceptable diktat which would inevitably lead to the detachment of Kosovo from the Serbian motherland.

The end result of the Rambouillet conference was somewhat confusing. Kosovo argued that its delegation had in fact accepted the text as the definite outcome of the negotiations and that it would probably sign, subject to con-sultation at home. This position was taken to avoid further dilution of the text. Throughout the conference process, the text had been fundamentally revised in order to tempt the FRY/Serbia into signing. It was feared that this would now continue, outside of the conference process, perhaps through another Holbrooke mission.

This attitude was consistent with indications given by the negotiators, who had in fact invented the idea of a follow-on meeting from the Rambouillet talks as a means of preventing their collapse. In their view, a further conference would be a kind of signature conference, in accordance with the precedent set by the 1995 agreement on Bosnia and Herzegovina. While the negotiators in Dayton had initialled the texts, the document was formally signed in Paris some weeks after negotiations had been concluded. By contrast, the FRY/Serbia regarded the pro-cess of negotiations as by no means terminated.

The Contact Group then issued Chairmen's Conclusions, which were perhaps not fully reflective of the intentions of either of the parties. It was noted that a

[35] Letter, 23 February, in Weller, *Crisis in Kosovo*, 471.

political framework was now in place and that the groundwork had been laid for finalizing the implementation chapters of the agreement, including the modalities of the invited international civilian and military presence in Kosovo. As it was essential that the agreement be completed and signed as a whole, the Contact Group indicated that the parties had committed themselves to attending a further conference, covering all aspects of implementation, on 15 March.[36] Hence, it appeared that the conference would neither be a simple signature conference, nor a conference at which discussions about a political settlement would be reopened. Instead, talks were apparently intended to focus only on implementation—the very issues which had been declared to be non-negotiable throughout the entire Rambouillet process thus far.

III. The Political Interim Settlement

A. The issue of status and the basic distribution of powers

The aforementioned Non-Negotiable Principles had reflected the FRY/Serbian demand that the territorial integrity of the FRY and its neighbouring countries be respected. The Kosovars had responded that they would be willing to attend the Rambouillet talks, provided a proposed settlement would not prejudice the status of Kosovo, in accordance with the approach that had been adopted in the initial Hill proposals. The first draft of the agreement presented to the conference was in accordance with this idea of leaving out express statements on issues on which no agreement was attainable. It contained, in what started out as the Draft Framework Agreement, merely a preamble, which recalled the commitment *of the international community* to the sovereignty and territorial integrity of the FRY. Hence, in signing this text, Kosovo itself would not have had to take an express view in this matter. There was also a reference to United Nations and OSCE principles. As these contain both the principle of self-determination and the rule of territorial unity, this reference was also acceptable to Kosovo, while simultaneously reassuring the FRY/Serbia. The Constitution (initially Annex 1) did not contain a preamble and, instead of addressing the status of Kosovo and the legal quality of its relations with the FRY or even Serbia, it focused on a reasonable division of competences.

When the second draft of the agreement was presented on 18 February, a preamble had been added which referred to 'democratic self-government in Kosovo grounded in respect for the territorial integrity and sovereignty of the Federal Republic of Yugoslavia, from which the authorities of governance set forth herein originate'. While the Contact Group attempted to assert that this was an insubstantive addition, it did in fact fundamentally change the nature of the entire

---

[36] Co-Chairmen's Conclusions, 23 February 1999, in Weller, *Crisis in Kosovo*, 471.

interim settlement. To avoid a failure of the Rambouillet process on account of this unilateral change made without explanation two days before the deadline for signature, the following compromise was ultimately adopted:

Desiring through this interim Constitution to establish institutions of democratic self-government in Kosovo grounded in respect for the territorial integrity and sovereignty of the Federal Republic of Yugoslavia and from this Agreement, from which authorities of governance set forth herein originate.

Even as amended, this provision almost led the Kosovo delegation to reject the agreement. Still, the formulation permitted Kosovo to argue that acceptance of the territorial integrity and sovereignty was limited to the interim period.[37] In any event, this commitment and the legal personality and powers of Kosovo were rooted in the agreement, rather than in a grant of autonomy by the FRY.

Another important change that had been made in the draft of 18 February related to the assignment of powers. According to Article I(2) of the initial draft of what was then Annex 1, Kosovo as an entity would enjoy responsibility for 'all areas' other than those where authority was expressly assigned to the FRY. Those areas of authority were enumerated exclusively and their exercise was subjected to important restrictions and safeguards for Kosovo. In the draft of 18 February, the express presumption in favour of Kosovo authority had been abandoned. Instead, a new paragraph had been added, indicating that Serbia, too, would exercise competences in relation to Kosovo, as specified in the agreement.

The FRY/Serbia insisted firmly on the inclusion of a further provision in the introductory section of the agreement (formerly the framework agreement), stating that the parties would only act within their powers and responsibilities in Kosovo as specified by the agreement. Acts outside those powers and responsibilities would be null and void. Kosovo would have all rights and powers set forth in the agreement, in particular as specified in the Constitution. While the FRY/Serbian delegation might have intended this provision as a safeguard against creeping jurisdiction by the Kosovo organs, the delegation of Kosovo interpreted it as a helpful confirmation that the powers of Kosovo were indeed based in the agreement, and not in a sovereign grant of rights by the FRY. In addition, this formulation supported the view that FRY/Serbian exercise of powers in relation to Kosovo would be strictly limited to competences that had been expressly granted to them.[38]

The issue of legal personality for Kosovo as a whole was also clarified in some measure through a provision concerning the communes. One of the difficulties

---

[37] A proposal to entitle Chapter 1 'Interim Constitution' was not adopted. However, given the overall title of the agreement, the specific reference to the interim period in the preamble, and the concluding provisions, this was not seen by the Kosova delegation as a significant setback.

[38] Federal functions were still expressly, and in the view of Kosovo, exhaustively listed: territorial integrity, maintaining a common market within the Federal Republic of Yugoslavia, monetary policy, defence, foreign policy, customs services, federal taxation, federal elections and other areas specified in this agreement.

with the initial Hill proposal was its insistence that Kosovo communes would be the basic unit of self-governance in Kosovo and that they would exercise all authority not assigned to other Kosovo organs. While the latter element was retained,[39] it was clarified in what was to become Article I(8) of Chapter 1 of the final text, that the communes were merely the basic unit of *local* self-government. The insertion of the word 'local' ensured that this provision no longer diluted the overall legal personality of Kosovo as a whole.

B. The Kosovo institutions and their powers

According to the agreement, the principal organs of Kosovo were the Assembly, the President of Kosovo, the government and administrative organs, judicial organs and the communes.[40] The Assembly was to be composed of a hundred and twenty members, of which eighty would be directly elected. The other forty members would be elected by members of qualifying national communities. Communities whose members constituted more than 0.5 per cent of the Kosovo population but less than 5 per cent were to divide ten of these seats among themselves. Communities whose members constituted more than 5 per cent of the Kosovo population (in fact only the ethnic Albanians and Serbs) would divide the remaining thirty seats equally.

As a result of FRY/Serbian pressure, the draft of 18 February had unilaterally introduced as an additional feature a second chamber of the Assembly. In that chamber of a hundred seats, the Turks, Goranies, Romanies, Egyptians, Muslims, and any other group constituting more than 0.5 per cent of the population (hence also including the ethnic Albanians and Serbs) would be equally represented. The chamber would have had the right of consultation in relation to legislative acts of the Assembly, and any of the groups represented within it could have initiated so-called 'vital interest motions' which would amount to an attempted veto of legislation.

The FRY/Serbian delegation abandoned the concept of the second chamber and focused instead on attempting to strengthen the power of veto of national communities in the Assembly. According to the initial draft and the draft of 18 February, the decision as to which legislative acts would violate the vital interests of a national community, and would thus be null and void, would have been taken by the Constitutional Court of Kosovo. The Kosovo delegation had grave reservations about the very concept of special powers for ethnic groups, including separate elections according to ethnic criteria. While strongly endorsing the notion of equal rights for members of all ethnic groups, the idea of separate representation appeared to grant to very small groups broad rights of co-decision which were unrepresentative and hence undemocratic. Moreover, the example of

---

[39] See also Art. VIII (5) of Chapter 1, and the important reference contained therein to Art. II (5)(b) of Chapter 1.

[40] On the national communities and their institutions, see the section which follows.

ethnic politics in Bosnia and Herzegovina had demonstrated the divisive nature of ethnic organization of a political system. Finally, a legislative system which was subjected to the constant threat of a veto by any ethnic group would result in perennial paralysis.

Despite these concerns, and in view of the strong position of the FRY/Serbia in this matter, the Kosovo delegation endorsed, however reluctantly, the concept of special representation for ethnic groups for the interim period. However, this concession was dependent on a judicial process to check vital national interest motions in the Assembly, in order to avoid arbitrary use of this procedure resulting in constant deadlock in the legislature. The Contact Group disregarded this view and gave way to a Serbian/FRY proposal for settling disputes about vital national interest motions outside of the judicial system. According to Article II(8)(c) of Chapter 1, the final agreement provided that decisions about such motions would be rendered by a panel comprising three members of the Assembly: one Albanian and one Serb, each appointed by his or her national community, and a third member of a third 'nationality' to be selected within two days by consensus of the presidency of the Assembly. As the Serb national community was guaranteed a member of the presidency of the Assembly (in fact, actually the President of the Assembly), it appeared that this nominating process itself could be blocked by a factual veto.

Decisions of the Assembly which had been challenged according to the vital national interest procedure were to be suspended in regard to the national community that brought the challenge, pending completion of the dispute settlement procedure. Hence, it might appear as though a Serb veto in relation to Assembly decisions had been introduced via the back door. However, as this veto would depend on an abuse of process in frustrating the nomination of the third member of the arbitration panel, the general dispute settlement mechanism attached to the agreement as a whole, or the general powers of the Constitutional Court, would probably be brought to bear on a matter of this kind. It should also be noted that decisions on the merits of a vital interest motion, while conducted by a political body, were to be made according to legal criteria.[41]

The substantive powers of the Assembly were reasonably wide, covering most aspects of governance. Importantly, this included the power to set the framework for, and to coordinate the exercise of, competences assigned to the communes. The first elections in Kosovo were to be held within nine months of the entry into force of the agreement, under international supervision.

The President of Kosovo was to be elected by the Assembly by a majority vote. The President's functions would include representation before international, FRY or republic bodies, the conduct of foreign relations consistent with the authorities of Kosovo institutions, proposing to the Assembly candidates for Prime Minister

---

[41] A vital interest motion shall be upheld if the legislation challenged adversely affects the community's fundamental rights as set forth in Art. VII, or the principle of fair treatment.

and for the principal courts of Kosovo, and so on. The government, also to be approved by the Assembly, would have general authority for implementing the laws of Kosovo. At least one minister would be a member of the Serb national community.

In comparison with earlier drafts, the powers reserved for the communes had been narrowed down. However, while there was provision for coordination on a Kosovo-wide basis, the police were to be organized on a communal basis and limited to a ceiling of 3,000 active law-enforcement officers throughout Kosovo. In addition, there was authority in relation to education, child care, the communal environment, and local economic issues.

The judiciary consisted of a Constitutional Court composed of nine judges. At least one judge was to be a member of the Serb national community and five other judges would have been selected from a list drawn up by the President of the European Court of Human Rights. The powers of review of the Constitutional Court were quite wide. They included, but were not limited to, determining whether laws were applicable in Kosovo and whether decisions or acts of the President, the Assembly, the government, the communes or the national communities were compatible with the Constitution.

The Supreme Court, comprised of nine judges including one member of the Serb national community, would hear final appeals from subordinated courts in Kosovo, including communal courts.

A special feature related to the right of citizens in Kosovo to opt to have civil disputes to which they were party adjudicated by courts in other parts of the FRY, which would apply the law applicable in Kosovo. In criminal cases, a defendant would be entitled to have a trial transferred to another Kosovo court designated by the defendant. In effect, this meant that a defendant could opt to be tried in the local court of a specific commune, which would be composed principally of members of his or her ethnic appurtenance. In criminal cases in which all defendants and victims were members of the same national community, all members of the judicial council would be from the national community of their choice, if any party so requested. A defendant in a criminal case could also insist that one member of the judicial council hearing the case was from his or her national community. This might include judges of courts in the FRY serving as Kosovan judges for these purposes.

C. Human rights and additional rights of national communities

The provisions on human rights were strangely short and undeveloped in the Constitution and throughout the agreement. There was no listing of fundamental human rights to be applied in Kosovo. Instead, Article VI(1) of the Constitution stated rather generally that all authorities in Kosovo must ensure internationally recognized human rights and fundamental freedoms. As opposed to the Dayton agreement, which included a long list of human rights instruments identifying what internationally recognized human rights and fundamental freedoms were, the agreement in Article VI(2) simply incorporated the terms of the European Convention for the protection of Human Rights and Fundamental Freedoms and its protocols which 'shall apply directly in Kosovo'. In this way, a very sophisticated body of human rights law, refined in decades of jurisprudence by the European Court and Commission of Human Rights, was instantly available throughout Kosovo. The Kosovo Assembly also had the power to enact into law other internationally recognized human rights instruments.

The rights and freedoms established in this way would have priority over all other law. Interestingly, all 'courts, agencies, governmental institutions, and other public institutions of Kosovo or operating in relation to Kosovo shall conform to these human rights and fundamental freedoms' (Article VI(3)). This means that FRY and republic authorities would also have had to exercise their competences in relation to Kosovo in accordance with these standards. As the FRY was not a party to the European Convention and its protocols, this would have placed it in an unusual position.

While the human rights provisions were compact, the additional rights granted to national communities were extensive, but not unlimited. Firstly, these rights were tied to the specific purpose of preserving and expressing their national, cultural, religious and linguistic identities. This was to be done in accordance with international standards and in accordance with human rights and fundamental freedoms.

More controversially, each national community could elect and establish its own institutions—a feature which it was feared would give rise to a parallel state structure within Kosovo. However, national community institutions would have to act in accordance with Kosovo law and not take discriminatory action. National communities could arrange for the inscription of local names of towns and villages in the language and alphabet of the respective community; issue information in that language; provide for education and schooling in that language and in national culture and history, reflecting a spirit of tolerance between communities and respect for the rights of members of all national communities; display national symbols, including those of the FRY and Serbia; protect national traditions on family law; arrange for the preservation of sites of religious, historical or cultural importance in cooperation with other authorities; implement public health and social services on a non-discriminatory basis; operate religious institutions in cooperation with religious authorities; and participate in NGOs.

National communities could also enjoy unhindered contact with representatives of their respective national communities within the FRY and abroad. They would be guaranteed access to and representation in the media and could finance their activities by collecting contributions from their members. Importantly, every person would have the right freely to choose to be treated or not to be treated as a member of a national community.

D. Final status

The draft presented to the parties at the outset of the conference restated the concluding provisions from previous Hill proposals providing for amendments to the accord to be adopted by agreement of all the parties. Each party was to be entitled to propose such amendments at any time. However, after three years, there would be a comprehensive assessment of the agreement under international auspices with the aim of improving its implementation and determining whether to implement proposals by either side for additional steps.[42] The means of undertaking this assessment, and the procedure to be adopted, were left unclear.

The Kosovo delegation argued strongly that, in accordance with the interim character of the agreement, provisions needed to be made for a further international conference on a final settlement for Kosovo. The decisions of that conference should be based on 'the will of the people of Kosovo', made manifest in a referendum. The negotiators pointed out that they were not authorized by the Contact Group to adopt language on a referendum. However, even the Non-Negotiable Principles had provided for 'a mechanism for a final settlement after an interim period of three years'. In the dramatic final phase of the conference, it was possible to obtain significant changes to the final provision that reflected this wording. The final text of what became Article I(3) of Chapter 8 reads:

Three years after the entry into force of this agreement, an international meeting shall be convened to determine a mechanism for a final settlement for Kosovo, on the basis of the will of the people, opinions of relevant authorities, each Party's efforts regarding the implementation of this Agreement, and the Helsinki Final Act, and to undertake a comprehensive assessment of the implementation of this Agreement and to consider proposals by any Party for additional measures.

This wording stops short of actually establishing a mechanism for a final settlement, contrary to what might have been expected from the language of the Non-Negotiable Principles. However, startlingly, it was accepted that this mechanism should be established and/or operate, inter alia, on the basis of the will of the people.[43] On the other hand, this mechanism would be created by 'an international meeting', whose composition, remit and authority was not defined. All organs of the international community had consistently ruled out the possibility of independence and it would not be surprising if the 'international meeting' were to adopt a similar view. These uncertainties were not entirely removed by the unilateral interpretation offered by the US in a draft side letter, which confirmed

[42] This formulation actually represented a slight retreat from the final Hill draft, put forward on 27 January, which had referred to a 'procedure' for considering such additional steps, to be determined taking into account the parties' roles in and compliance with the agreement.

[43] In a dramatic nocturnal negotiating session towards the very end of the conference, the Kosovo delegation was able to extract from the negotiators an even better formulation, referring to the 'expressed will of the people'. However, this concession was lost when the delegation was not immediately able to sign the final text and when the Contact Group overruled it afterwards.

that Kosovo could hold a referendum on independence after three years. In any event, that side letter was never formalized, given the failure of the Kosovo delegation to sign the agreement by the stipulated Rambouillet deadline.

IV. Implementation

The provisions for implementation contained in the Rambouillet text were complex and distributed throughout the interim agreement. They consisted principally of the introductory section of the agreement entitled Framework, Chapter 2 on Police and Public Security, Chapter 3 on the Conduct and Supervision of Elections, Chapter 4(a) on Humanitarian Assistance, Reconstruction and Development, Chapter 5 on the Civilian Implementation Mission in Kosovo, Chapter 6 concerning the Ombudsman and Chapter 7 on 'Implementation II', that is to say, military implementation. Due to constraints of space, it will only be possible to review some of the principal features of this implementation structure here.

A. Confidence building

Upon signature of the agreement, a ceasefire was to come into force immediately. Alleged violations of the ceasefire were to be reported to international observers and could not be used to justify the use of force in response. The status of police and security forces in Kosovo, including withdrawal of forces, was to be achieved according to Chapter 7. Paramilitary and irregular forces in Kosovo were deemed incompatible with the terms of the agreement. The latter provision gave rise to some difficulty, inasmuch as the KLA did not consider itself a paramilitary or irregular force. However, it was clear that it, too, was addressed through Chapter 7 of the agreement. All abducted persons or other persons detained without charge were to be released, including persons held in connection with the conflict in Kosovo. No one was to be prosecuted for crimes related to the conflict, except for persons accused of having committed serious violations of international humanitarian law. Persons already convicted of politically motivated crimes related to the conflict were to be released, providing these convictions did not relate to serious violations of humanitarian law.

The agreement confirmed the obligation, already contained in mandatory Security Council resolutions, to cooperate with the International Criminal Tribunal for the Former Yugoslavia in The Hague. This included the obligation to permit complete access to tribunal investigators and compliance with the orders of the Tribunal. This provision was contested at Rambouillet. Kosovo attempted to strengthen its scope, as did, albeit indirectly, the Tribunal itself. However, in the face of determined opposition from the FRY, a rather short paragraph was adopted which did not greatly improve on the obligations already contained in the demands of the Security Council. The parties also recognized the right of all persons to return to their homes, including those who had had to leave the region. There was to be no impediment to the normal flow of goods into Kosovo, including materials for the reconstruction of homes and structures. The FRY would not require visas, customs or licensing for persons or things connected with international implementation.

B. NATO-led implementation and the withdrawal of forces

The military implementation chapter was the most detailed element of the entire accord. The parties agreed that NATO would establish and deploy a force (KFOR) operating under the authority and subject to the direction and the political control of the North Atlantic Council through the NATO chain of command. However, contrary to much speculation afterwards, a Chapter VII mandate was to be obtained from the Security Council from the beginning. Other states would be invited to assist in military implementation. While this is not spelt out, it was envisaged that KFOR would be approximately 28,000 troops strong. This would include a sizeable Russian contingent according to the precedent of the Stabilization/Implementation Force (SFOR/IFOR) in Bosnia and Herzegovina. In accordance with that precedent, KFOR would be authorized to take such action as required, including the use of necessary force, to ensure compliance with Chapter 7. As opposed to the arrangements of Dayton, it was made clear from the beginning that KFOR would not only be available to ensure compliance with the military aspects of the agreement, but that it would also actively support civilian implementation by the OSCE and others as part of its original mandate. As in the Dayton agreement, the mandate of KFOR could have been broadened by further NATO action, in this instance acting through the North Atlantic Council.

A Joint Implementation Commission was to be established to consider complaints by the parties and other matters. It was to be composed of FRY military commanders and FRY/Serbian officials, Kosovo representatives and representatives of the military and civilian implementation missions. The agreement envisaged that final authority to interpret the provisions of Chapter 7 would rest with the KFOR military commander.

The regular armed forces of the FRY would have been subject to a rigorous regime of redeployment and withdrawal according to fixed deadlines. This included the removal of assets such as battle tanks, all armoured vehicles mounting weapons greater than 12.7mm and all heavy weapons of over 82mm. Within 180 days of the agreement coming into force, all VJ units, other than 1,500 members of a lightly armed border guard battalion deployed close to the border, would have had to be withdrawn from Kosovo. An additional 1,000 support personnel would be permitted in specified cantonment sites. The border guards were to be limited to patrolling the border zone and their travel through Kosovo was to be subject to significant restrictions. Moreover, the air defence system in Kosovo was to be dismantled and associated forces withdrawn, as with other FRY or Serbian forces, including the Ministry of Interior Police (MUP). The MUP would initially be reduced to a size of 2,500, and be entirely withdrawn upon the establishment of a Kosovo police within one year. Upon entry into force of the agreement, all other forces would have had to commit themselves to demilitarization, renunciation of violence, guaranteeing the security of international personnel, and so on. The definition of the term 'demilitarization' had been subject to some discussion, especially as it applied to the KLA. It would have included the surrender of heavy armaments and some small arms.

The military chapter was accompanied by two appendices, which were both published along with the agreement. The rather extravagant claims that they reveal a secret agenda by NATO for the virtual occupation of all of Yugoslavia made some time after the conclusion of the conference are entirely without substance. Appendix A established cantonment sites for FRY/Serbian forces. The famous Appendix B established what in other contexts would be the standard terms of a status of forces agreement for KFOR, very much in line with the precedent of IFOR/SFOR in Bosnia and Herzegovina and United Nations peacekeeping operations. A provision which permits transit through Yugoslavia for NATO and affiliated forces falls within these standard terms, although it may have been phrased more broadly than was strictly usual. If, as it was subsequently claimed, the terms of the appendix, or this particular provision, were what rendered Rambouillet unacceptable, it is unclear why the FRY did not seek clarification or even modification of this provision at the Paris follow-on conference. That conference was dedicated exclusively to negotiations on the implementation aspects of the agreement, which had not been available at Rambouillet itself.

C. Civilian implementation

The OSCE was to be charged with principal responsibility for the civilian elements of implementation, operating under a Chief of the Implementation Mission (CIM). The implementation mission would monitor, observe and inspect law enforcement activities in Kosovo, which would be established principally at communal level. The Kosovo police force of around 3,000 was to be only lightly armed. The authority of federal and Serbian police would have been very significantly restricted. Importantly, the CIM would have had final authority to interpret the provisions of the agreement in relation to civilian implementation.

All aspects of civilian implementation would have been coordinated and monitored by a Joint Commission, including federal, republic and Kosovo representatives and others, and chaired by the CIM who was to exercise a final right of decision in this rather powerful body. In addition, an ombudsman would monitor the realization of the rights of members of national communities and the protection of human rights and fundamental freedoms. Elections were to be held at communal and Kosovo level within nine months of entry into force of the agreement once the OSCE had certified that conditions had been established for a free and fair ballot. Finally, the agreement provided for the administration of humanitarian aid and reconstruction, principally through the organs of Kosovo, with strong involvement of the European Union. In fact, throughout the conference, the European Union, through its negotiator and representatives of the Commission, exercised considerable influence, also and especially in relation to this issue. Great emphasis was placed on careful planning, rapid and non-bureaucratic deployment of resources once needs had been identified, and close cooperation with the beneficiaries of such aid.

V. Conclusion

The Rambouillet conference on Kosovo represented a significant departure from the norm in international mediation. The presence of the parties at the talks had been ensured through the threat of the use of force by NATO. Acceptance of the political interim settlement for Kosovo was to be obtained, if necessary, through the threat or use of force. The implementation of the agreement was to be assured through the presence of a 28,000 strong NATO-led force, in addition to a sizeable OSCE contingent. Acceptance of this presence was also to be obtained through the threat of the use of force, if necessary. At the time of the conference, there existed no express United Nations Security Council mandate for the threat or use of force in relation to the parties. Instead, NATO had to rely on the justification of forcible humanitarian action in general international law to justify its position. However, the Security Council had expressly supported the Contact Group decision which required the parties to attend the conference, and backed NATO in this way.

In terms of its substance, the Rambouillet settlement might have represented a further step in the development of innovative mechanisms to resolve self-determination conflicts. In fact, it combines within it, and advances upon, some of the elements pioneered in the innovative responses to other crises that may have appeared irresolvable. The Dayton settlement provided for the retention of the territorial unity of a state (Bosnia and Herzegovina) which had come under unbearable pressure as a result of armed strife, while at the same time granting very substantive powers of self-governance to the entity that needed to be contained within it (Republika Srpska). The Good Friday Agreement on Northern Ireland and the Palestine accords introduced the concept of the allocation of authority at differing levels of governance, without necessarily prejudicing questions of legal status. Eritrea and Chechnya introduced the notion of an interim agreement pending an exercise of the will of the people.

Conceptually, one might argue that the conference represented an attempt by the international community to advance on these precedents by imposing reason upon parties who appeared unreasonable. The FRY/Serbia had presided, for more than a decade, over a policy of repression which had been clearly rejected. However, all attempts to reverse Belgrade's actions had failed. The Kosovars, on the other hand, had committed themselves to independence—an attitude which was deemed unreasonable by the international community. Hence, the international community, at the level of the Security Council, had identified at a general level the outcome that was to be obtained: significant self-governance with entrenched human rights within the FRY/Serbia. Rather than seeking to impose a permanent settlement, the Hill process revealed that the cooperation of both parties would be more likely if an interim agreement could be achieved. Insistence on an interim agreement was also more in line with the justification for an 'imposed' settlement, that is, the ongoing humanitarian emergency and destabilization of the region.

The actual terms of the settlement, anticipated in the basic Non-Negotiable Principles, had of course been refined over time in cooperation with the parties, through the Hill process. The definition of a reasonable political settlement which the parties could be expected to accept, at least for the interim, was therefore not quite as arbitrary as it seemed. The initial draft presented to the parties provided for a sensible sharing of authority without touching upon issues of status. However, when a second text was presented shortly before the conclusion of the talks, it had been fundamentally altered in accordance with Belgrade's demands. If the first version had been deemed to reflect that which was inherently reasonable, it was difficult to explain to Kosovo why a substantially different document was now equally as reasonable. Kosovo gave in on most matters relating to the assignment of public authority, or rather it was offered no choice in the matter. Hence, in terms of the assignment of public authority, the Rambouillet text fell short of restoration of the autonomous powers Kosovo had enjoyed before its status was unilaterally modified. In addition, it introduced the notion of national communities, which provided ethnic Serbs and others with very extensive and disproportionate powers of representation and co-decision making, to the point of undermining the functioning of the Kosovo institutions under the terms of the agreement.

On the issue of status, the FRY/Serbia obtained express recognition of the continued territorial integrity and even sovereignty of the FRY. This language had to be bought with reference to an expression of the 'will of the people' at the termination of the three-year period when it emerged that Kosovo would not sign. While it is clear that the wording 'will of the people' would have permitted the holding of a referendum, this would not, in fact, have necessarily determined the issue of status. Even according to the wording proposed in the US side letter, it was confirmed that the will of the people would be only one of the elements taken into consideration when determining the mechanism for a final settlement after three years. Given the fact that the establishment of the mechanism for a final settlement would rest in the hands of an international community which had declared itself consistently against the granting of independence for Kosovo, there was no automatic self-determination for Kosovo, although the case for it had been strengthened.

On the side of military implementation, the Contact Group itself, due to Russia's position, was unable to present a united view as to what was reasonable and could be imposed upon the parties. However, the FRY/Serbia gave up the opportunity to test to what extent it could advance its position on implementation at the follow-on Paris conference, which was expressly devoted to the issue of implementation. Most observers had expected an attempt to undermine NATO's determination to use force at Paris. Had the FRY/Serbia signed up to the political part of the agreement and offered, for example, to accept an OSCE or UN-led implementation mission of more limited dimensions, it is not at all certain that NATO could have maintained a consensus on the threat or use of force.

Instead, the FRY started to question the political settlement which it previously appeared to have regarded as a reasonable compromise and which, ironically, could have brought with it, for a period of at least three years, the international protection of the territorial integrity of that state. Evidently, Belgrade was unable to embrace the concept of self-rule for ethnic Albanians and a reversal of its policies in relation to that territory, co-administered by the organized international community. Perhaps there was also recognition that in the longer term it would be impossible to constrain an ethnic Albanian population in the FRY, if the tools of repressing that population had been removed from Belgrade.

Throughout the talks, significant rifts in the Contact Group were visible in relation to the political settlement, the implementation force and the threat or use of force as a tool in achieving a settlement. These divisions became more pronounced towards the conclusion of the conference, when collapse of the talks appeared likely. In fact, one might say that, towards the end, the talks were less about Kosovo and more about relations within the Contact Group. The rifts in the Contact Group, and the uncertain position of the Kosovo delegation itself, significantly undermined the effect of the threat of use of force. In view of this disunity, and of the actual conduct of the negotiations, at least in relation to the FRY/Serbia, the characterization of Rambouillet as a settlement imposed by a number of powerful states according to the model of the Concert of Europe appears somewhat shaky.

With the commencement of NATO action some weeks after Rambouillet, much thought has been expended on the question of whether Rambouillet represented a serious attempt to achieve a settlement, or whether it was instead a US 'set-up', designed to manoeuvre Yugoslavia into a position in which the initiation of military action appeared justified. The oscillating nature of the negotiations, and the very substantive concessions made to the FRY/Serbia, would appear to rule out such conspiracy theories. Similarly, the influence of other members of the Contact Group on the conduct of the talks is often underestimated. The Contact Group had developed the Hill package on which the Rambouillet text was based in principle. It had to approve by consensus all major developments in the drafts as the talks progressed. When the US unilaterally offered last-minute concessions to Kosovo to ensure that it would sign, these were in fact overruled in part by the Contact Group. Towards the end of the talks, there was a real sense that an agreement might be possible after all, although this was achieved through concessions which ultimately jeopardized Kosovo's ability to sign the agreement.

The conspiracy theory also fails to take into account the inability of the US to conceive and carry through long-term foreign policy. Had there existed a plan to 'frame' Yugoslavia, it would have been essential to ensure that the Kosovo Albanians were on board and conducted themselves according to the script. As developments at Rambouillet amply demonstrated, no such effort had been made. In fact, US policy-makers had failed to formulate an accurate understanding of the dynamics within the Kosovo delegation, and of the positions that its members were likely to adopt.

Whether or not the FRY/Serbia could reasonably have been expected to accept the Rambouillet package depends in the end on the standards applied in identifying what is reasonable. The defenders of the draft agreement and of the Rambouillet process would argue that this standard had been raised by Yugoslavia's own conduct over the previous decade. In fact, even up until the events of 1998, Serbia would probably have been able to satisfy international demands for the restoration of meaningful self-governance in Kosovo by accepting a more modest autonomy regime for the province. In the autumn of 1998, the FRY could have accepted a political settlement similar to the one on offer at Rambouillet in the shape of the Hill draft put forward on 2 November. Such a settlement would not have been attached to such strong implementation provisions, including a NATO-led presence. Instead, significant FRY/Serbian armed forces would have remained in the territory. After the Christmas offensive and the Racak massacre, conducted under the noses of the OSCE's unarmed verification mission, the attitude to implementation changed, at least among NATO states. It was no longer felt reasonable to expect the Kosovo Albanians to rely on further agreements or promises by the Belgrade government in the absence of the strong enforcement presence envisaged by the Rambouillet agreement.

The result of the Serbian failure to embrace Rambouillet, after its extraordinary campaign to expel virtually the entire ethnic Albanian population from its homeland, must strike the observer as somewhat ironic. It failure to engage sincerely resulted in the introduction of a NATO presence, without any significant opportunity for Belgrade to determine the modalities or powers of this force. Furthermore, no political settlement was in place to safeguard the territorial integrity of Serbia.

9

The Initiation of the NATO
Aerial Campaign and
the International Response

I. The Paris Conference

In the days following the conclusion of the Rambouillet talks, an intensive effort was mounted to persuade Kosovo to sign. The United States launched an Albanian-language television programme, attempting to explain the advantages of the agreement. US Senator Bob Dole, a long-standing supporter of the cause of the Kosovo Albanians, was dispatched to the region to try and persuade the KLA leadership to accept. Crucially, Hashim Thaci, who had appeared to obstruct acceptance of the agreement, apparently under instruction, now turned into a campaigner for acceptance. In a rather dangerous mission, he travelled throughout Kosovo, visiting every KLA district leader in turn. It was said that he managed to obtain the signature of all of them on a piece of paper endorsing the accord. On several occasions it appeared as if Kosovo would sign, even in advance of the follow-on conference. However, in the end, that signature came only later.

The Contact Group negotiators and the delegations of the FRY/Serbia and Kosovo assembled again at the Paris International Conference Centre on Avenue Kleber on 15 March 1999. As the attempt to isolate the delegations had not been successful previously, they were no longer constrained in their movements. The splendour of the Chateau Rambouillet was therefore exchanged for simple hotel accommodation.

On the first day of the follow-on conference, the Kosovo delegation presented the co-chairmen of the Conference and others with a formal letter, confirming the decision it had taken at Rambouillet to accept the interim agreement as presented on 23 February: 'We would be honoured to sign the Agreement in your presence at a time and place of your choosing', the letter stated.

Rather than offering an immediate opportunity to sign, the negotiators pressed Kosovo strongly to delay such a step, so as to permit further discussions with the FRY/Serbian delegation. After all, at the conclusion of the Rambouillet session, the FRY/Serbia had appeared to embrace the political elements of the settlement, at least in principle. It was hoped that there would now exist an opportunity to address FRY/Serbian reluctance to consider implementation, including military implementation. That issue had not really been up for discussion at Rambouillet, where the military implementation annex had been presented to the parties late in the game, without the opportunity to suggest changes.

In a significant about-turn, the Contact Group was now willing to discuss the modalities for implementation in some detail and offered a full week of discussions towards this end. That is to say, the conditions of the later famous Annex B on NATO implementation could have been discussed, had these really been the principal reason for Belgrade's refusal to sign. Annex B had been drafted in accordance with standard status of forces agreements and was modelled in some ways on the Dayton agreement. It would have permitted NATO access to Kosovo and, as is generally the case in status of forces arrangements, would have provided for an exemption from local jurisdiction. There would also have been a right of access to Kosovo via Yugoslavia—an issue that might well have been reconsidered in further talks.

However, the FRY/Serbia was not willing to exploit this opportunity to address its concerns in that respect. Instead, on the first day of the conference, the interlocutors from Belgrade greeted the three mediators with the words 'have you come to fuck us again?' Such language was not exactly conducive to negotiations, and turned the mediators in the discussion chamber a little pale.

Clearly, the Milosevic regime had decided that it would not engage in any further negotiations. Instead, it presented its own version of the political part of the agreement. Rather than focusing on limited changes, this counter-draft effectively sought to reopen discussions on the political settlement as a whole and start again from the beginning.[1] In fact, some of the proposed changes even fell outside of the Non-Negotiable Principles. The draft proposed a formal subordination of Kosovo to Serbia, abolished restrictions on the exercise of federal functions in Kosovo and correspondingly reduced the functions of the Kosovo Assembly. The office of the President of Kosovo would be abolished and its government replaced by a weakened Council of Ministers. There would be no Kosovo Constitutional or Supreme Court. In addition, the entire implementation chapters, both military and civilian, had simply been struck out, with the exception of OSCE election monitoring and provisions for the Ombudsman, although even those provisions were significantly altered. Even Chapter 4(a) on humanitarian assistance, reconstruction and economic development was deleted in its entirety.

This manoeuvre of walking away from everything that had been discussed at Rambouillet infuriated the negotiators, including Russian Ambassador Mayorski who had provided diplomatic cover for Serbia's earlier refusal to sign the Rambouillet draft. All hopes for a settlement had now been effectively dashed. The negotiators responded to the submission of the new draft by the FRY/Serbia by stating jointly in a formal letter 'the unanimous view of the Contact Group that

---

[1] Reproduced in Weller, *Crisis in Kosovo*, at 480.

only technical adjustments can be considered which, of course, must be accepted as such and approved by the other delegation'.[2] Hence it was confirmed that the exhausting process of seeking to tempt the FRY/Serbian delegation into accepting the agreement by making concessions on the political settlement had now been concluded. Instead, the talks would focus on implementation. Accordingly, over the days that followed, Kosovo was presented with the opportunity to discuss in detail the issues of economic reconstruction, civil implementation, the holding of elections by the OSCE, and military implementation with the relevant implementing organizations. The FRY/Serbian side did not take up this offer.

In the weeks following the Rambouillet conference, the Belgrade government had changed its initial, outwardly moderate positive assessment of the Rambouillet accords. When it was evident that Kosovo would definitely sign, Belgrade seemed to go out of its way to provoke a breakdown of the peace process, without feeling it necessary to deploy any diplomatic subtleties.

Essentially, Belgrade had decided to call NATO's bluff. In view of this attitude, subsequent claims that Rambouillet failed because the United States insisted inflexibly on the implementation chapters and offered no negotiations on the subject to Belgrade are misplaced. The entire follow-on conference had been called to address implementation, but there was no interest whatsoever in discussion on the part of the FRY/Serbia.

Given this deadlock, the text of the agreement in its form of 23 February was opened for signature on 18 March. In a formal ceremony, Kosovo signed the agreement, witnessed by only two of the three negotiators. The flat refusal of Ambassador Mayorski to witness the signature of Kosovo to the outcome of the Rambouillet and Paris talks is startling. After all, up to that moment at least the pretence had been maintained that the negotiators were serving the Contact Group, rather than the governments represented within it or even a particular party to the talks. In view of Belgrade's latest conduct, it had been hoped that unity in the Contact Group could now be restored. However, under the shadow of the looming implementation of the threat of the use of force, Moscow decided to dissociate itself from the conference result.

As is customary upon signature or ratification of legal instruments of this kind, the Kosovo delegation issued an interpretative statement at the moment of signature.[3] In so doing, it communicated certain understandings. It indicated that the text was now definitive and could not be subject to further modification, excluding purely technical changes. Kosovo also indicated that it regarded NATO-led implementation according to the provisions of the interim agreement to constitute a condition essential to the overall package and to the consent given by Kosovo. It committed itself to full cooperation with all implementing organizations and invited their early deployment. Kosovo confirmed its intention,

---

[2] Letter, 16 March 1999, Weller, *Crisis in Kosovo*, 490.
[3] Declaration of Kosovo, 18 March 1999, in Weller, *Crisis in Kosovo*, 490–1.

already indicated at the conclusion of the conference at Rambouillet, that at the termination of the interim period of three years the people of Kosovo would exercise their will through a referendum. This expression of the will of the people would be conveyed to the international meeting to determine the mechanism for a final settlement for Kosovo, consistent with the interim agreement, in particular Article I(3) of Chapter 8. Finally, the delegation noted again the intention of the KLA to exercise the opportunity to engage in a process of transformation and welcomed assurances as to cooperative bilateral contacts to carry out this process consistent with the interim agreement.

In a surreal act, the Serbian delegation to the talks then arranged signature of its own version of the agreement. It claimed that it had been 'signed by representatives of all ethnic communities' and that it was based exactly on the ten Contact Group principles.[4] The next day, Russian mediator Mayorsky declared that the Rambouillet document signed by the Kosovo delegation was invalid, as it contained elements that had not been approved by all members of the Contact Group. According to Mayorsky, the implementation annexes had been drawn up 'behind Russia's back' and without its approval.[5] Milosevic claimed:

As concerns the signed 'agreement', two documents were signed in Paris. One of the documents was signed by the representatives of all national communities from Kosovo, and these are the representatives of Kosovo. The other document was signed by the representatives of the Albanian separatist and terrorist movement, and they, of course, are not the representatives of Kosovo.[6]

The following day, one last attempt was made to engage the FRY/Serbian delegation in substantive discussions. When this attempt proved fruitless, the co-chairmen of the conference, the foreign ministers of the United Kingdom and France, issued a statement which indicated that the Kosovo delegation had seized the opportunity of peace and committed itself to the accords as a whole. Far from seizing this opportunity, the Yugoslav delegation had tried to unravel the Rambouillet accords, the statement continued.[7] The conference was, however, not terminated, but merely adjourned, pending acceptance by the FRY/Serbia.

The Belgrade government had used the break in talks since 23 February to deploy troop concentrations on the border with Kosovo and in Kosovo itself. These forces had already engaged in significant offensive operations during the Paris follow-on talks and now increased their activities still further, once again attacking entire villages and other civilian installations. In view of this situation, the OSCE Verification Mission in Kosovo was rapidly withdrawn on the day of

[4] Multi-ethnic Agreement on Kosovo Self-Government, signed 18 March 1999.
[5] No Alternative to a Political Solution, Tanjug, 19 March 1999.
[6] Reply of the President of the Federal Republic of Yugoslavia, Mr. Slobodan Milosevic, to the Message of the Co-Chairmen of the Rambouillet Meeting, Ministers of France and of Great Britain, Messrs Hubert Vedrine and Robin Cook, 22 March 1999. Text available at <http://emperors-clothes.com/docs/rambouillet-milosevic.htm>, accessed 6 October 2008.
[7] Statement, 19 March 1999, in Weller, *Crisis in Kosovo*, 493.

the adjournment of the conference. Within a few days the number of displaced persons had risen again, in very significant numbers.

II. The Initiation of Hostilities

On 22 March, the negotiators travelled to Belgrade, along with Richard Holbrooke, to make one final attempt to persuade the FRY/Serbia to cease offensive operations and to accept the Rambouillet accords. Again, no progress was achieved. Instead, the following day, the parliament in Belgrade voted to reject the interim agreement. That day, UN Secretary-General Kofi Annan expressed his grave concern at the escalating violence in Kosovo, referring to an ongoing offensive by Yugoslav security forces.[8]

Richard Holbrooke then returned to Brussels where NATO, having received a briefing on his discussions, authorized the launch of military operations against the FRY. The NATO Secretary-General explained that this action had been taken in order to 'avert a humanitarian catastrophe'.[9] The operations would be 'directed towards disrupting the violent attacks being committed by the Serb Army and Special Police Forces and weakening their ability to cause [a] further humanitarian catastrophe'.

The strong references to the unfolding humanitarian tragedy were meant to point to the legal justification for the operation, which remained one of humanitarian action. The three principal demands that were to be enforced militarily could be logically connected to that justification. In order to arrest further deterioration of the humanitarian situation, the use of excessive and disproportionate force by the FRY/Serbia would need to stop, as this practice had caused the large-scale displacement of civilians in Kosovo. This requirement was rather a cautious one, inasmuch as it did not appear to insist on an immediate ceasefire by Belgrade. The ongoing FRY/Serbian offensive against the KLA was therefore not necessarily rejected, but rather the means through which it was being conducted were condemned and subjected to counter-action.

In the absence of compliance with this demand, NATO would strike directly the military infrastructure actually engaged in excessive and indiscriminate attacks. This reference aimed at fulfilling the legal requirement of necessity, imminence of the threat to a civilian population, and proportionality of the forcible counter-measure.

A prospective further element of targeting would also be included, namely, that of weakening the future potential of the FRY/Serbia to engage in such activities. This slightly broader aim was justified with reference to the past record of

---

[8] Secretary-General Gravely Concerned at Escalation of Violence in Kosovo, 22 March 1999, Press release SM/SG6936.

[9] Press Statement by Dr Javier Solana, 23 March 1999, in Weller, *Crisis in Kosovo*, 495.

these forces, which had extended from involvement in probable genocide and ethnic cleansing in Croatia and in Bosnia and Herzegovina, to causing the initial exodus from Kosovo in 1998. Through this measure, Security Council demands for a troop withdrawal, and the FRY's own commitments in the Holbrooke agreement of October 1998, would be forcibly implemented. Again, as there existed no Security Council mandate to this effect, the use of force in this context needed to be justified with reference to an overwhelming humanitarian need.

The use of force in support of international efforts to secure Yugoslav agreement to an interim political settlement also mirrored an aim established by the United Nations Security Council to which no enforcement mandate was attached. It reflected a view that the humanitarian emergency could not be improved in the longer term in the absence of a settlement. However, the statement by the NATO Secretary-General was rather nuanced, inasmuch as it referred merely to the interim political settlement. The use of force by NATO was thus, at least according to this initial statement, not necessarily directed at ensuring acceptance of the Rambouillet package in its entirety. Instead, the Secretary-General referred to the more flexible requirement that a 'viable political settlement must be guaranteed by an international military presence'. On the other hand, the UK Prime Minister stated that the operation would have as its minimum objective the curbing of continued Serbian repression in Kosovo in order to avert a humanitarian disaster. It would therefore target the military capability of the Serbian dictatorship. To avoid such action,

Milosevic must do what he promised to do last October. End the repression; withdraw his troops to barracks; get them down to the levels agreed; and withdraw from Kosovo the tanks, heavy artillery and other weapons he brought into Kosovo early last year. He must agree to the proposals set out in the Rambouillet Accords, including a NATO-led ground force.[10]

The initiation of hostilities was strongly criticized by Russia and China in the United Nations Security Council, presaging the controversy over the moral and legal justification of NATO's action of the weeks to come. The extraordinarily rapid outpouring of refugees, as a result of the strategy of mass deportation employed by FRY/Serbian forces in Kosovo, also led to considerable soul-searching about the political wisdom and military effectiveness of the operation.

III. The International Response to the Use of Force

The UN Security Council convened, at the request of Russia, to consider the 'extremely dangerous situation caused by the unilateral military action of NATO

---

[10] UK Prime Minister's Statement on Kosovo, 23 March 1999, in Weller, *Crisis in Kosovo*, 495–6.

against the Federal Republic of Yugoslavia'.[11] During the Council meeting, Russia argued that the doctrine of humanitarian intervention is 'in no way based on the Charter or other generally recognized rules of international law'.[12] Belarus echoed this position:

... the use of military force against Yugoslavia without a proper decision of the only competent international body, which is undoubtedly the United Nations Security Council, as well as any introduction of foreign military contingents against the wish of the Government of Yugoslavia, qualify as an act of aggression, with all ensuing responsibility for its humanitarian, military and political consequences. Under these circumstances, no rationale, no reasoning presented by NATO can justify the unlawful use of military force and be deemed acceptable.[13]

Yugoslavia complained of a flagrant act of aggression in violation of the basic principles of the UN Charter and of Article 53. Yugoslavia also argued that an attempt had been made to impose a solution endorsing separatist objectives under pressure, blackmail and the threat of the use of force. This, it asserted, had been followed by an attack against Yugoslavia because it sought to solve an internal problem and had used its sovereign right to fight terrorism and prevent the secession of a part of territory that had always belonged to Serbia and Yugoslavia.[14]

China, too, was clear in its views: 'This act amounts to a blatant violation of international law ... We oppose interference in the internal affairs of other States, under whatever pretext or in whatever form'.[15] China added that 'it is only the Security Council that can determine whether a given situation threatens international peace and security and can take appropriate action'.

India found a clear 'violation of Article 53 of the Charter. No country, group of countries or regional arrangement, no matter how powerful, can arrogate to itself the right to take arbitrary and unilateral military action others.'[16] In addition to denying enforcement powers to a regional organization or arrangement in the absence of Council authorization, India also flatly opposed the doctrine of humanitarian intervention:

Among the barrage of justifications we have heard, we have been told that the attacks are meant to prevent violations of human rights. Even if that were to be so, it does not justify unprovoked military aggression. Two wrongs do not make a right.

When India invoked Article 2(7) of the Charter protecting the domestic jurisdiction of states from intervention, Slovenia responded by indicating that the previous Chapter VII resolutions on this issue had removed it from the exclusive jurisdiction of Yugoslavia. Slovenia also reminded the Council of a precedent from

---

[11] NATO Action against Serbian Military Targets Prompts Divergent Views as Security Council Holds Urgent Meeting on Situation in Kosovo, Press release SC/6657, 24 March 1999.

[12] Record of SC meeting 3988, S/PV/3988, 24 March 1999, 4.

[13] Record of SC meeting 3988, 15.   [14] Record of SC meeting 3988, 13f.

[15] Record of SC meeting 3988, 12.   [16] Record of SC meeting 3988, 15.

1971, when an Asian state had 'used force in a circumstance of extreme necessity', evidently referring to India's own armed intervention in East Pakistan.[17]

The United Kingdom offered a formal legal justification:

The action being taken is legal. It is justified as an exceptional measure to prevent an overwhelming humanitarian catastrophe. Under present circumstances in Kosovo, there is convincing evidence that such a catastrophe is imminent... Every means short of force has been tried to avert this situation. In these circumstances, and as an exceptional measure, military intervention is legally justifiable. The force now proposed is directed exclusively at averting a humanitarian catastrophe, and is the minimum judged necessary for that purpose.[18]

The Netherlands stated that:

The [UN] Secretary General is right when he observes in his press statement that the Council should be involved in any decision to resort to the use of force. If, however, due to one or two permanent members' rigid interpretation of the concept of domestic jurisdiction, such a resolution is not attainable, we cannot sit back and simply let the humanitarian catastrophe occur. In such a situation we will act on the legal basis we have available, and what we have available in this case is more than adequate.[19]

Unfortunately, the Netherlands representative did not expand on the exact nature of the legal basis for the operation. In particular, the statement is somewhat unclear as to whether this basis might be the humanitarian emergency itself, pointing to a general right to humanitarian intervention, or an argument that NATO states were exercising powers that would otherwise pertain to the Security Council. France seemed to emphasize the latter aspect when it indicated that 'the actions that have been decided upon are a response to the violation by Belgrade of its international obligations, which stem in particular from the Security Council resolutions adopted under Chapter VII of the United Nations Charter'.[20] Canada declared that 'humanitarian considerations underpin our action', also without referring to a specific legal basis for the operation.[21] Similarly, Germany presented a lengthy declaration on behalf of the EU, emphasizing the urgent humanitarian need for action without specifying the precise legal basis of the operation. These somewhat diffuse explanations reflected a sense among the majority of NATO members that action may have been necessary in this instance. However, it would not be helpful to expand on the exact legal nature of the justification, to avoid a precedent for the future. Indeed, prior to the launch of the aerial operation, the NATO Secretary-General had obtained a sense from all NATO governments that the operation would be lawful, expressly leaving it to each of them individually to determine exactly why this was the case.

---

[17] Record of SC meeting 3988, 19.
[18] Record of SC meeting 3988, 12.
[19] Record of SC meeting 3988, 8.
[20] Record of SC meeting 3988, 9.
[21] Record of SC meeting 3988, 5.

Opinion among states not directly involved in this issue also differed during the Security Council meeting. The Gambia declared that 'at times the exigencies of a situation demand, and warrant, decisive and immediate action. We find that the present situation in Kosovo deserves such treatment.'[22] Malaysia regretted that an absence of consensus in the Council had denied it the opportunity of pronouncing itself decisively on the matter and appeared to accept that it had become 'necessary' to act outside of the Council.[23] Argentina indicated that 'the responsibility lies with the Belgrade Government, since the objective of the military action is to avert a humanitarian catastrophe in Kosovo'.[24] Other states that showed understanding for the operation in view of the grave humanitarian circumstances were Slovenia, Bahrain, Albania, and Bosnia and Herzegovina. Gabon, on the other hand, indicated its opposition to the use of force as a matter of principle, having preferred further attempts at peaceful resolution.[25]

Belarus, India, and the Russian Federation introduced a resolution that would have expressed deep concern at the NATO use of force without authorization by the Security Council and affirmed that such unilateral use of force constituted a flagrant violation of the UN Charter, in particular Articles 2(4), 24 and 53. The resolution would have found that the use of force constituted a threat to international peace and security and demanded an immediate ceasefire.[26] However, introduction of this text proved to be something of a diplomatic blunder, overlooking the rather nuanced positions adopted even by states highly uneasy about the intervention. The draft received only three votes in favour (China, Namibia, Russian Federation) and twelve votes against. This result was somewhat unexpected, given that it would only have been necessary to abstain from voting in order to defeat the text, as would have ordinarily been the practice. The clear votes against the draft by five non-NATO states thus strengthened the position of the Alliance considerably.

In written communications to the Security Council, the Commonwealth of Independent States reinforced the Russian position that the action could not find justification in international law.[27] A similar submission was received from the Rio Group.[28] In a more balanced view, the Movement of Non-Aligned Countries emphasized the primary responsibility of the UN Security Council for matters of international peace and security, while focusing on the humanitarian situation that had resulted from the displacement campaign in Kosovo.[29] The Organization of Islamic States Contact Group on Bosnia and Herzegovina and the Kosovars, on the other hand, took note of the fact that the Security Council had been unable to discharge its responsibility in this instance and that in view of

---

[22] Record of SC meeting 3988, 7.   [23] Record of SC meeting 3988, 10.
[24] Record of SC meeting 3988, 11.   [25] Record of SC meeting 3988, 10.
[26] Draft Resolution submitted by Belarus, India and the Russian Federation, 26 March 1999 S/1999/328, in Weller, *Crisis in Kosovo*, 55.
[27] Letter of 26 March 1999, in Weller, *Crisis in Kosovo*, 63.
[28] Letter of 26 March 1999, in Weller, *Crisis in Kosovo*, 64.
[29] Letter of 9 April 1999, in Weller, *Crisis in Kosovo*, 66.

Belgrade's intransigence, 'decisive international action was necessary to prevent a humanitarian catastrophe and further violations of human rights in Kosova'.[30]

Overall, therefore, the initial responses by states and other international organizations were by no means as united against the NATO action as is sometimes supposed. While there were only a few formal legal justifications, a significant number of actors emphasized the humanitarian motivation of the operation without condemning it as a significant breach of international law.

IV. Action in the International Court of Justice

Faced with this somewhat ambiguous result, Yugoslavia brought an action in the International Court of Justice (ICJ), seeking, inter alia, cessation of the use of force by way of interim measures and a condemnation of the operation.[31] The ICJ is the highest judicial organ within the United Nations system. It is composed of fifteen senior international judges representing all the regions and ideological systems of the world. It tends to be a rather conservative body, which, according to its statute, needs to apply the law as it is, rather than developing it progressively. As the purported rule of humanitarian intervention would represent something of an innovation in post-1945 international law, it might have been difficult to find a majority of judges willing to support it in this instance. Hence, Yugoslavia's attempt to move the debate on the legitimacy of the operation to this forum.

For NATO or its member states, a finding by the Court that its action was unlawful would have been a very significant disaster. NATO states would find it very difficult to disregard a ruling by the ICJ. The issue of damages might arise. And, more immediately, should Yugoslavia succeed in obtaining a rapid pronouncement by the Court, this would have had a major effect on public opinion. Hence, Yugoslavia invoked an accelerated procedure, seeking interim measures of protection from the Court pending a full judgment. While a full case of this kind may take many years to be heard and decided, interim measures decisions are generally rendered within a few weeks. However, even in this condensed procedure, the applicant must be able to point to a prima facie basis of jurisdiction of the Court. That is to say, the ICJ can only hear cases in instances where the claimant and respondent have both accepted the right of the Court to make a ruling. Given the grave risk of a ruling on the substance of the matter, NATO governments therefore focused significant energy on denying that there existed such a jurisdictional link in this instance.

While the Court, in the end, declined to exercise jurisdiction on the merits, it did conduct an instant hearing on the interim measures application. Yugoslavia expanded on its charges of aggression and invoked the Nicaragua precedent. In

---

[30] Letter of 31 March, in Weller, *Crisis in Kosovo*, 65.
[31] Yugoslavia initiated proceedings through a letter dated 26 April 1999, adding a request for provisional measures on 28 April, in Weller, *Crisis in Kosovo*, 321f.

that case, which had found that the US had unlawfully intervened in Nicaragua, it had denied the availability of humanitarian justification for the use of force. It found that 'the argument derived from the preservation of human rights in Nicaragua cannot afford a legal justification of the conduct of the United States'.[32] Professor Ian Brownlie, appearing as Counsel and Advocate for Yugoslavia, argued that Article 2(4) of the UN Charter did not leave room for the doctrine of humanitarian intervention. Subsequent practice had not changed this position and no change in customary law had been proven, or even asserted, by NATO states. Instead, he argued that scholars had unanimously rejected the doctrine over the past thirty years, as confirmed in a famous 1984 UK Foreign Office memorandum, which had found that the best that could be said in favour of the doctrine of humanitarian intervention is that 'it is not unambiguously illegal', while 'the overwhelming majority of contemporary legal opinion comes down against the existence of a right of humanitarian intervention'.[33]

The actual hearing of the Court was of course focused mainly on the denial of jurisdiction of the Court by the NATO states. Belgium, however, offered a detailed legal justification for its position. First, Belgium claimed that the existing Security Council Resolutions 'provide an unchallengeable basis of the armed intervention. They are clear, and they are based on Chapter VII of the Charter.'[34] However, Belgium admitted that it was also necessary to develop the idea of armed humanitarian intervention. In support, it noted that 'NATO intervened to protect fundamental values enshrined in the jus cogens and to prevent an impending catastrophe, recognized as such by the Security Council'. Moreover, NATO had not questioned the political independence and the territorial integrity of Yugoslavia. Accordingly, this 'is an armed humanitarian intervention, compatible with Article 2, paragraph 4 of the Charter, which covers only intervention against the territorial integrity or political independence of a State'. Belgium relied on India's intervention in East Pakistan, Tanzania's intervention in Uganda, Vietnam in Cambodia, and ECOWAS interventions in Liberia and Sierra Leone—actions that had not been expressly condemned by the relevant United Nations bodies. Belgium also invoked a statement from a speech made by the UN Secretary-General at the University of Michigan, which indicated that it may be 'emerging slowly, but I believe [there] surely is an international norm against the violent repression of minorities that will and must take precedence over concerns of State sovereignty'.[35] The action was also in compliance with the requirements of humanitarian intervention: there was an imminent humanitarian catastrophe, this was recognized by the Security Council, which had determined that the situation constituted a threat to the peace and had identified Yugoslavia as the state responsible for the emergency.

---

[32] 1986 ICJ 134.
[33] *Legality of Use of Force Case* (Verbatim Record) (ICJ 1999), 10 May, CR 99/14, p 37.
[34] *Legality of Use of Force Case* (Provisional Measures) (ICJ, 1999), 10 May, CR 99/15.
[35] The speech took place on 30 April 1999.

As an alternative, Belgium invoked the doctrine of necessity, defined in what was then Article 33 of the UN International Law Commission Draft on State Responsibility. In this instance, a breach of a legal obligation would be justified by the need to safeguard, in the face of grave and imminent peril, values that are higher than those protected by the rule which has been breached.

The other respondents limited their submissions to the issue of jurisdiction, while reaffirming that the operation was motivated by an exceptional need to respond to an overwhelming humanitarian emergency. In addition to claiming justification for the NATO action on the basis of the 'humanitarian catastrophe that has engulfed the people of Kosovo', the acute threat of the actions of Yugoslavia to the security of neighbouring states, including the threat posed by extremely heavy flows of refugees and armed incursions into their territories, serious violations of humanitarian law and human rights obligations had been occasioned by forces under the control of Yugoslavia, in breach of the resolutions of the Security Council.[36]

The Court declined to grant provisional measures of protection as it did not see even a provisional basis of jurisdiction and eventually denied jurisdiction altogether without addressing the substantive arguments relating to the use of force.

V. Commissions of Enquiry

The debate on humanitarian intervention was continued, however, in a number of official or semi-official enquiries. The UK House of Commons Foreign Affairs Committee heard extensive evidence on the legality of the operation. It concluded that 'at the very least, the doctrine of humanitarian intervention has a tenuous basis in current international customary law, and that this renders NATO action legally questionable.'[37] However, the Committee also argued that the intervention was morally justified, and that it supported the development of new principles governing humanitarian intervention within the UN.

Similarly, a Netherlands committee of legal experts, commissioned by the Netherlands Ministry for Foreign Affairs, concluded that 'current international law provides no legal basis for such intervention, and also that no such legal basis is yet emerging.'[38] Somewhat inconsistently, the report continued to note, however, 'that it is no longer possible to ignore the increasingly perceived need to intervene in situations where fundamental human rights are being or are likely to be violated on a large scale, even if the Security Council is taking no action.' As

---

[36] *Legality of Use of Force Case* (Verbatim Record), (ICJ 1999), 11 May, CR 99/24.

[37] HC Session 1999–2000, Foreign Affairs Committee, Fourth Report, Kosovo, Volume 1, at li.

[38] Advisory Committee on Issues of Public International Law, Advisory Council on International Affairs, Roint Advisory Report, Humanitarian Intervention, Report No. 13, 13 April 2000.

a remedy, the report proposed that those wishing to intervene should turn to the UN General Assembly for authorization, instead of the Council.

A report of the Danish Institute of International Affairs offered a similar view. It clearly stated that 'under current international law there is no right for states to undertake humanitarian intervention in another state without prior authorization from the UN Security Council.'[39] This view was based on a review of practice during the Cold War years, and since 1990. Nevertheless, the report noted growing support amongst governments and legal experts in favour of a right to intervene. Moreover, the report found that criticism of unauthorized interventions had been muted. While this might 'evidence a greater acceptance that humanitarian intervention without Security Council authorization may be necessary and justified in extreme cases . . . these events do not amount to the conclusion that a legal right of humanitarian intervention without Security Council authorization has been established under international law. It is premature to assess whether such a right may be emerging under international law.'[40]

A high-level Independent International Commission on Kosovo, chaired by Richard Goldstone of South Africa and Carl Tham of Sweden, provided considerable evidence confirming the existence of a humanitarian necessity at the time of the intervention. It highlighted the 'need to close the gap between legality and legitimacy', apparently taking the view that the operation was not strictly legal, but should nevertheless not be condemned.[41] Accordingly, the Commission found that the 'time is now ripe for the presentation of a principled framework for humanitarian intervention which could be used to guide future responses to imminent humanitarian catastrophes and which could be used to assess claims for humanitarian intervention'.[42] In the view of the Commission, it would be for the General Assembly to adopt such a framework with a view to adapting the UN Charter to incorporate it.

The government of Canada established another international high-level commission to address the problem of humanitarian intervention. That Commission identified a 'responsibility to protect'. In its view:[43]

a. State sovereignty implies responsibility, and the primary responsibility of protection of its people lies with the state itself.
b. Where a population is suffering serious harm as a result of internal war, insurgency, repression or state failure, and the state in question is unwilling or unable to halt or avert it, the principle of non-intervention yields to the international responsibility to protect.

[39] Danish Institute of International Affairs, Humanitarian Intervention, Copenhagen, 1999, at 123.
[40] *Ibid.*
[41] Independent International Commission on Kosovo, Kosovo Report (Oxford: Oxford University Press 2000), 10.
[42] *Ibid.*
[43] International Commission on Intervention and State Sovereignty, The Responsibility to Protect, Ottawa, International Development Research Centre, 2001, ii.

The Committee emphasized, however, the expectation in principle that this responsibility be exercised through the means of the UN Security Council. It, too, considered the issue of unilateral humanitarian intervention, arguing that it would be impossible to find consensus on the matter. From this finding it drew the conclusion that the pressure on the Council increased to ensure through its own action that individual states or ad hoc coalitions did not feel constrained to act in the most extreme circumstances.[44]

VI. Conclusion

This review of the responses to the armed action against Yugoslavia, both in immediate response to the operation and after some time had passed, reveals a number of interesting facts. First, it is true to say that the Kosovo episode has generated division on the issue of the existence of a right to humanitarian intervention in general international law. A sufficient number of states formally and directly opposed this purported justification for the use of force to render its induction into the corpus of international custom easily possible. It is also noteworthy that some NATO states, including Germany and France, subsequently joined the ranks of the opponents of a right to unilateral action. France argued that the action had been justified with reference to authority contained in existing Security Council resolutions. Germany indicated that the operation was justified because circumstances had been very special, but expressly denied the existence of a rule of humanitarian intervention generally.

However, the wider debate reveals a significant number of states that have formally embraced the view that humanitarian intervention is lawful, at least when it becomes clear that a Security Council mandate cannot be obtained. A number of other states engaged sympathetically with the UN Secretary-General's proposal to re-consider the balancing of sovereignty and human rights. An even larger number of states indicated general understanding for the need to mount the operation, without offering a legal basis. While some of the opponents of the action (amongst them Russia, China, Cuba, Libya, and Vietnam) were very volatile in their condemnation of the intervention, few others joined in this particular chorus. Indeed, a reference to the doctrine of the responsibility to protect that was inspired by the events in Kosovo (and also the recollection of Bosnia and Herzegovina and Rwanda) has now been universally accepted in the 2005 World Summit Outcome Document.[45] International legal scholarship has reflected this development. While there are some who continue to deny the existence of the

---

[44] *Ibid.*, 54f.
[45] Outcome Document, Res 60/1, para. 138A/60/L.1, 20 September 2005.

doctrine of humanitarian intervention,[46] and some who argue that it unambiguously exists as a justification for the use of force,[47] a significant body of scholarship
takes the view that this doctrine is emerging in international law and practice,[48]
on the basis of a changed appreciation of the doctrine of sovereignty.[49]

[46] Peter Malanczuk, *Humanitarian Intervention and the Legitimacy of the Use of Force*
(Hingham, MA: Nijhoff International, 1993), Peter Hilpold, 'Humanitarian Intervention: Is there
a Need for a Legal Reappraisal?', *European Journal of International Law*, 12 (2001) 437–68.

[47] Arguing on the basis of an existing customary right: Christopher Greenwood, 'Humanitarian
Intervention: The Case of Kosovo', *Finnish Yearbook of International Law*, 10 (1999) 141–76.

[48] Detecting an emerging right: Steven Blockmans, 'Moving into UNchartered [sic] Waters: an
Emerging Right of Unilateral Humanitarian Intervention?', *Leiden Journal of International Law*,
12 (1999), 759–86; Antonio Cassese, 'Ex injuria ius oritur: Are We Moving Towards International
Legitimation of Forcible Humanitarian Counter-measures in the World Community?', *European
Journal of International Law*, 10(23) (1999), 23–30.

[49] John Currie, 'NATO's Humanitarian Intervention in Kosovo: Making or Breaking
International Law', *Canadian Yearbook of International Law*, 36 (1998), 303–33. Somewhat more
cautious is Alan James, 'The Concept of Sovereignty Revisited', in Albrecht Schnabel and Ramesh
Thakur, *Kosovo and the Challenge of Humanitarian Intervention* (New York: UN University Press,
2000), 334. For a more detailed review of the literature, see Marc Weller, 'Forcible Humanitarian
Action: The Case of Kosovo', in Michael Bothe, Mary Ellen O'Connell and Natalino Ronzitti
(eds), *Redefining Sovereignty: The Use of Force after the Cold War* (Ardsley, NY: Transnational
Publishers, 2005), 277.

10

The Conduct and Termination
of Hostilities

I. The Conduct of Hostilities

NATO had prepared for a phased air campaign. In its first phase, there would be a show of force. There would then follow a set of attacks against air defence and command and control installations in and around Kosovo. A third phase would take the conflict into Yugoslavia proper, hitting high value targets there. Throughout the seventy-eight day campaign, NATO launched 38,004 sorties, of which 10,484 were strike missions.[1]

NATO's determination to maintain the military operation in place was severely tested throughout the conflict. In addition to harsh protests and a disruption in cordial relations with Russia and China, NATO governments were unable to deliver an improvement of the situation on the ground in Kosovo. Although the operation was meant to serve humanitarian aims, it did not appear to inhibit the activities of Serbian forces. These had greatly intensified operations, which were no longer focused on engaging the KLA. Instead, the civilian population was now targeted in a huge campaign of forced displacement and terror.

NATO's initial aim of knocking out Serbian anti-aircraft and communications installations in a bid to gain air supremacy could not be met as rapidly as had been expected, due to very poor weather conditions. In addition, Serbian forces did not switch on their radar installations at critical times, making it difficult if not impossible to target them.

The attempt to engage Serbian ground forces in Kosovo was also fraught with difficulties. NATO planes had been instructed to operate from a height of at least 15,000 ft, so as to reduce the risk of being shot down over hostile territory. This made it very difficult to engage Serbian tanks and artillery, not to speak of the smaller mobile units employed to terrorize the local population. Low-tech decoys made of canvas and cardboard also deflected several of the attacks mounted on armoured units.

---

[1] Report by Secretary-General of NATO, Lord Robertson of Port Ellen, *The Kosovo Crisis*, 6 October 1999.

The NATO campaign also suffered setbacks due to a number of costly targeting errors. This included an accidental attack on a passenger train south of Belgrade, the destruction of a convoy of refugees on tractors and trailers in Kosovo, and the bombing of the Chinese embassy in Belgrade.

NATO's resolve to continue the armed campaign, which some had thought would last only a few days, was ironically kept in place by Slobodan Milosevic. Shortly before the start of the bombardment, an elaborate plan was set in motion to permanently rid Kosovo of its ethnic Albanian majority. This plan, apparently entitled 'Operation Horseshoe', required significant command, control and transport infrastructure and had been drawn up some time in advance of the NATO bombing. Entire populations were shipped out of towns and villages in cattle trucks towards uncertain destinations. There were also instances of mass murder of ethnic Albanian men. Those who were able to make their way to the border with Albania and Macedonia were stripped of their possessions before they were able to exit Serbia. Passports and identity documents of those forced out of the country were burnt or torn, to make return impossible. Even the licence plates were removed from the cars laden with refugees in order to ensure that the exodus was permanent. The UN Secretary-General protested on 30 March against the 'vicious and systematic campaign of "ethnic cleansing" conducted by Serbian military and paramilitary forces'.[2] Throughout the campaign, it is estimated that over half of the ethnic Albanian population of Kosovo, some 800,000 to 1.1 million civilians were forcibly removed from the territory. A very large number, around 500,000, were internally displaced. Houses were destroyed and property looted. According to figures from the US State Department, around 10,000 ethnic Albanians were murdered and dumped in mass graves.[3] As intended, the massive inflow of refugees—half a million in just the first two weeks of the operation—led to political instability in Macedonia and Albania. Macedonia at one stage closed its borders, fearing it would be overwhelmed by the more than 300,000 ethnic Albanians who had flowed in. NATO action increasingly focused not only on the armed campaign, but also on supporting assistance for the refugees who were experiencing serious hardship in cramped and undersupplied refugee camps. This led to unprecedented cooperation between the Alliance—which was after all an active combatant at the time—and humanitarian agencies.[4]

This highly visible policy of ethnic persecution made it easier for NATO to maintain the pace of the aerial campaign, despite public protest. Indeed, by early summer, the US and UK had started making preparations for a possible ground invasion of Kosovo. This eventuality was resisted by other NATO members, in

---

[2] UN Secretary-General, Statement of 30 March.

[3] US State Department Report, *Ethnic Cleansing in Kosovo: An Accounting*, December 1999. A detailed report, *Kosovo/Kosova—As Seen, As Told*, was also issued by the OSCE in 1999, offering great analytical detail in relation to this campaign of terror and expulsion.

[4] On the refugee crisis, see 'The Kosovo Refugee Crisis: An Independent Evaluation of UNHCR's Emergency Preparedness', *Refugee Survey Quarterly*, 19 (2000), 203–21.

particular Germany, as the German government was dependent on support from the pacifist Green Party. Support for the aerial campaign had been narrowly obtained, but it was clear that a ground offensive would not have been supported. Nevertheless, the UK in particular was pressing for arrangements to be made for ground deployments—a view that was gradually accepted by the US government. In preparation, NATO was authorized to start considering such options, and there were plans to beef up the presence of NATO troops in neighbouring states where they were conducting humanitarian missions, or were preparing for a peace implementation mission.

II. The Indictment by the ICTY

On 24 May 1999, exactly two months after the initiation of hostilities against Yugoslavia by NATO, the International Criminal Tribunal issued an indictment against the top leadership of FRY/Serbia. This action was to have a decisive impact on the development of the conflict, for it signalled a point of no return. It transformed NATO's use of force from an exercise in coercive diplomacy into an action which approximated a 'war' in the more traditional sense. In so doing, the Tribunal not only triggered a strategic shift in the armed conflict involving Kosovo. Its confident action also added a remarkable piece to the puzzle of an emerging international constitutional order.

The ICTY was established in 1993, in the wake of allegations of atrocities committed by military and paramilitary armed forces in the territory of Bosnia and Herzegovina and, previously, in Croatia. These atrocities appeared to be connected mainly with a campaign of 'ethnic cleansing' which had characterized the operations of Yugoslav armed forces and associated Bosnian Serb paramilitary formations and also Croatian militia operating in Bosnia and Herzegovina. The international response to the unfolding tragedy in Bosnia and Herzegovina was hesitant. Under the leadership of the states of the European Union, a policy of non-involvement and containment had been adopted. The rest of Europe was to be isolated from the consequences of the conflict until the parties themselves had had enough of the fighting and agreed to a negotiated peace proposed by the European Union. An ineffective UN presence was maintained in the territory, to give the illusion of international engagement, while actually serving the project of disengagement and containment. The establishment of the International Criminal Tribunal was driven by similar considerations. The lack of direct intervention to restrain the actors on the ground was to be compensated for by the distant threat of international accountability.

While the legal drafting body of the United Nations, the International Law Commission, had laboured in vain to establish a Permanent International Criminal Court, virtually since the judgments of Nuremberg and Tokyo had been handed down, establishment of the Yugoslav Tribunal occurred at a comparatively breathtaking pace. When the conflict in Bosnia and Herzegovina broke out in full force in 1992, the UN Security Council quickly confirmed that all parties were bound by their obligations under international humanitarian law.[5] It demanded that breaches of this law cease immediately[6] and, when there was no compliance, requested that the UN Secretary-General establish as a matter of urgency an impartial Commission of Experts to collect evidence of violations and suggest remedies.[7] In response to an interim report of the Commission, the Council decided on 22 February 1993 on the rapid establishment of an international tribunal for the prosecution of persons responsible for serious violations of international humanitarian law committed in the territory of the former Yugoslavia since 1991.[8] Drawing upon proposals made by several governments and international governmental and NGOs, the UN Secretary-General's office then produced a draft statute for the Tribunal by 3 May.[9] This proposal was endorsed by the Security Council in Resolution 827 (1993) of 25 May. Through the application of its Chapter VII powers, the Council instantly created an international body with objective international personality. That is to say, in the application of its extraordinary powers relating to international peace and security, the Council could effectively legislate into existence an international institution with jurisdiction at the level of the international community as a whole, or at least the entire UN membership. This action was a radical departure from the principle of state sovereignty in three ways:

- The decision privileged international community interest over the sovereign 'rights' of the state actors involved in the conflict;
- The decision created a supranational institution with objective powers without state consent;
- The decision equipped this supranational institution with truly independent decision-making authority.

As the Tribunal derives its authority directly from the Chapter VII enforcement powers of the Security Council, all UN member states are legally obliged to cooperate with it, and to recognize the pre-eminence of its jurisdiction. That jurisdiction extends to the prosecution of persons responsible for serious violations of international humanitarian law committed in the territory of the former Yugoslavia since 1991. It covers serious war crimes, genocide, and crimes against humanity. The latter includes murder, extermination, deportation, imprisonment, torture, rape, persecution on political, racial, and religious grounds, and other inhumane acts, whether committed in international or internal armed

---

[5] Resolution 764 (1992), S/RES/764 (1992).
[6] Resolution 771 (1992), S/RES/771 (1992).
[7] Resolution 780 (1992), S/RES/780 (1992).
[8] Resolution 808 (1993), S/RES/808 (1993).
[9] Report of the Secretary-General pursuant to para. 2 of Security Council Resolution 808 (1993), UN Document S/25704, 3 May 1993.

conflict and directed against any civilian population.[10] Those actually committing the acts, as well as those organizing and ordering their commission, can be held responsible.

While the existence of the Tribunal did not have the anticipated deterrent effect (the Srebrenica massacre, for example, was committed over two years after the Tribunal came into existence), it nevertheless established its international credibility as a professional legal body. Of course, its failure to obtain custody over the chief suspects in the Bosnian atrocities, Messrs Karadzic and Mladic over many years, dented its reputation somewhat. Although the Security Council gave consistent verbal support to the Tribunal, it failed to take effective action in the face of Yugoslav non-cooperation. In particular, no sanctions were adopted, despite repeated pleas from the Tribunal for strong measures to obtain Yugoslav cooperation.

Despite its limited staff, the Tribunal responded swiftly to reports of the initial massacres of ethnic Albanians in the Drenica region in the early phases of the hot conflict in Kosovo. On 10 March 1998, it issued an unusual public statement, confirming its view that its jurisdiction is 'ongoing and covers the recent violence in Kosovo'.[11] The Prosecutor indicated, in view of the scale of the fighting, the situation in Kosovo amounted to an internal armed conflict, bringing into operation the Tribunal's jurisdiction in relation to that territory.[12] The existence of internal armed conflict in Kosovo, at least by 1998, implies recognition of the status of the KLA as an organized armed movement controlling a significant portion of Kosovo territory. Yugoslav pleas that it was dealing with a band of gangsters or terrorists to be controlled by means of an internal 'police' action were no longer tenable at this point.

While some international organs started to refer to the KLA as an armed movement, others continued to label it a terrorist organization. The changed status of the KLA in a state of internal armed conflict, of course, did not entitle that organization to engage in 'terrorist' operations, such as the kidnapping and murder of Serbian civilians or the killing of members of Serbian security forces that fell into its hands. Instead, both the FRY/Serbian authorities and the KLA were bound to observe the rules of internal armed conflict. In effect, members of the KLA also became subject to the prosecutorial interests of the war crimes investigators who had begun to assemble evidence accordingly.

With respect to the FRY/Serbia, the Tribunal expressed its concern at numerous specific and credible allegations concerning willful killings (including a number of summary executions), wanton destruction (including the use of disproportionate force in attacking an area and devastation not justified by military

[10] Statute of the ICTY, Arts 1, 5, 25 May 1993.
[11] Prosecutor's Statement, 10 March 1998, in Weller, *Crisis in Kosovo*, 243.
[12] Communication from the Prosecutor, 7 July 1998, in Weller, *Crisis in Kosovo*, 243.

necessity after the attack has been successful), attacks against civilians (including reprisals) and plunder.[13]

The UN Security Council, in Resolution 1160 (1998) of 31 March, confirmed the jurisdiction of the Tribunal in relation to Kosovo and urged the office of the Prosecutor of the Tribunal to begin investigations.[14] Until October 1998, the Tribunal had been able to introduce investigators into the FRY/Kosovo to collect evidence on the ground. However, the FRY government then refused to grant visas to tribunal investigators, claiming that no jurisdiction existed.[15]

There then followed media reports which indicated that the secretive Holbrooke agreement had in some way purported to diminish the authority of the Tribunal in relation to Kosovo, leading to urgent requests for clarification from The Hague.[16] In the event, the authority of the Tribunal was rooted in Security Council resolutions and could not be affected by bilateral arrangements of any nature. When endorsing the principal elements of the Holbrooke agreement, the Security Council reiterated its call to Yugoslavia to cooperate with the Tribunal.[17] However, in contrast to the presence of NATO and associated forces in Bosnia and Herzegovina, the unarmed OSCE verifiers deployed in Kosovo pursuant to the Holbrooke agreement were not in a position to effect arrests of war crimes suspects.

Yugoslavia continued to refuse cooperation and access to the Tribunal's investigators, prompting the Security Council to adopt a further resolution which again called upon the FRY authorities, as well as the leaders of the Kosovo Albanian community, to cooperate fully with the Tribunal.[18] The situation was highlighted when the Chief Prosecutor attempted to enter Kosovo from Macedonia following news of the Racak massacre of January 1999. In an event captured on television and broadcast worldwide, she was refused entry and unceremoniously turned back by FRY border guards.[19] This dramatic footage helped to generate a climate in which the adoption of a more determined attitude by the Contact Group and NATO was made possible, leading to the summons of the parties to the Rambouillet conference.

While the Tribunal failed to gain access, it nevertheless proceeded to collect evidence as far as possible with a view to launching prosecutions. This included interviews by Tribunal staff of some of the 100,000 victims of forced displacement in the territories adjacent to the FRY. This activity was increased when, after the collapse of the Rambouillet process, the FRY/Serbia began its campaign of forced deportation of what seemed to be virtually the entire ethnic Albanian

---

[13] Statement by the Prosecutor, 4 November 1998, in Weller, *Crisis in Kosovo*, 246.
[14] Also Resolution 1199 (1998), 23 September 1998, S/RES/1199 (1998).
[15] Prosecutor's Statement, 7 October 1998, in Weller, *Crisis in Kosovo*, 244–5.
[16] President of the Tribunal Statement, 14 October 1998, in Weller, *Crisis in Kosovo*, 245.
[17] Resolution 1203, 24 October 1998, S/RES/1203 (1998).
[18] Resolution 1207 (1998), 17 November 1998, S/RES/1207 (1998).
[19] Letter by ICTY President to President of the Security Council, 16 March 1999, in Weller, *Crisis in Kosovo*, 249.

population of Kosovo. However, the limited resources of the Tribunal, compared to the scale of the unfolding tragedy, hampered its efforts in this respect.

An indictment was issued against five of the most senior leaders of the Federal Republic of Yugoslavia and Serbia:

- Slobodan Milosevic, President of the Federal Republic of Yugoslavia from 1997;
- Milan Milutinovic, President of Serbia from 1997;
- Nikola Sainovic, Deputy Prime Minister of the Federal Republic of Yugoslavia from 1998;
- Colonel General Dragljub Ojdanic, Chief of the General Staff of the Yugoslav Armed Forces (VJ); and
- Vlajko Stojiljkovic, Minister of the Interior of Serbia from 1998.

The Tribunal asserted that these individuals had planned, instigated, ordered, committed or otherwise aided a campaign of violence conducted by the forces of the FRY/Serbia in Kosovo. That campaign, it was alleged, consisted of a well-planned and coordinated campaign of destruction of property owned by Kosovo Albanian civilians. These civilians had also been systematically harassed, humiliated and degraded through physical and verbal abuse. The campaign of suppression had been followed by the unlawful deportation and forcible transfer of hundreds of thousands of Kosovo Albanians from their homes in Kosovo. This policy in turn was supported by increased attacks on civilian populations, including the widespread shelling of towns and villages, the burning of homes, farms, and so on, and the systematic seizure and destruction of identity documents and vehicle licences. In addition, the killing of Kosovo Albanians had occurred since the launch of NATO's armed operations on 24 March 1999 at numerous locations. It was alleged that the accused were linked to these activities by virtue of command responsibility and jointly indicted on three counts of crimes against humanity (deportation, murder, persecutions) and one count of violation of the laws or customs of war (murder).

The ICTY had asserted its claim to jurisdiction in relation to Kosovo ever since the outbreak of significant hostilities in the territory, followed by the initial wave of forced displacements, early in 1998.[20] However, the FRY had consistently denied this claim to jurisdiction, maintaining this approach even after the Security Council confirmed the position of the Tribunal in a Chapter VII resolution adopted in November 1998.[21] Needless to say, the Tribunal still had no direct access to Kosovo when it issued its indictment some two months after the massive campaign of displacement of Kosovo Albanians began in March.

[20] Prosecutor's Statement Regarding the Tribunal's Jurisdiction over Kosovo, 10 March 1998, and further statements in Weller, *Crisis in Kosovo,* Chapter 10.
[21] Resolution 1207 (1998), 17 November 1998, S/RES/1207 (1998).

In contrast to the work of the Tribunal in relation to Bosnia and Herzegovina, the absence of access to sites of alleged atrocities meant that no forensic evidence could be collected or preserved. No interviews could be conducted in Kosovo itself. Instead, the Tribunal had to rely on external sources to compile the materials supporting the indictment, including witness statements obtained by ICTY teams dispatched to the refugee centres in Albania and Macedonia. The Tribunal also received testimonies transmitted by NGOs operating in the region, and by some governments. Military intelligence may also have been made available. On this basis, the indictment does refer to some twenty specific incidents of deportations and alleged atrocities. It also features a longer general description of events in Kosovo and is accompanied by a list of individuals allegedly killed at specific locations. Overall, the events portrayed in the indictment do appear to support a picture of systematic and grave violations of humanitarian law. Given the debate surrounding the question of whether or not, in a situation of internal armed conflict, the Tribunal can consider atrocities to fall under the heading of grave breaches of the Geneva law (Article 2 of the Statute), it is noteworthy that the indictment only alleges 'ordinary' war crimes under Article 3 of the Statute.

Of course, the approach of the Tribunal to this case differs markedly from that exhibited in relation to Bosnia and Herzegovina. In the former, it focused initially on the actual perpetrators of specific, individual criminal acts. It did extend its interests to commanding officers (for example, General Mladic) and the political leader of the Republika Srpska, Radovan Karadzic. However, the leadership of the Federal Republic of Yugoslavia and Serbia, including especially Slobodan Milosevic, was initially spared. Given the magnitude of the suffering inflicted by the Yugoslav armed forces and Serbian units on the mainly Muslim population of Bosnia and Herzegovina early in that conflict, and the continued support and control of the local Serbian forces by Belgrade, this gave rise to allegations of excessive political prudence on the part of the Tribunal. No such caution was exercised in relation to the Kosovo indictment. Instead of seeking to isolate individual instances of atrocities and to link them to individual perpetrators, the Tribunal sought instead to establish a general pattern of violations. It then referred simply to Article 7 of the Statute, indicating that individual criminal responsibility includes committing, planning, instigating, ordering, or aiding and abetting in the planning, preparation, or execution of crimes.

The Tribunal did not exhibit significant evidence in relation to any such activities. No real attempt was made to demonstrate in a specific sense how any of the accused could be tied to the individual instances of atrocities that had been elaborated. Instead, the Tribunal described the official function of the indictees, asserting that the individuals 'had authority or control' over units, commanders and individuals engaged in atrocities by virtue of this function. In this way, the prosecutors appeared to be proceeding from a presumption of responsibility, as opposed to a more cautious approach that would rely on the construction of an actual chain of command relating to the individual acts in question, and the demonstration that specific commands leading to criminal conduct had actually been issued. Given the very widespread and systematic nature of the alleged offences involving a significant part of the official infrastructure of the FRY/Serbia, this approach appears justified. The difference in the Tribunal's approach, when compared to its action in relation to the conflict in Bosnia and Herzegovina, might perhaps be explained with reference to its external dimension. In contrast, Kosovo was, according to Belgrade, clearly a matter falling exclusively within its own domestic jurisdiction. Hence, no complicating issues of 'international' attribution of the acts of Yugoslav/Serbian forces arose and a presumption of command responsibility could be more easily maintained.

The effect of the indictment was potentially very significant. At the conclusion of the Bosnian war, Milosevic had emerged as an internationally lauded peacemaker upon whose cooperation the success of the settlement depended. A similar outcome must have been in Milosevic's mind in relation to Kosovo. NATO would launch its graduated air campaign to little effect against Belgrade's military infrastructure, which had been widely dispersed given the weeks of warning that were available. FRY/Serbia would have re-established control over Kosovo, having removed a large portion of the ethnic Albanian population in the process. NATO would cave in to internal political divisions and increasingly volatile public opinion and would not be able to sustain the use of force indefinitely. The option of the use of force having been exhausted, NATO would have to permit UN mediation to terminate the conflict on Belgrade's terms. That is to say, there would be confirmation of Yugoslavia's sovereignty in relation to Kosovo, Serbia would remain in political control of the territory and an enfeebled international UN presence would seek to implement a restricted autonomy regime within that framework. Under those circumstances, only a very limited number of refugees would return to Kosovo, easing the process of establishing full Serbian control in the long term.

The scale and swiftness of the ethnic cleansing campaign conducted in Kosovo jeopardized the success of this strategy, for it undermined public opposition to NATO's military action and bolstered NATO cohesion. The issuing of formal indictments against the top Yugoslav/Serbian leadership, however, completely frustrated Belgrade's aims. It was now clear that allegations of horrendous abuses and of a campaign of systematic ethnic cleansing (but not genocide, strictly speaking) in Kosovo were not spectres of NATO propaganda. Instead, the allegations had been confirmed by a body that was intrinsically connected to the UN Security Council, the international organ exercising primary responsibility in relation to international peace and security. The Tribunal could claim objectivity. And while human rights organs, including within the context of the UN, had unanimously condemned Yugoslav action in Kosovo, the Tribunal boasted the most specific judicial competence in relation to the matter. Moreover, it had the unique power to attach legal consequences directly to its findings and to seek to enforce them.

As such, President Slobodan Milosevic, the most prominent of the indictees, and his close associates were no longer an indispensable element to a resolution of the Kosovo conflict. Instead, they were to be considered as probable war criminals that needed to be defeated militarily. Indeed, this fact was reflected in the fact that at the end of the conflict, no peace settlement as such was concluded with the Belgrade leadership. Instead, the peace terms were established by way of the Security Council resolution, which only referred to certain documents that had been accepted by Milosevic and his associates.[22]

However, it would be wrong to see the relevance of the Tribunal's actions as focused exclusively on Yugoslav involvement in the conflict. While this may not have been widely appreciated at the time, the Tribunal's objective powers also applied, in principle, to NATO and its conduct in the conflict. Given the reluctance of some NATO states, and in particular the US, to subject any of its armed operations, or its service personnel, to any sort of international judicial review, including the International Criminal Court, this is a very interesting result.

The Kosovo indictment was powerful confirmation of the highly advanced nature of the ICTY. As an international judicial institution, the Tribunal outclasses its 'successor', the International Criminal Court (ICC) in some respects. The jurisdiction of the latter is founded in state consent and the implementation of its statute is vulnerable to significant political control. This control applies in part to the launching of proceedings by the ICC. At present, for instance, we can witness attempts in the UN Security Council to suspend potential action that may be taken by the ICC in relation to the Sudanese leadership regarding the possible genocide in Darfur.

In the case of the ICTY, prosecutors prepare indictments which are then reviewed by a judge of the Tribunal. Proceedings are then conducted exclusively according to judicial considerations. The ICC, on the other hand, can initiate proceedings through its prosecutors, but also on the basis of state application or Security Council action. While this might appear to broaden the scope of ICC activity, it is in fact greatly reduced by the principle of so-called 'complementarity'. Any single state is endowed with the procedural power to remove a case from the ICC. Conceptually, therefore, the ICC is a very different creature from the ICTY. The former functions until individual states decide to exercise jurisdiction. The latter permits the exercise of jurisdiction of states, but only until it resolves to exercise jurisdiction at the international level.

The Kosovo indictment therefore highlighted once again the radical and progressive nature of the decision to establish the ICTY in the first place. This applies to its establishment as a body with objective, genuinely supranational powers without regard to the classical structural requirement of state consent. The independent exercise of these powers in the case of Kosovo did have a profound political impact on the prosecution of the conflict. In that sense,

---

[22] Resolution 1244 (1999), see Joshka Fischer, *Die rot-gruenen Jahre* (Munich: Knaur, 2008), 184.

the Tribunal also played a strategic role, as its action effectively denied Belgrade any hope of achieving its principal aims. However, the Tribunal also exercised a strategic role in a wider, more significant sense. Not only did it insist on the application of fundamental principles of humanitarian law in circumstances of 'internal' or mixed armed conflicts, but it also clarified, or perhaps advanced, the doctrine of command responsibility in relation to a military and political leadership that launches a systematic and unlawful campaign of violence, but that cannot be tied directly to individual acts of atrocities. In so doing, it consolidated an important element of the substantive law of the emerging international constitution, which may have a useful impact on future instances of conflict.

III. Moves towards a Settlement

At the end of March, Russian Foreign Minister Ivanov travelled to Belgrade. He returned with an offer of some Serbian troop withdrawals from Kosovo and the launch of fresh negotiations in return for a suspension of NATO bombing. This offer was immediately rejected as it did not fulfil the NATO conditions stated at the outset of the campaign. Russia persisted, however, in its diplomatic initiative. A further proposal was made to suspend NATO hostilities over the Easter holidays, putting significant pressure on Germany and other key states, where the NATO action had been highly unpopular and threatened to lead to a breakdown of the governing coalition of Social Democrats and the Green Party. The initiative was refused, although NATO reduced military activities considerably during the Easter period.

Germany, responding to domestic opposition to the conflict, also sought involvement in the various peace initiatives that were being discussed. Berlin developed the so-called 'Fischer' Plan, named after its ambitious Foreign Minister, who was a member of the Green Party. The plan was first presented unilaterally by Germany on 12 April. It foresaw a total withdrawal of Serbian security forces, the deployment of an international peace force under a Chapter VII UN mandate and a single command, NATO aerial monitoring and various other elements. While this plan had been subject to consultation with the US and other allies, there was concern within NATO that the Alliance might become divided due to German eagerness to come to a peace deal. Nevertheless, NATO managed to maintain a public position of unity on the occasion of the celebration of its fiftieth anniversary in Washington DC in April. At the meeting NATO restated its conditions for a settlement, demanding that the Milosevic government must:[23]

Ensure a verifiable stop to all military action and the immediate ending of violence and repression in Kosovo

Withdraw from Kosovo his military, police and paramilitary forces;

---

[23] North Atlantic Council Statement on Kosovo, 23 April 1999.

Agree to the stationing in Kosovo of an international military presence;

Agree to the unconditional and safe return to all refugees and displaced persons, and unhindered access to them by humanitarian aid organizations; and

Provide credible assurance of this willingness to work for the establishment of a political framework agreement based on the Rambouillet accords.

NATO added that 'there can be no compromise on these conditions'. However, when compared to the eventual outcome, which removed Serbia from all governmental control over Kosovo and entirely replaced it with a UN mission, these conditions would indicate that Belgrade might, even at this late stage, still have had the option to negotiate a reasonable outcome.

In the meantime, President Rugova was made to appear in Prishtina, where he purportedly agreed, with Serbian President Milan Milutinovic, to a set of measures in relation to Kosovo, including a resumption of negotiations. In the meantime, Russia continued its diplomatic efforts, dispatching Special Envoy Viktor Chernomyrdin to Washington after further talks in Belgrade. During a long-drawn out meeting with Milosevic, who was reported to be calm and composed, Russia proposed a somewhat softer arrangement providing for a return of refugees, economic assistance to Yugoslavia, a resumption of negotiations on future status, a withdrawal of NATO forces from the immediate theatre and the deployment of a UN peacekeeping force including a significant Russian contingent.[24] Milosevic's own proposals, communicated through the Russian envoy on 3 May, provided for the beginning of a withdrawal of forces from Kosovo, which was to coincide with a suspension of NATO air strikes and a guarantee that there would be no ground invasion. This would be followed by UN-led negotiations about the deployment of a peacekeeping presence.[25]

This initiative was answered through a set of agreed principles on the political solution of the Kosovo crisis, adopted by the G-8 on 6 May 1999. The principles demanded an immediate and verifiable end to the violence and repression in Kosovo and the withdrawal from Kosovo of FRY/Serbian military, police and paramilitary forces. An 'effective international civil and security presence', endorsed and adopted by the United Nations, would be deployed. The US and other governments were insisting that this would need to be a NATO force, despite the weak formula of the declaration, reflecting the need to obtain Russian approval within the G-8 format. There would also be an interim administration established under Security Council authority. To organize for implementation of the plan, the political directors of the G-8 states were instructed to prepare elements of a UN Security Council resolution. This development proved important, inasmuch as it heralded a resumption of joint action by select NATO states and Russia on the basis of the agreed text.

---

[24] John Norris, *Collision Course: NATO, Russia, and Kosovo* (Westport, Ct: Praeger, 2005), at 59 (hereinafter Norris, *Collision Course*).
[25] Norris, *Collision Course*, 83.

A Troika of interlocutors, composed of Finnish President Martti Ahtisaari for the EU, Strobe Talbot for the US, and Viktor Chernomyrdin for Russia, was mandated to negotiate on the basis of these proposals. Over the next few weeks, very intensive negotiations took place. However, these were conducted largely within the Troika, where the US, with the EU, was seeking to persuade Russia to endorse a common proposal. Russia insisted on confirmation of the territorial integrity of Yugoslavia and was particularly adamant in rejecting NATO implementation of an agreement on the ground. Russia also sought sole control of the northern part of Kosovo by its own contingent in any peace force, triggering fears of a likely division of Kosovo. Hence, the actual negotiations were conducted within the former Contact Group, rather than in dialogue with Belgrade.[26]

Serbia accepted the G-8 principles, which had been expanded somewhat in the meantime, on 29 May and informed the UN Security Council of its decision on 1 June.[27] The Serbian Assembly endorsed the peace proposals two days later. However, NATO remained unwilling to suspend its military operations until a firm agreement on cessation of hostilities and the full withdrawal of Serbian forces had been achieved. By 9 June, a Military Technical Agreement was concluded, establishing a detailed plan for the withdrawal, although provision was also made for the reintroduction of a very small Yugoslav/Serbian military presence at a later stage, in reflection of provisions of the more detailed peace plan that had been accepted on 1 June. In the meantime, the G-8 had finalized work on a UN Security Council resolution, placing a proposed NATO or NATO-led peace force for Kosovo under a UN Chapter VII mandate, along with an international civilian interim administration. This text was adopted on 10 June as Resolution 1244 (1999). That resolution provided for a complete withdrawal of all Serbian security forces and the placing of Kosovo under exclusive UN control. A complete Serbian withdrawal then began, with NATO forces commencing deployment the following day. At that moment, some 200 Russian troops associated with the Bosnian peacekeeping mission arrived at Prishtina airport, seeking to place it under their control. This was meant to be followed by a more sizeable deployment of paratroopers that were being airlifted from Russia. It was speculated that this might have included some 7,000 to 12,000 troops, who would effectively take control of the mainly Serb inhabited regions of Kosovo.[28] NATO had some advance warning of the arrival of the Russian advance contingent and for some moments a risk of a direct military confrontation with them existed. A very tense situation among NATO Generals Wesley Clark and Michael Jackson was eventually resolved, leaving the small Russian contingent in place. However, the attempt to reinforce it was frustrated by the denial of the right of overflight by friendly states. Instead, the small Russian presence was used as a bargaining chip

[26] Generally, see Norris, *Collision Course*, chapters 6–8.
[27] Letter from Yugoslavia to the UN Secretary-General and the Security Council, 1 June 1999, UN Doc. S/1999/631, 7 June 1999.
[28] Norris, *Collision Course*, 218.

to achieve an agreement for a sizeable deployment of 3,500 Russian armed forces alongside NATO, placed under dual NATO and Russian control.

IV. Conclusion

The NATO aerial campaign was a highly risky operation. Most had expected that it would take rapid effect, much like the very short campaign of bombardment against Bosnian Serb forces in September of 1995 that almost instantly terminated the war in Bosnia. However, the Yugoslav armed forces and the Milosevic government proved far more resilient. Indeed, it is doubtful that public opinion would have allowed NATO to maintain the air operation very far beyond the time when a peace settlement was obtained. If a ground-based operations would have been mounted is also not entirely clear, although the prospect of such an operation may have contributed to the decision of the Belgrade government to withdraw.

NATO, and public resolve, were maintained and strengthened principally by Belgrade's ruthless campaign of ethnic cleansing, nearly stripping the territory of its ethnic Albanian majority population. The overt and systematic character of this campaign reflects a severe miscalculation on the part of the Milosevic government. In consequence of the drastic 'solution' to the Albanian 'issue' that was being attempted, the Milosevic government found itself indicted by the ICTY. From that point onwards, surrender, rather than a negotiated settlement, was the only possible outcome. In the end, Serbia was displaced from all control over Kosovo as a result of the conflict, with the UN being placed in complete authority over the territory for an open-ended period of time. This outcome made eventual independence virtually inevitable.

11

International Administration and
Moves Towards Final Status

In compliance with Resolution 1244 (1999), Kosovo was rapidly placed under international administration. While the Rambouillet draft had envisaged a period of interim governance of three years, the interim phase under the international presence lasted for eight and a half years. During this period, Kosovo authorities gradually took over most aspects of public policy, under the guidance of—or, from the Kosovar perspective, under the tutelage of—international administrators.

I. Interim Administration under
Resolution 1244 (1999)

Security Council Resolution 1244 (1999) was adopted on 10 June 1999 by fourteen votes to none (China abstaining). The entire text of the resolution is subject to Chapter VII of the United Nations Charter. Preambular paragraph 10 reaffirms the commitment of all UN member states to the sovereignty and territorial integrity of the Federal Republic of Yugoslavia and the other states of the region. In its very first operative paragraph, it addresses the issue of a political settlement, 'deciding' that a political solution to the Kosovo crisis shall be based on general principles established in two annexes to the resolution. In addition, the Council authorized the deployment under UN auspices of 'international civil and security presences'. The civil presence was to be 'controlled' by a Special Representative of the UN Secretary-General. While the military presence established by 'member states and relevant international organizations' was to coordinate closely with the civil presence, it was not subject to control by the UN Secretariat. It enjoyed a mandate to enforce the ceasefire, deter hostilities, ensure withdrawals and prevent the return of certain forces. It was also empowered to demilitarize the KLA; ensure public safety and order in the interim; conduct border monitoring; ensure freedom of movement for itself, the civil presence and other international organizations; and support, as appropriate, the civil presence.

The civil presence was charged with:

a. Promoting the establishment, pending a final settlement, of substantial autonomy and self-government in Kosovo, taking full account of Annex 2 of the
   Rambouillet accords (S/1999/648);
b. Performing basic civilian administrative functions wherever and for as long
   as required;
c. Organizing and overseeing the development of provisional institutions for
   democratic and autonomous self-government pending a political settlement,
   including the holding of elections;
d. Transferring, as these institutions are established, its administrative responsibilities while overseeing and supporting the consolidation of Kosovo's local
   provisional institutions and other peace-building activities;
e. Facilitating a political process designed to determine Kosovo's future status,
   taking into account the Rambouillet accords (S/1999/648);
f. In the final stage, overseeing the transfer of authority from Kosovo's provisional institutions to institutions established under a political settlement;
g. Supporting the reconstruction of key infrastructure and other reconstruction;
h. Supporting, in coordination with international humanitarian organizations,
   humanitarian and disaster relief aid;
i. Maintaining civil law and order, including establishing local police forces and
   meanwhile through the deployment of international police personnel to serve
   in Kosovo;
j. Protecting and promoting human rights;
k. Assuring the safe and unimpeded return of all refugees and displaced persons
   to their homes in Kosovo.

The UN interim administration for Kosovo was rapidly established in pursuance
of this mandate. In its Regulation No. 1999/1 of 25 July 1999, it established as
'the authority' of the administration that:

All legislative and executive authority with respect to Kosovo, including the administration of the judiciary, is vested in UNMIK and is exercised by the Special Representative
of the [UN] Secretary-General.

During the first phase of international governance by the Special Representative
of the UN Secretary-General (SRSG), Bernard Kouchner, Kosovar actors merely
exercised a power of consultation. However, fairly rapidly, a second phase was
started, providing early in 2000 for the Joint Interim Administrative Structure
(JIAS). This consisted of some twenty departments with responsibility for civil
administration. These departments were headed jointly by one local and one
international official. This was matched by the holding of municipal elections
and the establishment of local structures of self-government at the end of 2000.
A third phase provided for conditional self-government, to be realized under the
terms of the constitutional framework that was put forward in 2001.

II. The Constitutional Framework

The Constitutional Framework for Provisional Self-Government was issued on 15 May as UNMIK Regulation 2001/9. That is to say, its legal force is rooted in Regulation 1999/1 (subsequently amended), which vests supreme executive powers and also quasi-legislative powers in the SRSG. This power is, in turn, derived from the mandate contained in Security Council Resolution 1244 (1999).

The drafting of the document caused some friction among the Western members of the Contact Group (the Quint) throughout 2000. The United States was attempting to present a draft instrument that was based very much on Rambouillet, although the powers for Serbia/FRY had been significantly reduced in view of the recent conflict and its outcome. Others were arguing that it would be premature to offer any sort of consolidated interim constitution, which would accelerate the process of claims for statehood on the part of the Kosovo majority parties. Instead, individual regulations that would, over time and in stages, address issues normally contained in a constitutional document, should be issued.

The debate took a different turn with the appointment of a new SRSG, former Danish Minister of Defence Hans Haekkerup. With amazing expedition and the encouragement of a Presidential Statement by the Security Council, a consultative body of experts was established to draft a framework document (at the time, the use of the word 'constitution' was not accepted). This body was intended to be fully representative, but was generally boycotted by its Serb representatives. Some of the ethnic Albanian experts also resigned towards the end of the drafting process, when it emerged that the draft texts they had submitted would not be taken as the basis for the venture.

Thus, the text that emerged strongly reflected the internationalized nature of its drafting, through the UN's own legal adviser's office and other international experts, in particular an expert of the Venice Commission. Nevertheless, ethnic Albanian experts did have some influence in shaping the document, which eased the process that led all major ethnic Albanian political parties to embrace the document (albeit with reservations) as an acceptable interim solution. At the very end of the drafting process, an effort was also made to take account of the respective positions of the Serbian leadership and to accommodate them to some extent, despite their continued failure to participate formally in the drafting process.

Overall, therefore, an instrument emerged that served as a constitution for some seven years. There was no democratically legitimized constitutional drafting process, say, through a constitutional convention. Instead, the document was established internationally with the involvement (or in the case of the Serb community, with the possible involvement) of experts. Some of these experts were in fact affiliated with the principal political parties in Kosovo. Hence, local 'ownership' of the drafting process was fairly limited.

The Framework defined Kosovo in Article 1.1 as an entity under interim international administration which, because of its people, had unique historical, legal, cultural and linguistic attributes. There was an institutional and a functional layering of power. The institutional layers of authority were arranged in a comparatively simple way. There were municipalities, Kosovo-wide layers of provisional self-government, and the SRSG. Municipalities were the basic territorial units of local self-government, exercising responsibilities set forth in UNMIK legislation in force. Hence, as opposed to the Hill draft and the Rambouillet texts, the municipalities were no longer established as the residual source of all public authority not expressly assigned elsewhere.

The Framework also referred to '[n]ational communities and their members', where 'communities' was used as a substitute term for 'minorities', as a result of the latter's negative connotations in the region, and to the fact that it was not considered to be status neutral. There was no provision for parallel institutions for communities. Instead, the rights of communities were now defined in terms of traditional minority rights. That is to say 'communities of inhabitants belonging to the same ethnic or religious or linguistic group (communities) shall have the rights set forth in this Chapter in order to preserve, protect and express their ethnic, cultural and religious identities'. To this end, they could use their own language, receive education and have access to information in that language, as well as enjoy equal opportunities, and so on. They could also establish associations to promote their community interests and culture and to operate educational institutions. However, the communities were not equipped with institutions that exercised original state powers almost by way of full functional autonomy. Hence, this layer of public authority that was a crucial element of Rambouillet had simply disappeared.

The Kosovo-wide institutions enjoyed powers that were specifically enumerated in the Framework, and which extended to most aspects of public policy. They also had the authority to coordinate and supervise the exercise of public powers by the municipalities. This fact, together with the finding in Article 1.1 that 'Kosovo is an undivided territory throughout which the Provisional Institutions of Self-Government established by this Constitutional Framework...shall exercise their responsibilities', clearly subordinated the municipalities to the Kosovo-wide institutions. Hence, there was no original autonomy located within the municipalities, other than the specific power of municipal governance assigned in legislation.

A third institutional layer consisted of the SRSG who exercised certain 'reserved powers and responsibilities' that remained exclusively in his hands. These included, amongst others:

• Full authority to ensure that the rights and interests of communities were fully protected;
• Final authority to set financial and policy parameters and approve the Kosovo Consolidated Budget and its auditing;

- Dissolving the Assembly and calling for elections, especially when other institutions acted in violation of Resolution 1244 (1999);
- Monetary policy;
- Control of the customs service;
- Appointment, removal and disciplining of judges and prosecutors;
- Assignments of international judges and prosecutors and changes of venue of trials;
- International legal cooperation, conclusion and implementation of international agreements, and exercise of foreign affairs powers;
- Authority over law enforcement institutions and correctional facilities; and
- Control over the Kosovo Protection Corps, among others.

While the introduction to this provision suggested that these were exclusive powers, several provisions did in fact provide for the exercise of administrative authority in relation to them 'in cooperation' with the Kosovo institutions. Hence, there was also a gradual transfer of authority in these areas. In relation to other, exclusive international functions there was at least room for consultation and advice before decisions were made. However, the principle of unchallengeable supreme powers in relation to these issue areas was retained. Moreover, according to a concluding provision of the regulation, the SRSG retained a general right to oversee the provisional institutions and its officers and to take appropriate measures whenever their actions were inconsistent with Resolution 1244 (1999) or the Framework.

The unique character of the SRSG's role was also evident in the fact that he could 'effect' changes to the constitutional framework either at the initiative of a two-thirds majority of the Assembly, or at his own discretion. This provision cast some doubt on the character of the instrument as a 'constitution' and instead confirmed its *sui generis* character.

The Kosovo Assembly, the principal legislative organ of provisional self-government, consisted, and consists still, of 120 members elected by secret ballot in a nation-wide, single-district vote. One hundred of the seats are assigned proportionally to the votes cast for parties, citizens' initiatives (according to a fixed list system) or individual candidates. Additionally, twenty seats are reserved for 'the additional representation of non-Albanian Kosovo communities'. Ten of these fall to those declaring themselves representatives of the Kosovo Serb community; the others are divided amongst the Roma, Ashkali, Egyptian, Bosniak, Turkish, and Gorani communities.

The seven-member Presidency of the Assembly had to contain one member representing the Serb community and one member representing another minority community. However, there was no rotating presidency. Instead the President was nominated by the party that obtained the highest number of votes. There was also no provision for representation of other groups through, for instance, the Office of the Vice-President(s). The Presidency, which manages parliamentary business, should attempt to agree by consensus but, failing that, could decide by majority vote.

There was also no specific quota for representation in functional committees, other than the general exhortation that the membership should reflect the diversity of the membership of the Assembly. Chairs and Vice-Chairs of committees were appointed according to the strength of the parties in the Assembly.

There was, however, a Committee on the Rights and Interests of Communities, which consisted of two members from each of the communities represented in the Assembly (but only one Gorani representative). The Committee, which has been retained since independence, can adopt recommendations in relation to draft legislation or other matters by simple majority.

Decisions of the Assembly were to be passed by a simple majority of the members present and voting (the quorum being 50 per cent for decisions and 33 per cent for debates). Within forty-eight hours of approval of a law, any six members could submit a motion to the Presidency alleging a violation of vital interests of the community to which at least one of them belonged. A motion could be submitted on the grounds that the law or its provisions discriminated against a community, adversely affected the rights of a community or otherwise seriously interfered with the ability of a community to preserve, protect or express its identity.

Initially, an attempt at conciliation would be made by the Presidency, which would endeavour to put forward a consensus proposal. If that was not possible, a panel consisting of one member of the majority, one representative of the complainants and one presiding individual appointed by the SRSG was to issue a recommendation by simple majority. However, the Assembly remained at liberty to accept or reject the consensus proposal of the Presidency or the recommendation of the panel. An Assembly decision could, however, be reviewed for compatibility with the Constitutional Framework by a special chamber of the Supreme Court.

Overall, therefore, there existed no effective blocking mechanism for communities within the Constitutional Framework. There was also only limited provision for representation of minority groups. While it was confirmed that judges, the police and other public officials should be fully reflective of the diversity of the population, there was no rigid quota system as part of the Constitutional Framework, although this does not necessarily apply to implementing legislation and practices. The only concession to quota rules and minority representation was the determination that, out of the nine ministries established, two would be headed by minority representatives, one of them an ethnic Serb.

The Constitutional Framework operated reasonably efficiently over the years. However, it could not overcome two structural deficiencies. One was the ineffectiveness of the international administration. While vast resources were poured into it, it did not manage to come to grips with the major infrastructure issues that continued to plague Kosovo for many years. It was somewhat more successful in its attempt to help build indigenous institutions of governance. However, this was due less to its programmes of capacity building that appeared to focus on new and different issues every year, and rather more to the zeal of local parties and actors in taking over administrative functions, resulting in the establishment of a reasonably well-developed administrative system by the time of declared independence in early 2008.

The other problematic area concerned ethnic relations. The Serb community in the territory retained its links with Belgrade. Often it failed to engage with the Kosovo institutions or to participate in elections. This was most pronounced in territorially compact areas inhabited mainly by ethnic Serbs.

III. Standards Before Status

With Kosovo under international administration, a general sense prevailed among international actors that the status issue would be best left alone for as long as possible. Time might heal the wounds of history and memories of the 1999 conflict. A delay in status talks also seemed convenient for other reasons. It was clear that the majority population of Kosovo would not accept any deal short of independence. However, if independence was to ensue, this might have unhelpful consequences for Bosnia and Herzegovina; its mainly ethnic Serb Republika Srpska might also claim a right to independence. The same might apply to Abkhazia and South Ossetia, two regions of Georgia were that were administering themselves separately under the protection of Russian-led 'peacekeepers'. They, too, might declare themselves independent or merge with Russia—a concern that ultimately proved well founded.

While these might have been legitimate concerns in the eyes of international crisis managers, they were of little relevance to the population of Kosovo. To them, the period of ineffective and increasingly unpopular international administration appeared to stretch on endlessly.

The Rambouillet agreement would have foreseen discussions on a mechanism to address status by early 2002. In April of that year, the UN Secretary-General reported to the Security Council that he had asked his Special Representative to develop benchmarks against which progress in Kosovo could be measured.[1] Introducing the report to the Council, the Special Representative, Michael Steiner, claimed that significant advances had been made in Kosovo, arguing that it had entered a new phase. Referring to an 'exit strategy' for the Security Council, he added: 'The road is not endless. We have a vision of how to finish our job'.[2] Steiner noted that UNMIK was now transferring some responsibilities to the local institutions in the process of building substantial autonomy. This would mean moving closer to the beginning of the political process designed to

---

[1] Report of the Secretary-General on the United Nations Interim Administration Mission in Kosovo, UN Doc. S/2002/436, 22 April 2002.

[2] UN Doc. S/PV/4518, 24 April 2002, 3.

determine Kosovo's future status. However, he also noted that the time for this had not yet come:

Kosovo society and institutions will have to show that they are ready for this process—without prejudicing the outcome. We must make clear what is expected of them. Therefore, I am embarking on a benchmarks process. These benchmarks should be achieved before launching a discussion on status, in accordance with resolution 1244 (1999).[3]

The benchmark areas were drawn from the coalition agreement of the Kosovo parties that had been brokered by UNMIK after the recent elections in the territory. They related to:

- Existence of effective, representative and functioning institutions;
- Reinforcement of the rule of law;
- Freedom of movement for all;
- Respect for the right of all Kosovans to remain and return;
- Development of a sound basis for a market economy;
- Clarity of property title;
- Normalized dialogue with Belgrade;
- Reduction and transformation of the Kosovo Protection Corps in line with its mandate.

The Security Council endorsed this proposal that came to be known as the 'standards before status' policy.[4] However, it took until December 2003 for the eight standards to be developed and presented jointly by UNMIK and the provisional institutions of self-government in Kosovo (PISK). The standards were then still being put forward in a relatively compact form. Each of the issue areas was presented in relation to two or three more specific items which in turn were developed into particular requirements in bullet-point form. By March 2004, however, UNMIK bureaucracy had taken hold of the process. It had developed a Kosovo Standards Implementation Plan ranging over some 117 pages and covering so many items that they could only be listed as highly complex tables.[5]

It was foreseen that a status review process would commence concurrently with standards implementation. Such a review mechanism was formally endorsed by the Council on 12 December 2003, two days after the standards had been presented.[6] The international administration would assess periodically to what extent standards had been met, with a view to recommending whether or not the

[3] *Ibid.*, 4.

[4] Statement by the President of the Security Council, UN Doc. PRST/2002/11, 24 April 2002; also S/PRST/2003/1, 6 February 2003, where the terminology of 'standards before status' was formally adopted.

[5] Kosovo Standards Implementation Plan, 31 March 2004, available at <http://www.unmikonline.org/pub/misc/ksip_eng.pdf> (accessed 19 June 2008).

[6] Statement by the President of the Security Council, UN Doc. S/PRST/2003/26, 12 December 2003.

time was right for commencement of status talks. There was also provision for a comprehensive review of performance:

Reaffirming the 'standards before status' policy, the Council stresses that further advancement towards a process to determine future status of Kosovo in accordance with Resolution 1244 (1999) will depend on the positive outcome of this comprehensive review.

The Council went on to state that a 'first opportunity' for such a comprehensive review 'should occur around mid-2005'.

While the Kosovo authorities struggled mightily to develop even a computer-based matrix to understand and track the demands of the massive UNMIK standard implementation plan, this effort was soon overtaken by events and the shifting priorities of the international institutions.

IV. The March Riots and the Eide Reports

In March 2004, violent riots erupted, triggered by an incident along the dividing line between northern Kosovo (Mitrovica) and the rest of the territory. The North had remained under the control of a local majority of ethnic Serbs. The UN administration had been unable to establish a unified system of governance throughout Kosovo, leaving Mitrovica under a form of parallel administration steered from Belgrade. The riots were directed against ethnic Serbs and Serb religious and cultural monuments in many areas of Kosovo. They involved an uprising of over 50,000 people, allegedly spontaneous and guided via mobile phones. The rioting lasted over three days, reportedly leaving 19 people dead, 954 injured, 4,100 displaced, and 550 houses and 27 Orthodox churches and monasteries torched.[7] This showed how rapidly the situation might escalate in the territory. The Kosovo population might not be willing to remain subject to the standards before status policy forever and could easily opt for more direct action.

In the wake of the March riots, elements of the standards implementation projects were accelerated, including rule of law and security issues. Moreover, in view of the instability and tension that had manifested itself in the riots, the UN Secretary-General launched a general review process of the Kosovo operation.[8] This process was led by Ambassador Kai Eide, the Permanent Representative of Norway to NATO.

Ambassador Eide presented an initial report in August of 2004, which was only published some three months later, along with the Secretary-General's

[7] OSCE Mission in Kosovo, Department of Human Rights and Rule of Law, 'Human rights challenges following the March riots, 2004', 4.
[8] Report of the UN Secretary-General, UN Doc. S.2004/613, 30 June 2004.

own recommendations for future steps.[9] The Eide report noted the depth of dissatisfaction of the majority population with the international administration and the vulnerability of the Serb minority. It found that the standards-before-status policy lacked credibility and should be replaced by a 'priority-based and realistic standards policy'. Moreover, it predicted that the situation in Kosovo was likely to get worse rather than better. While there would never be an ideal time for moving on status, 'raising the future status question soon seems—on balance—to be the better option and is probably inevitable'. The UN should therefore initiate contacts with key government officials on this issue. In the meantime, the process of transferring power to the local actors should be accelerated. Further reviews of the performance of the Kosovo institutions should be conducted until mid-2005, when it was hoped that the comprehensive review that had been foreseen might open the way towards the initiation of status talks.

The UN Secretary-General consulted with governments, the OSCE and NATO before issuing his own recommendations, broadly in line with the Eide report.[10] However, these initial recommendations focused on strengthening the capacity of UNMIK and the responsibility of the local Kosovo institutions, not on the possible status process itself. He added, but only cautiously, that 'progress in all these aspects is essential for the success and sustainability of any future status process, and only if progress is sufficient will it be possible to consider moving gradually into talks on the future status of Kosovo'. However, with the Eide report, the sense spread in Kosovo that by mid-2005 a comprehensive review of implementation of the simplified standards would pave the way for status discussions.

After the reconfiguration of the standards before status process had taken place, the UN Secretary-General did indeed request a further comprehensive assessment of the conditions in Kosovo, asking in particular whether 'the conditions are in place to enter into a political process to determine the future status of Kosovo, in accordance with Security Council Resolution 1244 (1999) and relevant Presidential statements'.[11]

On 7 October 2005, Ambassador Eide reported to the Security Council that the record of standards implementation was uneven, but that nevertheless the time had come to move on status. Ambassador Eide added:

The future status process must be moved forward with caution. All the parties must be brought together—and kept together—throughout the status process. The end result must be stable and sustainable. Artificial deadlines should not be set. Once the process has started, it cannot be blocked and must be brought to a conclusion.[12]

---

[9] Letter dated 17 November from the Secretary-General addressed to the President of the Security Council, UN Doc. S/2004/932, 30 November 2004.

[10] *Ibid.*, Annex II.

[11] Letter dated 7 October from the Secretary-General addressed to the President of the Security Council, UN Doc. S/2005/635, 7 October 2005.

[12] *Ibid.*, Annex.

This final observation was critical for the design of the status process. It seemed inevitable that final status would have to lead to some form of independence, or at least disguised independence for Kosovo. Such a result, however, would hardly be acceptable to Belgrade. Hence, there was already a sense at this early stage that a settlement could not, in the end, be 'blocked', if it was to come about at all. A process would therefore need to be devised that would offer every opportunity for an agreement, but that might, ultimately, lead to a settlement in the absence of Serbia's consent.

On 24 October, the Security Council authorized the commencement of the status process.[13] The Council strongly urged the Kosovo leadership to increase their efforts to ensure implementation of standards. However, the policy of standards before status had now lost all credibility and the argument was made instead that Kosovo would want to comply with relevant standards in its likely future bid to seek Euro-Atlantic integration.

The Council supported the Secretary-General's intention to start a political process to determine Kosovo's future status, as foreseen in Security Council Resolution 1244 (1999). Reaffirming the framework of the Resolution, the Council welcomed the appointment of the Special Envoy to lead the process. The Council also encouraged the Contact Group, composed of France, Germany, Italy, the Russian Federation, the UK and the US, to remain closely engaged in the political process 'that will be led by the United Nations', and to support the Secretary-General's Future Status Envoy.

In agreement with the Council, the Secretary-General appointed Martti Ahtisaari, the former President of Finland who had helped negotiate the end of the NATO air campaign against Yugoslavia, as his Special Envoy for the Future Status Process for Kosovo.[14]

V. Conclusion

The UN, flanked by the EU, the OSCE and NATO, managed to establish a system of interim governance. While that governmental structure was established too late to prevent the displacement of ethnic Serbs and others in the immediate aftermath of the war, and was in many aspects ineffective, it did generally provide a reasonably stable and secure environment over a period that was significantly longer than had been initially envisaged. Moreover, it socialized the majority ethnic Albanian parties into the role of exercising governmental responsibility. However, the riots of March 2004 confirmed that the underlying ethnic

[13] Statement by the President of the Security Council, UN Doc. S/PRST/2005/51, 24 October 2005.
[14] UN Docs S.PRST/2005/51, 25 October 2005; S/2005/708, 24 October 2004; S/2005/709, 10 November 2005.

tension had not been resolved. It was also clear that pressure for independence would increase, rather than subside, as a result of prolonged interim administration. The standards before status process managed to channel the energy of the major political actors in the territory towards the aim of achieving benchmarks of good governance, including protection of minority communities. However, the policy itself was somewhat confused and initially excessively complex. Later, it was simplified and finally virtually abandoned, as the status process started to take shape.

12

The Vienna Final Status Negotiations

It has never been easy to square a circle. However, the Vienna negotiations on the final status for Kosovo appeared to represent an attempt at doing just that. The two parties to the negotiations, the government of the Republic of Serbia and the local authorities in internationally administered Kosovo, held diametrically opposed positions. It was known that Kosovo would not settle for anything other than independence. On the other hand, independence for Kosovo was utterly unacceptable to Serbia. Any mediator, however experienced, would have found it very difficult to generate a negotiating process that would be capable of overcoming this unpromising starting point. This looked like a zero-sum game if ever there was one.

I. Structural Factors Shaping Negotiations

The difficult negotiating environment was conditioned by a number of structural factors that were already noted in the introduction. First, Belgrade's position coincided with the strong emphasis placed by the classical international system on maintaining the territorial integrity and territorial unity of states.[1] Acceptance that statehood for Kosovo was possible might have been seen as an endorsement of the view that there existed, after all, an entitlement to self-determination and possible secession outside the narrowly constructed, classical colonial context.[2] This, it was feared, might lead to a proliferation of self-determination claims elsewhere, putting in jeopardy fragile states at risk of disintegration.[3]

---

[1] See Marc Weller, 'Why the Legal Rules on Self-determination Do Not Resolve Self-determination Disputes', in Marc Weller and Barbara Metzger (eds), *Settling Self-determination Conflicts* (Dordrecht: Martinus Nijhoff, 2008), 17–47. Biafra and Katanga are the principal examples of attempted but failed secession from the classical–modern period. Bangladesh is the exception proving the rule, given the specific circumstances of that case.

[2] The term 'colonies', in this sense, applies only to territories forcibly acquired during the period of imperialism by a distant metropolitan power, from which they are racially distinct and divided by an ocean, for the purposes of economic exploitation. To those covered by this definition the cases of Palestine, South Africa and secondary colonies (Western Sahara, Eastern Timor) were subsequently added.

[3] Indeed, as the debate in the UN Security Council covered in the following chapter relates, this argument was frequently invoked after Kosovo had declared independence.

A second structural factor shaping the dynamics of the final status process concerned the principle of state consent. It is a defining feature of the classical international system that obligations cannot be imposed upon states against their will. This applies with particular vigour in relation to issues that touch upon state sovereignty, notably questions relating to the territorial definition of states. For instance, when acting under Chapter VI of the United Nations Charter, which covers situations likely to endanger the maintenance of international peace and security, the UN Security Council can only recommend a possible settlement to states.[4] Even under Chapter VII of the Charter, concerning threats to the peace, breaches of the peace and acts of aggression, the Council has been very reluctant to use its enforcement powers to impose a territorial solution to a conflict in the absence of state consent.[5]

In this case, however, these hard principles of territorial integrity and territorial unity of states, and of state consent, came up against a number of softer challenges. As was noted in Chapter I, a re-evaluation of the principles of the classical system had set in, with increasing emphasis being placed on the rights of peoples and populations, at the expense of the claim to sovereignty inherent in the abstraction of the state.[6] Within this context a number of long-running self-determination disputes had finally been addressed, to the point of actually offering the option of self-determination and possible secession outside the colonial context that had hitherto been its almost exclusive preserve.[7]

Another factor concerned the growing recognition of the relevance in such cases of human rights. The suffering of the population in Kosovo under the Milosevic regime had been well documented.[8] The massive displacement of over half the population of the territory by Serbian military and paramilitary forces in 1999 had also left an indelible impression on policy-makers involved in the crisis.[9] There was a sense among major Western governments that, in view of this

[4] UN Charter, Art. 33(1).

[5] An example is furnished by Resolution 687 (S/RES/687, 1991), where the Council established a boundary demarcation commission in relation to the disputed boundary between Iraq and Kuwait. The mandate of that commission was expressly limited to finding and physically marking the boundary line that, it was claimed, already existed. Delegations on the Council made it clear at the time that they were not in any way supporting an imposition upon the parties of a new boundary arrived at through an arbitration process imposed upon Iraq by virtue of the Chapter VII resolution.

[6] The beginning of the process was inaugurated by the UN Secretary-General's seminal *An Agenda for Peace*, UN Doc. A/47/277, 17 June 1992, para. 17.

[7] These are Northern Ireland, Southern Sudan and Bougainville. Earlier, Eritrea had obtained independence through consent from the central authorities of Ethiopia. See Marc Weller, 'Addressing the Self-determination Dispute', in Weller and Metzger (eds), *Settling Self-determination Conflicts* (Dordrecht: Martinus Nijhoff, 2008), 387–407; also Marc Weller, *Escaping the Self-determination Trap* (Dordrecht: Martinus Nijhoff, 2008), *passim*.

[8] See Weller, *Crisis in Kosovo*, where the authoritative findings of international human rights bodies during this period are reproduced at 120–83.

[9] The authoritative finding of international agencies concerning this campaign of displacement are reproduced in Marc Weller, *The Kosovo Conflict* (Cambridge: Documents and Analysis, 2001), 160–319.

still quite recent history, it would simply not be realistic to place Kosovo under Serbian sovereignty once again.

This view was reinforced by anxiety that 'time [was] running out in Kosovo' and that 'the region could be plunged into new turmoil' if no settlement on status were forthcoming.[10] Indeed, there was a strong fear that any settlement short of independence would lead to an uncontrollable situation in Kosovo, rendering the position of the international administration untenable. This fear was only exacerbated by the riots of March 2004.[11]

The structure for the negotiations on Kosovo's final status was complex. The framework for the negotiations had been established by the UN Security Council, on the basis of the recommendations of Ambassador Eide and the UN Secretary-General. This framework was rooted in a general sense in Security Council Resolution 1244 (1999).

That resolution had reaffirmed the commitment of all member states to the sovereignty and territorial integrity of the Federal Republic of Yugoslavia (FRY) and the other states of the region. Acting under Chapter VII of the UN Charter, the Security Council had authorized the establishment of an international civil and security presence in Kosovo, providing for an interim administration there by the UN, 'under which the people of Kosovo can enjoy substantial autonomy within the Federal Republic of Yugoslavia'. Serbia, as the universal successor to the rights of the FRY (Serbia and Montenegro), would be able to invoke the provisions of Resolution 1244, including what might be perceived as a guarantee of its continued territorial integrity, to its benefit.[12]

However, the confirmation of the continued territorial unity of the FRY (now Serbia) in Resolution 1244 could be read in one of two ways. Either it applied to the interim period of UN administration or it applied beyond that, constraining options for a final status agreement on Kosovo. The resolution itself appeared to clarify that the UN mandate was concerned with 'promoting the establishment, pending a final settlement, of substantial autonomy and self-government in Kosovo': in other words, that the focus on autonomy would be limited to the interim period ('pending a final settlement'). The resolution also mandated 'facilitating a political process designed to determine Kosovo's future status, taking into account the Rambouillet accords'. The Rambouillet accords were interim agreements, preceding a final settlement to be adopted also on the

---

[10] International Crisis Group, *Kosovo: Toward Final Status*, Europe report 161, 24 January 2005, 1.

[11] See above, pp. 187–189.

[12] Serbia's universal succession was laid down in the Union Treaty with Montenegro, and the Constitutional Charter of the State Union, which stated in art 60 that Belgrade would inherit the FRY's legal rights and duties should Montenegro exercise the option of secession, which it eventually did: 'Should Montenegro break away from the state union of Serbia and Montenegro, the international instruments pertaining to the Federal Republic of Yugoslavia, Particularly UN SC Resolution 1244, would concern and apply in their entirety to Serbia as the successor.' The UN Security Council confirmed this arrangement in PRST/2003/1, 6 February 2003.

basis of the 'will of the people'.[13] This would not rule out independence as a final settlement.

Resolution 1244 also incorporated the statement by the Chairman on the conclusion of the meeting of the G8 foreign ministers held at the Petersberg Centre on 6 May 1999. That statement, which became the anchoring point for the cessation of hostilities against Yugoslavia in 1999, was annexed to the Resolution. It foresaw '[a] political process towards the establishment of an interim political framework agreement providing for a substantial self-government for Kosovo, taking full account of the Rambouillet accords and the principles of sovereignty and territorial integrity of the Federal Republic of Yugoslavia and the other countries of the region'. Again, self-governance under the sovereignty and territorial integrity of Yugoslavia appeared to be guaranteed for the 'interim' period only. Annex 2 to the Resolution, restating nine points accepted by the then FRY before the cessation of hostilities, contained a similar provision, adding that 'negotiations between the parties for a settlement should not delay or disrupt the establishment of democratic self-governing institutions'. Once more, it appeared that autonomous self-governance was linked to the period before final settlement.

Accordingly, it is at least possible to argue that the affirmation of the territorial unity and integrity of Yugoslavia in relation to Kosovo in Resolution 1244 related to the interim period of international governance, or Kosovo self-governance, pending a final settlement. This period, one might say, had been exhausted over some five years of internationally supervised self-governance under the provisional constitutional framework established in 2001. While substantial autonomy was prescribed for this interim period, the outcome of the final settlement was open. A final status settlement that included the option of independence was therefore not necessarily precluded by the terms of a Chapter VII resolution. Of course, Serbia continued to enjoy the protection of general international legal rules. As noted at the outset, international practice hitherto has certainly tended to favour the maintenance of territorial unity over the granting of independence.

While the Security Council had confirmed the leadership of the UN in the status process, in reality the Contact Group was to act as the controlling body for the negotiations and for the UN Special Envoy, Martti Ahtisaari. The functioning of the Contact Group had been disrupted since the outbreak of hostilities in 1999. Instead, the leading Western powers in this crisis had acted as the so-called Quint, composed of the US, UK, France, Italy and Germany. Now, it was felt important to resume cooperation with Russia in achieving a settlement result. Hence, Russia regained and retained an immediate blocking power at the level of the Contact Group over the actual conduct of the negotiations, rather than just over the eventual outcome, and only at the level of the Security

---

[13] The Rambouillet accords (see Weller, *Crisis in Kosovo*, 469) foresaw 'a mechanism for a final settlement for Kosovo, on the basis of the will of the people, opinions of relevant authorities, each Party's efforts regarding the implementation of this agreement, and the Helsinki Final Act...'.

Council. This arrangement was intended to ensure that Russia would be bound into the process at an early stage, so that the results of the negotiations would be guaranteed passage through the Security Council, given Russia's controlling involvement throughout. Moreover, Russia, it was thought, would be able to exercise influence upon Serbia and might help persuade Belgrade to negotiate constructively.

However, much as had happened under its purported leadership during the Rambouillet negotiations, the Group itself was divided. While some of the major West European governments and the United States were coming to accept that independence for Kosovo might be inevitable, Russia consistently opposed any such notion. Moreover, Russia was not willing to countenance the possibility of a settlement being imposed by the UN Security Council upon Serbia, if Belgrade refused a reasonable agreement. This stance seemed to lessen pressure on Belgrade, as it felt protected from the threat of an imposed settlement.

The Contact Group issued ten 'guiding principles' for a settlement on the status of Kosovo. Essentially, these principles set the red lines that were to be imposed by the mediators in the negotiations. They concerned compliance with human rights, democratic values and principles of Euro-Atlantic integration; assurances that mechanisms would be provided to ensure political participation remained open to all ethnic groups, including minority groups; provision for the return of refugees and the displaced; protection of cultural and religious heritage; regional stability and economic development; and the acceptance of continued international supervision of the implementation of the status package. It was also made clear that there would be no return to the situation that had prevailed in Kosovo preceding the NATO intervention. Moreover, the Contact Group added later that any settlement would need to be acceptable to the population of Kosovo—perhaps a reference to the possibility of a referendum on the results of the process. Of course, it was fairly clear that the Albanian population of Kosovo would not accept any result other than independence. On the other hand, even Russia could not argue successfully that a settlement could be realistically adopted if it was rejected by its intended beneficiaries.

The guiding principles also stipulated that '[a]ny solution that is unilateral or results from the use of force would be unacceptable. There will be no changes in the current territory of Kosovo, i.e., no partition of Kosovo and no union of Kosovo with any country or part of any country. The territorial integrity and internal stability of regional neighbours will be fully respected.' The remit for the negotiations therefore precluded any trading of territory for independence, for instance by offering a merger of the Mitrovica region with Serbia, perhaps compensated for by a transfer to Kosovo of the mainly Albanian-inhabited Presevo Valley of Serbia. Similarly, the possibility of a Greater Albania, consisting of a merger of Kosovo with Albania and perhaps claims for the incorporation of territories in Macedonia inhabited by ethnic Albanians, was to be ruled out for the long term.

II. The Format of Discussions

While the Contact Group steered the negotiations, the process was nevertheless formally a UN venture. The UN Secretary-General appointed not only the Special Envoy, Martti Ahtisaari, but also his deputy, Albert Rohan of Austria, who directed the actual talks. The mediators were supported by a secretariat, the UN Office of the Special Envoy for the Future Status Process for Kosovo (UNOSEK). Housed on the top floor of a modest office building in the centre of Vienna, this body consisted of expert advisers drawn mainly from the foreign ministries of the Contact Group states and some other governments or organizations. It was noticeable that the core team of advisers appeared to be carefully balanced, giving the key Contact Group states a direct voice and representation in the process. The legal drafting work of the secretariat was also supported by very experienced legal advisers from other expert institutions, including in particular the OSCE High Commissioner on National Minorities and the Secretariat of the Council of Europe Venice Commission.

While the accommodation of UNOSEK was modest, the mediation itself was conducted in some style. Building on the precedent of Rambouillet, the early rounds of the negotiations were conducted in splendid classical Viennese city palaces that were otherwise available for rent as venues for costume balls and similar entertainments. However, just as the follow-on process to the Rambouillet talks had been moved to a non-descript conference centre in Paris when impatience with the inability of the parties to come to an agreement reached a certain pitch, so, as time moved on, the Vienna talks migrated from the baroque glory of the city's most beautiful landmarks to the concrete charm of the UN conference centre on the outer ringroad.

The direct negotiations normally followed a certain pattern. The mediators would invite the delegations to Vienna for a period of several days, offering an agenda on just one issue area (say, decentralization) to be addressed over this period. They would invite the parties to come prepared with papers, offering views in relation to specific issues or questions that had been identified as worthy of discussion by the mediation team. In issuing these invitations, the mediators sometimes offered brief explanations of the areas they were hoping to address; in other instances they issued questionnaires, seeking to establish the positions or proposals of the parties on very specific points.

The direct negotiations were conducted at a large, horseshoe-shaped table in one of the Vienna city palaces. The parties would sit opposite one another on either side, with the UNOSEK team, often strengthened by representatives from the EU and other bodies, claiming the head of the table. At the beginning of each round of discussions, each delegation would usually be invited to a short, separate meeting with the Special Envoy, who would offer general words of encouragement to the parties. As noted above, the actual negotiations were then chaired for the most part by his deputy, Rohan.

Each party was restricted to seven representatives in the negotiating chamber. At the beginning of each round, the parties would make general opening statements, followed by prepared statements on the specific issues raised by the mediators. The sides would then answer queries from the mediation team, or engage one another directly. The Serbian side appeared generally unprepared to engage in much substantive discussion that went beyond its opening position or platform. Instead, it appeared at times to be seeking to provoke the Kosovo delegation into walking out by launching into historical debates or, occasionally, insults.

The delegation on the Kosovo side comprised the minister or ministers covering the appointed issue area for each individual negotiation session, representatives from the communities, and senior experts. Accordingly, its composition varied according to which issue was being discussed. The delegation operated under the guidance of the so-called 'all-party Unity Team' composed of President Fatmir Sejdiu (Democratic League of Kosovo, LDK); Prime Minister Agim Ceku (nominated to that post by the Alliance for the Future of Kosovo, AAK); the President of the Kosovo Assembly, Kole Berisha; Hashim Thaci, the leader of the Democratic Party of Kosovo (PDK) in opposition; and Veton Surroi, a leading intellectual heading the smaller Ora Party. The team was supported by a 'political–strategic group' made up of senior representatives of these mainstream parties together with, on occasion, some experts whose role was to develop positions for approval by the unity team and who participated in the day-to-day negotiating rounds. Both the Unity Team, and the political–strategic group reflecting the same party allegiances, were of course often fundamentally divided in their positions.

While Kosovo was represented at ministerial level or below, Serbia opted for an even lower level of representation from its foreign ministry alongside representatives from other authorities, experts, and its 'own' representatives of the communities in Kosovo. The question of the representation of the various communities in Kosovo led to a somewhat anomalous situation. The mediators and the Contact Group had urged Kosovo to ensure that these communities would have an input into the Kosovo delegation and be represented by it. In response, Kosovo had established a Community Consultative Council (CCC), which allowed community representatives to be briefed on the negotiations and to offer initiatives for presentation in Vienna. It was headed by Veton Surroi, who had been deputed for this purpose by the unity team, and was supported in this task by the European Centre for Minority Issues. In fact, acting through the CCC, the communities themselves took the lead in developing the very detailed platform on minority rights protection in the future Kosovo that was formally presented in Vienna by the Kosovo delegation.

The representatives of the Serb community in Kosovo adopted a seemingly ambiguous position. On the one hand, the community was formally represented in the delegation of Serbia. On the other hand, as negotiations progressed, the view spread among members of the Serb community that the interests of ethnic Serbs in Kosovo were not effectively represented by the Belgrade delegation. This applied in particular to the ethnic Serbs who lived outside of the northern area and who would be dependent on the solid protection of community rights throughout Kosovo—an issue more or less ignored by the Serbian delegation.[14] Accordingly, even the mainstream ethnic Serb parties in Kosovo, which had refused to participate in the Kosovo institutions of government since the March 2004 riots, nevertheless periodically joined the proceedings of the CCC and contributed to the construction of Kosovo's platform on minority rights. Thus the Serb community in Kosovo appeared to be represented on both sides in the negotiations. However, as Kosovo had declared its desire to offer maximum protection to communities and their members, it had no objection to this unorthodox situation.

Direct negotiation was combined with shuttle diplomacy, conducted through so-called 'expert missions' led by UNOSEK. These involved expert advisers from UNOSEK visiting the two capitals in order to refine their understanding of the positions of both parties on specific issues, and to float ideas about possible compromise solutions. In total, 26 such expert missions were launched. There were also occasions, especially during the final stages of the discussions, when a proximity format was adopted. On these occasions the delegations would work in separate rooms, with the mediators moving between them. Once it was felt that an issue area had been sufficiently explored, UNOSEK would produce papers purporting to reflect emerging areas of agreement. However, more often than not these papers merely served as invitations to the parties to state their disagreement and to oppose the texts as mis-stating their positions, rather than helping to consolidate agreement.

III. Basic Positions

Belgrade was primarily interested in the confirmation of its territorial sovereignty, even if it was willing to suspend the exercise of public power for a further period and to accept its significant limitation over the longer term. However, in a departure from its previous position at Rambouillet, it was now also interested in maintaining in the territory a robust and effective international security presence. This would transfer to the organized international community the duty to guarantee, by force if necessary, Kosovo's remaining within Serbia, in addition to the duty to protect the ethnic Serb population should riots break out again.

Before the negotiations commenced, the National Assembly of Serbia issued a mandate to its delegation, in which it invoked the protection of international law very extensively, declaring its:

firm belief that the UN Security Council is a reliable guarantor of respect of the international law and the entire world order...Accordingly, the National Assembly of the Republic of Serbia expects the UN Security Council to use the power of its authority to

---

[14] See Section IV below, entitled 'Content of the Negotiations'.

ensure that the inviolable principle of respecting sovereignty and territorial integrity is not violated in the case of Serbia and Montenegro either...Any attempt at imposing a solution towards de facto legalization of partition of the Republic of Serbia by a unilateral secession of part of its territory would be not only legal violence against a democratic state, but violence against the [sic] international law itself.[15]

Thus Belgrade's position was firmly aligned with the structural principles of classical international law noted previously, favouring territorial unity over demands for self-determination outside the colonial context. This seemed to place Belgrade in a comfortable position. No significant concessions would need to be made as the requirement of Serbia's consent to overcome this obstacle would control any outcome.

However, there were two risks. On the one hand, if Belgrade were to frustrate negotiations, the organized international community might reframe its operational parameters and make use of the enforcement powers of the UN Security Council under Chapter VII to overcome the lack of agreement. The Security Council had never previously been used in such a way, to decree that a sovereign state should lose territory in the interest of international peace and security.[16] However, the Council might claim such a power, and it might do so with some justification. The unresolved situation in Kosovo did constitute a genuine threat to international peace and security, and Belgrade's previous treatment of the ethnic Albanian population might also be invoked to justify such an extraordinary step.

Of course, this risk existed only to the extent that it was likely that the Council would be in a position to act decisively. In the event, Moscow provided assurances to Serbia that it would not permit the imposition of a solution against its will.

If collective action to overcome a lack of consent from Serbia was unlikely, there remained the prospect of unilateral action. There seemed to be several possibilities here, depending on how the negotiating process progressed. If negotiations failed as a result of Belgrade's perceived intransigence, international sympathy might lie with Prishtina. A declaration of independence would be the only way out, all avenues of negotiation having been exhausted. If negotiations stalled as a result of the parties' inability to agree, there would most likely be pressure for further talks. Kosovo would be impelled at least to delay unilateral action. Finally, if the talks were to collapse as a result of Kosovo's intransigence, even those governments that supported Prishtina's ambitions might find it very difficult to recognize unilaterally declared independence.

---

[15] Resolution of the National Assembly, 21 November 2005, <http://www.mfa.gov.yu/Policy/Priorities/KIM/draft_resolution_kim_e.html>, accessed 19 June 2008.

[16] Resolution 687 (1991) required Iraq to submit to a boundary demarcation process. However, it was deliberately a demarcation, and not a delimitation, exercise, in order to avoid any allegation that the Security Council was taking on the role of judge in a territorial dispute. S/RES/687 (1991). See n. 5 of this chapter, above.

Hence, during the negotiations it appeared that Serbia had opted for a strategy of seeking to gain time. It would participate in the negotiations to the extent necessary to avoid the allegation that it was obstructing the process. It might also hope that the Kosovo side would lose patience, or be unable to present a unified front, or be provoked into a walk-out, thereby becoming itself responsible for a failure of the process. During negotiations, Belgrade would also seek to lock in concessions from Pristina about the future of governance in Kosovo. These might be called upon in later negotiations on substantial autonomy, for instance in a further round of talks at the level of the UN Security Council.

In pursuit of this strategy Serbia published an opening 'platform' for the negotiations. The platform emphasized that there should not be any kind of imposed solution which would not bring about stability in the long term. Moreover, a negotiated solution would have the advantage of being 'situated between two unacceptable extremes—the status Kosovo and Metohija had in the period 1989–1999, and independence, i.e., the creation of a new Albanian state'.[17] Serbia also again directly invoked the structural principles of the classical international order to its benefit:

The future status of Kosovo and Metohija should fully conform to the fundamental principles and norms of the international community, as well as to the specific documents of the international community that affirm the sovereignty and territorial integrity of Serbia. Any settlement of the future status of Kosovo and Metohija that would go against the existing international law, infringing the sovereignty and territorial integrity of Serbia, could only represent an imposed solution, and as such would have to be declared illegitimate, illegal, and invalid by the relevant institutions of Serbia.

Rather than appearing to draw its own red line limiting the remit of the negotiations, Serbia therefore claimed that international legal rules would preclude a settlement leading to independence for Kosovo. This, of course, was not so. There is nothing in international law to stop a central government from agreeing to a secession by consent, as was the case between Ethiopia and Eritrea, for instance, or when Czechoslovakia dissolved by agreement. Indeed, on 15 March 2002 Serbia itself had concluded a union agreement with Montenegro, providing for the possibility of secession for both constituent republics.

The Serbian platform appeared to offer quite significant autonomous powers to Kosovo, including control over its own finances and access to international financial institutions. Kosovo would even have the right to maintain relations with states, provinces, and regional and international organizations, 'provided this does not require the status of a sovereign international subject'. On the other hand, it was also made clear that Serbia would retain and exercise certain powers in relation to Kosovo. In view of the experience of the ethnic Albanian population

---

[17] 'Platform on the Future Status of Kosovo and Metohija', 5 January 2006, <http://www.b92. net/eng/insight/strategies.php?yyyy=2006&mm=06&nav_id=35257>, accessed 6 October 2008.

of apartheid-like practices during the 1990s, it was known that Kosovo was unlikely to accept this proposition.

Another issue related to the form of the agreement. It was foreseen in the Serbian platform that the accord would not really be concluded by Kosovo. While, somehow, Kosovo would be a 'party to the agreement', the text would be signed and guaranteed by only Serbia and the UN, in view of Kosovo's lack of international legal personality. Through these complicated twists in its position, Belgrade unnecessarily undermined the credibility of its commitment to genuine and very wide-ranging self-government.

Kosovo's basic position, on the other hand, was very clear. From beginning to end Pristina insisted on outright independence. Kosovo was aware of the fact that the organized international community needed to achieve a final settlement, and needed to do so sooner rather than later. The international administration of Kosovo would not be viable for ever, especially if the aspirations of Kosovo for final status were being manifestly frustrated. Visits by leading international representatives coincided with mysterious explosions in and around Pristina, hinting at the threat that life in the territory could turn unpleasant if movement on status were to be delayed indefinitely. And whatever the divisions between the various factions of Kosovo politicians, they were all unified in their unwavering demand for independence. The Kosovo leadership could also deploy the 'trade union negotiator's ploy' of arguing that its home constituency would lynch it, or disown any result of negotiations, should it fall short of independence.

This uncompromising stance was, however, clad in a smile. Kosovo had been advised by the United States and others to 'negotiate generously' if it wished to see its hopes for status fulfilled. Accordingly, it indicated a willingness to be accommodating on issues of governance within Kosovo, including in particular the rights of communities, religious and historic monuments, and other issues of key interest to the organized international community.

Kosovo's position, however clear, was not free from risk. Prishtina could hardly refuse to participate enthusiastically in the very status process it had been demanding energetically for several years. On the other hand, it was not evident where the process might lead once initiated. True, Kosovo was represented in the talks in Vienna. But there were other, more powerful layers to these negotiations beyond its control: namely, the Contact Group and the Security Council. The Kosovo delegation received advice from experts who feared that the Vienna negotiations might focus only on practical issues of governance within Kosovo. Absent an agreement by Belgrade on the wider issues of status, Kosovo might be stuck with a claim that it had agreed to important concessions relating to decentralization, the treatment of communities and relations with Serbia. That 'settlement' without status might then be internationally imposed upon it by way of autonomy, at least for a further, undefined interim period.

Kosovo's concerns in this respect were nourished by the poor level of consultation between the Special Envoy and his delegation. When the formal invitation to the first round of talks arrived, there had been no briefing on the format of discussion, the agenda or the negotiating process. Nor had it been established whether or how the process might continue beyond Vienna. It was feared that, if the parties did come to an agreement there, the package might be undone to Kosovo's detriment at the level of the UN Security Council, where considerations of great power politics, rather than the interests of Prishtina, might dominate.

At least where process was concerned, the delegation from Belgrade enjoyed certain advantages over Kosovo. It could draw on its own, highly competent foreign ministry and its well-established international contacts. It was obvious to the mediators that they would discuss and agree the negotiating process with their diplomatic colleagues in Belgrade, as would ordinarily be the case. Kosovo was not treated in quite the same way.

According to Belgrade, the basic approach to the negotiations had been settled in these preliminary discussions between the Special Envoy and the Serbian side. In particular, it had been agreed that 'negotiations should begin with relatively concrete questions on the agenda' and should be conducted 'on a status neutral basis'.[18] Kosovo, principally interested in the status issue, was unaware of this agreement.

Lacking the stature and tools of diplomatic practice, Prishtina did not have the benefit of extensive preliminary consultations about the negotiating process. This problem was amplified by the inability of its leading politicians to organize themselves into an effective delegation that could seek such consultations early on. Instead, individual party leaders went off on individual missions for discussions with friendly governments, receiving reassurances in the process that all would be well in the end.

IV. Content of the Negotiations

The initiation of the first round of talks was a matter of some delicacy. In accordance with the principles outlined by Ambassador Eide in his second report to the UN Secretary-General, there was a presumption that the talks, once commenced, should not be 'blocked' by any party. Beginning the talks therefore had certain risks for both sides. If Serbia participated, it might thereby be signing up to a process that could ultimately endorse independence for Kosovo. Even if Belgrade were to object, it would be difficult to escape from the political dynamic that might develop. If Kosovo participated, Prishtina might in the end be stuck with a practical settlement on decentralization and minority rights, without any

---

[18] Letter from Boris Tadic and Vojislav Kostunica to the Foreign Ministers of the Contact Group and to the UN Secretary-General's Special Envoy, 18 May 2006, *Kosovo Perspectives*, no. 4, 26 May 2006, <http://www.kosovoperspectives.com/index.php?categoryid=22&selected=4&parentid=2&p202_articleid=330>, accessed 23 June 2008.

commitments on status. It was feared, therefore, that Belgrade might demand guarantees that independence would not be on the cards as a precondition for participation, while Kosovo might participate only if that option was expressly on the table.

To avoid deadlock on such possible preconditions, on 12 January 2006 the Special Envoy sent an invitation to the parties 'in furtherance of the political dialogue on the future status of Kosovo' to discuss the fairly technical decentralization issues. This was rather a cunning move, as there had existed a technical working group on this issue before the status process had commenced. Pretending merely to continue this dialogue therefore lessened the psychological hurdle of joining the first session of what were, after all, vital status talks. Similarly, the other issue that was to dominate the Vienna discussion, protection of religious and cultural heritage, had also already been discussed between the sides in a working group process. Moreover, this approach was in line with the undertaking given to Belgrade to engage initially only in 'status neutral' issues of a technical nature.

Another proposal of Ambassador Eide's had been to agree the agenda, format and procedure for the talks with the parties, so as to make the process transparent and predictable for both sides. This was not the case from the beginning. While the thematic emphasis of the talks appeared to correspond to the undertakings given to Belgrade, no longer-term plan was offered. However, the negotiations developed their own routine which stabilized over time, and longer-term agendas were shared later with both parties as the talks progressed.

In total, there were fifteen rounds of direct negotiations in Vienna throughout 2006. Belgrade was for the most part willing to discuss issues relating to ethnic Serb control over territory. During these discussions, Belgrade spent much time elaborating on the model of Swiss cantons when addressing decentralization. However, in the end the expositions of a Swiss expert on these matters were cut short by Ambassador Rohan, stating curtly that 'Kosovo is not Switzerland'. Still, the topic of decentralization claimed a great deal of negotiating time—over half of the sessions—and both sides engaged substantively with this issue. This engagement related in particular to the number and delimitation of municipalities that would enjoy powers of self-governance, and the extent of these powers. Belgrade was demanding the establishment of some fifteen new, mainly Serb-inhabited, municipalities. In some instances these might be small, including only several hundred inhabitants. In other instances the population balance was to be adjusted in favour of an ethnic Serb majority. There was also the proposal that displaced persons in Serbia be directed towards these new areas, rather than returning to their homes. Kosovo, on the other hand, contemplated the establishment of three new ethnic Serb municipalities, later upping the offer to five under intense international pressure.

There was also the difficult issue of whether or not municipalities could join to form collective units or regions—a proposal resisted by Kosovo, which feared the de facto division of the territory into a mainly Serb region that would administer itself through parallel structures. Moreover, there arose the issue of links between such regions and Serbia. The comprehensive proposal that emerged ultimately overruled Kosovo's objections on many of these issues.

As there were no discussions on issues that Kosovo wanted to pursue with Serbia, there was no room for the traditional 'trade-offs' that would ordinarily characterize negotiations of this kind (as had been the case at Dayton, or even the final phase of Rambouillet, for instance). Kosovo was pressed into making concessions on the basis of a hope that an overall package would ultimately develop in favour of establishing final status.

More progress could be made in three sets of discussions about the protection of religious and cultural heritage. While Kosovo favoured a functional approach to this issue the talks stalled over the very extensive claims by Serbia to territorial zones around historic and cultural monuments.

Only one session was devoted to economic problems.

The difference in attitude between the two sides became, ironically, most visible in relation to the issue of the protection of communities. To the representatives of the organized international community this issue was of key importance, wishing as they did to ensure that ethnic Serbs and others might live peaceably and without discrimination in Kosovo after status had been established. Indeed, before the first round of negotiations on this issue the Contact Group issued an exhortation to the Kosovo side to the effect that 'the more the vital interests of minorities are addressed the quicker a broadly acceptable agreement can be reached'.[19] It was presumed that Serbia would similarly press for solid protection of community rights. However, Belgrade was mainly interested in territorial solutions, arguing that ethnic Serbs would be safe only in areas under ethnic Serb control. It did not offer its own package of proposals for the protection of human and minority rights.

Prishtina, on the other hand, took the advice to 'be generous' to heart where community issues were concerned. It had spent a full year preparing a detailed catalogue of legally entrenched entitlements and institutional mechanisms for the protection of community rights. These had been developed in consultation with the communities in Kosovo and under the guidance of the European Centre for Minority Issues. Kosovo also informally involved senior advisers from the European human rights institutions in its preparatory work in this area. This approach offered two advantages to Kosovo. First, the involvement of these external agencies would improve the technical quality of its proposals. Second, it was known that the same international organizations supporting this process would also, later, advise the Ahtisaari team on the positions taken by the parties. In this

---

[19] 'Statement by the Contact Group on the Future of Kosovo', London, 31 January 2006, <http://www.unosek.org/docref/fevrier/STATEMENT%20BY%20THE%20CONTACT%20GROUP%20ON%20THE%20FUTURE%20OF%20KOSOVO%20-%20Eng.pdf>, accessed 19 June 2008.

way, they would have had the opportunity to observe the attempt of Kosovo to craft advanced provisions in this area and, indeed, to contribute to them.

The Kosovo authorities were more hesitant when it came to power-sharing issues. The experience of Bosnia and Herzegovina had taught the Kosovo delegation to be wary of short-term concessions in this area that would make the territory ungovernable in practice. This hesitancy extended to the issues of guaranteed ministerial appointments for members of ethnic minorities; guaranteed or reserved seats for community representatives in the Kosovo parliament, which would lead inevitably to an over-representation of minorities; and proposed veto powers for communities in relation to legislative projects affecting their 'vital interests'. Kosovo was concerned that such an approach would entrench ethnic division and a system of ethnic politics, rather than providing opportunities for interest-based politics to develop across ethnic lines. Hence, Prishtina argued during the negotiations that it should not be left indefinitely with a consociationalist post-conflict settlement, but should be given the opportunity to develop into a 'normal', diverse state.

However, the mediators held the line on power-sharing. They asserted that the Contact Group would not entertain a reduction in power-sharing mechanisms from those in the existing constitutional framework adopted by UNMIK in 2001. So far as reducing such provisions, it was argued, one might expect their enhancement, given the possible change in status. Hence, the Ahtisaari Comprehensive Proposal renders permanent many of the provisions of the constitutional framework that were originally intended to cover only a period of interim administration in the immediate post-conflict environment.[20] On the other hand, the mediators also resisted the attempts of the Serbian delegation to go beyond the constitutional framework and to resurrect provisions from the days of Rambouillet.[21] One such example relates to blocking powers in the Kosovo Assembly for representatives of the Serb community alone.

In fact, the issue of community rights was discussed in only two rounds of talks in August and September, over six months after the negotiations had opened. This discussion created an awkward situation for Belgrade. Kosovo had offered a comprehensive platform on this issue, ranging over some 70 pages of specific provisions for community protection. While Serbia was holding itself out as the protector of the communities in Kosovo, in fact it had little to say on the matter, emphasizing instead that decentralization would be the key to community protection.

---

[20] The final version of the Comprehensive Proposal adopted a compromise on the issue of guaranteed or reserved seats in the Kosovo Assembly, retaining the provisions from the constitutional framework for two electoral cycles before the application of a somewhat more modest form of representation.

[21] Rambouillet foresaw far more significant power-sharing for the Serb community, including harder blocking power and greater room for separate political and legal organization: see Marc Weller, 'The Rambouillet Conference on Kosovo', *International Affairs*, 75(2) (1999), 211–51.

Moreover, Serbia was unable to engage on these matters of crucial import-ance to its Kosovo constituency as its delegation seemed to have no instruc-tions in relation to issues that could be seen as 'constitutional', claiming that such an approach would prejudice status. This was, of course, a somewhat odd attitude, given that the parties were at the time supposed to be in the middle of status negotiations. In the absence of their own suggestions, the Serbian interlocutors pointed to an outdated proposal made by Belgrade in 2001, when the constitutional framework for Kosovo under UNMIK administration was discussed. That appeared to be a safe option in the absence of guidance from their capital, for that proposal had been approved by Belgrade—albeit some five years earlier.

This lack of preparedness to discuss constitutional issues at the level of the delegation, even at that late stage, jarred with Serbia's position at a higher level. As early as 18 May 2006 the Serbian President and Prime Minister had complained to the Contact Group and the Special Envoy that it had been a mistake to focus at the outset only on technical issues, such as decentralization and cultural her-itage. Belgrade argued that, as progress remained elusive in these areas, and as Prishtina had refused to make proposals in a way that was 'status neutral', con-trary to the promises of the Special Representative, it might now be appropriate to begin initial consultations on status. Belgrade proposed that there should be one round of negotiations on status, followed by four sets of discussions on the Kosovo constitution, covering community rights, security issues (including the demilitarization of Kosovo), economic issues and decentralization.[22] Two weeks later Belgrade reissued its platform, proposing again wide-ranging autonomy for a period of twenty years.

The Contact Group was responsive to the suggestions made in the letter from Belgrade. After some six months of talks according to the Vienna format, on 24 July 2006 a meeting was held at the level of heads of state and government to address status itself. Serbia was represented by President Boris Tadic and Prime Minister Vojislav Kostunica, with Kosovo's President, Fatmir Sejdiu, leading the Kosovo delegation. At that meeting the widely differing perspectives of both sides towards status became evident. Instead of managing to engage in a substan-tive discussion on specific status issues, the sides treated the mediators to their respective versions of recent history. Serbia also argued that Kosovo had failed to implement the standards laid out in the 'standards before status' policy and that the situation for ethnic Serbs in the territory remained intolerable. Serbia demanded wide-ranging protection for ethnic Serbs, but once again focused this demand on the issue of territorial control, rather than minority rights systems and mechanisms for political representation throughout Kosovo. 'Only if these

---

[22] See n. 18 above.

guarantees are ensured through decentralization would the Serbians in Kosovo create conditions for [a] normal life', Tadic argued.[23]

Kosovo, on the other hand, admitted that the situation on the ground was still far from perfect, but pointed to significant progress in governance in the territory. Moreover, it argued that further process would be impossible unless the status issue were finally resolved through independence.

Given this deadlock, the Contact Group focused the talks again on the practical issues that needed to be resolved. While acknowledging the flexibility shown by Prishtina on decentralization, it demanded further concessions. Kosovo, which had genuinely engaged with the arguments of the mediators and had changed its positions in response, was disappointed, increasingly feeling that Belgrade's attitude of sticking to its maximum position was being rewarded. Kosovo had given some ground and was now requested to give more, in the absence of movement on the other side.[24] However, the Contact Group also called upon Belgrade to exhibit much greater flexibility and to begin finally to consider 'reasonable and workable compromises for many of the issues under discussion'. Once again the Contact Group reiterated that 'once negotiations are underway, they can not be allowed to be blocked. The process must be brought to a close...The Contact Group will monitor the extent of constructive engagement on the part of both parties, and will draw conclusions accordingly.'[25]

This was a reminder of the threat that a settlement might be imposed upon Belgrade unless it showed genuine engagement in the talks. However, in view of Russia's attitude, the credibility of that threat may not have been high. At any rate, the Serbian delegation did not engage in a more substantive way during the negotiations that followed. Rather, its delegation started to threaten walk-outs and restated maximum positions on decentralization. Moreover, in a development outside the conference chamber, Belgrade arranged the suspension of cooperation between the municipal authorities in the north of Kosovo and UNMIK.[26] Apparently, Belgrade had concluded that the negotiation process was working against its interests and sought to devalue it.[27]

[23] 'Unofficial Transcript: What was Said in Vienna', *Kosovo Perspectives*, no. 14, 4 August 2006, <http://www.kosovoperspectives.com/index.php?categoryid=24&selected=14&parentid=2&p2 02_articleid=399>, accessed 23 June 2008.

[24] In fact, Kosovo significantly modified its position on decentralization at the end of August, in response to this pressure. Its updated proposals were much closer to the demands of the Contact Group and the eventual provisions contained in the comprehensive proposal. See 'Kosovo Delegation's Proposals for Decentralization', *Kosovo Perspectives*, no. 19, 8 September 2006, <http://www.kosovoperspectives.com/index.php?categoryid=22&selected=19&p202_articleid=416>, accessed 23 June 2008.

[25] Contact Group statement, Vienna, 24 July 2006, <http://www.unosek.org/docref/Statement_of_the_Contact_Group_after_first_Pristina-Belgrade_High-level_meeting_held_in_Vienna.pdf>, accessed 23 June 2008.

[26] Contact Group statement on the situation in northern Kosovo, 3 August 2006, <http://www.auswaertiges-amt.de/diplo/en/Aussenpolitik/RegionaleSchwerpunkte/Suedosteuropa/Kosovo-Kontaktgruppe060803.pdf>, accessed 18 October 2008.

[27] Belgrade claimed that the UN Special Envoy had indicated in a round of discussions on 8 August 2006 that Serbia might have to accept losing Kosovo as it was 'guilty as a nation': 'Report

On 20 September the Contact Group reiterated yet again its warning that no side would be able to prevent the process of resolving status from advancing. With the agreement of Russia, it now encouraged the Special Envoy to prepare a comprehensive proposal for a status settlement on this basis, so as to engage the parties in moving the negotiating process forward.[28] However, Moscow made its agreement highly conditional, adding in explanation: 'We consider it necessary that negotiations on the future status of Kosovo be preceded by a decision of the UN Security Council based on the results of the Council's review of the progress in the application of the standards. At the same time, it would be counterproductive to set any deadline for the negotiations on the status.'[29] In this way, Moscow appeared to be arguing (1) that status negotiations had not even commenced yet and (2) that it would retain a veto in the Council over the commencement of such negotiations. Hence, the agreement to the preparation of a comprehensive proposal document was conditioned by the assumption that this was not really a status document.

Russia adopted a further tactic to forestall action on status that might take the direction of independence. Moscow added in its statement that:

It is of principal importance to assume that the decision on Kosovo will be of a universal character. It will set a precedent. Any speculation about the uniqueness of the Kosovo case is just an attempt to circumvent international legal rules, which distracts from reality. What is worse is that attempts of that kind generate distrust of the international community as it creates an impression of double standards being applied to the settlement of crises in various regions worldwide and of rules being enforced arbitrarily, depending on each individual case.[30]

This view was in direct conflict with that held by the United States and some West European states, which hoped to present the case of Kosovo as a unique one, given its previous suppression and the prolonged period of international administration. From this perspective, a Council decision imposing a settlement might not be taken as establishing a precedent. It was known that China, Indonesia and several other states on the Council and beyond that were themselves experiencing secessionist campaigns were much concerned about that point.

Belgrade added to the pressure on the negotiating process by adopting a new constitution which confirmed that Kosovo was an integral and inseparable part

of the Serbian government negotiating team to the Serb parliament', *Kosovo Perspectives*, no. 20, 15 September 2006, <https://fco-stage.fco.gov.uk/resources/en/pdf/pdf17/fco_kosovo_ministerial_sept_2006>, accessed 18 October 2008.

[28] Contact Group ministerial statement, 20 September 2006, <http://www.unosek.org/docref/2006–09–20_CG%20_Ministerial_Statement_New%20_York.pdf>, accessed 19 June 2008.

[29] 'Russian position on Kosovo', *Kosovo Perspectives*, no. 21, 22 September 2006, <http://www.kosovoperspectives.com/index.php?categoryid=22&selected=21&p202_articleid=426>, accessed 19 June 2008.

[30] 'Russian position on Kosovo', *ibid.*

of Serbian territory, offering it a form of autonomy within the framework of Serbian sovereignty. The new constitution had emerged within a period of two weeks without any form of public consultation, and also without any involvement at all on the part of the Kosovars. The document was adopted unanimously on 30 September by all 242 members of the Serbian parliament present.[31] It was endorsed in a referendum held a month later, although only narrowly, voter turnout being poor.[32] There were also significant allegations of vote-rigging.[33] Ethnic Albanian voters from Kosovo were not eligible to participate.[34]

The Venice Commission of the Council of Europe later investigated the new constitution and its provisions for Kosovo. It found that 'the constitution itself does not at all guarantee substantial autonomy to Kosovo, for it entirely depends on the willingness of the National Assembly of the Republic of Serbia whether self-government will be realized or not'.[35]

On 3 October Russia demanded of the EU Presidency that talks be continued into 2007 should no agreement have been reached by the end of 2006. Moreover, as reported by the EU Presidency, the Russian Federation added that the Contact Group, in giving a mandate to generate a comprehensive proposal document, 'did not envisage the imposition of any solution on Belgrade without its consent and goodwill'.[36] Instead, the comprehensive proposal should be submitted 'to all sides for the purpose of engaging them in moving the negotiating process further. Russia added that it would 'not give its consent to any decision that would not be accepted by Belgrade—neither in the Contact Group, nor in the United Nations Security Council'.

V. Putting the Package Together

In the meantime, the various elements of a comprehensive settlement proposal had been put together on the basis of the negotiations up to this point. The overall proposal was therefore ready, for the most part, by the end of September. An end to the final status process had been promised by the Special Envoy before the end of the year. However, publication of the proposal was delayed several times

---

[31] Katarina Subasic, 'Serbia Adopts New Constitution in Bid to Keep Kosovo', *Agence France-Presse*, 29 September 2006.

[32] Boris Babic, 'Serbia Narrowly Passes New Constitution', German Press Agency, 29 October 2006.

[33] 'Serbian Leaders Bolstered by Approval of New Constitution Reasserting Claim on Kosovo', Associated Press, 30 October 2006.

[34] 'Serbia Passes New Constitution', *Der Spiegel*, 30 October 2006.

[35] European Commission for Democracy through Law, 'Opinion 405/2006 on the Constitution of Serbia', 19 March 2007, CDL-AD(2007)004, para 8.

[36] Letter from the EU Presidency to Member States of the Union, 3 October 2006, *Kosovo Perspectives*, no. 27, 3 November 2006, <http://www.kosovoperspectives.com/index.php?categoryid=22&selected=27&p202_articleid=27>, accessed 23 June 2008.

pending a series of elections to be held in Serbia. These delays increased the risk of protests and instability in Kosovo. However, the mainstream Kosovo politicians, some of whom were tough former resistance fighters who had been promising since early 2005 that independence was imminent, managed to maintain a surprisingly calm attitude in the territory. This may have been achieved in part by informal assurances from key players at a senior level that things would turn out all right in the end, provided Kosovo allowed events to take their course without disrupting the process.

Although it was the situation in Serbia that had caused publication of the proposals to be postponed, the Belgrade government's response to that delay was to call for the replacement of the UN Special Envoy and a resumption of talks. 'Serbia has not been informed about one letter of Ahtisaari's document and that shows that talks actually do not exist, but that Ahtisaari is attempting to replace the actual talks with controlled negotiations whose end has been predetermined.'[37]

When, on 2 February 2007, the draft settlement was finally shared with the parties, the Contact Group encouraged them once more to engage fully and constructively in order to advance the process on the basis of Resolution 1244.[38] However, the Russian Federation had already removed any pressure to negotiate seriously on the basis of the text. According to Serbian Prime Minister Vojislav Kostunica, President Vladimir Putin had offered fresh reassurances that the proposal would not be passed by the Security Council unless Belgrade had signed it.[39] On the eve of the follow-on negotiations, the Serbian parliament adopted a resolution rejecting the comprehensive package: 'The National Assembly of the Republic of Serbia concludes that the Proposal of UN Security-General's Special Envoy Martti Ahtisaari breaches the fundamental principles of international law since it does not take into consideration the sovereignty and territorial integrity of the Republic of Serbia in relation to Kosovo-Metohija.'[40]

Nevertheless, the mediators arranged for further direct negotiations, covering all parts of the comprehensive proposal, to continue for the second half of February. During that fortnight of talks, which were now chaired by Ahtisaari himself, Kosovo embraced the proposal in principle, offering modest suggestions for amendment. Belgrade returned to the negotiations with its own version of the proposal. Mirroring events at the Rambouillet follow-on conference

---

[37] Serbian Government Spokesman Srdjan Djuric, in *Kosovo Perspectives*, no. 28, 6 November 2006, <http://www.kosovoperspectives.com/index.php?categoryid=21&selected=28&p202_articleid=229>, accessed 23 June 2008.

[38] Contact Group Statement, 2 February 2007, <http://www.unosek.org/docref/Joint%20Contact%20Group%20Statement%202nd%20february%202007.doc>, accessed 23 June 2008.

[39] Radio Television Serbia, 'Status Proposal Won't Fly in UNSC If Not Acceptable to Serbia', 15 January 2007.

[40] Serbian Parliament, 'Resolution on UN Special Envoy Martti Ahtisaari's 'Comprehensive Proposal for the Kosovo Status Settlement', <http://www.mfa.gov.yu/Policy/Priorities/KIM/resolution_kim_e.html>, accessed 19 June 2008.

immediately preceding the initiation of hostilities in March 1999, the Serbian document was filled with deletions and amendments.[41] It referred to Kosovo consistently as 'The Autonomous Province of Kosovo and Metohija', which was to be governed in accordance with the Constitution of the Republic of Serbia and within its sovereignty.

During the discussions Serbia started to attack the Special Envoy personally and claimed that, in fact, no negotiations had yet taken place; that while the parties had put forward their own platforms for discussion, up to this point no actual dialogue had occurred. Moreover, while the draft document did not formally assign statehood to Kosovo, it equipped the territory with all the elements that typically appertain to states. Serbia demanded that the actual negotiations should now commence, at the very moment when the Contact Group and the UN mediator had thought that a final round of discussions was about to take place.

Despite its claim that there was as yet no agreed basis for discussion, Serbia nevertheless sought some changes to specific provisions in the package. Similarly, a few relatively minor changes were made at the suggestion of Kosovo. A final high-level meeting among the parties was held in March to review its final version, as amended in the light of the discussions that had been held. At the meeting, Serbia's President again rejected the package: 'Mr Ahtisaari's document is fundamentally not acceptable to us because it fails to reaffirm the sovereignty of the Republic of Serbia over Kosovo and Metohija and therefore brings into question the territorial integrity of our country.'[42] Prime Minister Kostunica added: 'We are issuing a timely warning that any attempt to impose a settlement on a free independent state would be tantamount to legal violence.'[43] He also confirmed that the decision of the Serbian National Assembly to reject the agreement was final and irrevocable and called on the Special Envoy to re-engage in negotiations on the basis of 'the substantive autonomy model'.[44]

VI. Content of the Ahtisaari Comprehensive Proposal

The Comprehensive Proposal for the Kosovo Status Settlement consists of a short framework agreement and twelve annexes. The agreement offers elements for a future constitution of Kosovo, detailed guidance on minority rights and community issues, decentralization and other issues, and provides for an international civil and military presence after the transition.

---

[41] See above, p. 151.

[42] Statement by the President of the Republic of Serbia, HE Boris Tadic, 10 March 2004, <http://www.mfa.gov.yu/Policy/Priorities/KIM/tadic100307_e.html>, accessed 6 October 2008.

[43] Statement by the Prime Minister of the Republic of Serbia, HE Vojislav Kostunica, 10 March 2007, <http://www.mfa.gov.yu/Policy/Priorities/KIM/kostunica100307_e.html>, accessed 6 October 2008.

[44] *Ibid.*

A. Status

The document is silent about the status of Kosovo. While it was transmitted to the Security Council along with a separate recommendation in favour of supervised independence, neither the framework text nor the annexes address this issue. But in contrast to Resolution 1244 (1999), there was no longer any mention of the need to preserve the continued territorial integrity of Yugoslavia (now Serbia) and of establishing mere autonomy or self-governance for Kosovo. Instead, the package provided everything that Kosovo would require in order to form itself into a state, and for others to recognize it as a state should they so wish.

In order to form a state, international law requires a clearly defined territory, a population that is attached to the territory and an effective government. That government must have the capacity to enter international relations. In line with the Non-Negotiable Principles of the Contact Group, Kosovo retained its own clearly defined territory. Furthermore, consistent with statehood, the package referred to the population traditionally resident in the territory, including refugees and the displaced, as 'citizens' of Kosovo.

The package also made it clear that Kosovo would have all the powers of governance that attach to statehood, covering the legislative, executive and judicial branches. According to UNMIK Regulation No. 1, adopted pursuant to Security Council Resolution 1244 (1999), 'All legislative and executive authority with respect to Kosovo, including the administration of the judiciary, is vested in UNMIK'. The package clearly provided that UNMIK's mandate would expire and 'all legislative and executive authority vested in UNMIK' would be transferred to the governing authorities of Kosovo. As UNMIK enjoyed 'all' public authority, and 'all' authority was to be transferred en bloc to the Kosovar authorities, Kosovo would have gained full public powers consistent with state sovereignty. Belgrade, on the other hand, was not mentioned at all in this context. It would retain no original or sovereign powers relating to Kosovo.

Would Kosovo really have obtained the sovereign powers needed to be able to claim that it exercised the functions of a state 'independently of others'—the requirement of sovereignty? It is true that the new institution of the International Civil Representative, and the International Steering Group of governments and organizations overseeing the transition, would continue to enjoy certain prerogatives for a period yet to be established. According to the package, Kosovo authorities would have had to give effect to the decisions of the relevant international bodies. However, the package emphasized repeatedly the principle that Kosovo's authority to govern 'its own affairs' is full and complete, subject only to temporary review and supervision in relation to certain specific areas. Such an arrangement would not have been inconsistent with the assumption or preservation of full sovereignty, as international practice has demonstrated.

Bosnia, for instance, retained its statehood during the period of international involvement of its affairs, as have many other states in other regions of the world that were subjected to a far more intensive international administration. Cambodia and Somalia are examples of established states that fell under full or partial international administration without effects on their statehood, Namibia and Eastern Timor obtained full statehood in the context of international administration.

Accordingly, the continued but far more limited international involvement in Kosovo would not have been inconsistent with its assumption of statehood. Moreover, the package foresaw that Kosovo itself would invite the activities of the international agencies. Hence, they would have undertaken their activities under the authority both of the United Nations Security Council (had it endorsed the package) and of Kosovo's consent.

While the international role in relation to Kosovo was to be limited in time, there were two restrictions to Kosovo's freedom of action that appear to have been intended to be permanent. The first related to certain human rights guarantees that were to be permanently anchored in the constitution. This posed no problem. A number of states remove human rights from the danger of ill-advised constitutional change including, for instance, Germany. The other provision concerned the abandonment of any territorial claims in relation to neighbouring states, including the acceptance of the boundary with Macedonia that was agreed by Belgrade. While it was controversial whether Belgrade then still had the power to address that issue when it concluded this deal, its agreement was endorsed by the UN Security Council at the time and could not now be re-opened.

Moreover, Kosovo was not to seek union with another state. Presumably this requirement was meant to be anchored permanently in a binding Security Council decision, had one been forthcoming.

The package confirmed the possibility of statehood in several other ways. It unambiguously assigned to Kosovo the capacity to enter into international relations, including the conclusion of treaties and membership in international organizations. It specifically requested that Kosovo sign and ratify the European Convention on Human Rights—an act that can only be performed by a state. The package even insisted that Kosovo should assume control of its air space—another function typically only exercised by a fully sovereign state.

If the package contained everything necessary to constitute Kosovo as a state, the next question that arose was whether it allowed enough room for the development of a state that could actually function in practice? In some other instances, including Bosnia and Herzegovina, international mediators insisted on constitutional provisions that have stunted the development of the state and led to consistent deadlock in its institutions. To answer this question, it is necessary to consider three principal issues. These are (1) the basic constitutional structure of the state, (2) the particular provisions that were foreseen in favour of communities, and (3) the future role of the international agencies.

B. Basic construction of the polity

The basic organization of Kosovo is that of a unitary state with a decentralized structure. That is to say, proposals for creating a federal-type system of autonomous and powerful 'cantons' according to the Swiss model were rejected. Such proposals would have risked the division of Kosovo. Instead the municipalities were established as the basic units only of local self-government. While they have 'full and exclusive powers' in relation to a range of issue, these apply only insofar as they 'concern local interest'. Moreover, these powers were to be exercised within the framework of central legislation. In principle, this design follows standard Western European practice on local governance.

Additional, primarily ethnic Serb, municipalities would be created. Mainly Serb municipalities were given enhanced competences relating to higher education, secondary health care, cultural affairs and arrangements concerning policing. Provision was made for a Serbian language university in Mitrovica and the use of Serbian curricula and textbooks in Serbian language schools.

As already noted, the provision for extensive cooperation between municipalities that decide to exercise their competences together was also controversial. According to the package, they would be entitled to establish common institutions, including a 'decision-making body' comprised of representatives from municipal assemblies. In Vienna, Kosovo objected to this proposal very strongly, explaining that this would offer the opportunities to certain municipalities to form, in effect, a third layer of governance between the central and the local. This would risk entrenching divisions in Kosovo, rather than furthering the integration of the territory, and introduce cantonization by the back-door. The Ahtisaari proposal ignored this objection. Similarly, direct financing for municipalities from Belgrade was retained in the document.

Particular interests of the communities were also recognized in provisions concerning the central Kosovo institutions. For two electoral periods, communities would continue to enjoy reserved seats in the Kosovo Assembly, in addition to those they might actually win in elections. Afterwards, the system would change to that proposed by Kosovo during the negotiations whereby the communities are guaranteed a certain number of seats in the Assembly. However, there was no double representation if more than those guaranteed seats were won in the elections.

There was also provision for power-sharing in relation to ministries and deputy ministers roughly in accordance with practice under international administration. Moreover, in accordance with European standards, there were detailed requirements for adequate representation of members of communities in the executive agencies and also in the prosecutorial and judicial branches. Somewhat painfully for Kosovo, there was a strong international representation in its future constitutional court. It was not clear how long these provisions would be in force.

Another important issue in the Vienna discussions related to the possible veto powers of the communities in the Assembly. Initially, the Kosovo delegation had proposed merely a conciliation process in the Assembly, followed by access to the Constitutional Court if the communities felt that their collective rights had been violated by a decision in the Assembly. However, Kosovo then offered a limited system of double majority in the Assembly instead, following the example of the Ohrid agreement on Macedonia. Accordingly, the Kosovo Assembly would only be able to adopt or modify certain, clearly enumerated pieces of legislation of key interest to the communities if the majority of representatives of communities in the Assembly also supported that change. This system guaranteed sufficient input of communities into decisions of vital importance to them, without exposing the Assembly to the risk of constant gridlock due to the application of a veto mechanism in all areas of legislation or decision-making.

C. Community rights

When presenting the Vienna package, Ahtisaari emphasized that the most important part related, in fact, to the rights of minorities or communities in Kosovo. In addition to the right of representation in the government, the Assembly and in the executive, the package did indeed contain a detailed list of rights for communities and their members, and of related obligations for Kosovo.[45] This listing was fully reflective of the position Kosovo had taken in Vienna, when submitting a very substantive framework document on community issues. In fact, the list of rights and obligations did not fully reflect all of the commitments Kosovo had been willing to accept during the negotiations. Instead, it converged with Council of Europe's human rights standards in this area, in particular the European Framework Convention for the Protection of National Minorities.

D. International presence

If a Security Council resolution had been forthcoming, this would have formalized the full transfer of authority from UNMIK to Kosovo, as well as the establishment of the office of the International Civil Representative, which would function under the guidance of the International Steering Group composed of France, Germany, Italy, Russia, the UK, USA, EU and European Commission, and NATO. The package emphasized that, in principle, Kosovo would be fully responsible for its own affairs. The International Civil Representative's mandate was limited to interpretation of the package and corrective measures in the event of its violation.

The International Civil Representative would also head the new EU Security and Defence Policy Mission addressing rule of law issues. It is in this area that

---

[45] For more details on the protection of communities, see Marc Weller, 'The Kosovo Constitution and Provisions for the Minorities of Kosovo', *European Yearbook of Minority Issues*, 6 (2006/2007) (Leiden, Boston: Martinus Nijhoff Publishers, forthcoming).

the mandate was perhaps not defined sufficiently clearly. The package merely declared that this mission would, after all, 'retain certain powers'. It was assumed that the EU mission would exercise support and monitoring functions and only intervene in certain circumstances that could be defined in greater detail.

The international military presence would continue to be NATO-led, ensuring a safe and secure environment and taking responsibility in relation to the building up of the new security force. Controversially for Kosovo, it was foreseen that the Kosovo Protection Corps, composed mainly of former KLA fighters would need to abolished. Instead, a smaller Security Force was envisaged.

E. The recommendation of the Special Envoy

On 26 March 2006 the UN Secretary-General forwarded the final version of the Comprehensive Proposal to the Security Council. While the proposal had been framed without any express reference to status, the submission also contained a recommendation on status by the Special Envoy—a recommendation fully endorsed by the Secretary-General.[46] The Comprehensive Proposal and the recommendation of the Special Envoy were deliberately separated, leaving room for the Security Council to endorse the substance of the settlement without necessarily confirming the status.

The recommendation on status was as follows:

The time has come to resolve Kosovo's status. Upon careful consideration of Kosovo's recent history, the realities of Kosovo today and taking into account the negotiations with the parties, I have come to the conclusion that the only viable option for Kosovo is independence, to be supervised for an initial period by the international community. My Comprehensive Proposal for the Kosovo Status Settlement, which sets forth these international supervisory structures, provides the foundations for a future independent Kosovo that is viable, sustainable and stable, and in which all communities and their members can live a peaceful and dignified existence.[47]

The Special Envoy added that, in the light of the recent history of the region, the 'autonomy of Kosovo within the borders of Serbia—however notional such autonomy may be—is simply not tenable'.[48] Similarly, continued international administration would not be sustainable. Instead:

Kosovo is a unique case that demands a unique solution. It does not create a precedent for other unresolved conflicts. In unanimously adopting resolution 1244 (1999), the Security Council responded to Milosevic's actions in Kosovo by denying Serbia a role in its governance, placing Kosovo under temporary United Nations administration and

---

[46] Letter dated 26 March 2007 from the Secretary-General to the President of the Security Council, UN Doc. S/2007/168, 26 March 2007.
[47] *Ibid.*, para. 5.
[48] *Ibid.*, para. 7.

envisaging a political process designed to determine Kosovo's future. The combination of these factors makes Kosovo's circumstances extraordinary.[49]

This statement was clearly aimed at persuading hesitant states on the Security Council to support the concept of supervised independence. Nevertheless, there remained significant reluctance to impose the Ahtisaari package by virtue of a Chapter VII resolution. Indeed, Russia, which had been part of the Contact Group process of guiding the negotiations throughout, now joined with Serbia in launching strong attacks on the UN Special Envoy, demanding fresh negotiations and a new mediator. However, other states were hesitant too. Indonesia, for instance, was keen to avoid a precedent in favour of independence. South Africa also voiced hesitations. Panama and Peru were undecided.

On 3 April the Security Council heard the Special Envoy introduce his proposal in confidential session. Serbia argued that the Envoy had exceeded his mandate by proposing to redraw Serbia's internationally recognized boundaries in a way that was consistent neither with the UN Charter nor with international law in general. It therefore demanded further negotiations under a new mediator. Kosovo, on the other hand, formally endorsed the Ahtisaari package in accordance with a declaration of the Kosovo Assembly on 5 March 2007.

VII. Conclusion

The negotiations on the final status of Kosovo were conducted in four dimensions. At the top level, the UN Security Council had set the overall negotiating framework in Resolution 1244 (1999). Serbia had expected that the resolution would confirm and preserve its territorial integrity when it agreed to the termination of hostilities with NATO in 1999. The UN administration would prepare the territory for self-governance. After an interim period, the territory would be returned to Belgrade's territorial jurisdiction, enjoying wide-ranging autonomy. In Belgrade's view, this design constrained options for final status. This, it asserted, was also in accordance with the emphasis of international law on the maintenance of the territorial integrity and unity of states. Accordingly, the negotiations would be 'status determined', focusing on the exact shape of an autonomy settlement, rather than on the question of whether autonomy or independence should be adopted.

The alternative view, adopted by many Western governments, noted that Resolution 1244 referred to autonomy only within the context of interim governance. There was no limitation on options for final status. Hence, the negotiations would be 'status open'.

[49] *Ibid.*, para. 15.

The UN Special Envoy adopted a third route. According to Belgrade, he agreed in advance of the talks that these would, at least in the first instance, be conducted in a way that is 'status neutral'. That is to say, there would be discussions on practical, technical issues first—issues that could be addressed irrespective of what agreement might emerge on status at a later stage. If there was to be no agreement on status, the Special Envoy would make his own recommendation on status to the Security Council on that issue. But this was to be a separable recommendation. That is to say, even if the Council failed to endorse his recommendation on status, it might still endorse—or, if need be, impose—the substantive comprehensive settlement package.

The substance of that package had been circumscribed at the second level by the Contact Group. It had made clear that Kosovo would enjoy more authority than it had in the years prior to the NATO intervention. However, the question of how much more authority remained unclear, as did the issue of whether this might extend to independence. Instead, certain base lines were drawn on minority rights, returns of the displaced and other topics.

At the third level, the Vienna negotiations, the parties were given the opportunity to build substantively upon those base lines. While the parties were not able to agree on many aspects, the mediators filled in the gaps between the positions of the parties with their own compromise proposals. These related mainly to decentralization and religious and cultural heritage. They also adopted a solid system for minority rights, although one that was somewhat less ambitious than that proposed by Kosovo.

A fourth layer of the negotiations concerned the domestic environment in Serbia and Kosovo. The Kosovo issue was one where compromises on status would be politically very costly to those who made them. In fact, neither side was willing or able to depart from its perceived popular mandate.

The original international script followed by the majority of states in the Contact Group anticipated that Serbia would not accept a settlement proposal granting independence to Kosovo. However, it was thought possible to persuade Serbia to protest against such a settlement publicly, while acquiescing silently. This acquiescence would be bought with promises of rapid EU accession and other incentives. Under such circumstances, it was thought, Russia would be willing to facilitate approval by the Security Council of the Ahtisaari package, as this would not really amount to a betrayal of its key ally.

Should Belgrade not acquiesce, there existed another option. As the UN Special Envoy had separated his recommendation in favour of supervised statehood from the substance of the Comprehensive Proposal, it might be possible to persuade the Council, including Russia, to accept only the substantive proposal, without reference to status. Kosovo would then still be bound into the commitments on decentralization, human rights and minority rights deemed essential by many governments. The replacement of UNMIK by an EU-led mission might still take place. Only the issue of status would be left unresolved at the level of the

Security Council, and could be determined instead through recognition of statehood by governments, in the event that it was eventually proclaimed by Kosovo.

When the Ahtisaari proposal was finally published, it did reflect in many parts the substantive compromises offered by the mediators after exhaustive discussion with the parties. However, the plan also went further. As there had been no in-depth discussions of 'constitutional' issues beyond problems of power-sharing in Vienna, the mediators offered certain provisions addressing the shape of the polity of Kosovo. These were meant to reflect and entrench the multi-ethnic character of the territory, democracy, human rights and other general principles. Most of these provisions did not directly address the issue of statehood. For instance, in the opening paragraph of the Comprehensive Proposal, Kosovo is described as a 'society', rather than a state or an autonomous unit.[50]

On the other hand, the general parts of the Comprehensive Proposal also address some aspects of the public powers to be enjoyed by Kosovo. Some of the functions assigned to Kosovo are typically only exercised by states. These include, for instance, 'the right to negotiate and conclude international agreements and the right to seek membership in international organizations' and the assumption of 'full ownership, responsibility and accountability for its airspace'.[51] Hence it could be said that elements of the general provisions of the plan were no longer strictly 'status neutral'.

In the end, Belgrade did not acquiesce in a settlement that would lead to independence. In this situation, the UN Security Council was unable to follow the recommendation of the Special Envoy and endorse supervised independence. However, it would not be possible to implement the second option. A vote in favour of the Comprehensive Proposal, without a pronouncement on status, would also be blocked as this was seen by Moscow, and by some other governments represented on the Security Council, as an indirect endorsement of independence. Hence the search for new approaches began.

---

[50] 'Comprehensive Proposal of the Kosovo Status Settlement', letter dated 26 March 2007 from the Secretary-General to the President of the Security Council, UN Doc. A/2007/168/Add.1, 26 March 2007, addendum, art. 1(1).

[51] *Ibid.*, annex 8, art. 7.

13

Further Negotiations and Unilateral Independence

The Ahtisaari plan for a comprehensive settlement of the status of Kosovo was greeted with some enthusiasm in Kosovo. While the plan itself did not touch the issue of status, it provided Kosovo with everything it would need for statehood. Moreover, it had been accompanied by a separate recommendation from the UN Special Envoy Martti Ahtisaari, declaring that supervised independence would be the only viable solution for Kosovo.[1] Final status seemed close. However, some two months after the unveiling of the Comprehensive Proposal, the mood swung the other way. It seemed as if the UN Security Council would not be in a position to act on the plan. Serbia, strongly backed by Russia, was demanded a fresh set of negotiations, arguing that the Ahtisaari process had been deeply flawed.

I. Further Negotiations

Several attempts were made to overcome the deadlock triggered by the varied reception of the Ahtisaari document in New York. First, the UN Security Council decided, on the initiative of Russia, to dispatch its own mission to Kosovo late in April 2007 in order to allow Council members to obtain first-hand information on progress made in Kosovo on the implementation of agreed standards and other matters.[2] During the visit to the region, Belgrade argued again that the Comprehensive Proposal amounted to an endorsement of independence—a result that could not be accepted. Instead of supervised independence, as proposed by the UN Special Envoy, the negotiations had not even begun to address the Serbian proposal of 'supervised autonomy' for Kosovo. That proposal would offer executive, legislative and judicial powers to Kosovo, while Serbia would retain control over foreign policy, defence, border control, monetary and customs policy and the protection of Serbian religious and cultural heritage and human

---

[1] See Chapter 12.
[2] Letter dated 19 April 2007 from the President of the Security Council to the Secretary-General, UN Doc. S/2007/220, 20 April 2007.

rights. Kosovo would also continue to be represented in Serbia's institutions.[3] The Kosovo authorities, on the other hand, maintained their insistence on independence. The mission concluded that the position of the sides on the Kosovo settlement proposal 'remain far apart'.[4]

Serbia then launched a formal 'Initiative to Commence a New State of Negotiations on the Status of Kosovo and Metohija'.[5] It argued that both the substance and the process of the Ahtisaari negotiations were totally unacceptable to Serbia. Hence, new negotiations should be commenced without the imposition of artificial time limits.

In the meantime, the EU and the US started to lobby in the Security Council in favour of elements of a draft resolution that would endorse the Ahtisaari package. There was no hope of achieving a resolution that would endorse Kosovo's independence outright. A more modest approach would simply seek endorsement of the substance of the Ahtisaari plan, and authorize the new implementation missions. Individual states would then have been free to take a view on recognition, without the Security Council having pronounced itself on statehood. However, at least the conditions for independence, including the very involving provisions for minority protection and guarantees against a possible merger of Kosovo with Albania or ethnic Albanian inhabited territories in Macedonia, would have been anchored at the level of a binding Chapter VII Security Council resolution.

The presentation of various different drafts in New York was flanked by intensive efforts by EU foreign ministers to change the attitude of the Russian government, involving a succession of visits to Moscow. These efforts were not successful. Similarly, attempts at achieving agreement at the G-8 meeting in Heiligendamm, Germany, of 6–8 June, failed. However, at that meeting, France stole the limelight somewhat from German Chancellor and host Angela Merkel. She had been supposed to 'deliver the Russians' on the Ahtisaari plan. Instead, newly elected President Nicolas Sarkozy proposed a further period of 120 days of negotiations. If, at the end of the period, there still was no agreement among the parties, the Security Council would endorse the Ahtisaari package.

The period of 120 days was the same as the transitional period that had been foreseen by the Comprehensive Proposal. Kosovo would have had 120 days from the endorsement of the proposal by the Security Council to adopt its constitution and the key pieces of legislation foreseen in it. At the conclusion of the period, the new international implementation mechanisms would take over and, presumably, Kosovo would be free to declare independence.

Two days after the conclusion of the Heiligendamm conference, US President George Bush visited Albania, promising rapid independence for Kosovo: 'The time

---

[3] Report of the Security Council Mission on the Kosovo Issue, UN Doc. S/2007/256, 4 May 2007.

[4] *Ibid.*, para. 59.

[5] Letter dated 25 May 2007 from the Permanent Representative of Serbia to the United Nations addressed to the Secretary-General, UN Doc. S/2007/312, 29 May 2007.

is now,' he proclaimed.[6] However, as it turned out, there were to be further negotiations after all. In July, Belgium, France, Germany, Italy, the UK and the US put
forward a formal draft resolution, reflecting elements of the French initiative in
favour of further negotiations. Instead of the formal endorsement of the Ahtisaari
package and the recommendation on status that had been expected at the end of
the 120-day period, it was less ambitious. The draft resolution recalled:[7]

the specific circumstances that make Kosovo a case that is sui generis resulting from the
disintegration of the former Yugoslavia, including the historical context of Yugoslavia's
violent break-up, as well as the massive violence and repression that took place in Kosovo
in the period up to and including 1999, the extended period of international administration under resolution 1244, and the UN-led process to determine status, and that this
case shall not be taken as a precedent by the Security Council.

Instead of referring to the territorial integrity of Serbia, it reaffirmed the Council's
commitment to a multi-ethnic and democratic Kosovo. The draft expressed its
appreciation for the work of the Special Envoy without formally endorsing his
comprehensive proposal. However, it did confirm that the status quo in Kosovo
would not be sustainable and that the unresolved situation in Kosovo constituted
a threat to international peace and security, opening the avenue for action under
Chapter VII of the UN Charter. The draft then provided for the opportunity of a
further round of negotiations, to be facilitated by the EU and the Contact Group.
The Council would review the situation further in the light of these negotiations.
At the end of the 120-day period, and irrespective of the outcome, the UNMIK
international civil presence in Kosovo would be replaced by an International Civil
Representative, nominated by the EU, who would head a European Security and
Defence Policy Rule of Law Mission in Kosovo. NATO would continue to lead
an international military presence.

The initial French proposal had been perceived by Russia and Serbia as a trap.
Further negotiations would merely provide a fig-leaf for the eventual and automatic endorsement of the Ahtisaari document upon expiry of the period of 120
days. The draft resolution placed before the Council did not suggest automatic
endorsement of the plan at that point. Nevertheless, the draft did arouse certain
suspicions. In exchange for the continuation of negotiations, the Council would
have agreed to put in place the implementation machinery for the Ahtisaari
plan. Accordingly, it would have been possible for the EU, the US and others to
recognize Kosovo without Security Council endorsement, and still to administer supervised independence as the Comprehensive Proposal foresaw, under a
Security Council mandate. 'It's kind of a hidden automaticity of the Ahtisaari
plan,' Russia's UN ambassador Vitaly Churkin noted.[8]

[6] Remarks by President Bush and Dr Sali Berisha, Prime Minister of Albania at Joint Press
Availability. Tirana, Albania, June 10 2007. Available at <http://fpc.state.gov/fpc/86270.htm>,
accessed 6 October 2008.
[7] UN Doc. S/2007/437, 17 July 2007.
[8] Evelyn Leopold, 'EU–US debate whether to call vote on Kosovo at UN', *Reuters*, 18 July
2007.

Russia's opposition killed the prospect of the adoption of the text, which was accordingly withdrawn by its sponsors before a vote could be held. Instead, the sponsors announced that they would now be pursuing the option of further, time-limited discussions. Should these not lead to agreement, 'we continue to believe that the Ahtisaari Plan is the best way forward'.[9]

In pursuit of this new initiative, the Contact Group dispatched a Troika of negotiators, led by Ambassador Wolfgang Ischinger of Germany for the EU, along with Alexander Botsan-Harchenko of Russia and Frank Wiesner of the United States. This initiative was welcomed by the UN Secretary-General, who requested a report on the venture by 10 December 2007, that is, after 120 days.

The Troika reaffirmed that it would act on the basis of Security Council Resolution 1244 (1999) and the Guiding Principles established by the Contact Group in November 2005. The Troika also agreed that 'while the Ahtisaari Settlement was still on the table, we would be prepared to endorse any agreement the parties might be able to reach'.[10]

The Troika clarified with the parties at the outset that it would not seek to impose any solution. Its principal role would be that of a facilitator of direct dialogue between the sides. However, in addition to such good offices, they might also act as mediators in the sense of 'taking an active role in identifying areas of possible compromise'. Essentially, therefore, the Troika mission offered an opportunity for Serbia to return to the drawing board and start the negotiations afresh. Kosovo, on the other hand, was reluctant to contemplate any move away from the Ahtisaari package which it had negotiated in good faith, believing it to be the definitive settlement.

Indeed, at one point the Troika even moved off the Contact Group principles. Ambassador Ischinger raised the issue of territorial exchanges, or a trade of northern Kosovo/Mitrovica for independence. This trial balloon was rapidly deflated when both sides rejected the suggestion. However, it was generally understood as an attempt by the Troika to open up all possible avenues for a settlement, even those that had previously been regarded as taboo. As the Troika put it in its final report: 'While it was broached, we did not dwell on the option of territorial partition, which was deemed unacceptable by both of the parties and the Contact Group'.[11] It therefore seemed that the Troika felt free to operate outside of the ten points for final status negotiations that had been issued by the Contact Group to guide the Ahtisaari negotiations. These had expressly and very clearly excluded any possibility of territorial adjustments.

In its initial discussions, Serbia requested that the Troika reach an international agreement over Kosovo's status that would support the essential autonomy of

[9] Statement issued by Belgium, France, German, Italy, the UK and the US, 20 July 2007. Available at <http://www.unosek.org/docref/2007-07-20%20-%20Statement%20issued%20by%20the%20co-sponsors%20of%20the%20draft%20resolution%20.doc>, accessed 6 October 2008.

[10] Letter dated 10 December 2007 from the Secretary-General to the President of the Security Council, UN Doc. S/2007/723.

[11] *Ibid.*, para. 10.

Kosovo. While Serbia had remained passive during much of the Ahtisaari talks, Belgrade now produced more concrete ideas for an autonomy solution that would offer powers of self-governance that went beyond those previously enjoyed by Kosovo. Belgrade would also reduce its own claims to powers it wished to exercise in relation to Kosovo. It was a proposal that might have appeared sufficiently reasonable to international negotiators to warrant further exploration had it been made in the context of the Ahtisaari negotiations. Kosovo would have come under very heavy pressure to defend its insistence on independence under those circumstances. However, after fifteen months of Ahtisaari talks, there was little inclination to start again from scratch and Kosovo restated its insistence on independence.

In the talks, Ambassador Ischinger recalled the experience of the two Germanies. Both states concluded a treaty in 1972, in which they agreed to disagree in their views of their respective legal positions. 'Let us resolve the practical issues here as well', Ischinger reportedly stated, 'Serbia is Serbia, and Kosovo is Kosovo. The two entities can agree to regulate economic cooperation and to form joint governing bodies, while temporarily shelving the dispute over Kosovo's status as either a province or an independent nation.'[12] It was not entirely clear whether 'temporarily shelving' meant refraining from declaring independence, or whether it meant that Kosovo would consider itself independent while Serbia would not.

The 1972 treaty between the two Germany's was, after all, concluded between two entities that were unquestionable states and in fact confirmed the statehood of the German Democratic Republic even in the eyes of the Federal Republic of Germany. The FRG had previously denied GDR statehood de jure, although not de facto. While it was concluded 'without prejudice to the different view of the Federal Republic of Germany and the German Democratic Republic on fundamental questions, including the national question' both sides agreed to develop normal, good neighbourly relations with each other 'on the basis of equal rights'.[13] The treaty confirmed that both 'States' would 'respect each other's independence and autonomy in their internal and external affairs'.

For Serbia, the idea of the Ischinger agreement therefore appeared to be another trap. Instead of offering a clear standstill for a further interim period during which the status quo on status would be maintained, the proposal seemed to imply that Kosovo would be entitled to proclaim independence and seek international recognition. The only benefit for Serbia would be that it would be entitled to continue to consider Kosovo part of its sovereign realm, which it could do anyway.

Nor was Kosovo particularly interested in this idea. Either it would involve freezing the campaign for independence for yet a further interim period. Or, if it

---

[12] Quoted in Gerhard Spoerl, Mission Impossible in the Balkans, *Spiegel Online International*. Available at <http://www.spiegel.de/international/europe/0,1518,522406,00.html>, accessed 6 October 2008.

[13] *Grundlagenvertrag* (Basic Treaty), 21 December 1972, Art. 6.

was not meant to include a standstill on status, then it would nevertheless add to the legitimacy of Serbia's opposition to its independence. However, the Ischinger initiative, which was also accorded the backing of the US, offered Prishtina a way out of the difficult dilemma of how to engage with the new round of negotiations. Kosovo did not wish to appear obstructive. On the other hand, the negotiations could only detract from the Ahtisaari package that Kosovo had endorsed.

Kosovo therefore embraced the notion of an agreement between the two sides that would address practical cooperation, although it did so on the assumption that Kosovo would be fully independent. Hence, it presented a proposal for an agreement with Serbia on how to manage cooperation and mutual relations after independence. In so doing, it acknowledged that Belgrade had certain legitimate interests and concerns that would warrant discussion, but that these were based on assumptions that had grown out of the Ahtisaari process. Of course, the very act of concluding a treaty with Belgrade might also have been taken as acknowledgement of its sovereign status.

Given the diverse views of the parties, the Troika merely succeeded in prompting the sides to declare that they would undertake not to undermine peace and stability during the further negotiating process.[14] The Contact Group reminded the parties in a statement on 27 September that the onus was on each of them to develop realistic proposals and that neither party could unilaterally block the process from advancing. It underlined that any future status settlement should focus on developing the special nature of the relations between both sides, especially in their historical, economic, cultural and human dimensions. Kosovo took this as an invitation to present its proposed draft agreement on future relations with Serbia. Belgrade, on the other hand, persisted in its view that autonomy with minimal powers reserved for Belgrade would best allow for the development of the relations between both sides.

While there were rumours that Belgrade might even propose a confederal arrangement between Serbia and Kosovo, such a proposal did not, ultimately, materialize. Serbian President Boris Tadic seemed to open that door when he referred to partnership under a common sovereign roof, promising to be 'very flexible with regard to the scope of self-governance for Kosovo'.[15] However, in substance, Belgrade continued to refer to substantial autonomy. This may have been due in part to the fact that it was known that Vojvodina would demand similar treatment within a new constitutional order if a confederal solution was to be adopted, leading to further loss of authority by Belgrade. However serious the willingness to go beyond wide-ranging autonomy, Serbia was

[14] Vienna Non-Paper, Read to both delegations on 30 August 2007 and confirmed in the presence of all the members of the Troika, Letter dated 10 December 2007 from the Secretary-General to the President of the Security Council, UN Doc. S/2007/723, 10 December 2007, Annex IV.

[15] Address by HE Mr Boris Tadic, the President of the Republic of Serbia, New York, 28 September 2007. Available at <http://bratislava.mfa.gov.yu/index.php?option=content&task=view&id=116&Itemid>, accessed 6 October 2008.

perhaps not best advised when presenting its proposed autonomy as a means of minority protection:

> It would be most useful for us to hear a well-substantiated argument that there is a national minority in Europe or anywhere in the world enjoying the rights more extensive in any segment than those outlined for Albanians in the proposal granting substantive autonomy to Kosovo. We are also inviting the Albanian side and the Troika alike to quote to us any example of a fuller exercise of minority rights... I can assure you that Serbia... will ... promptly amend its substantive autonomy model, all the way up to the red line where its sovereignty and territorial integrity become threatened. No national minority has ever been entitled to create a state within a state, and neither can the Albanian national minority be given the liberty to do so in the state of Serbia.[16]

Of course, to the ethnic Albanians of Kosovo, who constitute a 90 per cent majority in the territory, it was exactly the Serbian attitude of treating them as a minority in what they perceived as their own country that made their position on independence uncompromising. It appeared not only to the Kosovars, but also to the international negotiators, that Belgrade has learnt little from recent history, despite the forward-looking declarations of some of its interlocutors, including its President.

After the initial, fruitless discussions, the Troika offered its assessment of the negotiations' 'principal conclusions'. These were meant to identify areas of agreement.[17] This included a sense by both parties that there would be no return to the pre-1999 status and that Belgrade would neither govern Kosovo, nor establish a physical presence on its territory. Both sides would resolve all issues between them peacefully. Kosovo would be entitled to full integration into regional structures and both would move towards association and eventual membership of the EU and Euro-Atlantic arrangements. Prishtina would implement broad measures on behalf of Kosovo Serbs and other non-Albanian communities. Both sides would cooperate on issues of mutual concern, including economic and infrastructure issues and transport, minorities and cultural heritage protection, banking, public health and social welfare, and the fight against crime, and they would establish common bodies to implement such cooperation. Kosovo would manage its own public finances and enjoy unhindered access to international financial institutions. The international community would retain civilian and military presences in Kosovo after its status had been determined.

Having stated these areas of potential common positions (which were however not fully accepted as such by the parties), the mediators then reviewed all possible options of implementing them through different forms of legal relationships. These ranged from autonomy to confederal models and to full independence.

---

[16] Address of the Prime Minister of Serbia Vojislav Kostunica at the Direct Talks on the Future Status of the Province of Kosovo Metohija, New York, 28 September 2007. Available at <http://www.mfa.gov.yu/Policy/Priorities/KIM/kostunica280907_e.html>, accessed 6 October 2008.

[17] Letter dated 10 December 2007 from the Secretary-General to the President of the Security Council, UN Doc. S/2007/723, Annex VI: Principal Conclusions.

Particular examples, such as Hong Kong, were also put forward by Belgrade and explored. Serbia, again engaged in the negotiations at the presidential and prime ministerial levels, argued strongly that if the UK and China had been able to agree on the establishment of Hong Kong as a special administrative area within China's sovereign jurisdiction, such an approach should also be possible for Kosovo.[18] At a subsequent session, Belgrade presented a scholarly, comparative table of purportedly similar situations, covering Hong Kong, the Aaland Islands and Kosovo, as examples of autonomy.[19]

Belgrade also argued against the three main reasons Kosovo had advanced to oppose a reinstatement of autonomy.[20] The first argument was that Kosovo had now been under international administration for some eight years, and could not be expected to accept reintegration with Serbia. Belgrade pointed to the fact that Hong Kong had been administered by the UK for a century before being turned into a special administrative unit of China. Moreover, the UN interim administration had been mounted exactly in order to prepare for substantial autonomy for the territory. Second, autonomy would not disrupt regional stability. On the contrary, it was unilateral independence that would generate such instability and potential conflict. Third, Serbia was indeed offering meaningful autonomy, despite the record of its recent past, and was willing to accept virtually any solution as long as its sovereign claim remained in place.

At a high level negotiating meeting in Baden, Austria, President Tadic offered 'to Kosovo most competencies and symbols that are normally reserved only for sovereign countries':

Kosovo would have access to international financial institutions and other international and regional organizations except the UN, OSCE and Council of Europe. This would provide Kosovo with legitimacy in international and other lending institutions.[21]

Kosovo would have trade and cultural representative offices abroad.

Kosovo would have its own flag, anthem and national teams as they are accepted by international sporting federations.

Relations with Serbia would be normalized thus enhancing the prospects for stability and development of Kosovo.

[18] Serbian President Boris Tadic's Speech at the Fourth Round of Negotiations on Kosovo's Status, 5 November 2007. Available at by subscription at <http://www.predsednik.yu/mwc/default.asp?c=303500&g=20071105115746&lng=eng&hs1=0>, accessed 6 October 2008.

[19] *Kosovo Perspectives*, no. 82, 23 November 2007, Annex. Available at <http://www.kosovoperspectives.com/index.php?categoryid=23&selected=82&parentid=2&p202_articleid=1004>, accessed 6 October 2008.

[20] Serbian Prime Minister Vojislav Kostunica's Speech at the Fourth Round of Negotiations on the Future Status of Kosovo-Metohija, Vienna, 5 November 2007. Available at <http://www.kim.sr.gov.yu/admin/article/download/files/Statement%20of%20the%20Serbian%20Prime%20Minister%20at%20the%20fourth%20round%20of%20Vienna%20talks,%2005.11.2007.doc?id=5>, accessed 6 October 2008.

[21] President Tadic's Speech at the Negotiations on the Future Status of Kosovo and Metohija in Baden, 27 November 2007. Available at <http://www.predsednik.yu/mwc/default.asp?c=303500&g=20071127103315&lng=eng&hs1=0>, accessed 6 October 2008.

Kosovo's integration into the network of official regional relations and with Serbia would accelerate European integration. Serbia is prepared to ask for benefits of its relationship with the EU to be enjoyed by Kosovo.

Once more, one wonders what would have happened if Belgrade had engaged with the debate on status as openly and decisively in the run up to Ahtisaari talks, and substantively in the talks. During 2005/6, there had been much academic discussion about solutions that would offer substantive independence while not necessarily formally disrupting the territorial unity of Serbia (the 'Taiwan scenario'). Had Serbia opened the door for discussions along those lines a year and a half earlier, it would have been very difficult for Kosovo to resist the dynamic towards such a solution. This option was, after all, in compliance with the structural principles to which the entire organized international community was committed in principle. Had it been pursued earlier, it might have been imposed on Kosovo by the UN Security Council.

However, at this late stage, with the Ahtisaari Comprehensive Settlement Proposal in hand, Kosovo did not feel under significant pressure to address these points. Indeed, the presentation of the Serbian President was somewhat undermined by that of his Prime Minister, who referred again to the Albanians as a minority that would need to seek accommodation within the sovereignty of Serbia.[22] It seemed unlikely, after all, that even now, close to the abyss, Belgrade was really seriously willing to contemplate a solution beyond substantial autonomy.

In the end, Ambassador Ischinger introduced formally his earlier suggestion of an agreement between the two sides. He produced a draft containing some ten articles. Without taking a view on status, the parties would have agreed to exercise their powers separately, but to cooperate where mutually advantageous. 'Neither party shall be entitled to act on behalf of or in the name of the other party in foreign relations', the text reportedly added.[23] While the idea of the agreement to disagree on status had initially apparently attracted Russian backing, Moscow went cold on the initiative. Serbia apparently saw it as another form of the Treaty of Friendship and Cooperation that Kosovo had been proposing, essentially confirming its independence. Kosovo, on the other hand, could see little advantage in agreeing to the maintenance by Serbia of a position that was directed against its aspirations.

In total, there were ten negotiating sessions, including a final, intensive three-day conference held in Baden, Austria, in a last ditch gamble to foster agreement. True to form, the meeting was held, once more, in a splendid chateau. In the end the Troika concluded:

[22] Serbian Prime Minister Vojislav Kostunica's Speech at the Negotiations on the Issue of the Future Status of Kosovo-Metohija in Baden, 26 November 2007. Excerpts available at <http://www.osce.mfa.gov.yu/index.php?option=content&task=view&id=374&Itemid>, accessed 6 October 2008.
[23] Note 12, above.

After 120 days of intensive negotiations…the parties were unable to reach an agreement on Kosovo's status. Neither side was willing to yield on the basic question of sovereignty.[24]

By the year's end, the UN Secretary-General warned that the present impasse might lead to events on the ground taking on 'a momentum of their own, putting at serious risk the achievements and legacy of the United Nations in Kosovo. Moving forward with the process to determine Kosovo's future status should remain a high priority for the Security Council and for the international community.'[25] He added that, in the wake of the recent Kosovo elections that had brought to power former KLA leader Hashim Thaci, there was a high expectation that independence was imminent.

The Serbian parliament, on the other hand, adopted a further resolution committing itself to the protection of sovereignty, territorial integrity and the constitutional order of the Republic. It threatened the reconsideration of diplomatic relations with states recognizing an independent Kosovo and indicated that it might take action to protect the ethnic Serb population of the territory.[26] The Serbian government reiterated its proposals for autonomy and the need for more talks. However, reverting somewhat to its previous positions, the statement added that 'the Republic of Serbia cannot accept any request for secession by any of the twenty-seven national minorities which make [up] part of its citizenry'.[27] Again, this kind of approach, equating the position of the two million Kosovars with twenty-six, at that time quite tiny, minorities, removed any sense that innovative solutions seeking to circumvent the sovereignty issue might be explored.

II. Independence

Consultations in the UN Security Council continued from December onwards.[28] On 16 January, President Tadic of Serbia addressed the Security Council. He claimed that Belgrade had negotiated constructively over a period for two years. 'Substantial autonomy has figured in various models as a functioning, sustainable and successful solution. It has been proved that such solutions are in accordance with international law and that they are the only way to arrive at a compromise

---

[24] *Ibid.*, para. 10.
[25] Report of the Secretary-General on the United Nations Interim Administration Mission in Kosovo, UN Doc. S/2007/768, 3 January 2008.
[26] Resolution of the National Assembly on the Protection of Sovereignty, Territorial Integrity and Constitutional Order of the Republic of Serbia, 26 December 2007. Available at <http://www.mfa.gov.yu/Facts/resolution_kim_261207_e.html>, accessed 6 October 2008.
[27] Letter dated 4 January 2008 from the Permanent Representative of Serbia to the United Nations addressed to the President of the Security Council, UN Doc. S/2008/7, 7 January 2008.
[28] These consultations involved a number of countries additional to the Council membership that had requested to be heard; e.g., UN Doc. S/PV/5811, 19 December 2007.

in conflicts similar to the Kosovo conflict.'[29] Unilateral recognition of Kosovo's independence, he argued, would create a precedent causing unforeseeable consequences for other regions. Instead, he urged the resumption of negotiations on autonomy. Rather movingly, the President argued that Serbia should not be punished for the sins of its past, given that the previous government had been ousted by its people, nor could it be deprived of its rights on that account. While President Tadic warned that his government would use all legal and democratic means to preserve the sovereignty and territorial integrity of Serbia, he reaffirmed 'once again that Serbia will not resort to violence or war'.[30] This commitment was restated by Serbia's Foreign Minister, at a further meeting of the Council on 14 February, called by Russia and Serbia amidst reports that Kosovo's declaration of independence was imminent.[31] The Foreign Minister added:

The direct and immediate consequence of this act would be the destruction of the first principle of the United Nations, namely the sovereign equality of all member states. Such a precedent, imposed on the world community, would echo far, far away, into every corner of our globe. For we would discover that the rushing river of self-determination has become an uncontrolled cascade of secession. We all know that there are dozens of Kosovo-s [sic.] around the world, just waiting for secession to be legitimized, to be rendered an acceptable norm. Many existing conflicts would escalate, frozen conflicts would reignite, and new ones would be instigated.[32]

Serbia requested in vain that the Council should condemn the intent of the authorities in Prishtina to declare independence. Kosovo then declared independence on 17 February 2008. In their declaration, the members of the Kosovo Assembly noted that Kosovo 'is a special case arising from Yugoslavia's non-consensual breakup and is not a precedent for any other situation'. In substance:

We, the democratically elected leaders of our people, hereby declare Kosovo to be an independent and sovereign state. This declaration reflects the will of our people and it is in full accordance with the recommendations of the UN Special Envoy Martti Ahtisaari and his Comprehensive Proposal of the Kosovo Status Settlement.

We declare Kosovo to be a democratic, secular and multi-ethnic republic, guided by the principles of non-discrimination and equal protection under the law. We shall protect and promote the rights of all communities in Kosovo and creation the conditions necessary for their effective participation in political and decision-making process.

. . .

We hereby affirm, clearly, specifically, and irrevocably, that Kosovo shall be legally bound to comply with the provisions contained in this Declaration, including, especially the obligations for it under the Ahtisaari Plan. In all of these matters, we shall act

---

[29] Statement published by the Serbian Permanent Mission to the UN, UN Doc. S/PV.5821, 16 January 2008.

[30] *Ibid.*, 4.

[31] UN Docs S/2008/92, 12 February 2008; S/2008/93, 12 February 2008.

[32] Address Before the United Nations Security Council by H.E. Mr. Vuk Jeremić Minister of Foreign Affairs of the Republic of Serbia, New York, 14 February 2008. Available at <http://www. mfa.gov.yu/Policy/Priorities/KIM/jeremic140208_e.html>, accessed 6 October 2008.

consistent with principles of international law and resolutions of the Security Council of the United Nations, including resolution 1244 (1999). We declare publicly that all states are entitled to rely upon this declaration, and appeal to them to extend to us their support and friendship.

The Declaration was adopted unanimously, by 109 votes, including those of virtually all non-Serb minorities. The ten representatives of the ethnic Serb community, and one member of the Gorani community who supported them, had boycotted the meeting of the 120-member Assembly.

The Declaration had been drafted in conjunction with, and checked by, key governments. It was phrased in a way as to have important legal implications for Kosovo. Employing the international legal notion of a 'unilateral declaration', it created legal obligations *erga omnes*. These are legal obligations that all other states are entitled to rely on and of which they can demand performance. In this sense, an attempt was made to replace the binding nature of a Chapter VII resolution of the Security Council imposing the limitations on Kosovo's sovereignty foreseen in the Ahtisaari plan with a self-imposed limitation of sovereignty. In view of the fact that Kosovo had not yet adopted its new, Ahtisaari-compliant constitution at the time of the Declaration of Independence, this fact was of particular importance.

Serbia's parliament promptly adopted a decision purporting to annul this Declaration.[33] Serbia and the Russian Federation also immediately protested at the international level, demanding an urgent meeting of the Security Council which, for the first time in several months, would address the Kosovo issue in public.[34] The meeting was opened by the UN Secretary-General, who informed the meeting that the Kosovo Assembly had indeed declared independence by unanimous vote of all 109 deputies attending.[35] The Secretary-General noted that the Declaration confirmed Kosovo's full acceptance of the obligations contained in the Comprehensive Settlement Proposal as well as continued adherence to Resolution 1244 (1999). There had also been a strong commitment by the Kosovo Prime Minister to the equal opportunities of all inhabitants and a pledge that there would be no ethnic discrimination. The Secretary-General also noted a Letter from the EU High Representative for Common Foreign and Security Policy, stating that the EU would deploy a rule of law mission

[33] Decision on the Annulment of the Illegitimate Acts of the Provisional Institutions of Self-government in Kosovo and Metohija on their Declaration of Unilateral Independence, undated. Available at <http://en.wikisource.org/wiki/Decision_on_the_annulment_of_the_illegitimate_acts_of_the_provisional_institutions_of_self-government_in_Kosovo_and_Metohija_on_their_declaration_of_unilateral_independence>, accessed 6 October 2008.
[34] Letter dated 17 February 2008 from the Permanent Representative of Serbia to the United Nations addressed to the President of the Security Council, S/2008/103, 17 February 2008; Letter dated 17 February 2008 from the Permanent Representative of the Russian Federation to the United Nations addressed to the President of the Security Council, S/2008/104, 17 February 2008.
[35] UN Doc. S/PV/5829, 18 February 2008.

within the framework provided by Resolution 1244 (1999) and a EU Special Representative for Kosovo. The Secretary-General confirmed that, pending guidance from the Council, UNMIK would continue to exercise its mandate under Resolution 1244 (1999).

The Council then heard statements from the President of Serbia and the Russian Federation, condemning the Declaration of Independence in terms of their previous statements already discussed above. Serbia requested that the Secretary-General instruct his Special Representative in Kosovo, Mr Ruecker, to declare the act of secession null and void. 'The Special Representative has binding powers, and they have been used before. I request that he use them again.'[36] This demand was echoed by the Russian Federation. Russia also declared that the EU Rule of Law Mission had been launched without the mandate of the Council and was not covered by the existing authority contained in Resolution 1244 (1999).

Vietnam found that the Declaration of Independence was not in conformity with Resolution 1244 (1999), also stating its commitment to the doctrine of territorial integrity.[37] South Africa made a similar statement, indicating that the current developments in Kosovo would have serious implications for the international community that warranted further study.[38] China offered a rather measured assessment. It did not condemn or declare illegal the Declaration of Independence in an outright way. However, it did voice its concern:

Safeguarding sovereignty and territorial integrity is one of the cardinal principles of contemporary international law, as enshrined in the Charter of the United Nations. The issue of Kosovo's status does indeed have its special nature. Nevertheless, to terminate negotiations, terminate pursuit of a solution acceptable to both parties and replace such efforts with unilateral action will certainly constitute a serious challenge to the fundamental principles of international law.[39]

Indonesia also expressed its sense that negotiations had not yet been exhausted, referring in rather an indirect way to international legal principles.[40] Libya pointed to the unique circumstance of the case, which would preclude it from becoming a precedent.[41] Burkina Faso regretted the situation in general terms but declared that one could only take note of it at this stage.[42]

The states of the European Union confirmed their view that this situation was a very special and unique one. Belgium noted that:

Kosovo's independence is situated within a historical context that no one can ignore: the disintegration of Yugoslavia, which led to the creation of new independent States. The independence of Kosovo is part of this framework and can thus in no way be considered a precedent.[43]

[36] UN Doc. S/PV/5829, 7.   [37] UN Doc. S/PV/5829, 4.
[38] UN Doc. S/PV/5829, 16.   [39] UN Doc. S/PV/5829, 8.
[40] UN Doc. S/PV/5829, 12.   [41] UN Doc. S/PV/5829, 15.
[42] UN Doc. S/PV/5829, 15.   [43] UN Doc. S/PV/5829, 9.

Panama echoed this view, reminding the Council that Kosovo had 'enjoyed an autonomy much like the autonomy of the old republics of greater Yugoslavia, and an attempt was made to deprive it of that autonomy'.[44] The US added that the violent break-up of Yugoslavia, Milosevic's policies of repression and ethnic cleansing, and the adoption of Resolution 1244 (1999) removing Kosovo from Belgrade's control had all led to a unique situation. 'We have not, do not and will not accept the Kosovo example as a precedent for any other conflict or dispute'.[45]

Italy similarly expressed its sense that the independence of Kosovo was now a fact which had come about due to the impossibility of achieving a negotiated settlement.[46] The UK added that Resolution 1244 (1999) had not placed any limits on the outcome of a status process which, according to the Rambouillet Accords, was to be based on the will of the people of Kosovo: '...the substantial autonomy which Kosovo was to enjoy within the Federal Republic of Yugoslavia was an interim outcome pending a final settlement'.[47] Instead, Serbia had effectively ended any chance of a negotiated settlement which it unilaterally changed its constitution in the middle of the final status process.

Croatia declared that '[t]he recognition of independence is a sovereign decision of each individual state', indicating that it would form a view in the matter soon.[48] France similarly emphasized the national prerogative of deciding whether or not to recognize, in addition to the unique facts of the situation.[49] Costa Rica indicated that it had engaged in a very careful legal consideration of the issue:

We are convinced that Resolution 1244 (1999) and the 1999 general principles on a political solution to the Kosovo crisis set out in annexes 1 and 2 of that resolution, and the Interim Agreement for Peace and Self-government in Kosovo contain sufficient legal foundations to enable us to recognize the independence proclaimed yesterday. We believe that with this recognition, we are responding primarily to the will of the people of Kosovo—a people who find it impossible to live together with the Serb majority in the same country after the 1998 campaign of ethnic cleansing...[50]

The Council of the European Union, in its Conclusions on Kosovo adopted the following day, noted that EU member states 'will decide in accordance with national practice and international law, on their relations with Kosovo'.[51] This pragmatic approach avoided a split within the Union, which would have not been able to agree a common attitude on this issue. However, the Council was united in adding:

The Council reiterates the EU's adherence to the principles of the UN Charter and the Helsinki Final Act, inter alia the principles of sovereignty and territorial integrity and

[44] UN Doc. S/PV/5829, 21.   [45] UN Doc. S/PV/5829, 19.
[46] UN Doc. S/PV/5829, 11.   [47] UN Doc. S/PV/5829, 13.
[48] UN Doc. S/PV/5829, 16.   [49] UN Doc. S/PV/5829, 19.
[50] UN Doc. S/PV/5829, 17.
[51] 2851st External Relations Council meeting, Brussels, 6496/08 (Presse 41), 18 February 2008. Available at <http://www.consilium.europa.eu/ueDocs/cms_Data/docs/pressData/en/gena/98818.pdf>, accessed 6 October 2008.

all UN Security Council Resolutions. Its underlines its conviction that in view of the conflict of the 1990s and the extended period of international administration under SCR 1244, Kosovo constitutes a sui generis case which does not call into question these principles and resolutions.

This statement somewhat disguised that the EU had failed to meet the one clear target it had set itself in its attempt to manage this aspect of the Kosovo crisis. As opposed to the acrimonious debate about the recognition of Croatia and Slovenia in December of 1991, this time the EU member states wanted to present a united front and act together. In reality, the statement confirmed the inability of the EU to act as a unified entity in the matter of recognition. This admission appeared to confirm the sense of the US government that this affair had better be managed through strong leadership from Washington, rather than hoping for a consensus among the European states.

The situation was different, however, in relation to action on the ground. The EU had prepared to take over responsibility for the implementation of the Ahtisaari proposal since its publication. In April 2006 it had adopted a Joint Action on the Establishment of an EU Planning Team regarding a possible EU crisis management operation in the field of rule of law and possible other areas in Kosovo, followed by several amendments and extensions of the mandate.[52] On 14 December 2007, after the termination of the Troika mediation, the European Council declared its readiness to assist Kosovo through a European Security and Defence Policy Mission and a contribution to an International Civilian Office as part of the international presence in Kosovo. On 16 February, the day before independence was declared, the Council decided to launch the EULEX Kosovo mission in the wider area of rule of law. Simultaneously, Pieter Feith was appointed as EU Special Representative in Kosovo.[53] The mandate of the EULEX mission was, as foreseen in the Ahtisaari document, to assist Kosovo authorities in the legal and judicial field, in policing and customs issues, and to ensure the functioning of these institutions according to European best practices. It would become fully operational 120 days after the launch.

On 28 February 2008, the International Steering Group anticipated by the Comprehensive Proposal was constituted, appointing the EU Special Representative as the International Civilian Representative for Kosovo, exercising the functions and powers outlined in Annex IV of the Ahtisaari document. Given the absence of additional Security Council authority, the Steering Group became operational at the request of the Kosovo leadership.[54] However,

---

[52] Council Joint Action 2006/304/CFSP, 10 April 2006. Available at <http://eur-lex.europa.eu/LexUriServ/LexUriServ.do?uri=OJ:L:2006:112:0019:0023:EN:PDF>, accessed 18 October 2008.

[53] See Council of the European Union, S060/08, 16 February 2008. Available at <http://www.consilium.europa.eu/ueDocs/cms_Data/docs/pressData/en/gena/98772.pdf>, accessed 6 October 2008.

[54] Press Statement of the International Steering Group, Vienna, 28 February 2008. Available at <http://www.ico-kos.org/press/First%20meeting%20of%20the%20International%20Steering%20Group%20(ISG)%20for%20Kosovo.pdf>, accessed 6 October 2008.

subsequently, the role of the EU mission, and its relationship with UNMIK, became the subject of some controversy. Russia, at the Security Council, argued strongly that UNMIK would not be entitled to transfer its powers to Kosovo and the EU mission respectively, in the absence of a fresh mandate. While some EU states felt that the mission could proceed as planned from the moment of the coming into force of the Kosovo Constitution, others appeared to become more hesitant.

The UN Secretary-General then sought a consensus on how to proceed further. Consultations with the sides had revealed that they agreed on the need for an international presence. He proposed a way forward that would be 'status neutral'.[55] The Secretary-General noted that the unilateral declaration of independence, and the impending adoption of the Kosovo Constitution, 'would effectively remove from UNMIK its current powers as an interim civil administration'.[56] The Kosovo government had indicated, however, that it would welcome a continued UN presence in the territory provided that it would carry out only limited residual tasks.

The Kosovo Serbs, he reported, had engaged in protests, attacking customs service points on the Adminstrative Boundary Line to Serbia and forcibly seizing control over a courthouse in Northern Mitrovica. Kosovo Serbs were boycotting the Kosovo institutions, including the police, judiciary, transportation and municipal administrations.[57]

At the international level, the EU informed the UN that it would no longer fund the economic reconstruction pillar of UNMIK. Apparently, this decision had not been coordinated with UNMIK. On the other hand, the EU High Representative for the Common Foreign and Security Policy informed the Secretary-General of the willingness of the EU to play an enhanced role in the area of the rule of law in Kosovo 'within the framework provided by resolution 1244 (1999)'.[58]

In view of the risks of instability, and 'pending guidance from the Security Council', the Secretary General announced his intention to 'adjust operational aspects of the international civil presence in Kosovo'.[59] This would include an enhanced operational role for the EU in the area of rule of law, including, gradually, policing, justice, and customs throughout Kosovo. The OSCE would remain in place, addressing the promotion of democratic values and the protection of the interests of communities. UNMIK would take on a role of monitoring and reporting, facilitating arrangements for Kosovo's engagements in international agreements, facilitating Prishtina-Belgrade dialogue, and certain functions discussed with Belgrade. These functions were outlined in a letter of the Secretary-General to the Serbian President Boris Tadic. In particular, Kosovo

---

[55] Report of the Secretary-General on the United Nations Interim Administration Mission in Kosovo, UN Doc S/2008/354, 12 June 2008, para. 10.
[56] UN Doc. S/2008/354, para. 7.   [57] UN Doc. S/2008/354, para. 6.
[58] UN Doc. S/2008/354, para. 8.   [59] UN Doc. S/2008/354, paras 13–16.

Police Service operations in ethnic Serb-majority areas would remain under the overall authority of the UN. There would be additional local and district courts generated within Serb majority areas operating within the Kosovo court system under the applicable law and within the framework of Resolution 1244 (1999). A solution for the maintenance of a single customs area in Kosovo would be sought. There would be a joint committee on transportation and infrastructure including Serbia. NATO would continue to fulfil its existing security mandate, including with respect to boundaries, throughout Kosovo. Finally, the Serb Orthodox church would remain under the direct authority of its religious seat in Belgrade, retaining the sole right to preserve and reconstruct its religious, historical and cultural sites in Kosovo. It would be afforded international protection.[60]

Kosovo was informed of these steps, which would be of limited duration and without prejudice to the status of Kosovo.[61] The Secretary-General noted that his proposal might 'not fully satisfy all sides' but would at least be 'the least objectionable' course to all.[62] Indeed, during the debate in the UN Security Council of 20 June, Serbia's President Boris Tadic opposed Kosovo's adoption of its constitution as a 'usurpation' of the Council's mandate for UNMIK.[63] He also asserted that the reconfiguration of UNMIK would require a decision of the Security Council—a view echoed by Russia and Vietnam. Moreover, Serbia would not be able to endorse the suggestions of the Secretary-General as to the nature of this reconfiguration as this might be taken to give rise to a process of compromise in relation to the status of Kosovo. This issue was yet to be negotiated through the status process envisaged in Resolution 1244 (1999). Nevertheless, Serbia appeared to express itself in accord with the substantive areas of continued involvement foreseen by the UN Secretary-General for the UN civilian presence. Russia also did not oppose the substance of the Secretary-General's proposals, reminding him, however, that only the Council could decide on a transformation of UNMIK's mandate. The discussion in the Council was only a first step in this direction, and no action should be taken to 'reformulate' UNMIK without Council approval.[64]

The Council did not adopt a resolution on this issue. At the conclusion of the meeting, the Secretary-General indicated again that his proposal offered a balanced solution developed fully within the framework of Resolution 1244 (1999). The proposal was the result of an effort at compromise, having benefited from extensive consultations, he added. Emphasizing his own broad mandate provided by the UN Charter and Resolution 1244 (1999), he declared that the meeting had

[60] Letter dated 12 June 2008 from the Secretary-General to His Excellency Mr Boris Tadic, *ibid.*, Annex 1.

[61] Letter dated 12 June 2008 from the Secretary-General to His Excellency Mr Fatmir Sejdiu, *ibid*, Annex II.

[62] Plan to Reconfigure UN presence in Kosovo 'Least Objectionable Option', Ban, UN Press Release, 13 June 2008. Available at <http://www.un.org/apps/news/story.asp?NewsID=27013&Cr=Kosovo&Cr1=&Kw1=kosovo&Kw2=&Kw3=>, accessed 31 October 2008.

[63] See the record at UN Doc. S/PV.5917, 20 June 2008.   [64] *Ibid.*

given the Council an important opportunity to consider the matter. In this way, he appeared to lay the groundwork for an argument in favour of acquiescence by the Council in his proposal. The next day, Javier Solana welcomed the report of the Secretary-General, indicating that the reconfiguration of the civilian presence would allow the EULEX mission, in the framework of Resolution 1244 (1999), to intensify its deployment and move towards operational functions.[65]

Overall, therefore, it had been accepted by all that Resolution 1244 (1999) remained in place. Kosovo had somehow hedged its position, indicating that it would act 'in accordance with' the resolution, rather than accepting its continued validity de jure. It was also accepted by all sides that the UN civil presence would remain in place, providing a roof under which the new EULEX mission might operate. In practice, it seemed clear that most of UNMIK's functions would devolve on the EU mission, with the UN retaining a role mainly focused on reporting and monitoring, and facilitating dialogue between Kosovo and Belgrade. While Russia appeared to maintain that this plan had not been approved, it seemed as if the UN Secretary-General had done enough to give himself the space to implement this design without a further Security Council resolution.

III. Conclusion

The Ahtisaari Comprehensive Proposal provided Kosovo with the basic elements of statehood, without addressing the issue of status directly. However, when presenting his proposal, the UN Special Envoy attached a strong recommendation in favour of supervised independence. This was very fiercely resisted by Serbia and Russia. Other states represented in the Security Council were also unwilling to consider imposing such a settlement in the absence of Belgrade's consent. A further round of negotiations was therefore mounted, much to the discomfort of Kosovo, which had negotiated in Vienna in the expectation that the Ahtisaari talks were indeed the final status negotiations, rather than merely preliminary discussions.

The administration of the final phases of the negotiation process by the various actors involved raised a number of questions. It was surprising to see how easily the Comprehensive Proposal presented by Martti Ahtisaari was wiped away in July 2007 and replaced with entirely new negotiations once it encountered the opposition of Russia. Although formally conducted under UN authority, the initial mediation process had been carried forward under the quite close control of the Contact Group, which had included Russia. The US and the EU states were willing to grant Russia a controlling seat at the table, without insisting on collective responsibility for decisions taken. Hence, Russia felt free to disown the

---

[65] Council of the European Union, Press Release, S223/08, 21 June 2008.

outcome of the process it had supported, at least nominally, throughout. This outcome mirrored exactly the position at Rambouillet, where Russia had obtained the benefit of exercising influence and even control over the negotiations process without having to show commitment to it at the very end.

While Belgrade sought to offer very wide-ranging autonomy with minimum involvement in the governance of Kosovo in the new round of talks, Prishtina proposed instead modalities of cooperation with Belgrade on the basis of a treaty on international cooperation.

The failure of the Ischinger negotiations opened the way to unilateral action by Kosovo, coordinated with key states of the EU, the US and some other governments. This action triggered counter-measures by Belgrade, adopted with Russia's support. In particular, Serbia appeared to lay the groundwork for the de facto division of Kosovo, severing contacts between the Serbian authorities in the north of the territory and the UN administration. Local Serbian elections were also conducted in northern Kosovo, where a new regional assembly formed itself beyond the control and new constitutional order of Prishtina. Russia obstructed the handover from UNMIK to the EU mission that had started deploying in order to supervise independence.

This result was a slightly odd one. Through its unilateral Declaration of Independence, Kosovo had committed itself to all of the concessions agreed during the Ahtisaari process in the expectation of status. Belgrade could 'bank' on these concessions relating to its own interests in Kosovo, while still being able to actively oppose Kosovo in its quest for recognition. Moreover, having opposed the handover from UNMIK to EULEX, Belgrade managed to 'renegotiate' the Ahtisaari implementation system to some extent from the outside. It managed to retain a role for the UN in Kosovo, and a mechanism for itself to engage on Kosovo in relation to issues of core interest, such as religious heritage. This was placed expressly under the terms of Resolution 1244 (1999), confirming the continued applicability of the resolution.

On the other hand, while Serbia and Russia were in a position to make independence more difficult for Kosovo, while still relying on international action to ensure that the interests of the Serb community in Kosovo were fully protected, they could not prevent independence. This result goes very much against the grain of the classical international order, which strongly privileges territorial unity over claims to self-determination outside of the colonial context. In fact, until Serbia mounted its massive campaign of forced displacement during the 1999 conflict, the organized international community was united in its stand in favour of a restoration of autonomy and against the possibility of independence for Kosovo.

In addition to the brutality of its action against ethnic Albanians—set against the background of its campaign of possible genocide in Bosnia and Herzegovina—Belgrade's own inflexibility in the various international attempts of addressing the crisis rendered independence internationally acceptable, as least to the fifty-odd governments which have recognized Kosovan independence thus far. While Belgrade's position was fundamentally aligned with that of the international system as such, it failed to settle when a deal was on offer within that framework.

If Belgrade had offered very wide ranging self-governance to Kosovo while retaining only a nominal attachment to the territory at the beginning of the Vienna talks (the 'Taiwan solution'), Prishtina would have been very hard pressed to explain why full independence was still necessary. Such a moderate settlement might have been imposed upon Kosovo, reversing the dynamics of the negotiating process. However, in view of its internal politics, Belgrade appeared unable to exploit the fact that its interests were heavily privileged by the rules of the international system over those of Kosovo. Its actions were consistently one step out of synch with actual developments.

While the territorial integrity of Kosovo will remain under threat, the independence of the territory is unlikely to be reversed. The governments that have recognized Kosovo have advanced various, more or less persuasive, reasons to explain why this result does not set a precedent for other cases. In particular, it is asserted that the period of over eight years of international administration renders the case unique. Furthermore, the dissolution of the former Yugoslavia, and the fact that Serbia was the only surviving entity of that edifice, had rendered it impossible to return Kosovo to the autonomy status which it had enjoyed previously under the roof of the federation. In addition, it was asserted that Resolution 1244 (1999) had provided the option of a settlement in accordance with the wishes of the population of Kosovo. In the special circumstances that followed from the 1999 conflict, a return to autonomy would have been unrealistic.

All of these arguments were put forward in order to explain why Kosovo was a special and unique case that could not ever be a precedent for the future. However, these attempted explanations might nevertheless contribute ever so gently to the building of a new branch of the right to self-determination, rather than detracting from it. Kosovo does appear to be the first case of 'remedial self-determination'. In such a case, where a constitutionally relevant, defined segment of the state population has been persistently repressed, excluded from governance of its own area of compact habitation and from the central state, and exposed to a systematic and widespread campaign of its permanent displacement, the doctrine of territorial unity may lose its persuasive force. Instead, the will of the people, unambiguously expressed, may increasingly guide international action in dramatic and, admittedly, exceptional circumstances of this kind. Unfortunately, the abuse of this doctrine by Russia, acting in rather different circumstances, in relation to South Ossetia and Abkhazia, may have undermined this potential development.

14

The Drafting of the Kosovo Constitution and Special Provisions for Minorities in Kosovo

I. Background to the Constitutional Drafting

The prolonged struggle over the acceptance of the Ahtisaari plan at the UN Security Council had an important effect on the constitutional drafting process in Kosovo. The Ahtisaari Comprehensive Proposal had been issued, in its finalized form, on 26 March 2006.[1] The plan foresaw that a constitutional commission would be formed, with a view to generating a constitution within the 120-day interim period. This aim was in itself rather ambitious, given that the period was also supposed to accommodate a phase of public consultation on the document and the process of parliamentary approval. The tight time-scale added further to the pressure to commence at least preparations for constitution-making.

Of course, the local political parties had been anticipating this moment for many years. Even before the initial Kosovo Declaration of Independence of 1991, Kosovo had adopted its own constitution ranging over 140 articles.[2] Constitutional drafting attempts by Kosovar experts were again triggered by the abortive 1999 Rambouillet conference.[3] The PDK party which emerged from a segment of the KLA, sought to take over control of Kosovo immediately after the conclusion of hostilities in June 1999. It, too, came prepared with its own constitutional design, as did other parties over the period that followed. In fact, in the wake of the adoption of Security Council Resolution 1244 (1999) of June 1999, most of the major political parties had ready-made constitutions for an independent Kosovo waiting in their desk drawers.

These drafts were of differing quality, and were informed by the particular interests of the sponsor in question. For instance, the LDK strongly favoured

[1] Letter dated 26 March 2007 from the Secretary-General addressed to the President of the Security Council, UN Doc. S/2007/168/Add.1.
[2] Constitution of the Republic of Kosova, 7 September 1990, in Weller, *Crisis in Kosovo*, 65; Declaration of Independence, 22 September 1991, *ibid.*, 72.
[3] See Marc Weller, 'The Rambouillet Conference on Kosovo', *International Affairs*, 75(2) (1999), 211–52.

a presidential system with a directly elected president. Given the extraordinary adherence of the Kosovar population to their traditional voting preferences, President Ibrahim Rugova would be virtually guaranteed electoral victory. Correspondingly, other parties foresaw a president with far lesser powers and stature, merely to be appointed by the parliament.

In addition to the drafts generated within the framework of the political parties, there were also independent ventures supported by diaspora organizations. Finally, there was an outer wall of would-be constitution-makers in the form of international NGOs, which were keen to have an impact in Kosovo and eager to attach to themselves the label of constitutional advisers. The field of eager contenders in relation to any constitution-making venture was therefore quite dense, long before the question of a definite Kosovo Constitution ever arose.

Within international circles, discussions about a possible Kosovo Constitution began early in 2000, less than a year after the assumption of absolute power in the territory by the United Nations Mission in Kosovo (UNMIK). Bernard Kouchner, the energetic SRSG heading the administration, called a small secretive workshop to be held in the city of Prizren. That workshop was meant to settle the question of whether or not the Rambouillet document would still be of relevance when it came to constitutional drafting and propose a route towards establishing a constitution. The meeting had become necessary in view of international dispute on this issue. The US representatives, who had taken a lead role in the Hill process and at Rambouillet, seemed reluctant to abandon the political settlement that had so nearly been achieved there, and in which they had invested so much energy. Of course, this position overlooked the ultimate failure of those negotiations. The Rambouillet process had not really been about finding the best possible constitutional formula for a multi-ethnic, post-conflict society such as Kosovo. It had been about the future status of the territory, the question of war and peace, and the issue of the continuation or abandonment of a policy of repression in the territory. The decisions made by the parties and the mediators in the chateau were informed by the needs and pressures of the dramatic situation that had arisen as a result of the outbreak of fighting in Kosovo, the suffering of the civilian population and the prospect of NATO intervention. Rambouillet was not constitution-making. It was an attempt at maintaining or restoring peace.

In view of this background, the Rambouillet document foresaw arrangements for the governance of Kosovo that could hardly have worked in practice. The blocking powers and special rights of the Serb community were so extensive as to make the polity potentially ungovernable. The agreement was framed in such a way as to encourage parallel structures of governance, at least for the Serb community. Moreover, ethnic Serbs would continue to be governed in part through institutions in Serbia which would also have retained certain powers in relation to Kosovo as a whole.

Kosovo was aware of the practical difficulties involved in the Rambouillet at the time, but felt compelled to take account of the broader political picture and to accept its provisions. However, with the exclusion of any Serbian public authority in relation to Kosovo, as stipulated in Resolution 1244 (1999), such provisions were no longer appropriate. The attempt by Serbia to remove the larger part of the ethnic Albanian population from Kosovo during the conflict had undermined the legitimacy of its demands for a continued role for Belgrade while the territory was under international administration.

In addition to the dispute about the content of a future constitution—whether rooted in the Rambouillet accords or not—there was also uncertainty as to whether or not a constitutional document was necessary at all. It was felt by some hesitant members, even within the Quint (the Contact Group minus Russia), that anything resembling a constitution would not be in accordance with the concept of an interim period. Of course, Russia held that view with even greater conviction. A constitution might go too far in opening up the possibility of independent statehood.

After much soul-searching, it was decided to opt for a compromise. UNMIK had a mandate that permitted it to establish institutions of self-governance and to transfer authority to them. Institution-building did require a constitutional framework. However, such a framework should not prejudice final status. Thus, it was agreed that a Constitutional Framework for Provisional Self-government in Kosovo would be established. This was, however, only a framework, and it was focused expressly on the interim period of provisional self-government.[4]

Work on the framework proceeded with extraordinary rapidity under the new SRSG, Hans Haekkerup—an enigmatic Dane given to long silences in meetings he was meant to be chairing. However, the Kosovars, poised at the ready to whip out their constitutional drafts, were greatly disappointed by the constitutional process concerning 'their' country. While there was space for representation of the main political parties at the drafting table (along with minority representatives), they did not wield much influence. The Constitutional Framework that materialized was very much the baby of UNMIK legal office and advisers from other international organizations, who had been brought in especially for the task. It was perhaps a technically better document for it, and was completed with amazing expedition, but there was certainly no sense of local authorship. Indeed, the Kosovar members of the drafting body came under severe attack from their party bosses when the end result, enshrined in UNMIK Regulation 2001/9, of 15 May 2001, was made public.

The Constitutional Framework was a measured document. It certainly departed from Rambouillet.[5] The ethnic communities still enjoyed disproportionate

[4] See Marc Weller, 'Substantive Self-administration for Kosovo/a: From Rambouillet to the Adoption of a Constitutional Framework Document', in Kinga Gal (ed), *Minority Governance in Europe* (Budapest: ECMI/LGI, 2002) 293–309.

[5] See Marc Weller, 'Interim Governance for Kosovo: The Rambouillet Agreement and the Constitutional Framework Developed under UN Administration', in Marc Weller and Barbara

representation in bodies such as the Kosovo Assembly (the word 'parliament' was avoided, as some thought it might conjure up the image of a sovereign state) and in the ministries. They could launch complaints if they believed their vital interests to be under threat, but they could not block the functioning of the polity, as had occurred in Bosnia under Dayton. Moreover, the document made it clear that local self-governance, including of mainly ethnic Serb-inhabited municipalities, was not a licence for a quasi-merger with Serbia proper. While this was never actually implemented, the document at least formally opposed the phenomenon of 'parallel administration' of areas under ethnic Serb control, funded and directed to some extent by Belgrade.

The Framework provided for the gradual transfer of powers to Kosovo authorities, parallel to the process of institution-building. A significant amount of authority was in fact transferred, although the SRSG retained overall supremacy and so-called 'reserved powers' relating to justice, policing and other sensitive issues. The retention of some powers was used by Kosovar politicians as a handy excuse when it came to their own failings in terms of effective administration. Such failings were invariably blamed on the fact that ultimate control was, after all, retained by UNMIK, and that UNMIK had failed to transfer to the Kosovars the full powers they required to act effectively.

More powers, including those previously reserved, were transferred after the Eide Report of 2005, which signalled the possible beginning of the final status phase. By that time, the Kosovar authorities were meant to have engaged with some vigour in the implementation of the 'standards before status' policy, a set of benchmarks that were supposed to have been addressed by Kosovo prior to discussion of final status. However, in view of the confused nature of this highly complex policy, only limited progress had been made. UNMIK was blamed once again, given its refusal to hand over the 'hard' powers of particular relevance to some standards-related issues, notably community policy.

By 2006, the Ahtisaari process had begun. The Kosovars had assumed that this process, like Rambouillet, would be heavily focused on drafting a constitutional settlement, in addition to addressing status. By that time, and in contrast to Rambouillet, there were a number of competent local legal experts ready and available to lead the process from the Kosovo side. Notable amongst these were Professor Arsim Bajrami, a highly respected constitutionalist at Prishtina University, and Hajredin Kuci, Vice-President of the Democratic Party of Kosovo (PDK) led by Hashim Thaci, the first Prime Minister at the time of eventual independence. This, it seemed, would be the moment when the pre-existing constitutional drafts, presented by the parties in question, could finally be deployed. In fact, the Kosovars were planning to generate their own constitutional process, including a constitutional convention followed by broad discussion of an

Metzger (eds), *Settling Self-determination Disputes: Complex Power-sharing in Theory and in Practice* (Dordrecht: Martinus Nijhoff, 2008), 243–65.

eventual draft in the Kosovo Assembly. However, the Ahtisaari process, with its various twists and turns, was heading in a different direction.

II. The Ahtisaari Comprehensive Proposal and Its Impact on the Constitution

The Special Envoy of the UN Secretary-General in charge of the status process had agreed with the Serbian government that the initial status negotiations would focus exclusively on technical issues.[6] Serbia had nominated decentralization and the protection of historic monuments as topics for negotiation. Accordingly, the majority of the negotiating sessions in Vienna were given over to these issues of principal concern to the Serbian side.

As time progressed, the Kosovo delegation began to ask impatiently: when will we get to our constitution? The mediators answered with their own question: do you really want Serbia to lead the process of drafting your constitution? Accordingly, in contrast to Rambouillet, the basic constitutional arrangements for Kosovo that were not of special concern to Serbia were not actually broached in the negotiations. Instead of proposing a full constitutional text in the mould of Dayton, the Ahtisaari team intimated that, at the end of the negotiation process, they would only offer key elements that would need to be reflected in a future constitution for Kosovo. They did, at times, cast around for input from Kosovo into wider, more general issues that would be addressed in an eventual constitution. However, the final Ahtisaari package limited itself to those provisions in which Serbia, or the organized international community, had a legitimate interest.

As was noted above, the Ahtisaari Comprehensive Proposal for the Kosovo Status Settlement consisted of a set of general principles and twelve annexes. The first four annexes, covering constitutional provisions, human and community (minority) rights, decentralization, and the justice system were of particular relevance for the subsequent process of constitution-making. The General Principles and the constitutional annexes ensured that Kosovo would need to be a secular, democratic and multi-ethnic state based on the equality of all citizens. The General Principles confirmed that Kosovo could conclude international treaties and seek membership of international organizations. The draft added that 'Kosovo shall have no territorial claims against, and shall seek no union with, any State or part of any State'.[7]

Annex I also incorporated into Kosovo law the obligations of key international human rights instruments 'which shall be directly applicable in Kosovo'.[8] These instruments included the European Convention for the Protection of Human Rights and Fundamental Freedoms and its Protocol; the International Covenant on Civil and Political Rights; the Convention on the Elimination of All Forms

---

[6] See above, p. 203.   [7] General Principles, Art. 1.8.   [8] Annex I, Art. 2.3.

of Racial Discrimination; the Convention on the Elimination of all Forms of Discrimination against Women; the Convention on the Rights of the Child; and the Convention against Torture and Other Cruel, Inhumane or Degrading Treatment or Punishment.

Of course, there is debate as to whether these conventions, or some of the more general provisions they contain, can be applied directly within domestic law. Under the doctrine of 'self-executing' treaties, direct application is ordinarily reserved only for quite specific provisions capable of deciding concrete issues, rather than more programmatic entitlements. In fact, the Ahtisaari document required that provisions of the Universal Declaration of Human Rights and the Council of Europe Framework Convention for the Protection of National Minorities also be directly applicable. The former is a non-binding UN General Assembly resolution of a prescriptive nature. The latter was deliberately drafted as a 'framework' convention, as it was assumed that its provisions would not be directly enforceable. This problem, along with the fact that Kosovo would now have to apply the vast jurisprudence underpinning the European Convention on Human Rights as part of its domestic law, undoubtedly posed a significant challenge for the future.

The Ahtisaari document also addressed the issue of guaranteed representation of communities in the institutions of the state in Kosovo. There was also provision for an internationalized constitutional court. In addition, detailed arrangements were proposed for a continued international civil and military presence. The head of the civil presence, the International Civilian Representative (ICR), would retain corrective powers in relation to certain sensitive functions.

As already noted, Article 10 of the General Principles addressed the issue of constitution-making. It provided that, immediately upon entry into force of the settlement, a Constitutional Commission would be appointed by the Kosovo President in consultation with the Presidency of the Kosovo Assembly and the International Civilian Representative. Within 120 days, the Kosovo Assembly would approve the constitution emanating from this Commission, after certification by the ICR that it was compliant with all aspects of the Ahtisaari package. Should it not be possible to approve a new constitution within this period, UNMIK would amend the Constitutional Framework for Provisional Self-government in accordance with the settlement. That instrument would remain in force until a new settlement-compliant constitution could be adopted.

III. The Constitutional Drafting Process

With the presentation of the definitive version of the Ahtisaari proposal on 26 March 2007, it was assumed that the constitutional drafting process would finally get under way. In fact, the US Office in Prishtina, the Organization for Security and Cooperation in Europe (OSCE) and others had already found it necessary to organize a series of round tables and other events in order to keep Kosovo's own experts engaged. There was a fear that, without such engagement, they would simply proceed on their own with the constitutional process for which they had been planning. This, it was argued, might interfere with the higher politics being played out in New York and elsewhere.

The ethnic Albanian parties had disputed how the process would be organized, but they had all assumed that they would be in charge of it. Different formats were proposed, included the drafting of the constitution by a small, all-party group of experts, including representatives of the communities. Another proposal was that there should be a constitutional group of around forty, drawn from the Kosovo Assembly and from leading constitutional experts. In this way, there would have been a greater element of democratic accountability in the process, due to a stronger link with the Assembly. A third proposal foresaw an even larger constitutional convention, based in large part on the Kosovo Assembly.

The Ahtisaari draft resolved this issue. It foresaw a small group of twenty-one experts that combined professional expertise with representatives of Kosovo society. Fifteen members would be appointed by the Kosovo President, three would be appointed by the Assembly members holding seats reserved for the Kosovo Serb community, and another three members were to be appointed by the Assembly members holding seats reserved for other communities not in the majority in Kosovo. Moreover, legal advisers from international organizations present in Kosovo would also participate. In essence, therefore, the Ahtisaari team had clearly adopted the route of a small expert committee. It was thought that this option would make it more likely that a constitutional draft of good quality would emerge within a relatively short period of time.

The Ahtisaari document therefore resolved a power struggle that had emerged between the Kosovo Assembly, which demanded a leadership role in drafting the Kosovo Constitution, and the Unity Team, which consisted of the Kosovo President and Prime Minister, the President of the Assembly and the leaders of the two principal opposition parties, Hashim Thaci of the PDK and Veton Surroi of the Ora Party. As noted previously, the Unity Team was supported by a so-called Political-Strategic Group, composed of the second tier of the leadership of the main political parties and a few experts. Under the Ahtisaari formula, the Political Strategic Group became the nucleus of the Group of twenty-one constitutional drafters. The Assembly was mainly kept out of the process. As the Political–Strategic Group included the chief lieutenants of the main political parties represented in the Assembly, this was deemed acceptable, although it remained somewhat controversial.

The prolonged period of uncertainty that ensued regarding the fate of the Ahtisaari proposal also posed a dilemma. Kosovo was keen to progress on the constitution. It wanted to be able to generate a high quality document within the limited time of 120 days available according to the Ahtisaari document. Moreover, moving towards the adoption of a constitution would have increased pressure on the organized international community to move, finally, on status. Having a constitution ready would have enabled Kosovo to declare independence at any time.

It was precisely this scenario that prompted international representatives in Kosovo to inhibit the initiation of drafting by the Kosovars. Moreover, while Kosovo maintained that it would not countenance any changes to the final version of the Ahtisaari package, there was the possibility that further negotiations might bring about a different result. Hence, nothing should be done to prejudice such an outcome. The constitutional process would need to be put on ice.

It proved possible to rein in pressure for movement on this issue for some weeks. But by January 2007, a preliminary constitutional working group, jointly headed by Mr Thorbjorn Sohlstrom of the EU advance mission and Hajredin Kuci representing the Kosovo side, was established. That group would be composed in a similar way to the Constitutional Group provided for in the Ahtisaari draft. It would begin work, but only on the organization of the constitutional process.

By the early summer, however, preliminary arrangements no longer sufficed to occupy the working group. By then, the US Office in Prishtina had taken a very firm hold on the constitutional process, and adopted an interim strategy. It agreed to the establishment of a 'Pre-Constitutional Working Group' (PCG) that would continue to receive capacity building and conduct initial work on 'politically undisputable parts' of a constitution. This meant that the PCG might commence drafting work on issues that were not affected by the Ahtisaari document, albeit on the understanding that its work would not bind the actual Constitutional Group once it became operational. In reality, of course, it was clear that the work of the PCG would be decisive. While the PCG was operating without strong time pressure due to the uncertain fate of the Ahtisaari document, once the Ahtisaari package was finally accepted (if it ever was), the Constitutional Commission would have just thirty days to draft a constitution. Clearly, that would have been impossible without relying heavily on a pre-existing draft.

The US office, acting through a USAID project, also provided very detailed rules of procedure for the constitutional process. Part of this code was a mechanism for restricting the access of external, international experts to the constitutional process. The Kosovars were being bombarded by offers of support from institutions or individuals keen to provide expertise. Previous experience indicated that external experts who were not well versed in the larger political script might greatly complicate the process and their appointment was thus discouraged. Instead, USAID provided the group with its own experts. Although these had enjoyed distinguished careers in the US, they had little or no experience in the region and could not offer specific advice or guidance. In the end, only one international expert chosen by Kosovo, other than the representatives of international organizations that were part of the process, was admitted.

In its initial sessions, the PCG, headed by Hajredin Kuci, addressed issues of procedure and the work plan that had been proposed. While the US office asserted very strong guidance over this process, the Kosovars nevertheless met separately, without the presence of international representatives, in order to plan what they continued to regard as their constitutional process.

The work on the constitutional draft was divided into different working groups. These were:

1. Preamble
2. Founding Principles, Rule of Law and Transitional Provisions
3. Kosovo Institutions
4. Fundamental Rights and Freedoms
5. Security and Order
6. Community Rights
7. Judicial Power, Prosecution and Constitutional Court
8. Economic Relations
9. Local Self-Government
10. Independent Agencies and Ombudsperson

Each of the groups was assigned one or more expert representatives from the international organizations, in particular the OSCE. However, some of the groups managed to dodge international observation and offered their own, often rather wild, drafts. The low quality of some of these sections posed a significant problem. Once they had been put forward by the respective working group, it would be very difficult to revise them fundamentally without a loss of face for the original drafters. In order to gain control over the rather disparate process, it was agreed that a small 'comité de rédaction' should be established. While, nominally, such a committee would only have the function of 'harmonizing' the draft sections, in reality very fundamental revisions were necessary. The stalwart Professor Bajrami proved a valuable asset to this process. It was largely due to him, and the Chair of the Committee, Professor Hajredin Kuci, that the overall draft which ultimately emerged was of good quality and was based on input from local actors.

Throughout, this process was conducted in a rather ambiguous legal environment. It was not clear to the participants in the constitutional drafting process whether or not the 120-day transitional period foreseen by the Ahtisaari package was actually running or not. In fact, representatives of the organized international community did not know either. In particular, the decision over the summer to launch a fresh set of negotiations, also for a period of exactly 120 days until 10 December 2007, seemed to suggest that the clock had started to tick. However, as the new set of negotiations was not necessarily to be centred on the Ahtisaari document, that was apparently not the case.

By the end of 2007, it finally became clear that there would be no formal Security Council endorsement of the Ahtisaari plan. On 22 December, with the Declaration of Independence looming, there existed a consolidated draft of high quality. However, access to that draft was severely restricted by order of the US Office in Prishtina. Even senior members of international organizations present in Kosovo who had not been directly involved in the drafting support team were denied access, resulting in much backstabbing by those so deprived.

To prepare for public consultations on the constitution, members of the Working Group travelled to various regions of Kosovo, to explain the general principles of the work done so far. However, the actual text was only made public on 19 February 2008, immediately after the declaration of independence, when the PCG was transformed into the formal Constitutional Commission. At this point, a significant, but highly compressed, effort was made to consult, or at least inform, the public as to its content. This process lasted from 19 February to 4 March. The US Office had developed a high-tech Internet-based system of eliciting comments and suggestions from the public. Perhaps more effectively, the leading members of the group of twenty-one went on almost daily tours of the towns and villages throughout Kosovo in an attempt to introduce the constitutional draft and elicit comments. After this period of consultation, there was then a further opportunity for the Commission to consider revisions. While the principal elements of the document remained unchanged, some very useful changes were made as a result of the consultation, proving its worth despite the limited time available. For instance, the retrenchment of human rights in circumstances of public emergency was greatly improved in the final version.

The consultation process meant that there was no constitution in place by the time of the Declaration of Independence. The specific commitments of the Ahtisaari proposal were supposed to have been permanently anchored in both a Chapter VII Security Council resolution and in a constitution. Neither had been adopted. Instead, the organized international community had to content itself with a formal unilateral declaration in which Kosovo pledged its commitment to the Ahtisaari document and promised to reflect this commitment in its future constitution. The absence of an agreed constitution at that time significantly reduced the chances of Kosovo obtaining widespread recognition when it declared independence on 17 February.

By 2 April, the final version of the Constitution of the Republic of Kosovo was certified by the ICR and the Kosovo government for submission to the Kosovo Assembly, which adopted the text without modification on 9 April 2008. After a further preparatory period, the Constitution took effect on 15 June.

IV. Basic Constitutional Structures

The Constitution of Kosovo consists of 162 articles organized into fourteen chapters. The thirteenth and fourteenth chapters concern final and transitional provisions. The Kosovars were very keen to move elements of the Ahtisaari package that imposed temporary measures on Kosovo into that section, so as to ensure that the rest of the document had the appearance of a coherent and definitive constitution.

The Constitution of the Republic of Kosovo is fully compliant with the Ahtisaari document. In order to ensure this, it simply restated verbatim the key commitments of the Comprehensive Proposal that were mandatory. There was a debate within the Constitutional Commission as to whether it would be possible to rephrase some of those provisions. However, the international agencies involved wisely deemed it prudent to insist on a literal adoption of Ahtisaari language in certain key areas. These included, in particular, the provisions on communities. While this precluded the adoption of additional, more far-reaching provisions by the Kosovar drafters, it also reduced the risk of an accidental dilution of the Ahtisaari commitments.

The Preamble of the Constitution is very short. Its contents had triggered a long drawn-out battle with international community representatives. Kosovars were keen to reflect their struggle for statehood, including their sacrifices in the Preamble. However, this was deemed unacceptable, as such references might have suggested that Kosovo considered itself the home of a titular, ethnic Albanian nation to the exclusion of other communities.

The basic provisions of the Constitution confirm that Kosovo is a democratic state based on the equality of its citizens and the rule of law. The sovereignty of the state stems from its people. The state is indivisible and has no territorial claims against, nor shall seek union with, any state or part of any state, as required by the Ahtisaari document.

The Constitution, in Article 16, is identified as the highest legal act of the Republic. However, the Article also requires that Kosovo shall respect international law. Under Article 19, international law applies directly, except where not self-executing.

Chapter 13 of the Constitution contains the Final Provisions. Article 143 declares that, notwithstanding any provision of the Constitution:

1. All authorities in the Republic of Kosovo shall abide by all of the Republic of Kosovo's obligations under the Comprehensive Proposal for the Kosovo Status Settlement dated 26 March 2007. They shall take all necessary action for their implementation.
2. The provisions of the Comprehensive Proposal for the Kosovo Status Settlement dated 26 March 2007 shall take precedence over all other legal provisions in Kosovo.
3. The Constitution, laws and other legal acts of the Republic of Kosovo shall be interpreted in compliance with the Comprehensive Proposal for the Kosovo Status Settlement dated 26 March 2007. If there are inconsistencies between the provisions of this Constitution, laws or other legal acts of the Republic of Kosovo and the provisions of the said Settlement, the latter shall prevail.

Accordingly, contrary to Article 16 of the Constitution, the Ahtisaari document is in fact the highest legal authority in Kosovo. While the implementation powers provided for in the Comprehensive Proposal and in the Constitution are temporary, this requirement appears to be permanent. This is all the more noteworthy, given that the Ahtisaari document was a 'proposal', which nevertheless resulted in 'obligations' for Kosovo. Presumably, the source of obligation is the self-limitation of sovereignty offered by Kosovo in its Declaration of Independence.

Of course, the question of the permanence of these obligations is also addressed through provisions for possible constitutional amendments. According to Article 144, constitutional amendments can be made with the approval of two-thirds of all of the deputies of the Assembly, including two-thirds of all deputies of the Assembly holding reserved or guaranteed seats for representatives of communities that are not in the majority in Kosovo. However, even amendments that would pass this threshold must not 'diminish any of the rights and freedoms set forth in Chapter 2' of the Constitution. These are the general human rights and fundamental freedoms, not the additional community rights of Chapter 3. This requirement is to be enforced by the Constitutional Court, which must offer an assessment on this point prior to adoption of the amendment.

This opens up the possibility that Kosovo might amend Article 143 at some future date, thereby undercutting the primacy of the Ahtisaari package. However, the communities in Kosovo would be able to exercise a veto over such a decision. Moreover, while the ICR still exercises the powers assigned to him or her, the ICR can exercise 'final authority' in relation to the civilian aspects of the Comprehensive Proposal. Accordingly, during the period of supervised independence, a challenge to the Ahtisaari commitments could be overruled.

V. Special Arrangements for the Protection of Communities

It was clear to Kosovo that the protection of minorities (or 'communities', as they are consistently referred to in all the relevant documents) would be of key importance to international actors when considering whether or not to permit or recognize independence. This preoccupation with minority issues was well warranted, given the assault on ethnic Serbs at the conclusion of the 1999 armed conflict and during the March 2004 riots, and in view of the longer-term history of the region. However, ethnic Albanian politicians were tiring a little of the unrelenting international refrains on this issue. They feared that communities might receive so many privileges and advantages vis-à-vis the majority population, that, once again, the ethnic Albanians would be disenfranchised in their own country. Hence, while all majority politicians had learnt to repeat enthusiastically their commitment to minority protection in international fora, one could also discern a certain reluctance to engage on that issue in a more specific way.

Despite these hesitations, Kosovo was very proactive on the issue of communities. As such, it sought to remove the biggest stick with which it might be beaten in the upcoming status discussions. Kosovo needed no persuading that it should offer very generous provisions in this field—in fact, it was determined to lead the debate on this issue.

Kosovo's position on community rights was developed over a significant period of time, going as far back as 2005. First, an initial workshop was held to provide communities with an opportunity to articulate their interests. This proved challenging, as many of the community representatives could point to specific problems they were experiencing, but were unable to convert these into legislative proposals. However, through this process, the communities began to formulate initial demands and to discover a commonality of interests. The ethnic Serb parties, which at the time were boycotting the major Kosovo state institutions, also participated in this process. They were somewhat hesitant, however, as they considered themselves a titular nation instead of a community, and were expecting additional powers and protection in any final status settlement.

In a further round of discussions, the position of the communities was refined and introduced to the representatives of the majority parties. Reception of the proposals was generally positive. The work gained additional momentum when the Unity Team, the all-party leadership group for the status negotiations, came under pressure from the Contact Group and other actors. These demanded that Kosovo arrange for the formal inclusion of communities in the negotiating process. In response, the Community Consultative Council was established under the leadership of Unity Team member Veton Surroi, the brilliant leader of the Ora party, and with the support of the European Centre for Minority Issues.

The Council was made up of representatives of all communities sitting in the Kosovo Assembly. It took on a principal role in formulating the proposals on community issues that were to be submitted at the Vienna negotiations. Representatives of the communities assembled at a conference at Durres at the end of March 2006, furnishing detailed input into a questionnaire on community issues that had been put forward by the mediators. On the basis of this work, representatives of the Council then met together in Cambridge with experts from the Kosovo main political parties and drafted an initial version of a Kosovo platform on community issues. At a further event, held in Thessaloniki, this platform was finalized in discussions between communities and a larger group of ethnic Albanian officials and members of parliament. In the end, there emerged a roughly seventy-page Framework Document detailing Kosovo's position and intentions in relation to minority issues. This document had not only been generated with the strong involvement on the part of the Kosovo communities but, in its final drafting stages, Kosovo invited legal experts from the OSCE, the Council of Europe and other international bodies to review and discuss the document. In that way, it was assured that the Framework would be beyond reproach when it was reviewed in Vienna.

In fact, if there was criticism, it was that the Framework was too ambitious. In terms of rights, it went significantly beyond the Council of Europe Framework Convention for the Protection of National Minorities (FCNM). Furthermore, its institutional part provided for a rather complex array of implementation mechanisms that may not have been entirely realistic for a small entity like Kosovo. The Ahtisaari Comprehensive Proposal drew significantly on the Kosovo Framework Document, but then offered more modest provisions based closely on those of the FCNM.

The initial version of the Comprehensive Proposal was evaluated by the communities in a further workshop held in Antalya in February 2007, with a view to offering feedback for the final round of discussions on the Ahtisaari draft proposal held later that month.

Once the proposal was published in its final form on 26 March, the parties decided to build on the work with the communities and other actors that had led to the adoption of the larger framework document. On this basis, at a further major meeting held in Durres in May, a draft was generated for a Law on the Promotion and Protection of the Rights of Communities and Persons Belonging to Communities in Kosovo. This draft also profited from the input of the Serb-led Ministry of Communities and Return [sic], which eventually became its sponsor within the Kosovo government.

The draft was subject to intensive review by the International Civilian Office in Kosovo and was further refined through the input of all relevant international human rights agencies early in 2008. The Law was adopted by the Assembly immediately after independence, as part of the accelerated package of status-relevant legislation, to become operational upon the coming into effect of the Constitution on 15 June.

The minority protection system that ultimately emerged is thus fairly complex. First, there is the Ahtisaari document. It contains certain provisions on communities, non-discrimination and full equality in its General Principles, and a detailed listing of commitments in Annex 2. The next layer of protection consists of international conventions rendered directly applicable in Kosovo by virtue of the Ahtisaari document and the Constitution. This includes the FCNM. Then there is the Constitution itself. In addition to a wide catalogue of human rights and fundamental freedoms, it contains a chapter on community rights. While Kosovo was considering offering enhanced rights in that chapter, going beyond those envisaged by Annex 2 of the Ahtisaari document, this proposal was ultimately not pursued. As mentioned earlier, it was deemed preferable to restate exactly the wording of the Ahtisaari document in the Constitution, as this lessened the risk that the Constitution might fail to be certified by the ICR as fully Ahtisaari-compliant following the introduction of additions or changes, no matter how well-intentioned.

The next layer of protection is offered by the omnibus Law on Communities, noted above. Whilst that law expands on the constitutional provisions, very specific issues, such as language use, education provisions, decentralization and so on, are regulated in even greater detail in the specific legislative acts which cover them, such as the law on languages, education, etc. The Law on Communities and these laws are subject to the vital interest clause of the Constitution. They can only be amended or repealed with the support of the majority of the community representatives in the Assembly.

The substance of community rights on offer is broad. There is comprehensive protection against discrimination in full accordance with the relatively advanced EU legal standards in this field. Moreover, there is a proactive obligation on the part of the state to ensure full and effective equality in practice. The legislation clarifies that positive action towards this end cannot be considered discriminatory treatment in relation to the majority community.

There are broad rights of political participation. First, there is guaranteed representation for communities in the 120-member Kosovo Assembly. Ten seats are reserved for ethnic Serb representatives, and a further ten are reserved for other communities. In the first two electoral cycles, as provided in the Ahtisaari document, any seats won by parties representing communities will be added to the guaranteed seats. After two electoral cycles, only those seats won in excess of the number of the guaranteed seats will be added.

As already noted, a simple majority of deputies present claiming to represent communities in the Assembly is required in order to allow the passage of laws of vital interest to communities. This means that no single community has a blocking vote by itself, although the ethnic Serb group, with at least ten seats, would only need to find one ally among the other communities. There is a blocking vote for the Serb community alone, however, for constitutional amendments, which requires a two-thirds majority among the members representing communities.

There is provision for two deputy presidents of the Assembly, one appointed from the Serb community and one from another community. There is also provision for a Committee on Rights and Interests of Communities. That Committee is composed of one-third of members representing the ethnic Serb group, one-third representing other communities and one-third representing the majority community. At the request of any member of the Presidency of the Assembly, any proposed law can be submitted to the Committee. The Committee decides by simple majority vote whether it wishes to make a recommendation on the law within two weeks. However, there is no blocking power associated with such a recommendation and the conciliation procedure offered in the Framework Constitution was dropped.

Hence, there is a staggered mechanism relating to the interests of communities affected by legislation. Through the Committee on Rights of Interests, recommendations can be made on any legislation. In relation to particular, exclusively enumerated legislation of vital interest to communities, a simple majority of the members of the Assembly representing communities enjoys a blocking power. A third of the members representing communities can inhibit the adoption of constitutional changes.

There is also provision for a Community Consultative Council (CCC) associated with the Office of the President. The aim of this Council is to assist communities in gaining an additional voice in relation to legislative projects and many other issues of common concern. It is to be composed principally of representatives of community associations, although members of the Assembly representing communities may also be elected.

In the municipalities, which are to enjoy a 'high degree of local self-governance', communities that constitute a local minority also enjoy special rights of political participation through the institution of deputy chairs of local assemblies and deputy mayors.

There is also guaranteed representation of communities in the government. At least one minister is to be from the Kosovo Serb community, another from a further community. In addition, at least two Serb deputy ministers and two deputy ministers representing other communities are to be appointed. The composition of the civil service is to represent the ethnic diversity of the people in Kosovo, with an independent oversight board in charge of ensuring appropriate representation. That board must also reflect diversity.

Furthermore, there is guaranteed representation in the justice system. The Constitutional Court is composed of nine judges. At least two of these must represent communities not in the majority. During the phase of supervised independence, a further three judges are internationals, appointed by the President of the European Court of Human Rights. Hence, for that possibly extensive period, the ethnic Albanians are in a minority on the Constitutional Court.

At least three judges in the Supreme Court are to be from communities not in the majority in Kosovo, and at least two judges from communities will be represented on other appeals courts. The Kosovo Judicial Council, also appointed with due regard to ethnic balance, is to ensure that there is appropriate community representation throughout the entire justice system.

With respect to more specific minority rights, the Constitution and the Law on the Promotion and Protection of the Rights of Communities and Persons Belonging to Communities in Kosovo reflect and expand upon the catalogue offered by the Council of Europe Framework Convention. As the title of the latter makes clear, community rights can be enjoyed both by individual members of the communities and by the communities as a collective body.

The designation of communities entitled to the additional rights offered to them proved controversial throughout. On the one hand, it was clear that any future constitution would declare that Kosovo would be a multi-ethnic state of all its citizens. This would, however, prevent the specific recognition of ethnic Albanians as a titular nation, or of the other groups as recognized nationalities or communities. Given the lasting impact of communist ideology, this proved something of a problem. In the end, a compromise was found.

The Constitution defines communities as inhabitants (not citizens) belonging to the same national or ethnic, linguistic or religious group traditionally present on the territory of the Republic of Kosovo. This would equally include the ethnic Albanian community. The Law on Communities adds to this the requirement that these communities 'are not in the majority' in order to benefit from its application. That would restrict the scope of application of the more specific community rights granted precisely because a group is in a non-dominant, minority position. Still, the Law adds that members of the community in the majority in the Republic of Kosovo as a whole, who are not in the majority in a given municipality, shall also be entitled to enjoy the rights listed in the law.

At the insistence of the communities, and against the advice of international experts, the Law on Communities, which was adopted as part of the package of status-relevant legislation foreseen in the Ahtisaari plan, features a listing of the communities in question (Serb, Turkish, Bosniak, Roma, Ashkali, Egyptian, and Gorani). During the final phases of review, it was also proposed that the Croat community be included. However, in the end it was decided to follow the precedent set in the Constitutional Framework, which had only identified the groups listed above. The Law adds to the enumeration of communities ('and other communities'), leaving open the possibility that others will also meet the definition.

The constitutional chapter on community rights and the Law on Communities add a lengthy catalogue of specific rights. These concern identity and the preservation and advancement of community culture and religion, full and effective equality, access to the media and language rights. Albanian and Serbian are both statewide official languages. The Turkish, Bosnian, and Roma languages have the status of an official language at the municipal level or will be in official use as provided by the law on languages. Special provision is made for education in community languages, including the operation of institutions of higher education in Serbian. The ambitious targets set for achieving full and effective equality are to be pursued by the government, in coordination with the CCC, through an annual comprehensive strategy placed before the Kosovo Assembly.

The Kosovo Prime Minister launched a highly visible campaign of active engagement with communities upon the Declaration of Independence. Steps were set in motion to facilitate coordination of policy in favour of communities across ministries through the appointment of a high-level (ethnic Serb) coordinator for community policy in the office of the Prime Minster. Moreover, on 16 September 2008, the Kosovo President issued a decree putting in place a very advanced mechanism for political consultation of communities, the Community Consultative Council.

While Kosovo proceeded to implement its Ahtisaari commitments as if the Comprehensive Proposal, and its independence, had been endorsed by the UN Security Council, its unresolved legal position after the Declaration of Independence posed certain issues in relation to human and community rights. In particular, the question arose whether and, if so, how, the international human rights monitoring and implementation bodies could become active. If Kosovo's independence had been universally acknowledged, Kosovo would have gained membership to the relevant international organizations and subscribed to the relevant treaties and conventions. However, as the number of recognitions remains somewhat limited during the initial period of independence (52 at the time of writing in December 2008), it was deemed unlikely that such direct participation would be rapidly possible. In this context, the remaining shell of UNMIK would most likely continue to facilitate contact with international agencies, however uncomfortable this fact would be for the Kosovo authorities. During the previous period of UN administration, UNMIK had, for instance, concluded a formal agreement with the Council of Europe, providing for monitoring of the commitments contained in the Framework Convention for the Protection of National Minorities by the relevant implementation committee. UNMIK would be treated as the reporting agency, instead of either Serbia or the Kosovo authorities. However, the Kosovo authorities had contributed to UNMIK's implementation report. Given its loss of effective control in relation to Kosovo, Serbia had generally ceased reporting to the UN human rights treaty bodies and it was proposed that the Kosovo government might now offer reports channelled through UNMIK.

VI. Conclusion

The constitutional process in Kosovo was a highly unusual one. While the Ahtisaari Comprehensive Proposal had not offered detailed provisions for a constitution à la Dayton, it nevertheless contained important elements that required verbatim incorporation into the Kosovo Constitution. Moreover, there were other, less visible requirements. It was deemed important by international actors that the overall flavour of the Constitution should be open and welcoming to all communities in Kosovo. Hence, the historical references intended for the Preamble, drawing attention to the historical struggle of ethnic Albanians for independence, or the wish of the Serb community to be acknowledged as a 'titular' nation of Kosovo, was not accommodated.

The Kosovar experts and politicians involved in the drafting process were also seeking to ensure that the document would be a 'normal' constitution. They had no objections relating to the very extensive, and permanent provisions on human and minority rights that were anchored in the Constitution. However, they were hoping to avoid rendering permanent provisions relating to the transition from a post-conflict society, including in particular power-sharing guarantees. In that endeavour, they were not particularly successful. Instead, many elements of the constitutional framework document intended for the period of UN administration were simply transferred to the permanent constitution.

In accordance with the Ahtisaari document, there was also provision for direct applicability of a wide range of obligations drawn from international human rights instruments. Some of these provisions may not in fact be suited to operating as self-executing provisions. Moreover, it is not yet clear whether the Kosovo authorities can accommodate in their practice the very wide-ranging international human rights jurisprudence that attaches to the interpretation of these obligations. This will, undoubtedly, require a very considerable effort and international support.

Where minority rights are concerned, the system that was designed is somewhat complex, drawing on numerous layers of regulation from the international to subordinate Kosovo legislation. However, the system overall has been designed as one consistent whole, and it represents the most advanced set of minority rights provisions in Europe or anywhere else. Again, it remains to be seen whether such a comprehensive set of obligations can be fully implemented through Kosovo's limited institutional structure. At least during the initial phase of independent governance, a significant effort was made towards this end. This includes the establishment of the Community Consultative Council, that will give to Kosovo minorities an additional voice in the shaping of policy addressed to them.

Implementing the very ambitious set of provisions in full will certainly strain the resources and capacity of Kosovo significantly. Moreover, there is a risk that the perception in the territory that minority communities have excessive attention paid to them may increase. Already, a certain level of disengagement with community issues can be observed. While it is likely that international involvement and support in the administration of community issues will persist for some time, it remains to be seen whether a genuine interest in fostering and facilitating diversity will take root in the indigenous governing structures of Kosovo.

The lack of membership in international human rights treaties and mechanisms is also problematic. Kosovo may avail itself of the opportunity to report to these through the means of UNMIK. However its enthusiasm for this route may be limited, given its formal position on independence. It is somewhat surprising that issues of this kind were not foreseen and addressed with the Kosovo authorities in advance by the states involved in facilitating Kosovo's eventual independence.

It is true, of course, that the entire process of drafting the Constitution and the attached legislation featured heavy international involvement. While an effort was made to engage in wide-ranging consultations with the Kosovo population on the Constitution, a certain sense of lack of ownership over the process might not be entirely misplaced. After all, the constitutional drafting was carried out by a group of only twenty-one representatives, backed up by a team of advisers from the international implementation agencies present in Kosovo, and tightly managed by the US mission in Prishtina. On the other hand, given the significant element of continuity between constitutional framework and the new Constitution, there has been little public clamour about this fact. Instead, the political system has continued to function more or less as before. Whether the somewhat imperfect process of constitution-making will threaten the stability of the constitutional order of Kosovo in the future remains to be seen.

15

Conclusion

Foreign policy is not architecture, no matter what Dr Brzinski and others like to compare it to. In architecture, you make a plan down to the last nut, the last bolt, the last stress beam, and then you build the thing. Foreign policy, in my view, is more like jazz; it's an improvisation on a theme, and you change as you go along.[1]

This sentiment was expressed by Richard Holbrooke, one of the senior US policy-makers who shaped the international response to the crisis in Kosovo. In fact, Ambassador Holbrooke voiced this view shortly after he appeared to have delivered a settlement on this last remaining conflict arising from the dissolution of the former Yugoslavia—a settlement on Kosovo brought about by an unprecedented threat of force by NATO and dramatic negotiations with Slobodan Milosevic in Belgrade. It is a sobering assessment for those who have begun to see in the international response to the Kosovo crisis a new paradigm of international relations, a blueprint for a new world order, in either a positive or a negative sense. For, if anything is striking about this episode, it is the casual way in which policy was made at the highest levels, ultimately to the point of going to war in 1999.[2] Contrary to conspiracy theories of one kind or another, international policy develops in a haphazard and often contradictory way, in response to rapidly moving events and the shifting priorities of key actors. There was certainly no evidence of a grand strategy among any of the international actors involved in this episode over a period of some twenty years.

Given the ad hoc nature of policy-making in this instance, it is of course difficult to draw general lessons or conclusions. Nevertheless, the provisional outcome of the crisis—independence for Kosovo—is sufficiently incongruous with the classical structural principles of international relations to warrant some explanation. The explanation in this chapter comes in several parts, as indicated in the introduction:

  I. Changing Perceptions of Sovereignty
 II. Issues of Governance
III. Human Rights

---

[1] Richard Holbrooke, Press Conference, 28 October 1998. Transcript available at <http://www.mtholyoke.edu/acad/intrel/holb.htm>, accessed 6 October 2008.
[2] The term 'war' is not employed in a technical legal sense here.

I. Changing Perceptions of Sovereignty

The 1990s saw a significant debate about the meaning of sovereignty. This was by no means just an academic debate. International actors, including the UN Secretary-General, certain governments, such as Canada, along with institutions like the UN Security Council, were leading protagonists in this debate. Relevant action in other instances included Security Council authorization for the use of armed force in cases of overwhelming suffering of populations (including Somalia, Liberia, Cote d'Ivoire, Congo, and belatedly Bosnia and Herzegovina and Rwanda), forcible pro-democratic action (Haiti), and the establishment of international criminal tribunals in relation to Yugoslavia and Rwanda. The latter two cases, while important in terms of the development of international criminal law, also became bywords for a failure of the organized international community in addressing the plights of populations under imminent threat of extermination—generating a certain sense of 'never again' in this context. The willingness to privilege the interests of threatened populations over traditional conceptions of state sovereignty and non-intervention was made express in the debates triggered by the Kosovo case. The Netherlands made this point forcefully:[3]

Since 1945, the world has witnessed a gradual shift in that balance, making respect for human rights more and more mandatory and respect for sovereignty less and less stringent. An elaborate body of international human rights law has come to counterbalance the dictates of paragraphs 4 and 7 of Article 2. Today, human rights have come to outrank sovereignty. Increasingly, the prevailing interpretation of the Charter is that it aims to protect individual human beings, not to protect those who abuse them. Today, we regard it as a generally accepted rule of international law that no sovereign state has the right to terrorize its own citizens. Indeed, if the Charter were to be written today, there would be an Article 2 (8) saying that nothing contained in the present Charter shall authorize Member States to terrorize their own people.

Of course, progressive views of this kind did not remain unanswered. China, for instance countered:[4]

Sovereign equality, mutual respect for State sovereignty and non-interference in the internal affairs of others are the basic principles governing international relations today. In spite of the major changes in the post-cold war international situation, these principles

---

[3] A/54/PV.13, at 23.   [4] A/PV/54/8, at 16.

are by no means out of date. Any deviation from or violation of these principles would destroy the universally recognized norms governing international relations and would lead to the rule of hegemonism; if the notion of 'might is right' should prevail, a new gun-boat policy would wreak havoc, the sovereignty and independence by virtue of which some small and weak countries protect themselves would be jeopardized and international peace and stability would be seriously endangered.

Despite such hesitations, there definitely emerged an environment where the terms of the debate about sovereignty shifted, away from the abstraction of the state towards a sense of empowerment and protection of populations. This was evidenced, eventually, in the adoption of the doctrine of 'responsibility to protect'—a doctrine that grew out of the work of a Commission of Enquiry set up in the wake of the Kosovo intervention of 1999.[5]

II. Issues of Governance

The early 1990s also marked a revitalization of international pressure in favour of genuinely democratic governance. At least in instances of counter-constitutional coups, this doctrine was activated in the shape of international action. In fact, there is a surprisingly large list of international action in relation to coups or threats to democratic governance encompassing some twenty cases. Action taken ranges for collective condemnations to sanctions and even forcible action.[6]

The issue of Kosovo was, however, a slightly different case. In this instance, no coup against the central government had taken place. Instead, a significant group of constituents was being excluded from governance and participation in the overall state by the elected authorities. Moreover, the autonomy that had been provided to ensure self-governance for the ethnic Albanian population segment concentrated in Kosovo had been virtually removed in violation of constitutional procedures. Instead, direct governance from the centre based on repression had been instituted.

Initial attempts to address the Yugoslav crisis were very hesitant in engaging this issue, in view of the flat refusal by Belgrade to permit discussion of a problem which it was claimed fell within its *domaine réservé*. In view of the need seen by the mainly European crisis managers involved in the early phases of the crisis to address Croatia and Bosnia first, where dreadful atrocities were occurring, the issue of governance in Kosovo was noted but not vigorously pursued. While Western diplomats would reiterate the need to restore Kosovo's autonomy among themselves, the international conferences on Yugoslavia treated this issue in a

---

[5] See above, p. 162.

[6] These cases include Chad, Somalia, Angola, Nigeria, Gambia, Comores, Sireea Leone, Central African Republic, Sao Tome and Principe, Niger, Burundi, Lesotho, Guinea Bissau, Cote d'Ivoire, Togo and Mauretania, as well as Haiti, Peru, Guatemala and Equador, and Myanmar, Pakistan and Thailand.

peripheral way.[7] This extended into the phase of purported negotiations through the Special Group on Kosovo, that dragged on into the beginning of 1996.

However, while there was little early action to insist on, or enforce, a restoration of autonomy, the problem was not entirely ignored. At the universal level, outside of the context of immediate European attempts of crisis management, the UN Commission on Human Rights and other human rights bodies raised this issue in an impressively consistent way. Even the early phase of this episode therefore furnishes some evidence that an entitlement to autonomy may be anchored within the context of the right to democratic governance, at least where pre-existing autonomy arrangements have been unilaterally abrogated. This impression is strengthened when considering the position during the next phase of the crisis, when armed conflict erupted after the conclusion of the Dayton agreements. At that point, the international diplomatic process began to emphasize more forcefully the need to restore autonomy for Kosovo. Indeed, by 1998 this extended even to demands made by the Security Council under Chapter VII of the UN Charter. While such action can be explained in view of the Council's functions relative to the maintenance of international peace and security— rather than human rights as such—it was nevertheless also noteworthy in a human rights context. International bodies are traditionally reluctant to decree the structure of internal governance of states. While the principle of representation in government is raised on occasion, even human rights courts will generally allow a considerable 'margin of appreciation' to states in arranging their political system.[8] Political bodes, such as the UN Security Council, where sovereignty-conscious states such as China are present, would ordinarily be expected to be far more hesitant. However, in this case, it was generally accepted that the Kosovo population would, at least, be entitled to the return to the autonomy that was previously guaranteed, or perhaps to an even more wide-ranging form of autonomy or self-governance. At Rambouillet, the acceptance of autonomy at least for an interim phase was even to be enforced through the threat of force. Of course, at that stage, any prospect for a permanent return to autonomous government had disappeared, after a period of ten years of severe repression of the Kosovo population and after armed hostilities had led to a further polarization of the position on both sides. This was all the more so after the conflict of 1999 and the massive displacement crisis caused by the forced removal of a large segment of the ethnic Albanian population.

Overall, therefore, this episode does offer some support for those who argue that autonomy arrangements in favour of ethnic populations, in addition to traditional self-determination of peoples entitled to secession, can be matters of international concern. At least the maintenance in place of existing autonomy arrangements that have been unilaterally abrogated by the central government

---

[7] See above, p. Chapter 3, Section II.
[8] e.g., ECtHR, *Zdanoka v. Latvia* (Appls. 66289/01, Judgment of 6 June 2005).

can be subject to international action, both through international human rights action and through collective security mechanisms.

Would this mean that all ethnic peoples who live together in one part of a state can now invoke an entitlement to autonomy? Such a view would be premature. The Kosovo episode only relates to instances of the unilateral abrogation of a federally anchored autonomy. In that circumstance, the matter may raise human and minority rights issues at the international level. Where this internal wrong leads to potential or actual conflict, the matter can also be addressed by political organs, including the UN Security Council. There is also an increasing international expectation that minority communities should be allowed effective participation in the governance of the overall state, and in relation to affairs or regions of special interest to them. However, it remains up to the state to generate structures and mechanisms towards that end. Territorial autonomy may be one of them, but it is not the only option.[9]

III. Human Rights

Traditionally, efforts to achieve human rights compliance have relied on three requirements. First, the state concerned would need to adopt the international human rights norm in question. Second, it would need to consent to the application of human rights implementation mechanisms. And third, there would be the issue of securing implementation in cases of violations that have been confirmed by such mechanisms.

In this instance, Yugoslavia was a party to all or most relevant human rights instruments. According to the theory of the automatic succession to human rights treaties that was significantly strengthened through the Yugoslav episode, this was also the case during the time when the international legal status of Yugoslavia (Serbia and Montenegro) was not fully clarified, including its membership in international treaties and international organizations. Moreover, most of the rights at issue also formed part and parcel of the universal corpus of fundamental human rights that apply to all states under all circumstances. Yugoslavia's efforts to derogate from its human rights obligations were not effective in this respect. The application of fundamental human rights, such as the prohibition of genocide, crimes against humanity, torture or discrimination was not in doubt throughout the entirety of the crisis.

From the beginning, substantive violations of the human rights of the ethnic Albanian majority population were clearly identified by authoritative international agencies. The practices of the FRY/Serbian government were dissected

---

[9] See Marc Weller, 'Effective Participation of Minorities in Public Life', in Marc Weller (ed), *Universal Minority Rights* (Oxford: OUP, 2007), 477–516. In this sense, the propositions offered in the first Badinter opinion have not been accepted in practice.

with accuracy and in some detail. The human rights violations were named as such and publicly condemned. This condemnation extended beyond the specialized human rights agencies operating in the shadows of international politics and public interests. The principal political bodies of the regional European and the universal UN systems, such as the UN General Assembly, picked up the findings from specialized agencies and gave them a very public platform. Perhaps in view of Belgrade's record in relation to Bosnia and Herzegovina, there was no diplomatic subtlety in these pronouncements. They were clear and unambiguous.

It is also interesting to note that the relevant international agencies did not only restrict their findings to the human rights situation in a narrow sense. As has been noted already in the preceding section, there were also demands for the restoration of Kosovo's autonomous status. It was made clear that the FRY/Serbia could not claim the sovereign freedom to arrange for an ethnically-based political system of domination and discrimination within its area of territorial jurisdiction.

The international human rights bodies adapted their modalities of action throughout the course of the Yugoslav episode. In fact, various new procedures were triggered by it. The UN Commission on Human Rights started to hold special emergency sessions, summoning reluctant representatives from Belgrade for special hearings. As was noted already, the continuity of human rights obligations was confirmed, even in controversial cases of state succession. The UN High Commissioner on Human Rights established field presences. The reports and findings of the thematic rapporteurs, the country rapporteur for Yugoslavia and various other bodies were consolidated. The UN Secretary-General himself was charged with updating the UN General Assembly and other bodies on the situation. Admittedly, not all of these procedures were focused exclusively on Kosovo. However, through them, Kosovo was covered to a significant extent.

In addition to the regular human rights monitoring system, other traditionally silent actors became involved. The International Committee of the Red Cross issued public findings in relation to the situation. The OSCE reported on the violations in great detail and, in contrast to the confidential EU monitoring mission, ultimately published its reports. Indeed, it compiled a very comprehensive public dossier of human rights violations by Yugoslavia during the 1999 armed conflict. Moreover, the International Criminal Tribunal addressing crimes in the former Yugoslavia intervened in the Kosovo issue in a very high-profile way.

All of these activities, which were coordinated at least in part, point to a process of self-constitution of an integrated, regional and universal human rights monitoring system. Clearly, previous hesitations about interference in the sovereign domain of states were not of great relevance. There was no doubt that the organized international community was insisting on compliance with a number of core rules and principles that would have to be adhered to, whatever Yugoslavia's claims as to the nature of the crisis within its borders. Yugoslavia's diplomatic denials, formerly well received, were ignored by the international institutions, which formed their own views instead.

The clear findings of the human rights agencies in the end had quite a dramatic outcome. In view of the consistent reporting on Belgrade's practices during the preceding decade, there was a significant level of international understanding, although not necessarily outright support, for the 1999 NATO armed action. In view of the atrocities committed during the 1999 armed conflict, which were again well documented by international human rights agencies and NGO actors, there was no question upon the conclusion of the conflict of the FRY/Serbia exercising any sort of public authority in the territory. This was confirmed in the terms of Security Council Resolution 1244 (1999).

One must also note, however, that while the organized international community was relatively quick in condemning human rights violations in Kosovo, it was a long time before it acted decisively to terminate them. While international bodies were uncharacteristically undiplomatic in their condemnation of FRY/Serbian policies, no significant action was taken to enforce these demands for over a decade. In fact, if one considers the clarity of findings by a whole host of international bodies, adopted year after year throughout the 1990s, and determining that the situation in Kosovo was entirely intolerable and required immediate attention, the disjuncture between human rights monitoring and international action seems very pronounced indeed.

One reason for this reluctance to become involved relates to the nature of the struggle underpinning the human rights crisis. By the time the international agencies engaged with the crisis, it was no longer merely a human rights issue. With Kosovo's first declaration of independence in 1991, it had become a self-determination conflict—an issue approached with only the greatest hesitation by international actors.

It should also be noted that Yugoslavia, previously a leader of the neutral and non-aligned movement, was very well connected diplomatically. The rump Yugoslavia had retained a highly experienced diplomatic corps from that era. The Yugoslav Foreign Ministry was adept at erecting hurdles to international action against Yugoslavia. Their counterparts in Kosovo were former schoolteachers or professors of literature, unaccustomed to operating at the international level. This advantage might have yielded even more pronounced benefits, had Yugoslavia's diplomacy on the human rights front not been undermined by two factors. First, the horrors perpetrated in Bosnia were sufficiently dramatic to undercut the legitimacy and credibility of the league of gentlemen from Belgrade. Second, human rights abuses in Kosovo had been pursued through a formal programme of legislation in Serbia. It was not really possible to deny that a kind of apartheid had been established, as this fact was clearly evidenced in Serbia's official gazette.

Nevertheless, until 1997, Belgrade managed to keep a lid on international action. When it was faced with vocal condemnation of its human rights practices, it sought to terminate international access to Kosovo, for instance by withdrawing its consent to the OSCE Mission of Long Duration. It was only after the human rights crisis became a displacement crisis that more decisive international action was forthcoming.

IV. Forcible Humanitarian Action

As the crisis worsened, the UN Security Council adopted mandatory demands under Chapter VII of the Charter. Economic sanctions going beyond an arms embargo were, however, precluded by Russia. Even within the EU, traditional friends of Belgrade inhibited the development of a more comprehensive sanctions regime commensurate with the crisis.

When, finally, the crisis began to jeopardize regional stability throughout 1998, the threat of the use of force was adopted by the NATO states. Russia tolerated this threat, on the understanding that it would oppose the use of force in the event of the threat materializing. This knowledge may have given Belgrade a false sense of security. NATO had committed itself to the threat of the use of force and felt compelled to use it when the conditions it had stipulated were not fulfilled. When NATO actually launched its aerial campaign after the failure to achieve a negotiated settlement under the threat of the use of force at Rambouillet, Russia and others strongly opposed the operation.

Until 1999, it was generally thought that international precedent was gradually crystallizing around a new right to humanitarian intervention. There had been a considerable number of authorizations for the use of force in circumstances of humanitarian emergency coming from the UN Security Council. It was more problematic whether individual states, or coalitions of states, might also take action in the absence of a Council mandate. The two coalition interventions in Iraq (the Kurds in 1991 and the Marsh Arabs in the South in 1992) and the action by the Economic Community of West African States (ECOWAS) in Liberia appeared to offer a point of crystallization of a new justification of forcible humanitarian action. The UK government, in particular, had formally argued that such a legal right was now in existence, and offered specific legal criteria for its application, relating to the extend of the humanitarian emergency and its overwhelming nature, the fact that no other agency was addressing it, and the application of the minimum of force necessary to achieve the humanitarian aim.[10] While forcible humanitarian action had not been formally endorsed, at least in the case of Iraq, there had been very little international criticism.[11]

The condemnation of the NATO aerial operation by several states, including in particular Russia and China, gave the impression that the hesitant

[10] See above, p. 97.
[11] The Liberian action was, in fact, retroactively embraced by the UN Security Council. See Marc Weller, *Regional Peace-keeping and Peace-enforcement: The Liberian Crisis* (Cambridge: Cambridge University Press, 1994), 273.

development of the doctrine of humanitarian action had been terminated. The attempt of the UN Secretary-General to achieve a standard-setting document on humanitarian intervention in the UN General Assembly in the wake of the action backfired. Several additional states that had offered understanding at least of the humanitarian motives of the Kosovo operations joined in formally opposing the development of such a standard. Indeed, some NATO member states that had participated in the conflict now opposed the establishment of a general rule concerning humanitarian action. Therefore, a majority of international legal commentators formed the view that forcible humanitarian action was not, strictly speaking, legal, but might be considered legitimate in certain extreme circumstances.

Looking back on this issue with some distance of time, it is not clear that such view was entirely necessary. Both the debate in the UN Security Council and the consideration of the Secretary-General's proposals on humanitarian action in the General Assembly revealed a more nuanced picture. Outright condemnations of the operation were outnumbered by delegations that sought to emphasize that, in principle, forcible action requires a Security Council mandate, but who also pointed to the desperate humanitarian circumstances in this case. There was a definite, widespread recognition of the overwhelming need to protect populations at times of existential crisis. This sense later translated itself into support for the doctrine of responsibility to protect. That doctrine emphasizes in the first place the responsibility of the respective states to secure the well being of their constituents. Where they are unwilling or unable to do so, collective action at the level of the UN Security Council may be contemplated. Unilateral action is not encouraged, but there is room for an argument that it may be legitimate under exceptional circumstances of overwhelming need. In a somewhat ironic twist, Russia, too, now appears to have embraced this doctrine, when justifying its armed action relating to South Ossetia and Abkhazia. In that case, there was no evidence of an overwhelming humanitarian emergency, or even genodice, as Moscow has claimed, that triggered a necessary response.[12] Instances of abuse of this kind will not in the long term inhibit the strong power of attraction of this newly established doctrine, provided the organized international community clearly identifies them as such.

V. Self-Determination and Secession

In 1991 the US, UK and France mounted a humanitarian rescue operation on behalf of the Kurds of Northern Iraq.[13] However, the intervening paratroop

---

[12] See Marc Weller and Jonathan Wheatley, *The War in Georgia: Power Politics and the Failure of Conflict Prevention* (London: Hurst Publishers, forthcoming).

[13] See Marc Weller, *Iraq and Kuwait, The Hostilities and their Aftermath* (Cambridge: Cambridge University Press, 1993), Chapter 19.

forces came with strings attached. The Kurdish leaders of the region had to pledge that they would not exploit the humanitarian cover that was being provided for their civilian populations to advance their military campaign for an independent Kurdistan.[14] Hence, even where force has been used, ostensibly for humanitarian purposes, precautions were taken to ensure that this would not encourage or facilitate secession by the entity on whose behalf the intervention was mounted.

In relation to Kosovo, there was also a strong international consensus that enhanced self-government, or autonomy, would be the maximum that could be expected. Other than Albania, not a single state recognized Kosovo's claim to independence. Even when events on the ground had made a return to autonomy rather unlikely, Rambouillet represented an attempt to obtain the breathing space of at least three years of enhanced self-government. Signature by Kosovo of the Rambouillet accords was not only crucial in order to justify the use of force against Belgrade in case it refused the settlement. It was also meant to signal an undertaking by the Kosovar leadership that it would accept autonomy, rather than exploit the situation and (again) proclaim outright independence at least for an interim period if force should be used. That is why it was so important for the Western states to obtain, not only the signature of the moderate ethnic Albanian leadership under President Rugova, but also the agreement of the KLA.

Although Kosovo had declared full independence in 1991, it contented itself with the establishment of a parallel, unofficial system of government and peaceful resistance for a prolonged period of time. This initially moderate position was driven by a sense of pragmatism. Early on, before having declared independence, the Kosovo leadership had been given quite realistic legal advice, which indicated:[15]

Within the present international system, Kosovo's claim to self-determination will not be heeded. Even a carefully crafted argument which would not necessary broaden the application of the doctrine of self-determination and would not give rise to a precedent which might threaten other governments is likely to be ignored. Kosovo will have to decide whether it can survive in a state of limbo, seeking to consolidate its de facto rule over time in the face of Serb repression. In this position, it would consistently remain under the threat of a forcible restoration of effective control by Serbia. The only alternative is an armed campaign which will bring with it untold suffering for the civilian population of Kosovo and which it would not be likely to win. Instead, a gradual strategy of aligning the interests of the international community with those of Kosovo, given the dangers to the stability to the region, might be pursued. On balance, however, a rapid resolution of the issue is unlikely.

---

[14] Even after a US-led coalition invaded all of Iraq and toppled the Hussein government twelve years later, independence was not an option. Instead, Kurdistan was formed again into an autonomous region within Iraq. Iraqi Constitution, approved by referendum on 15 October, Art 117. Full text at <http://portal.unesco.org/ci/en/files/20704/11332732681iraqi_constitution_en.pdf/iraqi_constitution_en.pdf>, accessed 6 October 2008.

[15] Quoted in Weller, *Crisis in Kosovo*, 28.

The moderate Rugova government, which had been elected in 1992, was unwilling to risk the lives of those it purported to represent. Instead, it attempted to circumvent internal Serbian repression through the establishment of the parallel state structures in Kosovo.

At the international level, Kosovo deliberately did not argue on the basis of a wider right to self-determination applicable outside of the traditional colonial context. Such an argument, while politically persuasive to some, could also have applied to a wide range of other circumstances, be it the Kurds in Turkey, Iraq and Iran, the Basques in France and Spain, the Kashmiris in India, or the Tamils in Sri Lanka. A claim that ethnic groups of this kind might have a right to self-determination in the sense of unilateral secession would have been immediately opposed.

However, the Kosovo crisis took place in an environment of change. Since 1988, there has in fact been a very significant trend towards the settlement of self-determination conflicts. There have been some forty such settlements since the termination of the Cold War. While many of these have involved autonomy solutions, much like those suggested by Serbia, there were also signs of a new trend. In several settlements, a future option of self-determination has been built in, or independence accepted as a final outcome. These cases, amongst them, Czechoslovakia, Eritrea, Southern Sudan, Bougainville, and Northern Ireland, undermine the presumption that a change in status is generally excluded.[16] In fact, in 1996/7, Moscow accepted such an arrangement in relation to Chechnya, although it subsequently disowned it and forcibly reincorporated the entity. Serbia itself had agreed to a right of secession for Montenegro in a union treaty. Arguably, the Rambouillet agreement for Kosovo also foresaw such an option through its reference to a settlement based on 'the will of the people'.

The combination of this general trend opposing strict and automatic insistence on territorial integrity with the specific background facts of this case made the suggestion of independence for Kosovo somewhat more internationally acceptable. This was evident in the responses of states in the UN Security Council to the eventual 2008 declaration of independence. Even states which were deeply attached to the principle of territorial unity were quite cautious in their criticism of the event. Most interestingly, no state in the Council other than Russia and Serbia argued that the Declaration constituted an internationally unlawful act that would need to be resisted by the organized international community, for instance through a collective policy of non-recognition or even sanctions.

This is in marked contrast to cases of unilateral independence obtained in breach of a core rule of international law (*jus cogens*). In such cases, a positive obligation of non-recognition is extended to all states, along with a duty not to assist the unlawful entity in maintaining its purported independence. Examples

[16] See Weller, *Escaping the Self-determination Trap* (Dordrecht: Martinus Nijhoff, forthcoming), Chapter V.

are the Declaration of Independence of Southern Rhodesia in its offensive pursuit of the policy of apartheid, the purported independence of the Turkish Republic of Northern Cyprus after the Turkish armed invasion or the purported establishment of the Republika Srpska through a policy of ethnic cleansing and possible genocide.

In cases of this kind, it is not the disruption of the territorial unity as such that renders independence unlawful, but attendant factors such as a breach of the prohibition of apartheid, of aggression, or of ethnic cleansing or genocide. Kosovo's independence was not tainted in this way. Hence, it was not, per se, unlawful at the level of international law. Instead, it was treated simply as a fact that occurred. While Serbia was free to oppose this fact, third states were free to form a view as to whether or not they wished to recognize and establish diplomatic relations.

It is quite clear that all states involved would have preferred the question to have been settled by agreement between the parties, as was the case in Sudan, Papua New Guinea, Ethiopia and others. When Belgrade refused a settlement on the basis of the Ahtisaari Comprehensive Proposal, however, it turned out to be impossible to impose this result through Security Council action. Instead, Kosovo unilaterally declared independence.

Of course, in the end, Kosovo's Declaration of Independence was not quite so unilateral. Important limitations on its fledgling sovereignty had been negotiated, or rather imposed, by the Ahtisaari team, and reinforced by very strong pressure from the US government. Even in the absence of the Ahtisaari settlement, they were accepted as original limitations on Kosovo sovereignty. Hence, Kosovo was subject to all of the obligations that would have been contained in an eventual negotiated settlement, without the benefit of independence approved through the Security Council. Belgrade, on the other hand, could pursue its strategy of opposing independence through diplomatic isolation, and possibly by seeking the de facto division of Kosovo through other means. It could do so with the quiet assurance that the international actors it was so vigorously attacking for having facilitated independence would maintain its key interests in relation to Kosovo, notably the establishment of an extensive system of decentralization and the protection of the ethnic Serb population.

The wider meaning of this overall result for the doctrine of self-determination will remain controversial for some time, not least due to the latest actions of Russia in relation to Georgia. The states supporting Kosovo's eventual independence attempted to argue very strongly that Kosovo was quite unique and in no way a precedent for action in future cases. This, it was asserted, was due to three factors: Kosovo's status in a federal unit that had been removed by a federation that subsequently dissolved; the atrocities committed during the 1999 conflict; and the fact that the territory had been subjected to international administration for over eight years. While each of these factors might point to the uniqueness of the Kosovo episode, they could in fact also be taken as references to emerging new qualifications to the hitherto restrictive doctrine of self-determination.

The first factor relates to Kosovo's former federal status. While it was designated as an autonomous province of Serbia, it also enjoyed a full federal status under the 1974 federal constitution, on par with the six republics. Kosovo had argued from the beginning that it, too, had to be entitled to statehood once the overall federation dissolved. Otherwise, having lost its position and protection as part of a constituent unit of the federation, it would suddenly be trapped as a simple province within Serbia—a reduction and change in status that could not be accepted, especially in the light of the policy of repression administered by Belgrade.

However, while the states of the EU that were principally administering the dissolution of Yugoslavia had been ready to accept that the Yugoslav republics could become independent, they were unwilling to extend this privilege to Kosovo. As noted in the introduction, the organized international community had invested much in isolating the Yugoslav case from setting a wider international precedent in favour of a broad right of self-determination outside of the colonial context. The republics, it was felt, could claim a constitutionally based entitlement to self-determination that was entirely unique to the SFRY and that might therefore be given effect, without affecting international legal rules more generally. This was particularly true in the case of dissolution of the overall state.

While it was meant to prevent the setting of a new precedent, this approach did in fact establish a new kind of entitlement to self-determination: that of constitutional self-determination. According to this new precept, the organized international community would take note of a positive right to self-determination, even if such a right was only established in internal, constitutional law of the relevant state. However, in order to ensure that this new doctrine would remain highly restricted, it was limited to two circumstances. First, the state concerned had to be a full federation or confederation of a special kind. On the one hand, there are federations that have developed through a transfer of authority from the centre (devolution). In these cases, the constituent republics would not carry within them the original seeds of sovereignty, and they would not be able to achieve secession. However, there were also federal unions that had been created, at least nominally, through a coming together of entities that had enjoyed sovereign rights. This was the case in the USSR, and, according to the 1974 Constitution, the SFRY. Where the overall union dissolved in the latter type of case, the constituent republics would be able to regain sovereignty. In the case of the USSR this principle was therefore applied to the full union republics—Chechnya was not covered. Similarly, the organized international community ruled, initially, that Kosovo fell just below full republic status and would therefore not be able to claim independence along with the six full republics.

The second circumstance of constitutionally based self-determination was one where the constitution itself expressly assigned to the constituent units the right to secede. This practice was rare, but it existed, for instance, in the cases of the Soviet Union, and more recently, of Ethiopia. The 1974 Yugoslav Constitution did refer to a right to self-determination, although only in the preamble. That right appeared to be focused on the 'nations' of Yugoslavia. As the six republics were considered to the homeland of the titular nations of Yugoslavia (i.e., those major ethnic groups that did not have a kin state elsewhere), this provision was applied also only to the full republics.

With the need to explain Kosovo independence after all, although with a delay of close to twenty years, it might be tempting to 'rediscover' the status of Kosovo as a constituent unit of a dissolved federation as a ground for its independence. This was Kosovo's own argument in favour of independence throughout, and some governments have now started to embrace it.[17] This theory would restrain the precedental value of Kosovo's independence, as it is dependent on the constitutional particularities of this case.

There is, however, also the possibility that Kosovo will be seen as the fountainhead of another, new kind of self-determination. This would be the case of remedial self-determination. That doctrine, too, comes in two variants: lack of representation on the one hand, and repression on the other.

The first variant would hold that a significant segment of the population of the state that is structurally excluded from representation within it may lay claim to a right to secession. After all, the state is meant to represent the will of the governed. If it structurally excludes a territorially defined segment of the population from the process of forming a collective will, than this group must be entitled to form its own, independent political unit.

This theory is sometimes supported by reference to the Friendly Relations Declaration, adopted by the General Assembly by consensus on the occasion of the 25th anniversary of the United Nations in 1970. That document is generally regarded as an authoritative statement of essential principles of international law. When addressing self-determination, the resolution states:[18]

Nothing in the foregoing paragraphs shall be construed as authorizing or encouraging any action which would dismember or impair, totally or in part, the territorial integrity or political unity of sovereign and independent States conducting themselves in compliance with the principle of equal rights and self-determination of peoples as described above *and thus possessed of a government representing the whole people belonging to the territory without distinction as to race, creed or colour.* [emphasis added]

The final half sentence has been taken by some to establish that the principle of territorial integrity and unity of states is conditional. If a state does not possess a government representing the whole people belonging to the territory, the doctrine of territorial unity does not apply. Hence, secession becomes an option. However, in truth, this sentence was intended to apply only to colonial or analogous territories which, it was thought at the time, do not, by definition, possess a government representing the people of the territory. Nevertheless, this passage

---

[17] See above, pp. 232–233.   [18] Resolution 2625 (XXV), 24 October 1970, A/8082.

has been invoked in order to construct a right of remedial self-determination outside of the colonial context.[19] According to proponents of this argument, the restatement of this passage in the 1993 Vienna Declaration supports the application of self-determination in relation to post-colonial situations. After all, the declaration was adopted well after most instances of colonialism had been dissolved. Moreover, the text is slightly changed from the Friendly Relations declaration, now apparently making the application of territorial unity dependent on the existence of a government 'representing the whole people belonging to the territory *without distinction of any kind.*'[20] Moreover, it is also possible to find support for a remedial right to self-determination in cases of non-representation in the initial rulings of the Badinter Commission, determining that the SFRY was in a process of dissolution. The Commission had stated:[21]

[T]hat in the case of a federal-type state, which embraces communities that possess a degree of autonomy and, moreover, participate in the exercise of political power within the framework of institutions common to the Federation, the existence of the State implies that the federal organs represent the components of the Federation and wield effective power....

. . .

The composition and workings of the essential organs of the Federation, be they the Federal Presidency, the Federal Council, the Council of the Republics and the Provinces, the Federal Executive Council, the Constitutional Court or the Federal Army, no longer meet the criteria of participation and representativeness inherent in a federal state;

It may be questioned whether the Badinter Commission actually intended to suggest that a positive right to secession arises where a group does not enjoy full representation in the state.[22] In any event, thus far, it was not possible to find any support for this view in state practice. As was noted at the outset, the Iraqi Kurds, long precluded from representation in the state, were not offered independence when an intervention was mounted on their behalf, or in the wake of constitutional reconstruction following upon the 2003 invasion and occupation of the territory. Other population groups which have been persistently excluded from government of the overall state have also not been accorded an external self-determination status. However, it cannot be denied that the Kosovo case will, as independence consolidates, help strengthen this argument.

[19] See Christian Tomuschat, 'Self-determination in a Post-colonial World', in *id.* (ed), *Modern Law of Self-determination* (Dordrecht: Martinus Nijhoff, 1993), 1; but also see Patrick Thornberry, 'The Democratic or Internal Aspect of Self-determination with Some Remarks on Federalism', *ibid.*, 101.
[20] Emphasis added. UN Doc. A/CONF.157/23, 12 July 1993, para. 2.
[21] Opinion No. 1 of the Arbitration Commission on the former Yugoslavia, 29 November 1991, in Weller, *Crisis in Kosovo*, 81–2.
[22] Indeed, the principal author of the opinions denies this. See Alain Pellet, 'Note Sur la Commission d'Arbitrage de la Conférence Européenne Pour la Paix en Yugoslavie', *Annuaire Français de Droit International*, 37 (1991), 329–48, 339.

It is noteworthy that Russia, despite its vulnerability in this matter, expressly embraced this doctrine in the context of the operations concerning Abkhazia and South Ossetia:[23]

...Taking into account the appeals of South Ossetian and Abkhaz peoples, of the Parliaments and Presidents of both Republics, the opinion of the Russian people and both Chambers of the Federal Assembly the President of the Russian Federation decided to recognize the independence of South Ossetia and Abkhazia and to conclude treaties of friendship, cooperation and mutual assistance with them. Making this decision, Russia was guided by the provisions of the Charter of the United Nations, the Helsinki Final Act and other fundamental international instruments, including the 1970 Declaration on Principles of International Law concerning Friendly Relations among States. It should be noted that in accordance with the Declaration, every State has the duty to refrain from any forcible action which deprives peoples of their right to self-determination and freedom and independence, to adhere in their activities to the principle of equal rights and self-determination of peoples, and to possess a government representing the whole people belonging to the territory. There is no doubt that Mikhail Saakashvili's regime is far from meeting those high standards set by the international community.

Of course, in that instance, it was principally Russia that had precluded the establishment of an agreement providing for the full inclusion of Abkhazia and South Ossetia within the Georgian political system. Georgia had offered detailed provisions on representation for both territories by way of wide-ranging autonomy.[24] In view of Russia's obstruction of an autonomy settlement, it was a spurious argument to refer to the lack of representation of the two territories in the overall Georgian state. The states of the EU, any of which had accorded recognition to Kosovo, therefore rejected this argument. Instead, they demanded 'that a peaceful and lasting solution to the conflict in Georgia must be based on full respect for the principles of independence, sovereignty and territorial integrity recognised by international law, the Final Act of the Helsinki Conference on Security and Cooperation in Europe and United Nations Security Council resolutions. In this context, the Council deplores any action that runs contrary to a solution based on these principles.'[25] This statement would deny that Russia's invocation of the doctrine of remedial secession is in accordance with international law.

In fact, the Georgia conflict also highlighted the potentially problematic nature of the second type of proposed remedial secession. Russia argued:[26]

By the aggressive attack against South Ossetia on the night of 8 August 2008, which resulted in numerous human losses, including among the peacekeepers and other

---

[23] Statement by the Ministry of Foreign Affairs of Russia, 26 August 2008, Doc. 1246-26-08-2008. Text available at <http://www.un.int/russia/new/MainRoot/docs/off_news/260808/newen1.htm>, accessed 6 October 2008.

[24] See Marc Weller and Jonathan Wheatley, *The War in Georgia: Power Politics and the Failure of Conflict Prevention* (London: Hurst Publishers, forthcoming).

[25] Council of the European Union, Council Conclusions on Georgia, 2889th External Relations Council meeting, Brussels, 15/16 September 2008.

[26] See Statement by Russian Ministry of Foreign Affairs, above, n. 23.

Russian citizens, and by the preparation of a similar action against Abkhazia, Mikhail Saakashivili has himself put paid to the territorial integrity of Georgia. Using repeatedly brutal military force against the peoples, whom, according to his words, he would like to see within his State, Mikhail Saakashvili left them no other choice but to ensure their security and the right to exist through self-determination as independent States.

This argument suggests that active mistreatment or repression of a population may give rise to a right to remedial secession. Again, all the previous cases of forcible humanitarian action were carefully circumscribed, addressing only the humanitarian emergency and avoiding action that might strengthen a move towards secession. However, it is true that a number of governments stated expressly at the conclusion of the 1999 Kosovo conflict, and upon Kosovo's Declaration of Independence, that it was not possible to foresee Kosovo's return to Serbian control, in view of the atrocities and mass forcible displacement that had taken place. Such statements may well serve to strengthen the argument that a remedial right to self-determination could be developing over time, although Russia's invocation of the doctrine in circumstances that are somewhat different (Georgia had not engaged in conduct comparable to that of the Belgrade government in relation to Kosovo) may point to the risk of its abuse and may accordingly inhibit its development.

Two further propositions were made during the Kosovo conflict that relate to self-determination issues. First, there was the argument that the period of prolonged international administration strengthened Kosovo's case for independence. At first sight, it is not clear why international administration would be connected with an entitlement to self-determination and secession. While international administration often precedes or facilitates a change in the status of a territory (West Irian, Eastern Timor), this is not necessarily the case. However, there are a number of considerations that are relevant in this context. First, the prolonged period of administration generated a period of self-administration for Kosovo beyond the reach of Serbian authority. Once the Kosovo population had exercised self-governance independently of Belgrade, one might argue that this contributes to a legally protected de facto status. At least this would be the case where such self-administration is being conducted within the legally protected expectation of a change in status. Such an expectation existed through Resolution 1244 (1999), which did foresee a final status process after interim governance and self-governance. Of course, the outcome of that process was not determined by the resolution, although the reference in the resolution to the Rambouillet accords, which had required an agreement in accordance with the will of the people, could be taken to point in the direction of possible independence. What is more crucial in this instance, however, is the fact that the United Nations carried through the final status process foreseen in Resolution 1244 (1999). The outcome of this process was a clear recommendation in favour of independence of the UN Special Envoy, endorsed by the UN Secretary-General. In addition, it provided for a detailed settlement, accommodating the interests

Serbia had pursued during the negotiations, including those relating to decentralization and the protection of cultural heritage. Serbia did not fully cooperate in this process, or at least it refused to accept its outcome. As the process was nevertheless based on a Chapter VII mandate, one might argue that unilateral independence did become available when the negotiations proved fruitless due to the attitude of one party. In this sense, the legally established expectation of final status, coupled with independent administration over a period of eight years, and the frustration of the final settlement process, may be taken, together, to strengthen the case for independence in this case.

A final issue is that of conditional self-determination. In a number of settlements of self-determination disputes, the option of a referendum on independence is included, provided certain conditions are met. For instance, the Bougainville settlement requires performance of disarmament obligations and compliance with standards of good governance.[27] Several international NGOs active in ethnic conflict settlement suggested that conditional self-determination might also be an option for Kosovo.[28] Of course, the concept of 'earned sovereignty' is one that concerns principally the entity seeking independence. It does not add an additional entitlement to independence. Instead, it confirms that if, in principle, independence is available, it will only be granted in actual fact if the entity demonstrates is capacity for self-government.

This approach was of course applied in Kosovo, through the standards before status process. Kosovo was subjected to a very intensive, although at times confused, international standards process, and attempted to comply with it. While Belgrade has complained that ultimately independence came without fulfilment of all standards, this very criticism seems to suggest that independence might be a legitimate outcome if standards had been fulfilled. In any event, the application of the standards before status process certainly contributes to the argument that the period of UNMIK administration, including the administration of this policy, added to an expectation that independence would be available in the end.

---

[27] Article 4, Kokopo Agreement of 26 January 2001: 'The constitutional amendments will guarantee that the referendum will be held: no earlier than 10 years, and, in any case, no later than 15 years after the election of the first autonomous Bougainville Government, when the conditions listed below have been met, unless the autonomous Bougainville Government decides, after consultation with the National Government and in accordance with the Bougainville Constitution, that the referendum should not be held. The conditions to be taken into account include: weapons disposal, and good governance. The actual date of the referendum will be agreed after consultations by the autonomous Bougainville Government and the National Government.'

[28] International Crisis Group, 'Kosovo: Towards Final Status', *Europe Report* 161, 24 January 2005; Independent International Commission on Kosovo, *Why Conditional Independence? The Follow-up of the Kosovo Report* (Stockholm: Global Reporting Books, 2001); Public International Law and Policy Group, 'Kosovo Project', available at <http://www.pilpg.org/areas/peacebuilding/negotiations/kosovofinalstatus/index.html>, accessed 6 October 2007; Janusz Bugajski, *Achieving a Final Status Settlement for Kosovo* (Washington: Center for Strategic and International Studies).

VI. Hierarchies Among International Actors

The international system does not feature a very pronounced institutional hierarchy in the formal assignment of public functions to international organs. While it is now accepted that states and international organizations can exercise international constitutional functions, for example when criticizing the human rights performance of another state, or when acting together to reverse an act of aggression, it is not always clear which organs can exercise what competence and to what extent. The dispute about the legitimacy of action by a military alliance, NATO, to vindicate the humanitarian interests of a threatened population illustrates the sharp end of this dilemma. The same applies to the issue of the role of the UN Security Council in relation to the creation of statehood in this instance.

The post-Cold War crisis of the former Yugoslavia occurred at a time when collective security institutions were seeking to adapt to a changing world. There emerged a struggle for pre-eminence between conflict management agencies, a struggle which masked, to some extent, the conflict about the realignment of global power with the termination of the Cold War. The early episodes of the Yugoslav crisis demonstrated that the much-vaunted new European Security architecture was more myth than reality. The attempt to achieve a settlement for Kosovo gave rise once again to competition for pre-eminence between the OSCE, which Russia considered the principal authority in relation to peace and security in Europe, and the EU and its initially hesitant attempts to establish some kind of 'security identity' for itself. Moreover, the US and UK were fighting hard to preserve the dominant role of NATO.

During the period of the Kosovo crisis, the CSCE/OSCE underwent an important transformation from a Cold War mechanism of confidence-building to a conflict-management structure of quite incredible complexity. The early CSCE mission to Kosovo highlighted the progress that had been made in this respect. However, the subsequent inactivity of the CSCE/OSCE after Yugoslavia froze cooperation in light of its own suspension from the CSCE, were indications of the limitations of a mechanism still principally reliant on the cooperation of target states.

The EU, on the other hand, was desperately attempting to inject new impetus into the establishment of its security and defence identity. A first attempt to use the EU as a crisis mechanism had failed in Bosnia and Herzegovina. To the embarrassment of the Europeans, who had observed genocide take place unopposed, the crisis was finally resolved in a matter of days through the application of largely US airpower under a NATO umbrella. While some attempts at mediation were made, the EU was unable to assert its position early in the Kosovo crisis. In fact, Belgrade was able to remove its Special Envoy, Felipe Gonzales, from the equation by simply refusing him a visa.

278   Conclusion

In the later stages, the EU adopted sanctions outside the United Nations Security Council, but with great hesitation and only to a limited extent. The EU also took a leading role in the Contact Group and its attempts to achieve a peaceful settlement through its Special Envoy, Austrian diplomat Wolfgang Petritsch. The economic muscle of the Union was also brought to bear in the context of the Rambouillet talks, where considerable resources were promised for reconstruction and development of the region. The choice of a French chateau for the talks, rather than a US airbase in Ohio, was intended to symbolize the ability of the Europeans to address matters in their own region. The strong role of the US in the talks did, however, detract from this image somewhat.

The Western European Union (WEU) had also attempted to adapt to the times. It saw itself as the military arm of European security cooperation. However, the United Kingdom and the United States were not always enthusiastic about the development of structures which might devalue NATO. Hence, the WEU continued to expand on paper, ostensibly with the cooperation of NATO and its members, who promised to make certain assets available for its operations. In reality, however, the WEU was sidelined in most important instances, often reduced to a minor support role for NATO or other actors, and this led eventually to its demise.

NATO itself was also undergoing a process of transformation from a purely defensive alliance to a security organization with a broader remit. This had been powerfully demonstrated in the case of Bosnia and Herzegovina by its use of force, and by the subsequent deployment of IFOR/SFOR, the NATO-led peace-enforcement mission in that territory. There remained, however, significant transatlantic differences as to whether NATO operations might take place outside the context of a UN Security Council mandate.

The debate over the relationship between regional security and a universal system of collective security administered by the United Nations Security Council became especially pronounced in relation to the humanitarian intervention operation in Kosovo and the issue of final status. The provisions of Chapter VIII of the United Nations Charter, which require prior Security Council authorization for enforcement action by regional organizations or arrangements, had already been undermined by the earlier practice of the Economic Community of West African States (ECOWAS) in the case of Liberia and Sierra Leone, of the Southern African Development Community (SADC) in Lesotho and, to a lesser extent, of NATO in relation to Bosnia and Herzegovina, the latter being covered by a measure of Security Council authority.

During the first decade of the crisis, the Security Council distanced itself from exercising a lead role. Initially, member states were reluctant to involve the body in a dispute which seemed to have strong internal dimensions. Subsequently, more decisive action in the Council was blocked by Russia. The UN Security Council can only fulfil its pre-eminent role in relation to international peace and security if its members regard themselves, when voting in the Council, as agents of the international system as a whole, rather than as representatives of national interest. Of course, China and Russia are not the only states that, on occasion, fail to execute their functions in the Council in this way. However, Russia's determination to protect the FRY/Serbia from stronger Council action made the sidelining of the UN layer of collective security at the peak of the crisis almost inevitable. Belgrade could feel immune from the threat of tough economic sanctions. This made Milosevic even less inclined to accept the advice of Russian interlocutors and settle the conflict within a UN framework of weaker peace-keeping that would have offered opportunities for strong Russian involvement, as Moscow had intended. With no prospect of decisive action from the Council, and given the threat both in humanitarian terms and to the stability of the region, the only remaining option appeared to be the unilateral threat or use of force by NATO.

In the final phase of the crisis, the question of the pre-eminence of the Security Council arose again. A positive vote of the Council on the settlement package, including the recommendation of the Special Envoy, would have definitely resolved the issue of the status of Kosovo, even in the absence of consent by Belgrade. However, the opposite was not true. In general international law, statehood is not treated as being dependent on a grant of authority by the UN Security Council or other bodies. It could be declared without the need of a Council resolution and therefore outside of the controlling veto exercised by Russia. Unilateral action by Kosovo was possible, providing Prishtina was willing to risk a period of possible international isolation. Kosovo bought, however, a certain measure of international support by unilaterally accepting the Ahtisaari package, complete with a NATO backed military presence, even though it did not obtain UN sponsored universal recognition in return.

Overall, the entire episode reflects the international organizational transition undergone during the post-Cold War era. Institutions and mechanisms for the settlement of ethnic conflicts in Europe were only born in parallel with, or due to, the evolution of the conflict in Yugoslavia. By the time that these mechanisms were sufficiently effective to engage ethnic conflict, the crisis had deteriorated to an extend that diplomatic action alone was unable to resolve it. The attempt to link up the European regional dimension with the universal layer of legitimacy, the UN Security Council, through the means of the Contact Group was ultimately not successful. While Russia was willing to support common action to a certain point, ultimately, it was not willing to contribute to a posture that was sufficiently strong to persuade Belgrade to settle, both at Rambouillet and during the final settlement talks. This lack of unity transmitted itself to the Security Council, making action under the umbrella of the UN impossible. Nevertheless, the UN did exercise an important role in managing the period following on from the 1999 conflict, and in generating and sustaining the final status process under its umbrella, thus adding to its international credibility.

VII. Conference Diplomacy and Consent

It has been argued that international attempts to settle the Kosovo crisis occurred one step out of sync with developments on the ground. The EC/EU and other actors only engaged when the crisis had progressed to the point that the solution that was being proposed was no longer adequate.[29] If this is true, then it is also appropriate to say that Serbia's actions in relation to the crisis were not just one, but possibly two steps out of sync.

Had Serbia been willing to settle for a restoration of Kosovo's autonomy during the Carrington negotiations of the early 1990s, it might have been able to achieve such a result. Later, it might still have been possible to keep Kosovo within the remainder of the Yugoslav Federation by offering it the status of a republic. During the Hill negotiations, autonomy was still an option, although it would have had to have been balanced by a soft international presence in the territory. At Rambouillet, interim self-governance for Kosovo would have come with heavier, NATO-led implementation attached—in retrospect still a good deal for Belgrade, which lost all control over territory in consequence of the NATO air campaign. In fact, had Slobodan Milosevic been willing to accept the Rambouillet text, a rather different situation might have arisen. A NATO-led implementation force would have assumed effective control over the territory, while Belgrade continued to exercise important functions in relation to it. Such action by NATO would have underwritten the continued territorial unity of Serbia during the interim period which was not, in fact, necessarily restricted to three years—although this was perhaps not an enviable task in the longer term.

However, having rejected the Rambouillet agreement, and lost the war with NATO, a UN force replaced all Serbian authority in Kosovo. After the conflict, it was clear that there would no longer be universal international pressure for Kosovo to remain affiliated with Serbia. After all, Belgrade had nearly succeeded in forcibly removing close to a million ethnic Albanians from the territory, and internally displacing the rest. The UN civil administration, acting under a Chapter VII mandate of the Security Council, instead proceeded to build up institutions of self-governance in Kosovo. These institutions were also being prepared to assume the role of state institutions of Kosovo once the issue of final status was eventually resolved.

The Ahtisaari negotiations that followed presented Belgrade with an opportunity to rescue at least nominal affiliation with Kosovo, retaining its sovereign integrity on paper at least (the 'Taiwan solution'). However, from beginning to end, Belgrade offered only autonomy—a concept that was universally known to be unacceptable to the Kosovo Albanians in view of their previous experience

---

[29] This argument is made in Marc Weller, *Peace Lost: The Failure of Conflict Prevention in Kosovo* (Dordrecht: Martinus Nijhoff, 2008).

with it. While the offer of autonomy would, it was claimed, be very far-reaching, Belgrade somewhat oscillated in its proposals even in the crucial final phase of the Ischinger talks. At times, it claimed to be prepared to consider even a confederal solution, while at other times it referred to the Kosovo Albanians as one minority within Serbia along many others. This undermined the credibility of the Serbian position.

The Vienna negotiations themselves, according to an agreement with Belgrade, focused mainly on retaining control over parts of Kosovo through enhanced decentralization and the assignment of areas beyond Kosovo's control for reasons of historical and religious importance to Belgrade.

As the negotiations did not address any specific status or form of loose autonomy, it was left to a separate recommendation of UN Special Envoy Ahtisaari to raise that issue. However, his recommendation of supervised independence was not taken up in the Security Council. In addition to the threat of a Russian and perhaps a Chinese veto, several other states were also hesitant. Not only was it feared that endorsement of independence might generate an unhelpful precedent for the future, but there was concern for what was seen as disregard for the rule of consent in international relations. To impose such a dramatic result on Belgrade by virtue of a Chapter VII resolution would have been an important innovation in UN practice. While it could be argued that the Council could have acted in response to the genuine threat to regional peace and stability in Europe, this would have been a very major development in its practice. For, in addition to re-evaluating the relationship between self-determination and territorial unity, the Council would also have had to act inconsistently with a further classical, structural principle of international order: that of state consent.

To recall, classically, a state cannot be forced even to accept external settlement of a dispute, for instance through an international court, without its consent. It would be more radical still to propose the imposition of the substance of a settlement without the consent of the relevant state, especially where a dispute involving the territorial definition of that state is concerned. States represented in the UN Security Council were simply not prepared to take such a novel step.

A Chapter VII decision confirming or granting independence in this instance would not only have had legal effects in relation to Serbia, but would have clarified *erga omnes*—that is, in relation to all states—that Kosovo was a sovereign state. This would not have meant automatic membership in all international organizations and worldwide diplomatic relations for Kosovo, but its entitlement to be treated as a state and to invoke the fundamental rights of states would have been put beyond question.

However, even if the majority of states on the Security Council had been willing, in principle, to assign to that body the international constitutional function of deciding a self-determination dispute and determining or confirming status, in this instance the mechanisms would have failed due to the Russian veto. In one sense, this attitude of Russia and, indeed, of Serbia, was quite counterproductive.

For having blocked a role for the Security Council in the matter, they precluded a firm international grounding of important legal obligations incumbent upon Kosovo.

It was foreseen that Kosovo's acceptance of the Ahtisaari Comprehensive Proposal would be reinforced by a Security Council decision under Chapter VII. In that case, the original limitations on Kosovo's sovereignty would have been anchored very firmly in the international legal order. These limitations would have related to a possible future merger between Kosovo and a neighbouring state, minority rights provisions and other elements of the Ahtisaari package. As it stands now, these obligations have been enshrined in a self-limiting act contained in Kosovo's Declaration of Independence. While it is, in practice, highly unlikely that Kosovo will disown these commitments, they are legally less firmly established than they would have been under a Chapter VII resolution. Moreover, the implementation or enforcement of these commitments is subject to some legal ambiguity.

VIII. Outlook

The Kosovo episode is far from concluded. The northern part of the territory remains under separate, de facto control by Serbia. The UN and other agencies enjoy only very limited access there. Other, mainly ethnically Serb inhabited municipalities are also attempting to retain a system of parallel administration supported and funded from Belgrade. It remains unlikely that at least Northern Kosovo will be integrated with the rest of the territory in the near future. Instead, the prospect of a division of the territory is being raised on occasion. Such a step would lead the organized international community back to its very first actions in relation the Yugoslav crisis. While it accepted that independence would be possible for republics that wished it, it insisted that they retain their existing territorial definition. There was a strong rejection of the proposal instead to redraw boundaries according to ethnic appurtenance. This view appeared outmoded and repulsive in the integrated Europe that has been striving to generate a system of governance based on equal rights and the positive acknowledgement of diversity. Division along ethnic lines would reopen the question of the boundaries of Bosnia and Herzegovina (or, indeed, the question of its existence as a state) and of Macedonia.

While the Kosovo episode may have contributed to a modest strengthening of the claims of territorial units for self-determination, the further extension of this principle to self-determination to ethnic groups would indeed herald the beginning of a post-modern fragmentation of the state system that has thus far been avoided. If further conflict is to be averted, the lesson from the Kosovo episode must surely be that early engagement is required, before the one or other actor adds to the spiral of escalation and makes a balanced settlement impossible. Thus far, the organized international community has found it difficult to engage with the issue of Northern Kosovo—an issue that, incidentally, was also left virtually unaddressed in the Ahtisaari Comprehensive Proposal.

There is, however, some reason for hope. A very significant number of settlements of previously irresolvable self-determination conflicts have been achieved through innovative mechanisms in other regions. Increasingly, self-determination conflicts are no longer seen as an all-or-nothing game that can only result in either defeat of the secessionists or secession. A wide-ranging menu of settlement options has become available. The challenge remains to bring these to bear in a timely way, before unilateral action results in facts on the ground that can no longer be reversed, as Russia has recently demonstrated.

Beyond this lesson, what does the international administration of the Kosovo crisis tell us about the present state of the international system? Are we regressing into the old, classical world of real politics administered through the actions or conferences dominated by the great powers and by their threat or use of force? In this instance, some of the instruments of classical politics were indeed applied. However, the aim of such action was focused on the application of modern or post-modern values, such as the maintenance of human rights. Nevertheless, the unilateral enforcement of such values lessened the credibility of the international system of collective security. Russia is now pointing to its own interpretation of these values and has forcibly implemented it.

This does not mean, however, that the international action on Kosovo, when it finally came, was misplaced. It would be wrong to blame the purported demise of the UN Security Council, or of the stability of state borders, or Russia's use of force, on the Kosovo precedent. Rather, these developments reinforce the necessity to ensure that the international standards are sufficiently clear to permit a clear distinction between action that can be taken lawfully, even when collective security fails, on the one hand, and action that transgresses against the universal constitutional order on the other. The ability to make such distinctions will remain highly relevant in the increasingly fragmented and complex world in which we now find ourselves.

Bibliography

Adam, Bernard, *La guerre du Kosovo* (Paris: Complexe, 1999).

Ahrens, Geert, *Diplomacy on the Edge* (Baltimore, MA: John Hopkins University Press, 2007).

Akehurst, Michael, 'The Hierarchy of the Sources in International Law', *British Yearbook of International Law*, 47 (1974–5), 273–85.

Alfons, Michael, 'Of Standards and Status. The Role of the European Union in Kosovo: From UNSCR 1244 to the Future Status Talks', *Südosteuropa*, 54 (2006), 339–79.

Ali, Tariq, *Masters of the Universe? NATO's Balkan Crusade* (New York: Verso, 2000).

Altmann, Franz-Lothar, 'Kosovo 2005/06: Phased Independence?', *SWP Comments* (2005).

Amnesty International, *Kosovo: The Evidence* (London: Amnesty International, 1998).

Annan, Kofi A., 'Two Concepts of Sovereignty', *The Economist*, 18 September 1999.

Aspen Institute Berlin/Carnegie Endowment for International Peace, *Unfinished Peace, Report of the International Commission on the Balkans* (Washington: The Brookings Institution Press, 1996).

Abrahams, Fred, and Elizabeth Andersen, *Humanitarian Law Violations in Kosovo* (New York: Human Rights Watch, 1998).

Albright, Madeleine, *Madam Secretary: A Memoir* (London, Basingstoke, Oxford: Pan Books, 2004).

Auerswald, David P., and Phillip E. Auerswald (eds), *The Kosovo Conflict: A Diplomatic History Through Documents* (The Hague: Kluwer Law International, 2000).

Axt, Heinz-Jürgen, 'Internationale Implikationen des Kosovo-Krieges: wertorientierte Realpolitik statt Konfliktbearbeitung in Institutionen', *Südosteuropa*, 49 (2000), 68–87.

Bacevich, Andrew J., and Eliot A. Cohen (eds), *War over Kosovo: Politics and Strategy in a Global Age* (New York: Columbia University Press, 2001).

Baggett, Ted, 'Human Rights Abuses in Yugoslavia: To Bring an End to Political Oppression, the International Community Should Assist in Establishing an Independent Kosovo', *Georgia Journal of International & Comparative Law*, 27 (1999), 457–76.

Baldwin, Clive, 'Minority Rights in Kosovo under International Rule', Minority *Rights Group International Report* (2006), available at <http://www.minorityrights.org/download.php?id=158>

Banac, Ivo, *The National Question in Yugoslavia: Origins, History, Politics* (Ithaca: Cornell University Press, 1988).

Bandow, Doug, 'NATO's Hypocritical Humanitarianism', in Ted Galen Carpenter (ed.), *NATO's Empty Victory: A Postmortem on the Balkan War* (Washington DC: CATO Institute, 2000), 31–47.

Barnett, Neill, and Jeta Xharra, 'Decision Time: Will 2007 See a Verdict on Kosovo's Future?', *Jane's Intelligence Review*, 19 (2007), 28–35.

Bartkus, Viva Ona, *The Dynamic of Secession* (Cambridge: Cambridge University Press, 1999).

Basta, Lidija R. (ed.), *Constitutional Prerequisites for a Democratic Serbia* (Institute of Federalism, Etudes et colloques, 1998).

Batt, Judy, 'The Question of Serbia', *EU-ISS Chaillot Paper*, no. 81 (Institute for Security Studies, Paris, 2005).

Bedjaoui, Mohammed, *The New World Order and the Security Council: Testing the Legality of its Acts* (Dordrecht: Martinus Nijhoff, 1994).

Bejaski, Janusz, *Achieving a Final Status Settlement for Kosovo* (Washington: Center for Strategic and International Studies, 2003).

Belgrade Centre for Human Rights, *Human Rights in Yugoslavia 1999* (Belgrade: Belgrade Centre for Human Rights, 2000).

Bellamy, Alex J., *Kosovo and International Society* (New York: Palgrave, 2002).

Bellocchi, Luke P., 'Recent Developments: Self-determination in the Case of Chechnya', *Buffalo Journal of International Law*, 2 (1995), 183–91.

Bennett, Christopher, *Yugoslavia's Bloody Collapse: Causes, Course and Consequences* (London: Hurst, 1995).

Beran, Harry, 'A Liberal Theory of Secession', *Political Studies*, 32 (1984), 21–31.

Berman, Nathaniel, 'Sovereignty in Abeyance: Self-determination and International Law', *Wisconsin International Law Journal*, 7 (1988), 51–105.

Bethlehem, Daniel, and Marc Weller (eds), *The 'Yugoslav' Crisis in International Law: General Issues* (Cambridge: Grotius, CUP, 1997).

Bieber, Florian, and Židas Daskalovski (eds), *Understanding the War in Kosovo* (London and Portland: Frank Cass, 2003).

Bildt, Carl, *Peace Journey: The Struggle for Peace in Bosnia* (London: Weidenfeld and Nicolson, 1998). [Originally published in Swedish under the title *Uppdrag Fred* (Norstedts, 1997).]

Blair, Stephanie A., *Weaving the Strands of the Rope: A Comprehensive Approach to Building Peace in Kosovo* (Halifax: Centre for Foreign Policy Studies, Dalhousie University, 2002).

Blay, Sam K.N., 'Self-determination: A Reassessment in the Post-Communist Era', *Denver Journal of International Law and Policy*, 22 (1994), 275–315.

Blockmans, Steven, 'Moving into UNchartered [sic] Waters: an Emerging Right of Unilateral Humanitarian Intervention?', *Leiden Journal of International Law*, 12 (1999), 759–86.

Bodin, Jean, *Six livres de la République* (Paris, 1576).

Booth, Ken (ed.), *The Kosovo Tragedy: The Human Rights Dimensions* (London, Portland: Frank Cass, 2001).

Bozzo, Luciano, and Carlo Simon-Belli, *The Kosovo Quagmire: Conflict Scenarios and Methods for Resolution* (Milan: F. Angeli, 2000).

Brilmayer, Lea, 'Secession and Self-determination: A Territorial Interpretation', *Yale Journal of International Law*, 16 (1991), 177–202.

Brownlie, Ian, 'Humanitarian Intervention', in John Norton Moore (ed.), *Law and Civil War in the Modern World* (Baltimore: John Hopkins University Press, 1974).

—— and C.J. Apperley, 'Kosovo Crisis Inquiry: Memorandum on the International Law Aspects', *International and Comparative Law Quarterly*, 49 (2000), 878–905.

Bruha, Thomas, 'The Kosovo War before the International Court of Justice—A Preliminary Appraisal', in Christian Tomuschat (ed.), *Kosovo and the International Community: A Legal Assessment* (The Hague, London, New York: Martinus Nijhoff Publishers, 2002), 287–316.

Brunner, Georg, 'Völkerrecht und Selbstbestimmungsrecht in Kosovo', in Jens Reuter and Konrad Clewing (eds), *Der Kosovo Konflikt. Ursachen, Verlauf, Perspektiven* (Klagenfurt: Wieser-Verlag, 2000), 117–35.

Buchheit, Lee C., *Secession: The Legitimacy of Self-determination* (New Haven, CT: Yale University Press, 1978).

Buckley, Mary, and Sally N. Cummings (eds), *Kosovo: Perceptions of War and Its Aftermath* (London, New York: Continuum, 2001).

Buckley, William Joseph (ed.), *Kosovo: Contending Voices on Balkan Interventions* (Grand Rapids, Michigan, Cambridge, UK: William B. Eerdmans Publishing, 2000).

Bugajski, Janusz, R. Bruce Hitchner, and Paul Williams, *Achieving a Final Status Settlement for Kosovo* (Washington: Center for Strategic and International Studies, 2003).

Burger, James A., 'International Humanitarian Law and the Kosovo Crisis: Lessons Learned or to be Learned', *International Review of the Red Cross*, 837 (2000), 129–45.

Büschenfeld, Herbert, *Kosovo—Nationalitätenkonflikt im Armenhaus Jugoslawiens* (Cologne: Aulis Verlag Deubner, 1991).

Byman, Daniel L., and Matthew C. Waxman, 'Kosovo and the Great Air Power Debate', *International Security*, 24(4) (2000), 5–38.

Calic, Marie-Janine, *Kosovo Policy Study. A Three-Step Approach to Conflict Prevention in Kosovo* (Ebenhausen: Stiftung Wissenschaft und Politik, 1997).

Campbell, Greg, *The Road to Kosovo: A Balkan Diary* (Boulder: Westview Press, 1999).

Caplan, Richard, *A New Trusteeship? The International Administration of War-torn Territories*, Adelphi Paper 341 (Oxford University Press for International Institute for Strategic Studies, 2002).

—— 'International Diplomacy and the Crisis in Kosovo', *International Affairs*, 74 (1998), 745–61.

Carpenter, Ted Galen (ed.), *NATO's Empty Victory: A Postmortem on the Balkan War* (Washington DC: CATO Institute, 2000).

Cass, Deborah Z., 'Rethinking Self-determination: A Critical Analysis of Current International Law Theories', *Syracuse Journal of International Law and Commerce*, 18 (1992), 21–40.

Cassese, Antonio, 'Ex Injuria Ius Oritur: Are We Moving Towards International Legitimation of Forcible Humanitarian Counter-Measures in the World Community?', *European Journal of International Law*, 10(23) (1999), 23–30.

Chandler, David, *From Kosovo to Kabul: Human Rights and International Intervention* (London, Sterling, Va.: Pluto Press, 2002).

Chesterman, Simon, 'Building Democracy through Benevolent Autocracy: Consultation and Accountability in UN Transitional Administrations', in Edward Newman (ed.) *The UN Role in Promoting Democracy: Between Ideals and Reality* (Tokyo: United Nations University Press, 2004), 86–112.

—— *Just War or Just Peace? Humanitarian Intervention and International Law* (Oxford: Oxford University Press, 2001).

——*Kosovo in Limbo: State-Building and 'Substantial Autonomy'* (New York: International Peace Academy, 2001).

Chiclet, Christophe, and Bernard Ravenel, *Kosovo: le piège. Les cahiers de Confluences* (Paris: Harmattan, 2000).

Chomsky, Noam, *The New Military Humanism: Lessons from Kosovo* (London: Pluto Press, 1999).

Clark, Howard, *Civil Resistance in Kosovo* (London and Sterling: Pluto Press, 2000).

Clinton, Bill, *My Life* (New York: Vintage Books, 2005).

Cockell, John C., 'Civil-Military Responses to Security Challenges in Peace Operations: Ten Lessons from Kosovo', *Global Governance*, 8 (2002), 483–502.

Cohen, Lenard J., *Broken Bonds: Yugoslavia's Disintegration and Balkan Politics in Transition* (Colorado, Oxford: Westview, 1993).

Corrin, Chris, 'Developing Democracy in Kosova. From Grassroots to Government', *Parliamentary Affairs*, 55 (2002), 99–108.

Corten, Olivier, and Barbara Delcourt, *Droit, legitimation et politique exterieure: l'Europe et la guerre du Kosovo* (Brussels: Bruylant, 2001).

Colombus, Frank (ed.), *Kosovo-Serbia: A Just War?* (Commack: Nova Science, 1999).

Craven, Matthew, 'The European Community Arbitration Commission on Yugoslavia', *British Yearbook of International Law*, 66 (1995), 333–411.

Crawford, James, 'State Practice and International Law in Relation to Secession', *The British Yearbook of International Law*, 69 (1998), 85–117.

Crawford, Timothy W., 'Pivotal Deterrence and the Kosovo War. Why the Holbrooke Agreement Failed', *Political Science Quarterly*, 116 (2002), 499–523.

Currie, John, 'NATO's Humanitarian Intervention in Kosovo: Making or Breaking International Law', *Canadian Yearbook of International Law*, 36 (1998), 303–33.

Czaplinski, Wladyslaw, 'The Activities of the OSCE in Kosovo', in Christian Tomuschat (ed.), *Kosovo and the International Community: A Legal Assessment* (The Hague, London, New York: Martinus Nijhoff Publishers, 2002), 37–44.

Daalder, Ivo H., and Michael E. O'Hanlon, *Winning Ugly: NATO's War to Save Kosovo* (Washington: Brookings Institution Press, 2000).

Danilov, D.A., Arkadii Moses, and Timofei Viacheslavovich Bordachev, *Kosovskii krisis: novye evropeiskie realii* (Moscow: Institut Evropy RAN, 1999).

Daskalovski, Židas, 'Claims to Kosovo: Nationalism and Self-Determination', in Florian Bieber and Židas Daskalovski (eds), *Understanding the War in Kosovo* (London and Portland: Frank Cass, 2003), 13–30.

Dauphinee, Elizabeth Allen, 'Rambouillet: A Critical (Re)Assessment', in Florian Bieber and Židas Daskalovski (eds), *Understanding the War in Kosovo* (London and Portland: Frank Cass, 2003), 101–21.

Decaux, Emmanuel, 'La Conférence de Rambouillet: Négociation de la dernière chance ou contrainte illicite?', in Christian Tomuschat (ed.), *Kosovo and the International Community: A Legal Assessment* (The Hague, London, New York: Martinus Nijhoff Publishers, 2002), 45–64.

Detrez, Raymond, *Kosovo, de uitgestelde oorlog* (2nd edn, Antwerp: Houtekiet, 1999).

Dimitrijević, Vojin, 'The 1974 Constitution as a Factor in the Collapse of Yugoslavia or as a Sign of Decaying Totalitarianism', in Nebojša Popov (ed.), *The Road to War in Serbia:*

Trauma and Catharsis (Budapest: Central European University Press, 2000). [First published in Serbian as *Srpska strana rata* (Republika, Belgrade, 1996).]

Duijzings, Ger, Dusan Janic, and Shkelzen Maliqi (eds), *Kosovo-Kosova: Confrontation or Coexistence* (Nijmegen: Peace Research Centre, University of Nijmegen, 1997).

Dujak, Sabina, 'Politische und rechtliche Argumentationslinien der serbischen/jugoslawischen Führung', in Joseph Marko (ed.), *Gordischer Knoten Kosovo/a: Durchschlagen oder entwirren?* Schriftenreihe der Europäischen Akademie Bozen, Bereich 'Ethnische Minderheiten und regionale Autonomien', 3 (Baden-Baden: Nomos, 1999), 47–55.

Egan, Patrick T., *Kosovo Intervention and Collective Self-Defence* (London: Frank Cass, 2001).

Ehrhart, Hans-Georg, and Albrecht Schnabel (eds), *The Southeast European Challenge: Ethnic Conflict and the International Response* (Baden-Baden: Nomos, 1999).

Eldridge, Justin L.C., *Kosovo: Land of Uncertainty* (London: Frank Cass, 2001).

Elsie, Robert, *Kosovo: In the Heart of the Powder Keg* (New York: Columbia University Press, 1997).

European Action Council for Peace in the Balkans/Public International Law and Policy Group of the Carnegie Endowment for International Peace, *Kosovo: From Crisis to a Permanent Solution* (Amsterdam: European Action Council for Peace in the Balkans, 1997).

Everts, Daan W., 'The OSCE Mission in Kosovo', in Institute for Peace Research and Security Policy at the University of Hamburg (ed.), *OSCE Yearbook 2001* (Baden-Baden: Nomos, 2002), 137–48.

—— 'The OSCE Mission in Kosovo—Two Years into Institution-building', *Helsinki Monitor*, 12 (2001), 245–56.

Falk, Richard A., 'Kosovo, World Order, and the Future of International Law', *American Journal of International Law*, 93 (1999), 847–57.

Federal Republic of Yugoslavia, *Proposed Programme of the Federal Government for Resolving Problems in the Area of the Education and Culture of the Albanian Minority in Kosovo and Metohija* (Belgrade: Federal Republic of Yugoslavia, 1992).

Felgenhauer, Pavel, 'The Tactics and Strategic Goals of Russia's Stand on the Independence of Kosovo (ARI)', *Analyses of the Royal Institute*, 125 (November 2007), available at <http://www.realinstitutoelcano.org/analisis/ARI2007/ARI125–2007_Felgenhauer_Kosovo_Russia.pdf>.

Felix, Antonia, *Wesley K. Clark: A Biography* (New York: Newmarket Press, 2004).

Fischer, Joschka, *Die rot-grünen Jahre: Deutsche Außenpolitik—vom Kosovo bis zum 11. September* (Cologne: Verlag Kiepenheuer & Witsch, 2007).

Fox, Gregory H., and Brad R. Roth (eds), *Democratic Governance and International Law* (Cambridge: Cambridge University Press, 2000).

Franck, Thomas M., 'Lessons of Kosovo', *American Journal of International Law*, 93 (1999), 857–60.

—— 'The Emerging Right to Democratic Governance', *American Journal of International Law*, 86 (1992), 46–91.

Friis, Lykke, and Anna Murphy, 'Negotiating in a Time of Crisis: The EU's Response to the Military Conflict in Kosovo', EUI Working Papers, RSC 2000/20 (European University Institute, May 2000). Available at <http://www.iue.it/RSCAS/WP-Texts/00_20.pdf>.

Gardner, Hall, Elinore Schaffer, and Oleg Kobtzeff (eds), *Central and Southeastern Europe in Transition: Perspectives on Success and Failure Since 1989* (Westport and London: Praeger, 2000).

Gazzini, Tarcisio, 'NATO Coercive Military Activities in the Yugoslav Crisis (1992–1999)', *European Journal of International Law*, 12 (2001), 391–436.

—— 'Considerations on the Conflict in Chechnya', *Human Rights Law Journal*, 17 (1996), 93–105.

Ghai, Yash (ed.), *Autonomy and Ethnicity: Negotiating Competing Claims in Multi-ethnic States* (Cambridge: Cambridge University Press, 2000).

Gießmann, Hans J., 'Aus der Traum! Der Krieg auf dem Balkan und das Versagen der NATO', *WeltTrends*, 22 (1999), 113–18.

Glamotchak, Marina, and Diane Masson, 'Kosovo: le débat du statut', *Politique étrangère*, 70 (2006), 147–58.

Glennon, Michael J., *Limits of Law, Prerogatives of Power: Interventionism after Kosovo* (New York and Basingstoke: Palgrave, 2001).

Glenny, Misha, *The Fall of Yugoslavia* (2nd edn, London: Penguin Books, 1993).

Greenwood, Christopher, 'Humanitarian Intervention: The Case of Kosovo', *Finnish Yearbook of International Law*, 10 (1999), 141–76.

Gross, Leo, 'The Peace of Westphalia, 1648–1948', *American Journal of International Law*, 42(1) (1948), 20–41.

Grossi, Rafel Marianao, *Kosovo: los límites del intervencionismo humanitario*, Colección Estudios internacionales (Buenos Aires: Galerno, 2000).

Guichard, Catherine, 'International Law and the War in Kosovo', *Survival*, 41 (1999), 19–34.

Hajrullahu, Arben, *Langfristiger Frieden am Westbalkan durch EU-Integration. Der EU-Integrationsprozess als Chance für die Überwindung des serbisch-kosovarischen Konfliktes* (Baden-Baden: Nomos, 2007).

Harris, David J., *Cases and Materials on International Law* (5th edn, London: Sweet and Maxwell, 1998).

Hasani, Enver, *Dissolution of Yugoslavia and the Case of Kosova. Political and Legal Aspects* (Tirana: Albanian Institute for International Studies, 2000).

Hayden, Robert M., *Blueprints for a House Divided: The Constitutional Logic of the Yugoslav Conflict* (Ann Arbor: University of Michigan Press, 1999).

Heintze, Hans-Joachim, 'Die völkerrechtliche Verantwortlichkeit der Föderativen Republik Jugoslawien und die Massenflucht aus dem Kosovo', *Association for the Study of the World Refugee Problem Bulletin*, 37 (1999), 9–15.

—— 'Überlegungen zur Lösung des Kosovo-Problems aus der Sicht des Völkerrechts. Möglichkeiten und Grenzen der Gewährung von Autonomie', in Günther Bächler, Reiner Steinweg, and Arno Truger (eds), *Friedenbericht 1995* (Zürich: Rügger, Chur, 1995), 236–47.

Helsinki Committee for Human Rights in Serbia, *Kosovo: Law and Politics: Kosovo in Normative Acts Before and After 1974* (Helsinki Committee for Human Rights in Serbia, 1998).

Heraclides, Alexis, 'Ethnonationalist and Separatist Conflict Settlement in Kosovo', in Thanos Veremis and Evangelos Kofos (eds), *Kosovo: Avoiding another Balkan war* (Athens: Hellenic Foundation for European and Foreign Policy, 1998), 389–443.

—— 'The Kosovo Conflict and its Resolution: In Pursuit of Ariadne's Thread', *Security Dialogue*, 28 (1997), 317–31.

Herring, Eric, 'From Rambouillet to the Kosovo Accords: NATO's War against Serbia and Its Aftermath', in Ken Booth, *The Kosovo Tragedy: The Human Rights Dimensions* (London: Frank Cass, 2001).

Hibbert, Reginald, 'The Kosovo Question: Origins, Present Complications and Prospects', David Davies Memorial Institute of International Studies, Occasional Paper 11 (1999).

Hilpold, Peter, 'Humanitarian Intervention: Is there a Need for a Legal Reappraisal?', *European Journal of International Law*, 12 (2001), 437–68.

—— 'Sezession und humanitäre Intervention—völkerrechtliche Instrumente zur Bewältigung innerstaatliche Konflikte?', *Austrian Journal of Public and International Law*, 54 (1999), 529–602.

Hosmer, Stephen T., *The Conflict over Kosovo: Why Milosevic Decided to Settle When He Did* (Santa Monica, Arlington, Pittsburgh: RAND, 2001).

Hoxhaj, Enver, 'The Politics of Ethnic Conflict Regulation in Kosovo', LSE Centre for the Study of Global Governance, Discussion Paper 39 (2005), available at <http://www.lse.ac.uk/Depts/global/Publications/DiscussionPapers/DP39.pdf>.

Hubrecht, Joël, *Kosovo 1981–1989, 1999–2001: établir les faits* (Paris: Esprit, 2001).

Human Rights Watch, *Open Wounds: Human Rights Abuses in Kosovo* (New York: Human Rights Watch, 1993).

Independent International Commission on Kosovo, *The Kosovo Report: Conflict-International Response—Lessons Learned* (Oxford: Oxford University Press, 2000).

—— *Why Conditional Independence? The Follow-up of the Kosovo Report* (Stockholm: Global Reporting Books, 2001).

Institute of History. Academy of Sciences of the Republic of Albania, *The Truth on Kosova* (Tirana: Encyclopaedia Publishing House, 1993).

International Commission for the Balkans, *The Balkans in Europe's Future* (Sofia: Centre for Liberal Strategies, 2005), available at <http://www.balkan-commission.org/activities/Report.pdf>.

International Crisis Group, 'Kosovo Countdown: A Blueprint for Transition', International Crisis Group Europe Report (December 2007), available at <http://www.crisisgroup.org/home/index.cfm?id=5201&l=1>.

—— 'Kosovo: No Good Alternatives to the Ahtisaari Plan', International Crisis Group Europe Report (May 2007), available at <http://www.crisisgroup.org/home/index.cfm?id=4830&l=1>.

—— 'Kosovo Status: Delay is Risky', International Crisis Group Europe Report (November 2006), available at <http://www.crisisgroup.org/home/index.cfm?id=4497&l=1>.

—— 'Kosovo Status: Difficult Months Ahead', International Crisis Group Europe Briefing (December 2006), available at <http://www.crisisgroup.org/home/index.cfm?id=4585&l=1>.

—— 'Kosovo: Toward Final Status', International Crisis Group Europe Report (January 2005), available at <http://www.crisisgroup.org/library/documents/europe/balkans/161_kosovo_toward_final_status.pdf>.

—— 'Reality Demands: Documenting Violations of International Humanitarian Law in Kosovo 1999', International Crisis Group Europe Report (June 2000), available at <http://www.crisisgroup.org/home/getfile.cfm?id=542&tid=1865&type=pdf&l=1>.

International Helsinki Federation for Human Rights, *From Autonomy to Colonization: Human Rights in Kosovo 1989–1993* (Vienna: International Helsinki Federation for Human Rights, 1993).

—— *Human Rights in the OSCE Region: Europe, Central Asia and North America (Events of 2006)* (Vienna: International Helsinki Federation for Human Rights, 2007).

Ipsen, Knut, 'Der Kosovo-Einsatz—Illegal? Gerechtfertigt? Entschuldbar?', in Dieter S. Lutz (ed.), *Der Kosovo-Krieg—Rechtliche und rechtsethische Aspekte (Demokratie, Sicherheit, Frieden, 127)* (Baden-Baden: Nomos, 2000), 101–5.

Islami, Hivzi, *Demographic Reality in Kosova* (Prishtina: Academy of Sciences and Arts in Kosova, Kosova Information Center, 1994).

Ismajli, Rexhep, *Kosova and the Albanians in former Yugoslavia* (Prishtina: Academy of Sciences and Arts in Kosova, Kosova Information Center, 1994).

Jahn, Egbert, 'Nie wieder Krieg! Nie wieder Völkermord!' Der Kosovo-Problem als europäisches Problem', Working Paper 14 (Mannheimer Zentrum für Europäische Sozialforschung, 2000), available at <http://www.mzes.uni-mannheim.de/publications/wp/wp-14.pdf>.

James, Alan, 'The Concept of Sovereignty Revisited', in Albrecht Schnabel and Ramesh Thakur, *Kosovo and the Challenge of Humanitarian Intervention* (New York: UN University Press, 2000).

Janjic, Dusan, and S. Maligi (eds), *Conflict or Dialogue: Serbian-Albanian Relations and Integration of the Balkans—Studies and Essays* (Subotica: Open University, 1994).

Janning, Josef, and Martin Brusis (eds), *Exploring Futures for Kosovo: Kosovo Albanians and Serbs in Dialogue—Project Report* (Munich: Research Group on European Affairs, 1997).

Jatras, James George, 'NATO's Myths and Bogus Justifications for Intervention', in Ted Galen Carpenter (ed.), *NATO's Empty Victory: A Postmortem on the Balkan War* (Washington D.C.: CATO Institute, 2000), 21–9.

Jelavich, Barbara, *History of the Balkans: Twentieth Century*, II (Cambridge: Cambridge University Press, 1983).

Jerkovic, Nebojsa (ed.), *Kosovo and Metohija: An Integral Part of the Republic of Serbia and FR of Yugoslavia. Documents and Facts* (Belgrade: Review of International Affairs, 1995).

Joskimovich, Vojin, *Kosovo Crisis: a Study in Foreign Policy Mismanagement* (Los Angeles: Graphics Management Press, 1999).

Joyner, Daniel H., 'The Kosovo Intervention: Legal Analysis and a More Persuasive Paradigm', *European Journal of International Law*, 13 (2002), 597–619.

Judah, Tim, *Kosovo: War and Revenge* (2nd edn, New Haven and London: Yale University Press, 2002).

—— 'Kosovo's Moment of Truth', *Survival*, 46 (2006), 73–83.

—— 'Kosovo's Road to War', *Survival*, 41(2) (Summer 1999), 5–18.

—— 'The Growing Pains of the Kosovo Liberation Army', in Michael Waller, Kyril Drezov, and Bülent Gökay (eds), *Kosovo: The Politics of Delusion* (London and Portland: Frank Cass, 2001), 20–4.

—— *The Serbs: History, Myth and the Destruction of Yugoslavia* (New Haven and London: Yale University Press, 1997).

Jurekovic, Predrag, 'Die serbische Kosovopolitik im Lichte der ungelösten Statusfrage', *Europäische Sicherheit*, 54 (2005), 12–15.

Karakostanoglou, Veniamin, 'The Ethnic Conflict in Kosovo: A Test Case for International Borders?', in Heinz-Jürgen Axt (ed.), *Beiträge zur Stabilisierung Südosteuropas aus deutscher und griechischer Sicht. Ergebnisse der deutsch-griechischen Konferenz der Südosteuropa-Gesellschaft und des Institute for Balkan Studies, Thessaloniki vom 26. bis 28. September 1994 in Berlin*, Südosteuropa Aktuell 20 (Munich: Südosteuropa-Gesellschaft, 1995), 152–63.

Kaser, Karl, 'Die Verhandlungen in Rambouillet und Paris: die Fragen der Souveränität Jugoslawiens und der Unabhängigkeit für Kosovo', *Südosteuropa*, 49 (2000), 51–67.

Kemp, Walter A. (ed.), *Quiet Diplomacy in Action: The OSCE High Commissioner on National Minorities* (The Hague, London, Boston: Kluwer Law International, 2001).

King, Iain, and Whit Mason, *Peace at Any Price. How the World Failed Kosovo* (Ithaca: Cornell University Press, 2006).

Kohen, Marcello G. (ed.), *Secession* (Cambridge: Cambridge University Press, 2006).

Kohl, Christine von and Wolfgang Libal, *Kosovo—Gordischer Knoten des Balkan* (Vienna, Zürich: Europaverlag, 1992).

Koji, Teraya, 'Emerging Hierarchy in International Human Rights and Beyond: From the Perspective of Non-derogable Rights', *European Journal of International Law*, 12(5) (2001), 917–41.

Kokott, Juliane, 'The Development of the Human Rights Situation in Kosovo 1989–1999', in Christian Tomuschat (ed.), *Kosovo and the International Community: A Legal Assessment* (The Hague, London, New York: Martinus Nijhoff Publishers, 2002), 1–35.

Kokkalis Foundation, *NATO and Southeastern Europe: Security Issues for the Early 21st Century. A Joint Conference Report by The Kokkalis Foundation and The Institute for Foreign Policy Analysis* (Athens, Greece and Cambridge, Massachusetts: Kokkalis Foundation and Institute for Foreign Policy Analysis, 1999).

Kola, Paulin, 'Albania, its Isolation and the Albanian National Question, with Particular Emphasis on Kosova, 1941–1992', Ph.D. thesis, on file at the London School of Economics (2000).

Korovilas, James P., 'The Economic Sustainability of Post-conflict Kosovo', *Post-Communist Economies*, 14 (2002), 109–21.

Koskinen, Pirkko K., *Kosovon paikka: Balkanilla, historiassa ja tulevaisuudessa* (Helsinki: WSOY, 2000).

Kosovo Institute for Policy Research and Development, 'Analysis of the Comprehensive Package for the Status of Kosovo', KIPRED Policy Brief No. 5 (February 2007), available at <http://www.kipred.net/site/documents/Analysis_of_the_Comprehensive_Package_for_the_Status_of_Kosovo.pdf>.

—— 'Kosovo Future Status Process Knowledge–Attitudes–Practices (KAP) Survey', KIPRED Occasional Paper (July 2006), available at <http://www.kipred.net/site/documents/Kosovo_Future_Status_Process_Knowledge_Attitudes_Practices.pdf>.

—— 'Kosovo: The Unprecedented State', KIPRED Policy Brief No. 6 (July 2007), available at <http://www.kipred.net/site/documents/Kosovo%20The%20Unprecedented%20State%20.pdf>.

Kostovicova, Denisa, *Kosovo: The Politics of Identity and Space* (London: Routledge, 2005).

—— 'Parallel Worlds: Response of Kosovo Albanians to Loss of Autonomy in Serbia', Keele European Centre Research Papers, Southeast Europe Series 2 (Keele European Research Centre, 1997).

—— and Bülent Gökay, *Kosovo: Myths, Conflict, War* (Keele European Research Centre, 1999).

Krause, Joachim (ed.), *Kosovo: humanitäre Intervention und kooperative Sicherheit in Europa* (Opladen: Leske and Budrich, 2000).

Krieger, Heike (ed.), *The Kosovo Conflict and International Law: An Analytical Documentation 1974–1999* (Cambridge: Cambridge University Press, 2001).

Krisch, Nico, 'Legality, Morality, and the Dilemma of Humanitarian Intervention after Kosovo', *European Journal of International Law*, 13 (2002), 323–35.

Krstic, Branislav, *Kosovo: Causes of the Conflict, Reconciliation of Rights* (Belgrade: Liber Press, 2001).

Küntzel, Matthias, *Der Weg in den Krieg: Deutschland, die NATO und das Kosovo* (Berlin: Elefanten Press, 2000).

Kupchan, Charles A., 'Independence for Kosovo: Yielding to Balkan Reality', *Foreign Affairs*, 84 (2005), 14–20.

Kuperman, Alan J., 'Averting the Third Kosovo War', *The American Interest*, 3 (2008), 52–8.

Lampe, John R., *Yugoslavia as History: Twice There Was a Country* (Cambridge: Cambridge University Press, 1996).

Landry, Tristan, *La Bosnie hier, le Kosovo aujourd'hui—et demain? Les pourquoi de la guerre dans les Balkans* (Paris: Harmattan, 1999).

Largantaye, Bertrand de, and Tamara Buschek, *Kosovo after 10 December 2007: What's at Stake for the European Union* (Groupement d'Etudes et de Recherches 'Notre Europe', Paris, 2007), available at <http://www.notre-europe.eu/uploads/tx_publication/Kosovo10Dec.2007-en.pdf>.

Lauwers, G., and S. Smis, 'New Dimensions of the Right to Self-determination: a Study of the International Response to the Kosovo Crisis', *Nationalism and Ethnic Politics* (2000), 43–70.

Layne, Christopher, 'Miscalculations and Blunders Lead to War', in Ted Galen Carpenter (ed.), *NATO's Empty Victory: A Postmortem on the Balkan War* (Washington D.C.: CATO Institute, 2000), 11–20.

Lawyers Committee for Human Rights, *Kosovo: Protection and Peace-Building: Protection of Refugees, Returnees, Internally Displaced Persons and Minorities* (New York: Lawyers Committee for Human Rights, 1999).

Leicht, Lotte, 'Milošević, Menschenrechte und der Kosovo', *WeltTrends*, 22 (1999), 123–6.

Leurdijk, Dick, and Dick Zandee, *Kosovo: From Crisis to Crisis* (Aldershot: Ashgate, 2001).

Lilic, Stevan, 'Die Verfassung der Republic Serbien', in Joseph Marko and Tomislav Boric (eds), *Slowenien–Kroatien–Serbien, Die Neuen Verfassungen* (Vienna: Böhlan, 1991).

Littman, Mark, *Kosovo: Law and Diplomacy* (London: Centre for Policy Studies, 1999).

Lobore, Robert, *Brandherd Kosovo* (Taunusstein: Driesen, 2002).

Locke, John, *Two Treatises on Government* (Cambridge: Cambridge University Press, 1988).

Lord Byron Foundation for Balkan Studies, *The Kosovo Dossier: A Collection of Essays and Articles, Including Papers Presented at the International Conference 'The End of the*

American Century' Held in London in April 1999 (London: Lord Byron Foundation for Balkan Studies, 1999).

Lowe, Vaughan, 'International Legal Issues Arising in the Kosovo Crisis', *International and Comparative Law Quarterly*, 49 (2000), 934–43.

Loquai, Heinz, *Der Kosovo-Konflikt: Wege in einen vermeidbaren Krieg: Die Zeit von Ende November 1997 bis März 1999 (Demokratie, Sicherheit, Frieden, 129)*, Eine Veröffentlichung aus dem Institut für Friedensforschung und Sicherheitspolitik an der Universität Hamburg (Baden-Baden: Nomos, 2000).

Lukic, Reneo, 'The Sovereignty of the Republics under the Preliminary Draft of the Federal Constitution', *New Yugoslav Law*, 14 (1963), 27.

Lutz, Dieter S. (ed.), *Der Kosovo-Krieg—Rechtliche und rechtsethische Aspekte (Demokratie, Sicherheit, Frieden, 127)*, Eine Veröffentlichung aus dem Institut für Friedensforschung und Sicherheitspolitik an der Universität Hamburg (Baden-Baden: Nomos, 2000).

Magnusson, Kjell, *Rambouilletavtalet—Texten, förhandlingarna, bakgrunden* (Centre for Multiethnic Research, Uppsala University, 1999).

Malanczuk, Peter, *Humanitarian Intervention and the Legitimacy of the Use of Force* (Hingham, MA: Nijhoff International, 1993).

Malone, Linda A., 'Seeking Reconciliation of Self-determination, Territorial Integrity and Humanitarian Intervention', *William and Mary Law Review*, 41 (2000), 1677–82.

Malcolm, Noel, *Kosovo: A Short History* (New York: New York University Press, 1998).

Maliqi, Shkelzen, 'A Demand for a New Status: The Albanian Movement in Kosova', in Veremis, Thanos and Evangelos Kofos (eds), *Kosovo: Avoiding another Balkan War* (Athens: Hellenic Foundation for European and Foreign Policy, 1998), 207–38.

—— 'Kosovo: otpor nenasiljem' [Kosovo: Non-violent Resistance], *Erasmus*, 10 (1995), 6–11.

Marko, Joseph (ed.), *Gordischer Knoten Kosovo/a: Durchschlagen oder entwirren?*, Schriftenreihe der Europäischen Akademie Bozen, Bereich Ethnische Minderheiten und regionale Autonomien, 3 (Baden-Baden: Nomos, 1999).

Meier, Viktor, *Yugoslavia: A History of its Demise* (London: Routledge, 1999).

Merkel, Reinhard (ed.), *Der Kosovo-Krieg und das Völkerrecht*, Edition Suhrkamp 2152 (Frankfurt am Main: Suhrkamp, 2000).

Meron, Thedor, 'On a Hierarchy of International Human Rights', *American Journal of International Law*, 80 (1986), 1–23.

Mertus, Julie A., *Kosovo: How Myths and Truths Started a War* (Berkeley, Los Angeles, London: University of California Press, 1999).

—— 'Legitimizing the Use of Force in Kosovo', *Ethics and International Affairs*, 15 (2001), 133–50.

Minnesota Advocates for Human Rights, *The Minnesota Plan: Recommendations for Preventing Gross Human Rights Violations in Kosovo* (Minneapolis: Minnesota Advocates for Human Rights, 1993).

Minority Rights Group International (ed.), *Preventing the Spread of War in the Balkans: Report of the Brussels Action Seminar on Human Rights and Democracy in Kosovo/a* (London: Minority Rights Group International, 1993).

Mitra, Saumya, *Kosovo: Economic and Social Reforms for Peace and Reconciliation*, World Bank Technical Paper 509 (Washington, D.C.: World Bank, 2001).

Morand, Charles-Albert (ed.), *La crise des Balkans de 1999. Les dimensions historiques, politiques et juridiques du conflit du Kosovo* (Brussels: Bruylant, 2000).

Motes, Mary, *Kosova Kosovo: Preludes to War 1966–1999* (Homestead, Florida: Redland Press, 1998).

Murphy, Sean, *Humanitarian Intervention* (Philadelphia: University of Pennsylvania Press, 1996).

Norris, H.T., 'Kosova, and the Kosovans: Past, Present and Future as seen through Serb, Albanian and Muslim Eyes', in F. W. Carter and H. T. Norris (eds), *The Changing Shape of the Balkans*, SOAS/GRC Geopolitics Series, 5 (London: UCL Press, 1996), 9–23.

Norris, John, *Collision Course: NATO, Russia, and Kosovo* (Westport and London: Praeger, 2005).

O'Connell, Mary Ellen, 'The UN, NATO, and International Law after Kosovo', *Human Rights Quarterly*, 22 (2000), 57–89.

O'Neill, William G., *Kosovo: An Unfinished Peace* (Boulder and London: Lynne Rienner Publishers, 2001).

Onuf, Nicholas G., and Richard K. Birney, 'Peremptory Norms of International Law: Their Source, Function and Future', *Journal of International Law and Policy*, 4 (1974), 187–98.

Oschlies, Wolf, *Kosovo '98: I. Ursachen und Kulmination eines alt-neuen Balkan-Konflikts* (Cologne: Bundesinstitut für Ostwissenschaftliche und Internationale Studien, 1998).

—— *Kosovo '98: II. Breitenwirkung und (mögliche) Lösungen des Konflikts* (Cologne: Bundesinstitut für Ostwissenschaftliche und Internationale Studien, 1998).

Owen, David, *Balkan Odyssey* (London: Victor Gollancz, 1995).

Pakoviác, Aleksandar, *The Fragmentation of Yugoslavia: Nationalism and War in the Balkans* (New York: St. Martin's Press, 2000).

Paris, Roland, 'Kosovo and the Metaphor War', *Political Science Quarterly*, 117(3) (2002), 423–450.

Pavlowitch, S.K., *A History of the Balkans, 1804–1945* (London, New York: Longman, 1999).

Pellet, Allain, 'L'activité de la commission d'arbitrage de la Conférence européenne pour la paix en Yougoslavie', *Annuaire français de droit international*, 39 (1993), 286–303.

—— 'Note Sur la Commission d'Arbitrage de la Conférence Européenne Pour la Paix en Yugoslavie', *Annuaire Francais de Droit International*, 37 (1991), 329–48.

Petkovic, Ranko, and Gordana Filipovic (eds), *Kosovo: Past and Present* (Belgrade: Review of International Affairs, 1989).

Petritsch, Wolfgang, and Robert Pichler, 'Kosovo—Entscheidung in der Statusfrage', *Europäische Rundschau*, 33 (2005), 59–78.

—— and Robert Pichler, *Kosovo, Kosova: der lange Weg zum Frieden* (2nd edn, Klagenfurt, Vienna, Ljubljana: Wieser Verlag, 2005).

—— Karl Kaser, and Robert Pichler, *Kosovo Kosova: Mythen Daten Fakten* (Klagenfurt, Vienna, Ljubljana: Wieser Verlag, 1999).

Pettifer, James, *Kosova Express: A Journey in Wartime* (London: Hurst & Company, 2005).

—— 'The Kosovo Liberation Army: The Myth of Origin', in Michael Waller, Kyril Drezov and Bülent Gökay (eds), *Kosovo: The Politics of Delusion* (London and Portland: Frank Cass, 2001), 25–9.

—— and Miranda Vickers, *The Albanian Question: Reshaping the Balkans* (London and New York: I.B. Tauris, 2007).

Phillips, David L., 'Comprehensive Peace in the Balkans: The Kosovo Question', *Human Rights Quarterly*, 18 (1996), 821–32.

Pichl, Elmar F., 'Kosovo in den jugoslawischen Verfassungssystemen: 1974 bis 1998', in Joseph Marko (ed.), *Gordischer Knoten Kosovo/a: Durchschlagen oder entwirren?* Schriftenreihe der Europäischen Akademie Bozen, Bereich Ethnische Minderheiten und regionale Autonomien, 3 (Baden-Baden: Nomos, 1999), 75–86.

Pipa, Arshi, 'The Political Situation of the Albanians in Yugoslavia with Particular Attention to the Kosovo Problem', *East European Quarterly*, 23 (1989), 159–81.

—— and Sami Repishti (eds), *Studies on Kosova*, East European Monographs 155 (Boulder: East European Monographs, 1984).

Placzek, Norbert, *Der Kosovo-Konflikt. Genese und Perspektive*, Arbeitspapier 2, (Hamburg: Universität Hamburg, Forschungsstelle Kriege, Rüstung und Entwicklung, 1996).

Pond, Elizabeth, 'Balkanische Eiertänze: welcher Endstatus für das Kosovo?', *Internationale Politik*, 60 (2005), 82–9.

Popov, Nebojša (ed.), *The Road to War in Serbia: Trauma and Catharsis* (Budapest: Central European University Press, 2000). [First published in Serbian as *Srpska strana rata* (Belgrade: Republika, 1996).]

Poulton, Hugh, and Suha Taji-Farouki (eds), *Muslim Identity and the Balkan State* (London: Hurst, 1997).

Pradetto, August, 'Die NATO, humanitäre Intervention und Völkerrecht', in Dieter S. Lutz (ed.), *Der Kosovo-Krieg—Rechtliche und rechtsethische Aspekte (Demokratie, Sicherheit, Frieden, 127)*, Eine Veröffentlichung aus dem Institut für Friedensforschung und Sicherheitspolitik an der Universität Hamburg (Baden-Baden: Nomos, 2000), 135–55.

—— *Konfliktmanagement durch militärische Intervention?—Dilemmata westlicher Kosovo-Politik* (Hamburg: Institut für Internationale Politik an der Universität der Bundeswehr Hamburg, 1998).

Preuß, Ulrich K., 'Zwischen Legalität und Gerechtigkeit', in Dieter S. Lutz (ed.), *Der Kosovo-Krieg—Rechtliche und rechtsethische Aspekte (Demokratie, Sicherheit, Frieden, 127)*, Eine Veröffentlichung aus dem Institut für Friedensforschung und Sicherheitspolitik an der Universität Hamburg (Baden-Baden: Nomos, 2000), 37–51.

Prorok, Christiane, *Ibrahim Rugova's Leadership* (Frankfurt am Main, Berlin and Bern: Peter Lang, 2004).

Provost, Rene, *International Human Rights and Humanitarian Law* (Cambridge: Cambridge University Press, 2002).

Pugh, Michael, 'Civil-Military Relations in the Kosovo Crisis', *Security Dialogue*, 31 (2000), 229–42.

—— 'Rubbing Salt into War Wounds: Shadow Economies and Peacebuilding in Bosnia and Kosovo', *Problems of Post-Communism*, 51 (2004), 53–60.

Pula, Gazmend, 'Kosova-Republic in a New (Con-)Federation Via Re-Federalization of Yugoslavia. General Considerations, Preconditions, Processes and Relevant Features', *Südosteuropa*, 46 (1997), 184–196.

—— 'Modalities of Self-Determination—The Case of Kosova as a Structural Issue for Lasting Stability in the Balkans', *Südosteuropa*, 45 (1998), 380–410.

—— 'The Serbian Proposal for the Partitioning of Kosova—Accents of Albanian Reaction', *Südosteuropa*, 45 (1996), 639–42.

Qosja, Rexhep, *La question Albanaise* (Paris: Fayard, 1995).

Quane, Helen, 'A Right to Self-Determination for the Kosovo Albanians?', *Leiden Journal of International Law*, 13 (2000), 219–27.

Ramcharan, B.G. (ed.), *The International Conference on the Former Yugoslavia: Official Papers, Volume 1* (The Hague, London, Boston: Kluwer Law International, 1997).

—— *The International Conference on the Former Yugoslavia: Official Papers, Volume 2* (The Hague, London, Boston: Kluwer Law International, 1997).

Ramet, Sabrina P., *The Three Yugoslavias* (Washington DC: Woodrow Wilson Centre Press, 2006).

Rapp, Christopher G., Kosovo: *The Ethno-National Dilemma and Policy Options for Conflict Resolution* (Monterey: Naval Postgraduate School, 1998).

Rasmussen, Niels Aadal, *Kosovo Independence: De Jure Versus De Facto,* DIIS Report 14 (Copenhagen: Danish Institute for International Studies, 2005).

Ratsch, Ulrich, Reinhard Mutz, and Bruno Schoch (eds), *Friedensgutachten 2000* (Münster, Hamburg, London: LIT Verlag, 2000).

Rattner, Steven, *Promoting Sustainable Economies in the Balkans: Report of an Independent Task Force* (New York: Council on Foreign Relations, 2000).

Rauert, Fee, *Das Kosovo: eine völkerrechtliche Studie,* Ethnos 55 (Vienna: Braumüller, 1999).

Redman, Michael, 'Should Kosovo be entitled to Statehood?', *The Political Quarterly*, 73 (2002), 338–43.

Reisman, Michael W., 'Kosovo's Antinomies', *American Journal of International Law*, 93 (1999), 860–2.

Reljić, Dušan, 'Bedrohliche Weiterung der Kosovo-Krise', *SWP-Aktuell*, 4 (2008). Available at <http://www.swp-berlin.org/common/get_document.php?asset_id=4639>.

Reka, Blerim, *Kosova: A Case for Preventive Diplomacy* (Prishtina: Grafika Reznigi, 1994).

Repishti, Sami, 'The Evolution of Kosova's Autonomy', in Arshi Pipa and Sami Repishti (eds), *Studies in Kosova* (Boulder: East European Monographs, 1984), 195–232.

Research and Documentation Centre Sarajevo (RDCS), 'Documenting the victims of conflict', (Sarajevo: RDCS), available at <http://www.idc.org.ba/aboutus/documenting_the_victims.htm>, accessed 6 October 2008.

Reuter, Jens, and Konrad Clewing (eds), *Der Kosovo Konflikt* (Ursachen, Verlauf, Perspektiven, Klagenfurt: Wieser, 2000).

—— and Melpomeni Katsaropoulou, 'Die Konferenz von Rambouillet und die Folgen', *Südosteuropa*, 48 (1999), 147–55.

Rezon, Miron, *Europe's Nightmare: The Struggle for Kosovo* (Westport: Prager, 2001).

Rieff, David, *et al.*, 'A Symposium on Kosovo', *Journal on Human Rights*, 1 (2002), 111–32.

Riegler, Henriette, 'Der Kosovokonflikt: Bestandsaufnahme und Lösungsszenarien', Working Paper 28 (Vienna: Österreichisches Institut für Internationale Politik, 2000).

Roberts, Adam, 'NATO's 'Humanitarian War' Over Kosovo', *Survival,* 41(3) (1999), 102–23.

Roth, Hugo, *Kosovski iskoni: pozadina aktuelnih zbivanja na Kosovu i Metohiji* ['Kosovo Origins: The Background to the Present-day Situation in Kosovo and Metohia'] (Belgrade: N. Pasic, 1996).

Rousseau, Jean Jacques, 'Of the Social Contract', in Victor Gourevitch (ed.), *Rousseau, The Social Contract and other later Political Writings* (Cambridge: Cambridge University Press, 1997).

Roux, Michel, *La guerre du Kosovo: dix clés pour comprendre* (Paris: Découverte, 1999).

—— *Les Albanais en Yougóslavie, Minorités national territoire et développement* (Paris: Editions de la Maison des sciences de l'homme, 1992).

Rrecaj, Besfort, *Kosova's Right to Self-determination and Statehood: Masters Thesis* (Pristina: University College 'Victory', 2006).

Rüb, Matthias, *Kosovo—Ursachen und Folgen eines Krieges in Europa* (Munich: Deutscher Taschenbuch Verlag, 1999).

Rugova, Ibrahim, Marie-Françoise Alain and Xavier Galmiche, *La Question du Kosovo* (Paris: Fayard, 1994).

Safran, William, and Ramon Maiz (eds), *Identity and Territorial Autonomy in Plural Societies* (London: Frank Cass, 2000).

Salla, Michael, 'Kosovo, Non-violence and the Break-up of Yugoslavia', *Security Dialogue*, 26 (1995), 427–38.

Salvoldi, Giancarlo, and Lush Gjergji, *Kosovo: non violenza per la riconciliazione* (Bologna: EMI, 1999).

Saxer, Urs, 'Kosovo und das Völkerrecht: ein Konfliktmanagement im Spannungsfeld von Menschenrechten, kollektiver Sicherheit und Unilateralismus', *Basler Schriften zur europäischen Integration*, 42/43 (Basel: Europainstitut der Universität Basel, 1999).

Schmid, Thomas (ed.), *Krieg im Kosovo*, Reinbek bei Hamburg: Rowohlt Taschenbuch Verlag, 1999.

Schnabel, Albrecht (ed.), *Kosovo and the Challenge of Humanitarian Intervention: Selective Indignation, Collective Action, and International Citizenship* (Tokyo and New York: United Nations University Press, 2000).

Schwartz, Stephen, *Kosovo: Background to a War* (London: Anthem Press, 2000).

Seidel, Gerd, 'A New Dimension of the Right of Self-Determination in Kosovo?', in Christian Tomuschat (ed.), *Kosovo and the International Community: A Legal Assessment* (The Hague, London, New York: Martinus Nijhoff Publishers, 2002), 203–215.

Shaw, Malcolm N., *International Law* (5th edn, Cambridge: Cambridge University Press, 2003).

Shawcross, William, *Deliver Us From Evil: Warlords and Peacekeepers in a World of Endless Conflict* (London: Bloomsbury, 2001).

Silber, Laura, and Allan Little, *The Death of Yugoslavia* (London: Penguin, 1995).

Smith, Mark A., *Kosovo's Status: Russian Policy on Unrecognised States* (Camberley: Conflict Studies Research Centre, Defence Academy of the United Kingdom, 2006).

Spillmann, Kurt R., and Joachim Krause (eds), *Kosovo: Lessons Learned for International Cooperative Security*, Studies in Contemporary History and Security Policy, 5 (Bern and Berlin: Peter Lang, 2000).

Stahn, Carsten, 'Constitution Without a State? Kosovo under the United Nations Constitutional Framework for Self-Government', *Leiden Journal of International Law*, 14 (2001), 531–61.

Stavileci, Esat, *Albanian Question at the Crossroads of Peaceful Solution* (Prishtina: The Independent Association of Jurists of Kosova, 1995).

—— *Kosova and Albanians: Between Negation and Independence* (Prishtina: The Independent Association of Jurists of Kosova, 1995).

—— Reka Blerim, and Arsim Bajrami, 'Kosova: Political, Constitutional and International Law Arguments', *Kosova Law Review* (1996).

Steiner, Henry J., *International Human Rights Law in Context: Law, Politics, Moral. Text and Materials* (Oxford: Oxford University Press, 2000).

Stowell, Ellery C., *Intervention in International Law* (Washington, D.C.: John Byrne Co., 1921).

Sturesjö, Örjan, 'Kosovo, ett jugoslaviskt dilemma', *Världspolitikens dagsfrågor*, 4, (Stockholm: Utrikespolitiska institutet, 1990).

Sundhaussen, Holm, 'Der Gegensatz zwischen historischen Rechten und Selbstbestimmungsrechten als Ursache von Konflikten: Kosovo und Krajina im Vergleich', in Philipp Ther and Holm Sundhaussen (eds), *Nationalitätenkonflikte im 20. Jahrhundert*, Forschungen zur osteuropäischen Geschichte 59 (Berlin: Osteuropa-Institut der Freien Universität Berlin, 2001), 19–33.

Surroi, Veton, 'Kosova and the Constitutional Solutions', in Thanos Veremis and Evangelos Kofos (eds), *Kosovo: Avoiding Another Balkan War* (Athens: Hellenic Foundation for European and Foreign Policy, 1998), 145–72.

—— 'Mehrheit und Minderheit in Kosovo: Albaner contra Serben', *Internationale Politik*, 52 (1997), 49–52.

Tarifa, Fatos, and Peter Lucas, 'The End of Balkan History: Serbia Should Let Go of Kosovo and Move On', *Policy Review Online* (2007), 141–6, available at <http://www.hoover.org/publications/policyreview/5516471.html>.

Tavernier, Paul, 'Responsabilité pénale? L'action du tribunal pénal international pour l'ex-Yougoslavie', in Christian Tomuschat (ed.), *Kosovo and the International Community: A Legal Assessment* (The Hague, London, New York: Martinus Nijhoff Publishers, 2002), 157–79.

Terrett, Steve, *The Dissolution of Yugoslavia and the Badinter Arbritration Commission* (Aldershot: Ashgate 2000).

Thomas, Robert (2000), *Kosovo, Serbia and the West: NATO's Balkan War* (London: Hurst, 2000).

Thornberry, Patrick, 'The Democratic or Internal Aspect of Self-determination with Some Remarks on Federalism', in *Christian Tomuschat* (ed.), *Modern Law of Self-determination* (Dordrecht: Martinus Nijhoff 1993).

Thürer, Daniel, 'Die NATO-Einsätze in Kosovo und das Völkerrecht', in Dieter S. Lutz (ed.), *Der Kosovo-Krieg—Rechtliche und rechtsethische Aspekte (Demokratie, Sicherheit, Frieden, 127)*, Eine Veröffentlichung aus dem Institut für Friedensforschung und Sicherheitspolitik an der Universität Hamburg (Baden-Baden: Nomos, 2000), 129–33.

Tomuschat, Christian (ed.), *Kosovo and the International Community: A Legal Assessment* (The Hague, London, New York: Martinus Nijhoff Publishers, 2002).

—— (ed.), *Modern Law of Self-determination* (Dordrecht: Martinus Nijhoff, 1993).

—— 'Self-determination in a Post-colonial World', in *Christian Tomuschat* (ed.), *Modern Law of Self-determination* (Dordrecht: Martinus Nijhoff, 1993).

—— 'Völkerrechtliche Aspekte des Kosovo-Konflikts', in Dieter S. Lutz (ed.), *Der Kosovo-Krieg—Rechtliche und rechtsethische Aspekte (Demokratie, Sicherheit, Frieden, 127)*, Eine Veröffentlichung aus dem Institut für Friedensforschung und Sicherheitspolitik an der Universität Hamburg (Baden-Baden: Nomos, 2000), 31–5.

Transnational Foundation for Peace and Future Research, *UNTANS: Conflict Mitigation for Kosovo* (Lund: The Transnational Foundation for Peace and Future Research, 1996).

Triantaphyllou, Dimitrios (ed.), *What Status for Kosovo?* Institute for Security Studies, Chaillot Papers 50 (October 2001).

Trifunovska, Snezana, *Former Yugoslavia through Documents: From its Dissolution to the Peace Settlement* (The Hague, Boston: Martinus Nijhoff, 1999).

Troebst, Stefan, 'Conflict in Kosovo: Causes and Cures—An Analytical Documentation', in Hans-Georg Ehrhart and Albrecht Schnabel (eds), *The Southeast European Challenge: Ethnic Conflict and the International Response (Democracy, Security, Peace, 121)* (Baden-Baden: Nomos, 1999), 85–116.

—— 'Conflict in Kosovo: Failure of Prevention?—An Analytical Documentation, 1992–1998', European Centre for Minority Issues, Working Paper No. 1 (May 1998). Available at <http://www.ecmi.de/download/working_paper_1.pdf>.

—— 'The Kosovo Conflict', in *SIPRI Yearbook 1999* (Oxford: Oxford University Press, 1999), 47–62.

Tuerk, Danilo, 'Reflections on Human Rights: Sovereignty of States and the Principle of Non-intervention', in Morten Bergsmo (ed.), *Human Rights and Criminal Justice for the Downtrodden: Essays on Honour of Asbjorn Eide* (Dordrecht: Martinus Nijhoff, 2003).

United Kingdom. Ministry of Defence, *Kosovo: Lessons from the Crisis*. Presented to Parliament by the Secretary of State for Defence by Command of Her Majesty (Stationery Office, London, 2000).

—— Parliament. Select Committee on Foreign Affairs, *Kosovo, Fourth Report, Volume I: Reports and Proceedings of the Committee* (London: House of Commons, Select Committee on Foreign Affairs, 2000).

—— Parliament. Select Committee on Foreign Affairs, *Kosovo, Fourth Report, Volume II: Minutes of Evidence and Appendices* (London: House of Commons, Select Committee on Foreign Affairs, 2000).

United States Institute for Peace, 'Kosovo Final Status: Options and Cross-border Requirements', Special Report 91 (Washington: United States Institute for Peace, 2002).

United States. Congress. 'Commission on Security and Cooperation in Europe, Kosovo's Displaced and Imprisoned: Hearing before the Commission on Security and Cooperation in Europe', 106th Congress, 2nd Session (Washington, D.C.: The Commission, 2000).

—— Congress. Commission on Security and Cooperation in Europe, 'Repression and violence in Kosovo', 18 March 1998; 'Kosovo, the Humanitarian Perspective', 25 June 1998; two hearings before the Commission on Security and Cooperation in Europe, 105th Congress, 5th Session (Washington, D.C.: GPO, 1998).

—— Congress. House of Representatives, 'The Future of Kosovo, Hearing before the Committee on International Relations', U.S. House of Representatives, 108th Congress, 1st Session, 21 May 2003 (Washington, D.C.: GPO, 2003).

—— Congress. Senate. Committee on Foreign Relations. Subcommittee on European Affairs, 'Kosovo, One Year after the Bombing: Hearings before the Subcommittee on European Affairs of the Committee on Foreign Relations', United States Senate, 106th Congress, 2nd Session, 8 June 2000 (Washington, D.C.: GPO, 2000).

Bibliography 301

—— Congress. Senate. Committee on the Judiciary. Subcommittee on Immigration, 'The Kosovo Refugee Crisis: Hearing before the Subcommittee on Immigration of the Committee on the Judiciary', United States Senate, 106th Congress, 1st Session, on the Current Kosovo Refugee Situation and the Scope and Adequacy of the Response of the United States and the International Community, 14 April 1999 (Washington, D.C.: GPO, 2000).

—— Congressional Research Service, 'Kosovo and US Policy: Background and Current Issues', CRS Report for Congress (Washington: CRS, 2007).

—— Senate, 'The Crisis in Kosovo: Hearings before the Subcommittee on European Affairs of the Committee on Foreign Relations', United States Senate, 105th Congress, 2nd Session, 6 May and 24 June 1998 (Washington, D.C.: GPO, 1998).

Valki, László, 'The Kosovo Crisis and International Law', *Südosteuropa*, 49 (2000), 259–71.

Védrine, Hubert [with Dominique Moïsi, transl. by Philip H. Gordon], *France in an Age of Globalization* (Washington, D.C.: Brookings Institution Press, 2001).

Veremis, Thanos, and Evangelos Kofos (eds), *Kosovo: Avoiding another Balkan War* (Athens: Hellenic Foundation for European and Foreign Policy, 1998).

—— and Dimitrios Triantaphyllou (eds), *Kosovo and the Albanian Dimension in Southeastern Europe: The Need for Regional Security and Conflict Prevention* (Athens: Hellenic Foundation for European and Foreign Policy, 1999).

Vetter, Reinhold, 'Konditionierte Unabhängigkeit' für Kosovo', *Südosteuropa*, 52 (2003), 66–85.

Vickers, Miranda, *Albania: From Anarchy to a Balkan Identity* (New York: New York University Press, 1997).

—— *Between Serb and Albanian: A History of Kosovo* (London: Hurst, 1998).

—— *The Albanians: A Modern History* (rev. edn, New York: Tauris, 1997).

—— 'Tirana's Uneasy role in the Kosovo Crisis, 1998–1999', in Michael Waller, Kyril Drezov and Bülent Gökay (eds), *Kosovo: The Politics of Delusion* (London and Portland: Frank Cass, 2001), 30–6.

Vincent, Marc, and Birgitte Refslund Sorensen (eds), *Caught Between Borders: Response Strategies of the Internally Displaced* (London: Pluto Press, 2001).

Vrieze de, Franklin, *De Kosovo-diplomatie: waarom de voorspelde oorlog niet werd voorkomen* (Antwerp: Pax Christi Vlaanderen, 2000).

—— 'Kosovo: Stable and Explosive', *Helsinki Monitor*, 6 (1995), 43–51.

—— 'Toward Self-government in Kosovo', *Helsinki Monitor*, 13 (2002), 11–25.

Vuckovic, Milan, *Stanovnistvo Kosova u razdoblju od 1918. Do 1991. Godine* [Status and history of Kosovo from 1918 to 1991] (Munich: Slavica Verlag Kovac, 1996).

Vukovic, Illija, *Autonomastvo i separatizam na Kosovu* (Belgrade: Nova Knjiga, 1985).

Walker, William G., 'OSCE Verification Experiences in Kosovo: November 1998–June 1999', in Ken Booth, *The Kosovo Tragedy: The Human Rights Dimensions* (London: Frank Cass, 2001).

Wall, Andru E. (ed.), *Legal and Ethical Lessons of Nato's Kosovo Campaign* (Newport: Naval War College, 2002).

Waller, Michael, Kyril Drezov, and Bülent Gökay (eds), *Kosovo: The Politics of Delusion* (London and Portland: Frank Cass, 2001).

Weckel, Philippe, 'Les devoirs de l'attaquant à la lumière de la campagne aérienne en Yougoslavie', in Christian Tomuschat (ed.), *Kosovo and the International Community:*

A Legal Assessment (The Hague, London, New York: Martinus Nijhoff Publishers, 2002), 129–55.

Wedgwood, Ruth, 'NATO's Campaign in Kosovo', *American Journal of International Law*, 93(4) (1999), 828–34.

Welfens, Paul J.J., *Der Kosovo-Krieg und die Zukunft Europas: Diplomatieversagen Kriegseskalation, Wiederaufbau, Euroland* (Munich: Olzog, 1999).

Marc Weller, 'Access to Victims: Reconceiving the Right to Intervene', in Wybo P. Heere (ed.), *International Law and The Hague's 750th Anniversary* (The Hague: Kluwer, 1999).

—— 'Effective Participation of Minorities in Public Life', in Marc Weller (ed.), *Universal Minority Rights* (Oxford: Oxford University Press, 2007), 477–516.

—— *Escaping the Self-determination Trap* (Dordrecht: Martinus Nijhoff, forthcoming).

—— 'Forcible Humanitarian Action: the Case of Kosovo', in Michael Bothe, Mary Ellen O'Connell and Natalino Ronzitti (eds), *Redefining Sovereignty: The Use of* Force after the Cold War (Ardsley: Transnational Publishers, 2005), 277–333.

—— 'Interim Governance for Kosovo: The Rambouillet Agreement and the Constitutional Framework Developed under UN Administration', in Marc Weller and Barbara Metzger (eds), *Settling Self-determination Disputes: Complex Power-sharing in Theory and in Practice* (Dordrecht: Martinus Nijhoff, 2008), 243–65.

—— *Iraq and Kuwait: The Hostilities and Their Aftermath* (Cambridge: Grotius, 1993).

—— 'Missed Opportunities of Conflict Prevention in Kosovo', in Luc van de Goor and Martina Huber (eds), *Mainstreaming Conflict Prevention: Concept and Practice* Aktuelle Materialien zur Internationalen Politik, 60/10 (Baden-Baden: Nomos, 2001), 238–68.

—— *Peace Lost: The Failure of Conflict Prevention in Kosovo* (Dordrecht: Martinus Nijhoff, 2008).

—— 'Peace-keeping and Peace-enforcement in the Republic of Bosnia and Herzegovina', *Heidelberg Journal of International Law [Zeitschrift fuer auslaendisches oeffentliches Recht und Voelkerrecht]*, 56 (1996), 70–177.

—— *Regional Peace-keeping and Peace-enforcement: The Liberian Crisis* (Cambridge: Cambridge University Press, 1994).

—— (ed.), *The Crisis in Kosovo 1989–1999: From the Dissolution of Yugoslavia to Rambouillet and the Outbreak of Hostilities* (Cambridge: Documents & Analysis, 1999).

—— 'The International Response to the Dissolution of the Socialist Federal Republic of Yugoslavia', *American Journal of International Law*, 86 (1992), 569–607.

—— (ed.), *The Kosovo Conflict: Forced Displacement, the Conduct and Termination of Hostilities and the Renewed Search for a Settlement* (Cambridge: Documents & Analysis, 2001).

—— 'The Kosovo Constitution and Provisions for the Minorities of Kosovo', *European Yearbook of Minority Issues,* 6 (2006/2007) (Flensburg: European Centre for Minority Issues, forthcoming).

—— 'The Kosovo Indictments', in Ken Booth (ed.), *The Kosovo Tragedy: Human Rights Dimensions* (London and Portland: Frank Cass, 2001).

—— 'The Rambouillet Conference on Kosovo', *International Affairs*, 75(2) (1999), 211–52.

—— 'The Self-determination Trap', *Ethnopolitics*, 4 (2005), 1–42.

—— 'The Vienna Negotiations on the Final Status of Kosovo', *International Affairs*, 84(4) (2008), 659–81.

—— 'Why the Legal Rules on Self-determination Do Not Resolve Self-determination Disputes', in Marc Weller and Barbara Metzger (eds), *Settling Self-determination Conflicts: Complex Power-sharing in Theory and in Practice* (Dordrecht: Martinus Nijhoff, 2008), 17–47.

—— and Daniel Bethlehem (eds), *The Yugoslav Crisis in International Law: The General Issues, Part I*. Cambridge International Documents Series, 5 (Cambridge: Cambridge University Press, 1997).

—— and Jonathan Wheatley, *The War in Georgia: Power Politics and the Failure of Conflict Prevention* (London: Hurst Publishers, forthcoming).

—— and Stefan Wolff, *Autonomy, Self-governance and Conflict Resolution* (London: Routledge, 2005).

Wellman, Christopher Heath, *A Theory of Secession* (Cambridge: Cambridge University Press, 2005).

Williams, Paul, Rebecca Grazier, and James Hooper, Simulating Kosovo: Lessons for *Final Status Negotiations*, Special Report 95 (Washington D.C.: United States Institute of Peace, 2002).

Wirth, Kerstin A., 'Kosovo am Vorabend der Statusentscheidung: Überlegungen zur rechtlichen Begründung und Durchsetzung der Unabhängigkeit', *Zeitschrift für ausländisches öffentliches Recht und Völkerrecht*, 67 (2007), 1065–1106.

Wolfke, Karol, 'Jus Cogens in International Law', 6 *Polish Yearbook of International Law* (1974), 145–163.

Wood, Michael, 'The Law on the Use of Force: Current Challenges', *Singapore Yearbook of International Law*, 11 (2007), 1, 10.

Woodward, Susan L., *Balkan Tragedy: Chaos and Dissolution after the Cold War* (Washington D.C.: The Brookings Institution, 1995).

World Bank, 'Kosovo: Building Peace through Sustained Growth. The Economic and Social Policy Agenda', Report (1999).

Yannis, Alexandros, *Kosovo under International Administration: An Unfinished Conflict* (Athens: Hellenic Foundation for European and Foreign Policy, 2001).

Youngs, Tim and Tom Dodd, 'Kosovo'. Research Paper 98/73 (London: House of Commons Library, 1998).

Zajmi, Gazmend, *Dimensions of the Question of Kosova in the Balkans: Individuality and the Question of Kosova as a Question of Self-determination* (Prishtina: Academy of Sciences and Arts of Kosova, Kosova Information Center, 1994).

Zemanek, Karl, 'Human Rights Protection vs Non-intervention', in Lal Chand Vorah *et al.* (eds), *Man's Inhumanity to Man, Essays in Honour of Antonio Cassesse* (The Hague: Kluwer Law International, 2003).

Zhirinovskii, Vladimir, and German I. Moro, *Kosovo I Metokhiia: regional' nyi konflikt mezhdunarodnogo znacheniia* (Moscow: Izd. Gos. Dumy, 1999).

Zygojannis, Phillip A., *Die Staatengemeinschaft und das Kosovo: Humanitäre Intervention und internationale Übergangsverwaltung unter Berücksichtigung einer Verpflichtung des Intervenienten zur Nachsorge*, Veröffentlichungen des Walther-Schücking-Instituts für Internationales Recht an der Universität Kiel, 145 (Berlin: Duncker & Humblot, 2003).

APPENDIX 1

United Nations Security Council Resolution S/RES/1244 (1999), 10 June 1999

RESOLUTION 1244 (1999)

Adopted by the Security Council at its 4011th meeting, on 10 June 1999

The Security Council,

Bearing in mind the purposes and principles of the Charter of the United Nations, and the primary responsibility of the Security Council for the maintenance of international peace and security,

Recalling its resolutions 1160 (1998) of 31 March 1998, 1199 (1998) of 23 September 1998, 1203 (1998) of 24 October 1998 and 1239 (1999) of 14 May 1999,

Regretting that there has not been full compliance with the requirements of these resolutions,

Determined to resolve the grave humanitarian situation in Kosovo, Federal Republic of Yugoslavia, and to provide for the safe and free return of all refugees and displaced persons to their homes,

Condemning all acts of violence against the Kosovo population as well as all terrorist acts by any party,

Recalling the statement made by the Secretary-General on 9 April 1999, expressing concern at the humanitarian tragedy taking place in Kosovo,

Reaffirming the right of all refugees and displaced persons to return to their homes in safety,

Recalling the jurisdiction and the mandate of the International Tribunal for the Former Yugoslavia,

Welcoming the general principles on a political solution to the Kosovo crisis adopted on 6 May 1999 (S/1999/516, annex 1 to this resolution) and welcoming also the acceptance by the Federal Republic of Yugoslavia of the principles set forth in points 1 to 9 of the paper presented in Belgrade on 2 June 1999 (S/1999/649, annex 2 to this resolution), and the Federal Republic of Yugoslavia's agreement to that paper,

Reaffirming the commitment of all Member States to the sovereignty and territorial integrity of the Federal Republic of Yugoslavia and the other States of the region, as set out in the Helsinki Final Act and annex 2,

Reaffirming the call in previous resolutions for substantial autonomy and meaningful self-administration for Kosovo,

Determining that the situation in the region continues to constitute a threat to international peace and security,

Determined to ensure the safety and security of international personnel and the implementation by all concerned of their responsibilities under the present resolution, and acting for these purposes under Chapter VII of the Charter of the United Nations,

1. Decides that a political solution to the Kosovo crisis shall be based on the general principles in annex 1 and as further elaborated in the principles and other required elements in annex 2;

2. Welcomes the acceptance by the Federal Republic of Yugoslavia of the principles and other required elements referred to in paragraph 1 above, and demands the full cooperation of the Federal Republic of Yugoslavia in their rapid implementation;

3. Demands in particular that the Federal Republic of Yugoslavia put an immediate and verifiable end to violence and repression in Kosovo, and begin and complete verifiable phased withdrawal from Kosovo of all military, police and paramilitary forces according to a rapid timetable, with which the deployment of the international security presence in Kosovo will be synchronized;

4. Confirms that after the withdrawal an agreed number of Yugoslav and Serb military and police personnel will be permitted to return to Kosovo to perform the functions in accordance with annex 2;

5. Decides on the deployment in Kosovo, under United Nations auspices, of international civil and security presences, with appropriate equipment and personnel as required, and welcomes the agreement of the Federal Republic of Yugoslavia to such presences;

6. Requests the Secretary-General to appoint, in consultation with the Security Council, a Special Representative to control the implementation of the international civil presence, and further requests the Secretary-General to instruct his Special Representative to coordinate closely with the international security presence to ensure that both presences operate towards the same goals and in a mutually supportive manner;

7. Authorizes Member States and relevant international organizations to establish the international security presence in Kosovo as set out in point 4 of annex 2 with all necessary means to fulfil its responsibilities under paragraph 9 below;

8. Affirms the need for the rapid early deployment of effective international civil and security presences to Kosovo, and demands that the parties cooperate fully in their deployment;

9. Decides that the responsibilities of the international security presence to be deployed and acting in Kosovo will include:
   a. ring renewed hostilities, maintaining and where necessary enforcing a ceasefire, and ensuring the withdrawal and preventing the return into Kosovo of Federal and Republic military, police and paramilitary forces, except as provided in point 6 of annex 2;

    b. Demilitarizing the Kosovo Liberation Army (KLA) and other armed Kosovo Albanian groups as required in paragraph 15 below;

    c. Establishing a secure environment in which refugees and displaced persons can return home in safety, the international civil presence can operate, a transitional administration can be established, and humanitarian aid can be delivered;

    d. Ensuring public safety and order until the international civil presence can take responsibility for this task;

    e. Supervising demining until the international civil presence can, as appropriate, take over responsibility for this task;

    f. Supporting, as appropriate, and coordinating closely with the work of the international civil presence;

    g. Conducting border monitoring duties as required;

    h. Ensuring the protection and freedom of movement of itself, the international civil presence, and other international organizations;

10. Authorizes the Secretary-General, with the assistance of relevant international organizations, to establish an international civil presence in Kosovo in order to provide an interim administration for Kosovo under which the people of Kosovo can enjoy substantial autonomy within the Federal Republic of Yugoslavia, and which will provide transitional administration while establishing and overseeing the development of provisional democratic self-governing institutions to ensure conditions for a peaceful and normal life for all inhabitants of Kosovo;

11. Decides that the main responsibilities of the international civil presence will include:

    a. Promoting the establishment, pending a final settlement, of substantial autonomy and self-government in Kosovo, taking full account of annex 2 and of the Rambouillet accords (S/1999/648);

    b. Performing basic civilian administrative functions where and as long as required;

    c. Organizing and overseeing the development of provisional institutions for democratic and autonomous self-government pending a political settlement, including the holding of elections;

    d. Transferring, as these institutions are established, its administrative responsibilities while overseeing and supporting the consolidation of Kosovo's local provisional institutions and other peace-building activities;

    e. Facilitating a political process designed to determine Kosovo's future status, taking into account the Rambouillet accords (S/1999/648);

    f. In a final stage, overseeing the transfer of authority from Kosovo's provisional institutions to institutions established under a political settlement;

    g. Supporting the reconstruction of key infrastructure and other economic reconstruction;

    h. Supporting, in coordination with international humanitarian organizations, humanitarian and disaster relief aid;

    i. Maintaining civil law and order, including establishing local police forces and meanwhile through the deployment of international police personnel to serve in Kosovo;

    j. Protecting and promoting human rights;

    k. Assuring the safe and unimpeded return of all refugees and displaced persons to their homes in Kosovo;

12. Emphasizes the need for coordinated humanitarian relief operations, and for the Federal Republic of Yugoslavia to allow unimpeded access to Kosovo by humanitarian aid organizations and to cooperate with such organizations so as to ensure the fast and effective delivery of international aid;

13. Encourages all Member States and international organizations to contribute to economic and social reconstruction as well as to the safe return of refugees and displaced persons, and emphasizes in this context the importance of convening an international donors' conference, particularly for the purposes set out in paragraph 11(g) above, at the earliest possible date;

14. Demands full cooperation by all concerned, including the international security presence, with the International Tribunal for the Former Yugoslavia;

15. Demands that the KLA and other armed Kosovo Albanian groups end immediately all offensive actions and comply with the requirements for demilitarization as laid down by the head of the international security presence in consultation with the Special Representative of the Secretary-General;

16. Decides that the prohibitions imposed by paragraph 8 of resolution 1160 (1998) shall not apply to arms and related matériel for the use of the international civil and security presences;

17. Welcomes the work in hand in the European Union and other international organizations to develop a comprehensive approach to the economic development and stabilization of the region affected by the Kosovo crisis, including the implementation of a Stability Pact for South Eastern Europe with broad international participation in order to further the promotion of democracy, economic prosperity, stability and regional cooperation;

18. Demands that all States in the region cooperate fully in the implementation of all aspects of this resolution;

19. Decides that the international civil and security presences are established for an initial period of 12 months, to continue thereafter unless the Security Council decides otherwise;

20. Requests the Secretary-General to report to the Council at regular intervals on the implementation of this resolution, including reports from the leaderships of the international civil and security presences, the first reports to be submitted within 30 days of the adoption of this resolution;

21. Decides to remain actively seized of the matter.

Annex 1
Statement by the Chairman on the conclusion of the meeting of the G-8 Foreign Ministers held at the Petersberg Centre on 6 May 1999

The G-8 Foreign Ministers adopted the following general principles on the political solution to the Kosovo crisis:

• Immediate and verifiable end of violence and repression in Kosovo;

- Withdrawal from Kosovo of military, police and paramilitary forces;
- Deployment in Kosovo of effective international civil and security presences, endorsed and adopted by the United Nations, capable of guaranteeing the achievement of the common objectives;
- Establishment of an interim administration for Kosovo to be decided by the Security Council of the United Nations to ensure conditions for a peaceful and normal life for all inhabitants in Kosovo;
- The safe and free return of all refugees and displaced persons and unimpeded access to Kosovo by humanitarian aid organizations;
- A political process towards the establishment of an interim political framework agreement providing for a substantial self-government for Kosovo, taking full account of the Rambouillet accords and the principles of sovereignty and territorial integrity of the Federal Republic of Yugoslavia and the other countries of the region, and the demilitarization of the KLA;
- Comprehensive approach to the economic development and stabilization of the crisis region.

Annex 2
Agreement should be reached on the following principles to move towards a resolution of the Kosovo crisis:

1. An immediate and verifiable end of violence and repression in Kosovo.

2. Verifiable withdrawal from Kosovo of all military, police and paramilitary forces according to a rapid timetable.

3. Deployment in Kosovo under United Nations auspices of effective international civil and security presences, acting as may be decided under Chapter VII of the Charter, capable of guaranteeing the achievement of common objectives.

4. The international security presence with substantial North Atlantic Treaty Organization participation must be deployed under unified command and control and authorized to establish a safe environment for all people in Kosovo and to facilitate the safe return to their homes of all displaced persons and refugees.

5. Establishment of an interim administration for Kosovo as a part of the international civil presence under which the people of Kosovo can enjoy substantial autonomy within the Federal Republic of Yugoslavia, to be decided by the Security Council of the United Nations. The interim administration to provide transitional administration while establishing and overseeing the development of provisional democratic self-governing institutions to ensure conditions for a peaceful and normal life for all inhabitants in Kosovo.

6. After withdrawal, an agreed number of Yugoslav and Serbian personnel will be permitted to return to perform the following functions:
   - Liaison with the international civil mission and the international security presence;
   - Marking/clearing minefields;
   - Maintaining a presence at Serb patrimonial sites;
   - Maintaining a presence at key border crossings.

7. Safe and free return of all refugees and displaced persons under the supervision of the Office of the United Nations High Commissioner for Refugees and unimpeded access to Kosovo by humanitarian aid organizations.

8. A political process towards the establishment of an interim political framework agreement providing for substantial self-government for Kosovo, taking full account of the Rambouillet accords and the principles of sovereignty and territorial integrity of the Federal Republic of Yugoslavia and the other countries of the region, and the demilitarization of UCK. Negotiations between the parties for a settlement should not delay or disrupt the establishment of democratic self-governing institutions.

9. A comprehensive approach to the economic development and stabilization of the crisis region. This will include the implementation of a stability pact for South-Eastern Europe with broad international participation in order to further promotion of democracy, economic prosperity, stability and regional cooperation.

10. Suspension of military activity will require acceptance of the principles set forth above in addition to agreement to other, previously identified, required elements, which are specified in the footnote below. A military-technical agreement will then be rapidly concluded that would, among other things, specify additional modalities, including the roles and functions of Yugoslav/Serb personnel in Kosovo:

    Withdrawal

    • Procedures for withdrawals, including the phased, detailed schedule and delineation of a buffer area in Serbia beyond which forces will be withdrawn;

    Returning personnel

    • Equipment associated with returning personnel;
    • Terms of reference for their functional responsibilities;
    • Timetable for their return;
    • Delineation of their geographical areas of operation;
    • Rules governing their relationship to the international security presence and the international civil mission.

Notes

Other required elements:
    • A rapid and precise timetable for withdrawals, meaning, e.g., seven days to complete withdrawal and air defence weapons withdrawn outside a 25 kilometre mutual safety zone within 48 hours;
    • Return of personnel for the four functions specified above will be under the supervision of the international security presence and will be limited to a small agreed number (hundreds, not thousands);
    • Suspension of military activity will occur after the beginning of verifiable withdrawals;
    • The discussion and achievement of a military-technical agreement shall not extend the previously determined time for completion of withdrawals.

Kosovo Declaration of Independence
17 February 2008

Convened in an extraordinary meeting on February 17, 2008, in Pristine, the capital of Kosovo,

Answering the call of the people to build a society that honors human dignity and affirms the pride and purpose of its citizens,

Committed to confront the painful legacy of the recent past in a spirit of reconciliation and forgiveness,

Dedicated to protecting, promoting and honoring the diversity of our people,

Reaffirming our wish to become fully integrated into the Euro-Atlantic family of democracies,

Observing that Kosovo is a special case arising from Yugoslavia's non-consensual breakup and is not a precedent for any other situation,

Recalling the years of strife and violence in Kosovo, that disturbed the conscience of all civilised people,

Grateful that in 1999 the world intervened, thereby removing Belgrade's governance over Kosovo and placing Kosovo under United Nations interim administration,

Proud that Kosovo has since developed functional, multi-ethnic institutions of democracy that express freely the will of our citizens,

Recalling the years of internationally-sponsored negotiations between Belgrade and Pristina over the question of our future political status,

Regretting that no mutually-acceptable status outcome was possible, in spite of the good-faith engagement of our leaders,

Confirming that the recommendations of UN Special Envoy Martti Ahtisaari provide Kosovo with a comprehensive framework for its future development and are in line with the highest European standards of human rights and good governance,

Determined to see our status resolved in order to give our people clarity about their future, move beyond the conflicts of the past and realise the full democratic potential of our society,

Honoring all the men and women who made great sacrifices to build a better future for Kosovo,

Kosova Declaration of Independence

1. We, the democratically-elected leaders of our people, hereby declare Kosovo to be an independent and sovereign state. This declaration reflects the will of our people and it is in full accordance with the recommendations of UN Special Envoy Martti Ahtisaari and his Comprehensive Proposal for the Kosovo Status Settlement.

2. We declare Kosovo to be a democratic, secular and multi-ethnic republic, guided by the principles of non-discrimination and equal protection under the law. We shall protect and promote the rights of all communities in Kosovo and create the conditions necessary for their effective participation in political and decision-making processes.

3. We accept fully the obligations for Kosovo contained in the Ahtisaari Plan, and welcome the framework it proposes to guide Kosovo in the years ahead. We shall implement in full those obligations including through priority adoption of the legislation included in its Annex XII, particularly those that protect and promote the rights of communities and their members.

4. We shall adopt as soon as possible a Constitution that enshrines our commitment to respect the human rights and fundamental freedoms of all our citizens, particularly as defined by the European Convention on Human Rights. The Constitution shall incorporate all relevant principles of the Ahtisaari Plan and be adopted through a democratic and deliberative process.

5. We welcome the international community's continued support of our democratic development through international presences established in Kosovo on the basis of UN Security Council resolution 1244 (1999). We invite and welcome an international civilian presence to supervise our implementation of the Ahtisaari Plan, and a European Union-led rule of law mission. We also invite and welcome the North Atlantic Treaty Organization to retain the leadership role of the international military presence in Kosovo and to implement responsibilities assigned to it under UN Security Council resolution 1244 (1999) and the Ahtisaari Plan, until such time as Kosovo institutions are capable of assuming these responsibilities. We shall cooperate fully with these presences to ensure Kosovo's future peace, prosperity and stability.

6. For reasons of culture, geography and history, we believe our future lies with the European family. We therefore declare our intention to take all steps necessary to facilitate full membership in the European Union as soon as feasible and implement the reforms required for European and Euro-Atlantic integration.

7. We express our deep gratitude to the United Nations for the work it has done to help us recover and rebuild from war and build institutions of democracy. We are committed to working constructively with the United Nations as it continues its work in the period ahead.

8. With independence comes the duty of responsible membership in the international community. We accept fully this duty and shall abide by the principles of the United Nations Charter, the Helsinki Final Act, other acts of the Organization on Security and Cooperation in Europe, and the international legal obligations and principles of international comity that mark the relations among states. Kosovo shall have its international borders as set forth in Annex VIII of the Ahtisaari Plan, and shall fully respect the sovereignty and territorial integrity of all our neighbors. Kosovo shall also refrain from the threat or use of force in any manner inconsistent with the purposes of the United Nations.

9. We hereby undertake the international obligations of Kosovo, including those concluded on our behalf by the United Nations Interim Administration Mission in Kosovo (UNMIK) and treaty and other obligations of the former Socialist Federal Republic of Yugoslavia to which we are bound as a former constituent part, including the Vienna Conventions on diplomatic and consular relations. We shall cooperate fully with the International Criminal Tribunal for the Former Yugoslavia. We intend to seek membership in international organisations, in which Kosovo shall seek to contribute to the pursuit of international peace and stability.

10. Kosovo declares its commitment to peace and stability in our region of southeast Europe. Our independence brings to an end the process of Yugoslavia's violent dissolution. While this process has been a painful one, we shall work tirelessly to contribute to a reconciliation that would allow southeast Europe to move beyond the conflicts of our past and forge new links of regional cooperation. We shall therefore work together with our neighbours to advance a common European future.

11. We express, in particular, our desire to establish good relations with all our neighbours, including the Republic of Serbia with whom we have deep historical, commercial and social ties that we seek to develop further in the near future. We shall continue our efforts to contribute to relations of friendship and cooperation with the Republic of Serbia, while promoting reconciliation among our people.

12. We hereby affirm, clearly, specifically, and irrevocably, that Kosovo shall be legally bound to comply with the provisions contained in this Declaration, including, especially, the obligations for it under the Ahtisaari Plan. In all of these matters, we shall act consistent with principles of international law and resolutions of the Security Council of the United Nations, including resolution 1244 (1999). We declare publicly that all states are entitled to rely upon this declaration, and appeal to them to extend to us their support and friendship.

Pristina, 17 February 2008
President of the Assembly of Kosova
Jakup KRASNIQI

Index

Printed and bound by CPI Group (UK) Ltd, Croydon, CR0 4YY